65.00

The Seventh-day Men

The Seventh-day Men

Sabbatarians and Sabbatarianism in England and Wales, 1600–1800

BRYAN W. BALL

CLARENDON PRESS · OXFORD

1994

Oxford University Press, Walton Street, Oxford OX2 6DP
Oxford New York Toronto
Delhi Bombay Calcutta Madras Karachi
Kuala Lumpur Singapore Hong Kong Tokyo
Nairobi Dar es Salaam Cape Town
Melbourne Auckland Madrid
and associated companies in
Berlin Ibadan

Oxford is a trade mark of Oxford University Press

Published in the United States
by Oxford University Press Inc., New York

British Library Cataloguing in Publication Data
Data available

Library of Congress Cataloging in Publication Data
The Seventh-day Men : Sabbatarians and Sabbatarianism in England
and Wales, 1600–1800 / Bryan W. Ball.
Includes bibliographical references and indexes.
1. Sabbatarians—Great Britain—History—17th century.
2. Sabbatarians—Great Britain—History—18th century.   3. Sabbath—
History of doctrines—17th century.   4. Sabbath—History of
doctrines—18th century.   I. Title.
BX9680.S33B35   1994   263'.2'094209032—dc20   93–30811
ISBN 0–19–826752–5

1 3 5 7 9 10 8 6 4 2

Typeset by Graphicraft Typesetters Ltd., Hong Kong
Printed in Great Britain on acid-free paper by
Bookcraft (Bath) Ltd., Midsomer Norton, Avon

ACKNOWLEDGEMENTS

THIS book has been in the making for ten years, since the collection of material began in earnest in 1983. During that time I have become indebted to many individuals whom it is now my pleasure to acknowledge.

In the first place my thanks go to Neal C. Wilson, at that time President of the General Conference of Seventh-day Adventists, and to W. Duncan Eva, Administrative Assistant to the President and formerly Vice-President of the General Conference, for their endorsement of the idea to research and write a history of the Sabbatarian movement which appeared in England and Wales in the wake of the Reformation. Their subsequent support of the project as it has grown has ensured its eventual accomplishment. My thanks are due also to the General Conference for support which enabled the research to proceed unhindered.

I am also deeply indebted to Dr Geoffrey Nuttall, once my mentor at New College, the University of London, whose exceptional knowledge of the rise and development of Nonconformity in England and Wales has again been so willingly shared. His unwavering interest, supply of information, suggestions for investigation, and criticism of the manuscript in draft have been a constant encouragement.

The quest for information has taken me to many libraries, county record offices, and archival collections in England, Wales, and North America. The helpful efficiency of the staff in each place deserves recognition. In particular, I must express appreciation to John Creasey, librarian, and Janet Barnes, senior assistant librarian, at Dr Williams's Library, London; Susan Mills, librarian at Regent's Park College, Oxford; Janet Thorngate and Don Sanford of the Seventh Day Baptist Historical Society, Janesville, Wisconsin; and to the staff in Duke Humfrey's reading room at the Bodleian Library, Oxford. Their courtesy and professional assistance has lightened the frequently tedious task of research.

I am also grateful to Oscar Burdick for generously providing so many bibliographical details from his own researches relating to the Sabbatarian literature listed in Appendix IV.

Dennis Porter and Hugh Dunton read the final draft of the manuscript and made many helpful suggestions. John Dunnett provided linguistic assistance, and Jacqueline Peet helped with the illustrations and the indices. Steve Smith, Maurice Ashton, and Ian Howie provided much-needed technical assistance at various stages of the manuscript's development. I am grateful to each of them. And I am again indebted to my wife for her support, and for preparing the manuscript through several revises. The errors and omissions which remain are, of course, my own. My colleagues at Avondale College and Wahroonga deserve thanks for their understanding and willingness to believe that years of research would finally come to fruition.

A significant portion of my life, albeit together with other responsibilities, has been occupied by this study. I share it now in the hope that it may contribute in some small way to a better understanding of the religious past, that common bond in the European heritage which, for so many, consciously or unconsciously, continues to shape the present.

B.W.B.

Martinsville, NSW
January 1993

CONTENTS

ILLUSTRATIONS

ABBREVIATIONS

AL	Angus Library, Regent's Park College, Oxford
AUSS	*Andrews University Seminary Studies*
BAR	John Rippon, *The Baptist Annual Register*
BB	W.T. Whitley, *A Baptist Bibliography*
BBC	Bristol Baptist College Library
BDBR	R.L. Greaves (ed.), *A Biographical Dictionary of British Radicals in the Seventeenth Century*
BL	British Library
Bodl.	Bodleian Library, Oxford
BQ	*Baptist Quarterly*
BRO	Buckinghamshire Record Office
BrRO	Bristol Record Office
CR	A.G. Matthews, *Calamy Revised*
CSPD	*Calendar of State Papers, Domestic*
CSPI	*Calendar of State Papers, Ireland*
DDR	Durham Diocesan Records
DNB	*Dictionary of National Biography*
DRO	Durham County Record Office
DWB	*Dictionary of Welsh Biography*
DWL	Dr Williams's Library, London
EDR	Ely Diocesan Records
ERO	Essex Record Office
FMM	B.S. Capp, *The Fifth Monarchy Men*
GL	Guildhall Library, London
GRO	Gloucestershire Record Office
HMC	*Historical Manuscripts Commission Reports*
HRO	Hampshire Record Office
HWRO	Hereford and Worcester Record Office
INB	'Index to Notable Baptists', *TBHS*, vii
JEH	*Journal of Ecclesiastical History*
JQR	*Jewish Quarterly Review*
LAO	Lincolnshire Archives Office
MGA	W.T. Whitley (ed.), *Minutes of the General Assembly of the General Baptist Churches in England*
MYM	Mill Yard Minutes

NLW	National Library of Wales, Aberystwyth
NoRO	Northamptonshire Record Office
NPNF	*A Select Library of Nicene and Post-Nicene Fathers of the Christian Church*
NRO	Norfolk Record Office
ODCC	*The Oxford Dictionary of the Christian Church*
OR	G.L. Turner, *Original Records of Early Nonconformity under Persecution and Indulgence*
ORO	Oxfordshire County Record Office
PDM	*Protestant Dissenters' Magazine*
PHCB	Pinners' Hall church book
PRO	Public Record Office
SDBEA	*Seventh Day Baptists in Europe and America*
SDBHS	Seventh Day Baptist Historical Society, Janesville
SDBM	*Seventh Day Baptist Memorial*
SM	*Sabbath Memorial*
SO	*Sabbath Observer*
SP	State Papers
SR	*Sabbath Recorder*
SRO	Suffolk Record Office
STC	D. Wing, *Short Title Catalogue . . . 1641–1700*
TBHS	*Transactions of the Baptist Historical Society*
TCD	Trinity College, Dublin
TCHS	*Transactions of the Congregational Historical Society*
TJHSE	*Transactions of the Jewish Historical Society of England*
TUHS	*Transactions of the Unitarian Historical Society*
UCL	University Library, Cambridge
VCH	*Victoria County History*
WRO	Wiltshire Record Office
YDR	York Diocesan Records

Further details of sources will be found in the Bibliography.

Introduction

T HE Seventh-day Men of the seventeenth and eighteenth centuries were so called by their contemporaries in England and Wales because they observed Saturday as the divinely appointed day of rest and Christian worship. They were also known widely as Sabbatarians, or Sabbatharians, frequently as Jews, sometimes as Fifth Monarchy Men, and occasionally merely as Anabaptists. Such confusing uncertainty concerning the identity of the Saturday Sabbatarians highlights an important fact, common also to some other religious movements of the time. They have not always been well understood, even in their own age. The congregation of 'Jewes' reported at Amersham in 1669 and the Fifth Monarchy Men reported at Southampton in the same year[1] were almost certainly both Seventh-day groups. Peter Chamberlen, one of the most prominent and influential seventeenth-century Sabbatarians, complained to William Sancroft in 1680 that he had been 'traduced . . . as a Jew' to the Archbishop.[2] Francis Bampfield, another leading Sabbatarian, who in 1682 was described as a 'Christian Jew', had previously been listed as a Presbyterian, a Nonconforming minister, even simply as a clerk.[3] John Sullins, well known in his locality as leader of the Bledlow Sabbatarians, was still designated a Presbyterian several years after his conversion to the Saturday Sabbath.[4] Such ambiguities and apparent discrepancies underline the need, recognized for some time now, for a more definitive record of the Seventh-day movement in its entirety.

The passing of three and a half centuries since the doctrine of the Seventh-day Sabbath was first openly promulgated in England has produced a more mature climate in which to examine the

---

[1] G.L. Turner (ed.), *Original Records of Early Nonconformity under Persecution and Indulgence*, i (1911), 81, 143.

[2] Bodl. MS Tanner 160, fo. 71. On Chamberlen, see Ch. 3 and Appendix III.

[3] F.H.A. Micklewright, 'A Congregation of Sabbatarian and Unitarian Baptists', *Notes and Queries*, 191 (1946), 95; *OR* ii. 1132; *CSPD* 1671–2, 597; 1672, 292. On Bampfield, see Chs. 4 and 5.   [4] *OR* ii. 834. On Sullins, see Ch. 6.

Sabbatarian movement and its theology. That the Seventh-day Men observed the Saturday Sabbath and met on that day for worship and edification has always, of course, been beyond question. That the majority did so from the standpoint of Christian obedience rather than from any Judaizing legalistic motivation,[5] that some of them, perhaps many during the mid-seventeenth century, adopted Fifth Monarchy views, and that most were antipaedobaptist is now also all beyond doubt. Such clarifications have helped to set the Sabbatarian movement in a more objective light, as they also help to counter the loose and often misleading allusions found in some of the contemporary records.

This study documents the existence, and examines the character, of Saturday Sabbatarianism in England and Wales from its appearance during the early seventeenth century[6] to its decline several generations later. It was a movement more extensive than hitherto recognized,[7] and more persistent than many of the contemporaneous sects that previously have attracted attention. Quakers, Diggers, Levellers, Ranters, Seekers, Fifth Monarchy Men, the Family of Love,[8] *et al.*, are all thoroughly established as part of the rich kaleidoscope of seventeenth-century religious life in England. With few exceptions they flourished for a decade or two, perhaps half a century at the most, and then disappeared. The Seventh-day Men appeared at various points all over the country between 1600 and 1750, establishing themselves in over sixty identifiable discrete or mixed-communion congregations, and probably in many others which cannot now be positively identified, and bearing witness to their Sabbatarian doctrine in countless instances of individual and family observance of the Seventh-day Sabbath. They produced a vigorous literature in defence of their practice of Saturday-

---

[5] The stigma of Judaizing was never far away. An earlier critic of the Sabbatarian movement noted 'a vein of Jewishness running through the leaders': Micklewright, *Notes and Queries*, 191: 95.

[6] Almost certainly not its first appearance in England; see Ch. 1, *passim*.

[7] Whiting referred to eleven known congregations: C.E. Whiting, *Studies in English Puritanism from the Restoration to the Revolution, 1660–1688* (1931), 84. Dr Payne later published a document that identified eighteen groups: E.A. Payne, 'More about the Sabbatarian Baptists', *BQ* 14: 165. A nineteenth-century observer noted that in the preceding two centuries there had been 'several congregations in London' and in many English counties, as well as 'many Sabbatarians that were not members anywhere', Robert Burnside, *Remarks on the Different Sentiments Entertained in Christendom Relative to the Weekly Sabbath* (1825), 113.

[8] *ODCC* comments briefly on each of these seventeenth-century sects.

keeping.[9] They attracted many men of influence and position to their ranks. Their distinctive tenet has been taken up and perpetuated in the confessions and practice of Christian denominations currently active in many parts of the world. They, too, deserve recognition as part of the religious heritage of the English-speaking world.

Little notice has been paid previously to the Sabbatarian movement as such, even though some of its more prominent adherents have occasionally attracted interest. The ponderous two-volume *Seventh Day Baptists in Europe and America* (1910)[10] gave some eighty pages out of 1,500 to early Seventh Day Baptist[11] history in England, but unfortunately is quite inadequate, and frequently inaccurate, and can only be cited with care.[12] A recent more scholarly history of the Seventh Day Baptist Church in North America, *A Choosing People: The History of Seventh Day Baptists*,[13] surveys the seventeenth-century English origins of that denomination, but fails to correct many of the errors in the earlier *SDBEA*, and likewise suffers in some respects from lack of access to the primary source materials. Standard early Baptist histories generally seem unaware of the Seventh-day movement as such,[14] a somewhat strange phenomenon in view of the evidence that now points to a widespread dissemination of Seventh-day views at the time the Baptist Church was itself developing. More recent Baptist histories allude more

[9] See Appendix IV for the pro-Sabbatarian literature to 1750, and the Bibliography for some of the more salient printed works and manuscripts *contra*.

[10] A third volume, dealing with later Seventh Day Baptist history, was added in 1972.

[11] The form 'Seventh Day Baptist' is used throughout when referring to the present-day denomination of that name, in deference to current practice, but in distinction to 'Seventh-day Baptists', 'Seventh-day Men', 'Seventh-day churches', etc., as used of the Sabbatarian movement during the seventeenth and eighteenth centuries, and following *The Oxford Dictionary for Writers and Editors*.

[12] Similarly C.H. Greene's series 'History of Seventh Day Baptists', *SO* 1/4–28, 2/1–28, 3/1–8, contains some fundamental inaccuracies, e.g. that Edward Brerewood, Thomas Broad, and John Tombes were Sabbatarians, 1/196, 212; 2/125.

[13] Don A. Sanford, *A Choosing People: The History of Seventh Day Baptists* (Nashville, 1992).

[14] Most references to Sabbatarianism in these early works are to prominent individuals. Thomas Crosby, *The History of the English Baptists* (4 vols., 1738–40), speaks generously of the Stennetts, John James, and Francis Bampfield, but makes little or no mention of the Sabbatarian movement. Joseph Ivimey, *History of the English Baptists* (4 vols., 1811–30), mentions only James, Bampfield, and the early Stennetts, and the two main London Sabbatarian churches. Adam Taylor, *The History of the English General Baptists* (2 vols., 1818), refers to the Mill Yard church, and to James, and to Joseph Davis, sen.

easily to the Sabbatarian wing within the Baptist Church in the seventeenth and eighteenth centuries,[15] but fail to convey any real sense of its extent. J.T. Dennison's *The Market Day of the Soul*, while brief, and not primarily focused on Saturday Sabbatarianism, is useful, although the exchange between Thomas Bampfield and John Wallis[16] was clearly not 'the final skirmish' in the debate over whether Saturday or Sunday was the true Christian Sabbath.[17]

A few articles in *Transactions of the Baptist Historical Society* and the *Baptist Quarterly* have in the main been devoted to notable Sabbatarians.[18] W.T. Whitley and E.A. Payne each contributed a brief piece on the wider movement, the latter being the first to publish the important record from the Llanwenarth Baptist church relating to Sabbatarian congregations *c*.1690.[19] Other occasional articles, such as B.R. White's study on John Traske in *Transactions of the Congregational Historical Society*[20] and F.H. Amphlett Micklewright's contributions in *Notes and Queries*,[21] have also drawn attention to individual Sabbatarians or to the movement itself, without commenting on it in any detail, or even being aware of its true extent. D.S. Katz's *Sabbath and Sectarianism in Seventeenth-Century England* again revolves around three or four prominent Sabbatarians, and is essentially concerned with any connection they or their colleagues may have had with contemporary Judaism. It is confessedly not a 'history of the Seventh-Day Baptists', or of the Sabbatarian movement.[22]

---

[15] W.T. Whitley, *A History of British Baptists* (1923); B.R. White, *The English Baptists of the Seventeenth Century* (1983); R. Brown, *The English Baptists of the Eighteenth Century* (1986). [16] See below, 161–2.

[17] J.T. Dennison, Jr., *The Market Day of the Soul: The Puritan Doctrine of the Sabbath in England, 1532–1700* (1983), 135. Dennison states that the Puritan Sabbath 'was flanked on the left by the "medieval" position of the Court party and on the right by the Seventh-day or Saturday-Sabbatarians', p. xii.

[18] e.g. J.W. Thirtle, 'A Sabbatarian Pioneer—Dr Peter Chamberlen', *TBHS* 2, and 'Dr Peter Chamberlen: Pastor, Propagandist, and Patentee', *TBHS* 3; [W.T. Whitley], 'Trask in the Star-Chamber, 1619' (date later amended to 1618), *TBHS* 5; [W.T. Whitley], 'Bampfield's Plan for an Educated Ministry', *TBHS* 3.

[19] W.T. Whitley, 'Seventh Day Baptists in England', *BQ* 12; E.A. Payne, 'More about the Sabbatarian Baptists', *BQ* 14. The Llanwenarth record is reproduced in this study in Ch. 8.

[20] B.R. White, 'John Traske (1585–1636) and London Puritanism', *TCHS* 20/7.

[21] Micklewright, *Notes and Queries*, 191: 5, and 'Some Further Notes on Mill Yard Meeting House', *Notes and Queries* 191: 7, 8, 9 (1946).

[22] D.S. Katz, *Sabbath and Sectarianism in Seventeenth-Century England* (Leiden, 1988), p. xii.

1 Berkshire
2 Breconshire
3 Buckinghamshire
4 Cambridgeshire
5 Devon
6 Dorset
7 Durham
8 Essex
9 Gloucestershire
10 Hampshire
11 Herefordshire
12 Hertfordshire
13 Huntingdonshire
14 Kent
15 Lincolnshire
16 London/Middlesex
17 Monmouthshire
18 Norfolk
19 Northamptonshire

20 Northumberland
21 Nottinghamshire
22 Oxfordshire
23 Radnorshire
24 Somerset
25 Staffordshire
26 Suffolk
27 Surrey
28 Warwickshire
29 Wiltshire
30 Worcestershire
31 Yorkshire

MAP 1 Counties in England and Wales in which Saturday Sabbatarianism appeared during the seventeenth and eighteenth centuries (County boundaries after Bowles' map of England and Wales, 1773. Used by permission of the British Library)

Most of the Seventh-day Men now known to have existed during the seventeenth and eighteenth centuries lived in England south of a line drawn roughly from the Humber to the Severn. Sabbatarians were also found in Durham and Northumberland during the seventeenth century,[23] in the south-east corner of Wales between 1650 and 1750,[24] and in Ireland during the seventeenth century and later.[25] Several concentrations of Sabbatarians developed in relatively small areas in various parts of the country, usually keeping Seventh-day observance alive in those localities for several generations. Thus, for example, an initially strong and lingering Sabbatarian presence in found in north-east Norfolk, in parts of Gloucestershire, in the Chilterns, in Dorset, and in London. In many instances, a geographical affinity with an earlier Lollard movement will be noted. It will be suggested that a theological affinity may also have existed.

From a confessional perspective, there were some notable exceptions to the general rule that most Sabbatarians were also Baptists. The two names most frequently associated with early Sabbatarian doctrine in England, John Traske and Theophilus Brabourne,[26] were both paedobaptist. Brabourne himself claimed that the Saturday/Sunday issue was the most debated point in the Church of England *c.*1660.[27] Joseph Stennett, noted always for his moderation, stated nearly half a century later, in 1704, that there were Saturday observers beyond Baptist ranks, noting specifically some 'in the communion of the Church of England'.[28] Thirty years later mention might have been made of John Wesley, then still very much an Anglican.[29] There is also evidence that Independent

[23] See below, Ch. 10.   [24] See below, Ch. 8.   [25] See Appendix I.
[26] On Traske and Brabourne, see below, Ch. 2.
[27] Theophilus Brabourne, *Of the Sabbath Day, which is now, the Highest Controversie in the Church of England*...(1660), title-page. Cf. Whitley, *BB* i. 91–660, and see Appendix IV.
[28] Joseph Stennett, *An Answer to Mr David Russen's Book Entitled, Fundamentals Without a Foundation, or a True Picture of the Anabaptists* (1704), 228.
[29] Although the Sabbath observance of Wesley and other early Oxford 'Methodists' appears to have been of a different kind from that of Sabbatarians more broadly understood. By 1733, when Wesley wrote to John Clayton regarding the Saturday Sabbath, they 'were becoming Ritualists', adding to biblical norms of faith and practice the requirements of ecclesiastical canons and decretals, L. Tyerman, *The Oxford Methodists* (1873), 32. Clayton continued to be 'consulted about such questions as the observance of Saturday as the Sabbath, in addition to Sunday as the Lord's Day', W.J. Townsend, H.B. Workman, George Eayrs, *A New History of Methodism* (1919), i, 145–6. The Holy Club's leaning to liturgical observance is a good example of that formal scrupulosity unleavened by the doctrine of gospel obedience, of which so

paedobaptist congregations existed in Gloucestershire during the eighteenth century.[30] As late as 1795 John Evans noted that Sabbatarians were found 'principally, if not wholly' among Baptists.[31] Baptist Sabbatarians, always in the majority, were somewhat unequally divided between the Calvinistic Particular Baptists and the Arminian General Baptists. While the former eventually outnumbered the latter, the first and last Baptist Sabbatarians in England and Wales were probably General Baptists, deriving respectively from the forerunners and the survivors of the well-known Mill Yard church in London.

The dates proposed as parameters for this study are, of course, no more than approximations. Religious convictions and their associated practices rarely arise and decline to coincide conveniently with the calendar. There is no known evidence at present to indicate congregational observance of the seventh day before 1617, though it is quite feasible that undetected Sabbatarian groups did exist before that, perhaps as later manifestations of a lingering Lollard practice. Certainly, one of the most interesting facts to emerge from this study regarding earlier Sabbatarianism is confirmation of Seventh-day observance in Lollard circles very early in the fifteenth century.[32] The date traditionally given for the appearance of Baptist Sabbatarian congregations, the early 1650s,[33] is clearly too late. Groups observing the seventh day had formed in London, Colchester, and King's Stanley by the early to mid-1640s, and perhaps in Tewkesbury, Salisbury, and Devon before that. Richard Baxter admits to deciding in favour of Sunday observance *c.*1640–1, after having studied himself 'into full satisfaction in this matter'.[34] It is substantial enough evidence of a widespread interest in the subject

---

many opponents of the wider Sabbatarianism were justifiably suspicious. Even so, the use of the term Sabbath for Saturday, and the Holy Club's observance of the Saturday Sabbath 'as a festival in itself', are of interest, particularly in the context of a resurgence of Sabbatarianism in the 1720s and 1730s. It is also of note, in the light of other practices prevalent in wider Sabbatarian circles, that the young John Wesley advocated baptism by immersion and abstinence from blood and things strangled, G.R. Balleine, *A History of the Evangelical Party in the Church of England* (1933), 8, 9. [30] See below, Ch. 7.

[31] John Evans, *A Sketch of the Several Denominations into which the Christian World is Divided* (1795), 98.

[32] See Ch. 1.   [33] e.g. White, *English Baptists*, 8.

[34] Richard Baxter to Thomas Bampfield, 16 Jan. 1671, DWL, Baxter MS 59.6, fo. 248ᵛ.

at that time. Traskite Sabbatarians existed in London, if nowhere else, during the 1630s, most probably in continuity of the practice established by their founder *c.*1617. Archbishop George Abbot objected to the use of the word Sabbath in a bill brought before Parliament in 1621, on the grounds that 'many of late times have runn to Judaisme', and some 'have written for the very day'.[35] John Sprint's 'Sabbatary Christians' were those who in 1607 held that 'the Jewish Sabbath of the seventh day in the week . . . is never to be abolished, being no less necessary for us to observe now than it ever was for the Jews'.[36] All in all, 1600 is an appropriate starting-point for the examination of a movement that came clearly into the open shortly thereafter.

By 1800 most of the Sabbatarian congregations which had appeared during the preceding two centuries had become defunct. This includes those that had first come to light with a visible congregational identity during the eighteenth century. There were, however, a few notable exceptions. Salisbury and Watlington both persisted beyond 1800, if only in name. The two leading London churches, Mill Yard and Pinners' Hall/Curriers' Hall, survived until the 1960s and the 1860s respectively. Both had played an important role in maintaining the continuity of Saturday observance in London and in many other parts of the country, and in ensuring its acceptance in the New World. The Ashchurch–Natton congregation in Gloucestershire also continued into the twentieth century, having held tenaciously to Seventh-day principles for the greater part of three centuries. By this time others, principally Seventh-day Adventists from North America and, later, Seventh Day Baptists from the Caribbean, had appeared to perpetuate the tradition of Seventh-day observance in the British Isles. Beyond the finer details of historical accuracy it is now evident that the Saturday Sabbath persisted as a recognizable element in English religious life throughout the seventeenth and eighteenth centuries.

Perhaps the most significant contemporary account of Sabbatarianism in the seventeenth century comes from Henri Misson's *Memoires et Observations faites par un Voyageur en Angleterre* (1698), translated by John Ozell as *M. Misson's Memoirs and*

---

[35] W. Notestein, F.H. Relf, and H. Simpson (eds.), *Commons Debates, 1621* (1935), iii. 299.

[36] John Sprint, *Propositions Tending to Prove the Necessary Use of the Christian Sabbath, or Lord's Day* (1607), 2.

Observations in his Travels over England (1719). Misson had travelled widely throughout the country during the 1690s, and apparently had encountered enough Seventh-day congregations and individual Sabbatarians to have been persuaded of their socio-religious significance and of their essential orthodoxy. Sabbatarians received more comment in Misson's record than all the mainstream Nonconformist denominations and other contemporary sects put together. Describing English religious life of the time, Misson refers briefly to Presbyterians, Independents, Quakers, and Anabaptists, and then lists some of the more eccentric sects which flourished in England during the latter half of the seventeenth century. Dismissing Muggletonians, Wilkinsonians, Adamites, Hetheringtonians, Familists, *et al.* as 'fools' with 'fantastical opinions',[37] Misson then comments as follows on the Sabbatarian movement. It is a valuable account, both for its detachment and its detail:

Here and there also you meet with a Millennarian; but I know there is a particular Society, though it makes but little noise, of People, who though they go by the Name of Sabbatarians [fn. 'the common people call them Seventh-Day Men'] make Profession of expecting the Reign of a Thousand Years without participating in the other opinions which are ascribed to the ancient Millenarians. These Sabbatharians are so call'd, because they will not remove the Day of Rest from Saterday to Sunday. They leave off work betimes on Friday Evening, and are very rigid observers of their Sabbath. They administer Baptism only to adult People [fn. 'in other respects they subscribe to our Confession of Faith']; and perhaps they are blameable in these two Things only because they look upon them to be more important than they really are. The major Part of them will eat neither Pork, nor Blood, nor things strangled, but they do not absolutely forbid the Use of those meats; they leave it to the Liberty of every Conscience. For the rest, their Morality is severe, and their whole outward Conduct pious and Christian-like. Were it only for this one Opinion or Belief of theirs concerning the absolute Necessity of keeping the Sabbath on Saturday without paying any Regard to the next Day, which is the first Day in the week, and which we call Sunday with the author of the Revelations; that alone would be enough to make them unavoidably a Society by themselves.[38]

By the end of the seventeenth century the Seventh-day Men, like other Nonconformist groups, had recovered from the rigours of post-Restoration repression, had re-established disseminated

[37] John Ozell (tr.), *M. Misson's Memoirs and Observations in his Travels over England* (1719), 233–4. [38] Ibid. 235.

congregations, and had perhaps formed others. They now appeared to a foreign observer as a coherent and respectable religious body. They subscribed to believers' baptism, espoused a moderate millenarian eschatology,[39] favoured a diet which excluded pork and blood, recognized the liberty of individual conscience, and in general conveyed the impression of being thoroughly representative of fundamental Protestant values and the epitome of Nonconformist rectitude. On account of their Sabbatarian convictions alone, however, they were, as Misson concluded, 'unavoidably a society by themselves'. We may be reasonably sure that this description of Sabbatarians and Sabbatarianism at the turn of the century is an accurate picture of the majority of the Seventh-day Men who are the focus of this study.

Any attempt to understand the Sabbatarian movement in its own particular context must take into account two fundamental and related factors. The Seventh-day Men were thoroughly Protestant, and they were thoroughly Puritan. They were motivated by the quest for a biblical faith purged of human accretions and restored to its primitive apostolic purity. In this, of course, they were one with Puritans and Protestants of all shades of opinion. That which distinguished Sabbatarians, however, was a deep conviction that it was necessary to take the arguments which characterized Protestantism and Puritanism to a logical conclusion. In the matter of the Sabbath it had become patently clear to the Seventh-day Men that both Protestants and Puritans had stopped well short of that. Their search, in short, was for a completed Reformation.

Thus the essential Protestant impetus to free the Church from all Roman influences realized its ultimate and perhaps most controversial fulfilment in Sabbatarian theology. The Seventh-day Men believed that Sunday observance was a late modification of original apostolic practice, introduced to the Christian Church in early times and perpetuated thereafter by Rome. The origin of Sunday-keeping to them was post-apostolic and the practice itself extra-biblical. The title of one of the earlier seventeenth-century pro-Sabbatarian publications put the point succinctly: *The Doctrine of the Fourth Commandement, Deformed by Popery; Reformed and Restored to*

---

[39] Russen classed Sabbatarians with 'Millenaries or Chiliasts', *Fundamentals without Foundation, or, a True Picture of the Anabaptists in their Rise, Progress and Practice. Written for the use of such as take 'em for saints, when they are not so much as Christians* (1703), 78–9.

its Primitive purity.[40] The first known Sabbatarian writer of the period, Theophilus Brabourne, who hoped to change Anglican practice regarding Sabbath observance rather than cause schism, argued that the Church of England in respect of the Sabbath had been 'as wheat . . . covered in the chaff of popery'. Sunday observance was an 'error to be imputed to the Romish church', rooted in tradition rather than in Scripture. The Protestant task, including Sabbath reformation, was therefore a 'battle against Rome, in defending the ground of religion'.[41] Thomas Tillam, who later disgraced himself in the eyes of his fellow Sabbatarians, rejoiced that a knowledge of the true Sabbath had broken through 'the Romish fogs that had long obscured it under the heathenish title of Saturday, or Saturn's day'.[42] The anonymous author of *The Moralitie of the Fourth Commandement* (1652) argued that the Church of Rome had 'adulterated the very letter of the second and fourth commandement most wickedly'.[43] It was a reference to the difference in wording between the Ten Commandments as portrayed in Roman Catholic catechisms and the original wording in Exodus 20. It was an important point to Sabbatarians, as we shall note shortly. The authors of the 1657 *Appeal* to Parliament regarding Sabbath observance argued that the change from Saturday to Sunday was the work of Rome, 'the Man of sin', and should not be sanctioned by an English Parliament. They therefore urged, 'We do hereby, in God's stead, exhort you to reduce the Lord's holy Sabbath to its proper day.'[44] There can

---

[40] By James Ockford, or Oakford, 1650. On Ockford, see Ch. 5.

[41] Theophilus Brabourne, *A Discourse upon the Sabbath Day* (1628), 62. A manuscript copy of Brabourne's *Discourse* is in the Bodleian Library, MS Tanner 378.

[42] Thomas Tillam, *The Seventh-Day Sabbath Sought out and celebrated, or, the Saints last Design upon the Man of sin . . . being a clear discovery of that black character in the head of the little Horn, Dan. 7.25. The Change of Times & Laws. With the Christians glorious Conquest over that mark of the Beast, and recovery of the long-slighted seventh day, to its antient glory* (1657), 52. On Tillam, see Chs. 9, 10.

[43] *The Moralitie of the Fourth Commandement* (1652), 53–4.

[44] William Saller and John Spittlehouse, *An Appeal To the Consciences of the chief Magistrates of this Commonwealth, touching the Sabbath-day* (1657), 12. 'We cannot but stand in admiration, that you should take upon you . . . to countenance, and much more to establish such a day [Sunday] for the Lord's holy Sabbath, as hath no warrant from the Scriptures . . . and to restrain the people of this Commonwealth from working on that Day, wherein Jehovah himself hath commanded, or at least, freely permitted them to labour in', 11, 12. The *Appeal* fell on deaf ears in 1657, and apparently was never considered by the parliamentary committee appointed to examine its claims. The *Appeal* was reprinted, and expanded, in 1679.

be little doubt that the Seventh-day Men saw themselves as thorough-going Protestants determined to see the last traces of Roman influence removed from the life and doctrine of the English Church.

This belief, that the day of Christian rest and worship had been changed from Saturday to Sunday on the authority of Rome, had an important eschatological dimension. In fact, it derived much of its strength from an interpretation of certain prophecies of Daniel and the Revelation. Standard historicist prophetic interpretation of the period designated that the Little Horn power of Daniel, chapter 7, symbolized the Papacy. This view had been at the heart of Protestant theology from the beginning. The four preceding kingdoms of Babylon, Medo-Persia, Greece, and Rome had been prefigured in the metal image of Daniel 2 and the four beasts of Daniel 7.[45] Both were apocalyptic prophecies pertinent to the unfolding course of world history. Historicism demonstrated that the four kingdoms which successively dominated world affairs between c.600 BC and AD 476 gave rise in time to the Little Horn power, which arose from the fourth beast of Daniel 7. Of the many features given in the text which helped to identify this power as the Papacy, the attempt to 'change times and laws'[46] was of particular significance to Sabbatarians. Thus, it was 'that little Horn', 'Antichrist . . . who hath destroyed the fourth commandment'.[47] Brabourne was concerned that by continuing to observe Sunday he would be an 'accessary to the sin of changing God's tymes', a 'brand' of that 'wicked man prophecied of in Dan. 7: 25'.[48] A lawyer, Thomas Bampfield, argued that the bishops of Rome 'though they pretended to dispense with the laws of the church, could not alter or dispense with the law of God'. Hence 'the law to alter the Seventh day to the First' was proposed on the basis of a spurious authority.[49] The renowned

---

[45] Dan. 2: 31–45; 7: 2–7. On historicist interpretation, see V.N. Olsen, *John Foxe and the Elizabethan Church* (1973), 24 ff., and 83 ff., B.S. Capp, *The Fifth Monarchy Men* (1972), 23 ff., and B.W. Ball, *A Great Expectation: Eschatological Thought in English Protestantism to 1660* (Leiden, 1975), Ch. 2, 'Apocalyptic Interpretation and the End of the Age'. L.E. Froom's massive *The Prophetic Faith of our Fathers* (4 vols., Washington, DC, 1946–64) should be consulted, but needs in places to be treated with caution.   [46] Dan. 7: 25.

[47] *The Moralitie of the Fourth Commandement*, 53.

[48] Brabourne, *Discourse*, 28.

[49] Thomas Bampfield, *An Enquiry Whether the Lord Jesus Christ made the World, and be Jehovah, and gave the Moral Law? And Whether the Fourth Command be Repealed or Altered?* (1692), 135 (the first so numbered). On Bampfield, see *DNB* and Ch. 6.

Peter Chamberlen wrote an open letter to the Lord High Chancellor and the English judiciary in 1682, arguing that the 'Triple-Crowned-Little-Horn-Changer of Times and Laws' had changed the Sabbath, 'giving the lie to the Seventh day', saying 'that the First day is the Sabbath of the Lord'.[50]

It is quite impossible to grasp fully the significance of the Sabbatarian movement apart from its concern with the change of the Sabbath from Saturday to Sunday, the authority for that change, and the eschatological nexus in which it had been anticipated in apocalyptic prophecy. The import of all this for the Sabbatarian community, and the thoroughly Protestant character which it accordingly appropriated, may be seen clearly in the work of Francis Bampfield, a learned and respected seventeenth-century Sabbatarian apologist. Bampfield was concerned, as were his fellow Sabbatarians, to defend the authority of the moral law as revealed in the Ten Commandments. In that respect Rome, the papal Antichrist, was the 'Anomous one', the lawless one, since it had changed the very law of God, the Ten Commandments, precisely as Daniel had predicted:

The Antichristian party have mangled the ten Words; for thus they publish them in their Psalters and Catechisms:

1. I am the Lord God: thou shalt have no other God but me.
2. Thou shalt not take the Name of God in vain.
3. Remember to sanctifie the holy days.
4. Honour thy father and mother.
5. Thou shalt not kill.
6. Thou shalt not commit adultery.
7. Thou shalt not steal.
8. Thou shalt not bear false witness.
9. Thou shalt not desire thy neighbours wife.
10. Thou shalt not desire thy neighbours goods.

Here they wholly leave out the second Commandment: They thrust the weekly Seventh-day Sabbath of *Jehovah*, out of Fourth Word, and substitute their own unscriptural holy days; they turn the last Word into two. They teach religious reverence to be done to Creatures, as to Angels, to Souls departed, to the Cross, &c they teach Invocation of Saints; they allow blasphemous Oaths; they teach Will-worship, Idolatry, Superstitions, and

[50] Peter Chamberlen, *Englands Choice* (1682), 2, 3. Chamberlen also asked William Sancroft for clarification of the Little Horn of Dan. 7 on the grounds that the Archbishop's response would 'tend to the healing of those divisions' afflicting the nation, Bodl. MS Tanner 35.

their fabulous feigned Traditions, and such vows as are unwarrantable and unlawful, they lay aside the weekly Seventh-day Sabbath, and set up days of mens inventing, instituting and imposing. . . . They dispense with the whole Decalogue, by Usurpation; If the Pope command what Christ doth forbid, or if he forbid what Christ doth command, yet they require their people to obey them, contrary to Christs Law.[51]

The argument for Rome's complicity in changing the Sabbath and 'mangling' the Ten Commandments is contextualized here in terms that any informed Protestant of the day would have understood.

The strength of such convictions should not be underestimated. They led men like Bampfield, an accomplished Hebraist and one of the most distinguished preachers of his day, to endure calumny, persecution, imprisonment, and ultimately death. The Sabbath was no mere whim, no passing fad. It was not even an option. To those who had been convinced of its legitimacy, it was a matter of truth, conscience, obedience to the known will of God, and ultimately a mark of human response to grace and the gospel. Hence Sabbatarians believed that their Protestant brothers should be informed of the origins of Sunday observance and the claims of the original Seventh-day Sabbath.

If to the Seventh-day Men Protestantism had failed, then so had Puritanism. And it had failed at precisely the same point as had Protestantism more broadly understood. It had not gone far enough. It had not followed its own arguments for thorough biblical reform to their logical conclusion, a Church reformed in every respect according to the teachings of the Bible. Such a reformation was not merely a reshaping of practice according to the dicta of Scripture, but more specifically a restoration of the purity of life and faith of the early Church. Sabbatarians believed that their insistence on the Seventh-day Sabbath called the Christian Church back to its original practice. It was hard for them to understand why others, with similar motives, could not grasp the logic of their position.

The Seventh-day Sabbath was, of course, but one practice of the early Church felt to be in need of restoration. Its reappearance in the religious life of Jacobean and Caroline England was accompanied by the rediscovery and re-emphasis of other biblical practices believed to have been observed in the apostolic Church. As it became

---

[51] Francis Bampfield, *Septima dies, Dies Desiderabilis, Sabbatam Jehovae. The Seventh-Day-Sabbath the Desirable Day* (1677), 129. Bampfield uses 'word' here to mean commandment, as occasionally do other writers of the period.

ever more apparent that the established Church was not going to initiate further reforms, so those who had waited impatiently became more vocal and more active. The appearance of Independent and Baptist congregations made possible the corporate observance of many such practices. Baptists in particular were among the most zealous advocates of a thoroughly biblical faith, and it was in many Baptist congregations that observance of the Saturday Sabbath was re-established, together with believer's baptism, foot-washing, anointing with oil, abstinence from unclean meats, and, in some cases, the laying on of hands. It was all part of a spontaneous movement in English Christianity to restore that which centuries of papal accretions and deletions had obfuscated. The Seventh-day Men saw themselves, as did others, as restorers of the old paths, as thoroughgoing reformers, making it possible for all who would to return to primitive, apostolic purity.

Thus the past and the future meet in Seventh-day theology. The impetus to return to the original teachings of Christ and the apostles becomes also a characteristic of the latter-day 'remnant'. Eschatological conviction derives from a sense of conformity to apostolic practice. The idea of a people prepared for the coming of the Lord frequently finds expression in Sabbatarian literature. Occasionally it gives rise to excess, as the following pages will reveal. But in the main it is the conviction of a people honestly and earnestly seeking to live in harmony with what they perceive to be the revealed will of God. Indeed, they find themselves depicted in prophecy. The latter-day 'remnant' are known as those who 'keep the commandments of God, and the faith of Jesus'.[52] Sabbatarians who, like most of their contemporaries in the seventeenth century, believed that they lived in the last days were thus at pains to be found faithful. 'It greatly concerns us', wrote Edward Stennett, a leading Sabbatarian, 'to show ourselves the remnant of the woman's seed'. The woman was the Church, and the remnant her latter-day descendants, specifically characterized as 'keeping the commandments of God, and the faith of Jesus'. But it was also a direct link with the apostolic Church. Stennett continues, 'And be followers of those churches of Christ which were in Judea which . . . did keep and observe the seventh-day Sabbath.'[53] The past and the future

[52] Rev. 12: 17.
[53] Edward Stennett, *The Insnared Taken in the Work of his Hands, or an Answer to Mr John Cowell . . .* (1677), 159. This rare work has a second title-page, dated 1679. On Stennett, see Chs. 4 and 6.

here come together to shape the present. History and eschatology impinge on the life of the believing community, a life which is lived in the consciousness of future events. So Tillam adds that the Sabbath 'in these very last days' has become 'the last great controversy between the saints and the men of sin', with the saints being assured of 'victory over the mark of the beast'.[54]

Perhaps one further emphasis may be noted. The Sabbath, like the law that enshrined it, and indeed like the Lord's day when observed in the stricter Puritan tradition, had many uses. It was a day of rest, a day of worship, a day of communion with one's God, and a day for reflection, meditation, and spiritual growth, part of a broader rule of life for all who were believers in Christ. And, in the words of one of its seventeenth-century advocates, it was a 'preservative against atheism'.[55] The argument was simple enough. The weekly observation of a divinely appointed day of rest inevitably focused the mind on the Creator. The Sabbath, in short, was integral to the survival of belief. Could those whose convictions are traced in this study have looked into the twentieth century, they would undoubtedly have seen a link between its atheism and agnosticism and the corresponding disrespect for the day instituted by the Creator as a recurring memorial of his acts and his being. That, too, fairly represents the Protestant and the Puritan impetus.

To the twentieth-century mind, shaped by secularism, it may all sound a little intense, a little eccentric, perhaps a little self-confident. In their own eyes, however, the Seventh-day Men sought only that which most of their contemporaries in other branches of the Church in England also sought—a thorough reformation of Christian teaching and practice in harmony with Scripture and according to apostolic norms. Anything other would be less than truly Puritan and less than truly Protestant. And the Seventh-day Men could not in conscience settle for that.

Something remains to be said regarding sources and methodology. The information which appears in the following chapters has been gathered from original manuscripts, primary printed works, diocesan records, personal correspondence, news-sheets, church books, and Nonconformist records deposited in more than fifty libraries and archival collections in England and Wales. Several

---

[54] Tillam, *Seventh-Day Sabbath*, 1.
[55] William Saller, *A Preservative against Atheism and Error* (1664).

church books held by individual Baptist churches have also been consulted, as has material in the Seventh Day Baptist Historical Society archives in Janesville, Wisconsin. Helpful information has also been received by correspondence from a number of historians and archivists where a personal visit has not been possible or practicable. A number of standard reference works have also been useful, and these are cited in the footnotes where appropriate, and included in the bibliography. County records have proved invaluable sources of information, although in view of the massive amount of material held in many of these offices, it cannot be claimed that an exhaustive search has been made for the relevant data. Indeed, further work in many of these archives would probably yield additional valuable information. It is quite conceivable that further Sabbatarian groups may yet come to light.

The foregoing should not be interpreted to signify an abundance of material relating to Sabbatarian history. While as far as the London churches are concerned, and in respect of the Sabbatarian movement in some other areas, such as Gloucestershire and Norfolk, and also in the case of certain better-known individuals, there is adequate information, the opposite is more often the case. In many instances, even after considerable research, the history of a given congregation remains fragmentary, at best. Tantalizing gaps remain, and questions go unanswered. In some cases, proof of the existence of a Sabbatarian group depends on one or two surviving pieces of information, incontrovertible in themselves, but totally inadequate to convey any idea of the life of the congregation or its constituent members. Boston, Braintree, Harwich, and Great Yarmouth are good examples of congregations whose existence is beyond doubt but concerning which thorough research has failed to produce any significant detailed information. Reference is made occasionally in the text to this frustrating lack of evidence and the difficulties thus posed in the attempt to put together a coherent account of the Sabbatarian movement. I must ask my critics, at least on this point, to be sympathetic.

There are in general two reasons for this paucity of information. Either the records have been destroyed, intentionally or unintentionally, or they were not kept properly in the first place. Thus the diocesan records for much of Dorset prior to 1731 were destroyed by fire at Blandford in that year. A chest containing original materials relating to early Welsh Baptist history had been disposed of before Joshua Thomas went in search of it *c.*1775. The church books of the Natton congregation, still extant in the early years of this century, have since disappeared. Baptist church books covering the post-Restoration period are generally scarce. Some were deliberately destroyed to avoid providing incriminating evidence to the authorities. In other instances, as at Tewkesbury, records for the period were kept in cipher, for the same reason. Diocesan visitation records and consistory court records vary considerably in content and quality. In some dioceses the records relating to seventeenth-century Nonconformist activity are full and well preserved. Elsewhere, such records are scanty and of little value, or have deteriorated to the point of being unusable. Sometimes such records were well kept for decades, then cease abruptly before recommencing several years later. Given the conditions of the age and the lapse of time since the first appearance and subsequent development of the Sabbatarian movement, it is gratifying that sufficient information has survived to make possible even a limited and imperfect reconstruction. And it must be said that the sources which do remain have frequently yielded unexpected treasures. Exeter, Hay-on-Wye, Alderminster, Cheltenham, and Oddington are good examples of localities where a hitherto unknown Sabbatarian presence has now come to light.

The first two chapters are essentially foundational. Chapter 1 briefly surveys earlier periods in which Seventh-day beliefs appeared, including some important antecedents in the British Church, thereby attempting to set the later Sabbatarian movement in an appropriate historical and theological context. Chapter 2 concentrates on two early seventeenth-century English Sabbatarians, John Traske and Theophilus Brabourne, both of whom were seminal to the subsequent development of Saturday Sabbatarianism in England and Wales. Thereafter the movement itself is traced chronologically within geographical and regional areas rather than chronologically for the country as a whole. W.T. Whitley tried the latter method but was unsuccessful in that it proved too confusing.[56] The approach followed here has the disadvantage perhaps of being rather obvious, perhaps unimaginative, but the advantage of being more logical and consistent. An attempt has been made wherever possible to link developments and people in various parts of the country, thereby

---

[56] Whitley's manuscript is in the Angus Library, Regent's Park College, Oxford. Another similar manuscript attributed to Whitley is held by the Seventh Day Baptist Historical Society.

to convey a sense of coherence. Individuals such as Edward and Joseph Stennett, Francis and Thomas Bampfield, Peter Chamberlen, Thomas Tillam, Robert Cornthwaite, Edmund Townsend, and Joseph Davis belong to the whole Sabbatarian fraternity, and their names, and the names of others with similar influence, will be found in several chapters. Undergirding the whole is a theology which found expression in the preaching and writing of these men and their colleagues, and the biblical and theological convictions which distinguished the Seventh-day Men and made them what they were are examined in differing contexts, again to provide a sense of coherence to the movement as a whole.

Sabbath and Sabbatarianism refer throughout, unless otherwise indicated, to the Saturday Sabbath and to those who felt constrained to observe it as the day of rest and worship, rather than to Sunday and those who, particularly under the Puritan impetus, felt the necessity to observe that day in the stricter terms of the fourth commandment. Sabbatarianism has, of course, been widely understood in this latter sense for some time, particularly by historians of the later sixteenth and seventeenth centuries. The real Sabbatarian controversy was, however, as to whether Saturday or Sunday should be kept holy as the Sabbath, and not whether Sunday should be called the Sabbath and kept more strictly, as the Puritans insisted, or whether it should be called the Lord's day, as advocates of the Dominical party maintained. Or so the Sabbatarians who appear in the following chapters would have argued. New style dates are used throughout, and spelling and punctuation have usually been modernized, except in titles, where in text and footnotes original spelling and punctuation have been retained. The Baptist historian Dr E.A. Payne expressed the hope that one day there would be a 'comprehensive monograph' on the whole Sabbatarian movement.[57] This study is an attempt to make that hope a reality.

[57] *BQ* 14, 161.

1

Precedents and Antecedents

IT is clear that the Seventh-day movement, as it began to emerge in England early in the seventeenth century, did so within the context of what has become known as the Sabbatarian controversy. The first known advocate of the seventh day, John Traske, and the first English publications promoting observance of the seventh day, Theophilus Brabourne's *A Discourse upon the Sabbath Day* (1628), and *A Defence of . . . the Sabbath Day* (1632),[1] all appeared in London as this broader Puritan Sabbatarian movement gained momentum. Bishop Francis White's *Treatise of the Sabbath-Day* (1635), judged by Cox to have been the most notable work in the entire controversy after Peter Heylyn's *History of the Sabbath* (1636), was written specifically at the direction of Charles I to counter Brabourne's *Defence*. White speaks patronizingly of the views of both the Seventh-day Men and the Puritans who argued that the requirements of the fourth commandment had been transferred to Sunday as 'Sabbatarian Novelty',[2] and Heylyn refers variously to 'Jewish fancies', 'Jewish Sabbatarian rigours', and 'new Sabbath speculations'.[3] The relevance of this wider Sabbatarianism to the appearance of Seventh-day views will be noted in greater detail in the concluding section of this chapter.

It is equally clear that many other influences from a rich religious past came together to form the background for the appearance in England of the Seventh-day movement. It has recently been argued that the broader Sabbatarianism was not, in fact, a unique Puritan phenomenon at all, as has traditionally been claimed, but rather the natural outgrowth of a medieval Sabbatarian emphasis, maturing at a time when respect for the Bible as God's authoritative word had received new life.[4] The Seventh-day Men would have understood

---

[1] On Traske and Brabourne, see below, Ch. 2.

[2] Francis White, *A Treatise of the Sabbath-Day; containing a Defence of the Orthodoxall Doctrine of the Church of England, against Sabbatarian Novelty* (1635), title-page.

[3] Peter Heylyn, *The History of the Sabbath* (2nd edn. 1636), sig. A6ᵛ, 252–4.

[4] K.L. Parker, *The English Sabbath: A Study of Doctrine and Discipline from the Reformation to the Civil War* (Cambridge, 1988), *passim*.

this argument well, since they contended that the seventh day of the week had been observed both in England and on the Continent at various periods in the Church's history. Thomas Bampfield even contended that the seventh day had been kept in England in unbroken succession until the thirteenth century, and that there had been no law for the observance of Sunday until the time of Edward VI.[5] Most advocates of the seventh day, however, would have been content to point to antecedents in the early Church, in medieval or contemporary Europe, or in the East, including parts of what is now North Africa, particularly Ethiopia. Surprisingly, little direct connection seems to have been made by Seventh-day writers with the Celtic Church in Britain, or with the Lollard movement, both of which might have been called to their aid with benefit.

None the less, the Seventh-day Men entered the field with a strong sense of history on their side. Many of them demonstrated in their numerous publications a detailed knowledge of church history, especially of the writings of the Fathers, and could match reference for reference with the best of their opponents. On one matter of historical import, most writers in the Sabbatarian controversy seem to have agreed with those who propounded the seventh day. Christians with Seventh-day convictions had existed within the Church from the very earliest times. This is not to compromise all those who hotly contended that such an assertion did not include apostolic times. This chapter surveys the more salient Sabbatarian antecedents to the English Seventh-day Men, some of which they themselves knew well, and some of which they cited in their attempt to persuade others of the essential correctness of their position.

THE EARLY CHURCH

The desire of Protestantism in general and of Puritanism in particular to return to the archetype of New Testament teaching and practice has already been noted.[6] The clearest expression of this orientation is seen in Independent and Baptist writers who wanted the Church reformed in all respects, constitutional and practical as well as

---

[5] Bampfield, *An Enquiry*, 117–19. The *Enquiry* attracted a reply from John Wallis, mathematician and Savilian professor of geometry at Oxford, entitled *A Defence of the Christian Sabbath in answer to a Treatise of Mr Tho. Bampfield*, 2 parts (Oxford, 1692, 1694).

[6] Cf. C.H. and K. George, *The Protestant Mind of the English Reformation 1570–1640* (Princeton, NJ, 1961), 382, and Ball, *A Great Expectation*, 26.

theological, according to the first principles of Christ. Saturday Sabbatarians, most of whom were both Independent and Baptist, believed that they were working according to this principle in pointing out that the seventh day had been widely observed in the early Church for more than a hundred years. They were supported in this contention, although for quite different reasons, by those of the Anglican establishment who opposed all forms of Sabbatarianism and who contended that the requirements of the Sabbath commandment had not been transferred to Sunday as the Puritans maintained, but that the observation of the Lord's day rested on entirely different grounds.[7] Hence many seventeenth-century authorities from quite opposite camps bear witness to the observance of the seventh day in the first four centuries or so of Christian history.

Theophilus Brabourne, whose early writings became almost a point of reference for writers of various opinions in the ensuing Sabbatarian debate, clearly presented his case for Seventh-day observance in the early Church in an exchange in 1654 with John Collings of Norwich.[8] Brabourne cited Athanasius and the Council of Laodicea in support of his argument that the seventh day had been observed at least until the middle of the fourth century. Athanasius had urged that the Sabbath should be kept in a manner which freed it from any taint of Judaizing. 'We assemble on the Sabbath day, not as if we were infected with Judaisme, but . . . that we may worship Jesus the Lord of the Sabbath.'[9] The Council of Laodicea (AD 364) finally prohibited the observance of the old seventh day under pain of excommunication: 'Christians shall not Judaise and be idle on the Sabbath, but shall work on that day; but the Lord's day they shall especially honour, and, as Christians, shall, if possible, do no work on that day. If, however, they are found Judaising, they shall be shut out from Christ.'[10] Some twenty years previously Brabourne had been called to account for his earlier writings advocating the seventh day, and he now described for the

---

[7] Representative writers of the so-called Prelatical or Dominical view include John Prideaux, *The Doctrine of the Sabbath, Delivered in the Act at Oxon, anno 1622* (1634); White, *Treatise*; Heylyn, *History*; John Pocklington, *Sunday No Sabbath* (1636); Gilbert Ironside, *Seven Questions of the Sabbath briefly disputed, after the Manner of the Schools* (Oxford, 1637). Pro-Sabbatarian writers are noted below, 42, n. 97.

[8] On Collings, or Collinges, DD, Presbyterian, ejected from St Stephen's, Norwich, 1662, see *DNB*, s.v. Collinges, and *CR*.

[9] Theophilus Brabourne, *A Reply to Mr Collings Provocator Provocatus* (1654), 63.   [10] Ibid. Cf. *NPNF*, 2nd series, xiv. 148.

first time how in the discussions between himself and the Archbishop of Canterbury, William Laud, and the Bishop of Ely, Francis White, both the Archbishop and the Bishop had agreed that the Sabbath had been observed in the early Church. Brabourne maintained that it was essentially the evidence presented above which had convinced the prelates.[11] White eventually conceded a degree of Seventh-day observance in the post-apostolic Church in his *Treatise of the Sabbath-Day*, written in 1635 as 'a defence of the Orthodoxall [*sic*] doctrine of the Church of England against Sabbatarian Novelty'—Brabourne being the chief culprit.[12]

James Ockford (or Oakeford) cited Socrates, the fifth-century Greek church historian, in support of his assertion that the Seventh-day Sabbath had been observed in the early Church for about four centuries. Socrates had recorded that for the first two centuries virtually all Christian churches in the world had kept the original Sabbath with the exception of Rome and Alexandria. 'Almost all churches throughout the world celebrate the sacred mysteries on the Sabbath [fn. "i.e. Saturday"] of every week, yet the Christians at Alexandria and Rome, on account of some ancient tradition, have ceased to do this.'[13] Sozomen, a contemporary of Socrates, confirms this Sabbatarian tradition by saying, 'The people of Constantinople, and almost everywhere, assemble together on the Sabbath, as well as on the first day of the week, which custom is never observed at Rome or at Alexandria.'[14]

Peter Heylyn, one of Charles I's chaplains, and the most erudite seventeenth-century historian of Sabbatarianism, agreed that the seventh day had been kept by the early Church, and confirmed that some observed both Saturday and Sunday. In support of the assertion that 'the old Sabbath was kept holy by the primitive Christians', Heylyn offers as evidence the fourth-century Apostolic Constitutions, Theophilus of Antioch, and the Council of Laodicea, adding Gregory of Nyssa, whom he cites as rebuking those who had neglected to observe the Sabbath: 'With what face, saith the Father,

[11] Brabourne, *Reply to Mr Collings Provocator Provocatus*, 65.

[12] White, *Treatise*, 189.

[13] James Ockford, *The Doctrine of the Fourth Commandement, Deformed by Popery; Reformed and Restored to its Primitive purity* (1650), 27; cf. *NPNF*, 2nd series, ii. 132.

[14] Ockford, *Doctrine of the Fourth Commandement*, 27; cf. *NPNF*, 2nd series, ii. 390. On Sozomen and Socrates, see W. Smith and H. Wace, *A Dictionary of Christian Biography*, iv (1887), and *ODCC*.

THE
DOCTRINE
OF THE
FOURTH
Commandement,

Deformed by Popery;

Reformed & Restored to its Primitive purity.

Wherein is clearely proved by Scripture,
Arguments, and Reasons, that *the Seventh day of
the week,* and not the first, *viz.* the day called Saturday [and
not the day called Sunday] *is the true Christian Sabbath,*
the time Instituted and commanded by God himself, for the day, or time, of his publique worship, in the time of the Gospel, as it was
in the time of the Law.

*Objections answered, and the truth cleared, by Gods
unworthy Servant,* **J.O.**

The seventh day is the Sabbath of the Lord thy God. In it
thou shalt do no work, &c. Exod. 20. 10.

*Blessed is the man that doth this, and the son of man which layeth
hold on it, and keepeth the Sabbath from polluting of it,* Isa. 56. 2
Be doers of the word, & not hearers only, deceiving your own selvs.
Jam. 1. 22. *For not the hearers of the law are justified before
God, but the doers of the Law shall be justified,* Rom. 2. 13.

London, Printed by *G. Dawson,* and are to be sold by *Iohn Hides*
in *Blew Anchre Alley* neer *Pauls Alley.* 1650.

F<small>IG</small>. 1 Title-page of James Ockford's *The Doctrine of the Fourth
Commandement,* 1650

wilt thou look upon the Lord's day which hast dishonoured the Sabbath? Knowest thou not that these two days are sisters and that whosoever doth despise the one doth affront the other?'[15] In Heylyn's view observance of the seventh day began to decline in the West towards the end of the fourth century, although in the East the seventh day 'retained its wonted credit, little inferior to the Lord's day, if not plainly equal' until Augustine. The seventh day was known specifically as the Sabbath, while the first day was referred to as the Lord's day, both being observed as days of rest, but not 'infected any whit with Judaisme'. Meetings for worship were held on the Sabbath, but the day was not otherwise observed in the strict Jewish sense 'like a Sabbath'.[16]

Others throughout the seventeenth century, who themselves had no allegiance to the seventh day, recognized that it had been observed in early Christian history. Edward Brerewood, in 1611, emphasized the significance of the seventh day in the Eastern Church 'three hundred years and more' after Christ,[17] and Edmund Porter, a prebendary of Norwich, put Seventh-day observance generally 'long after Origen's time'.[18] John Ley, who was greatly disturbed that the Sabbath had 'become as a ball betwixt two rackets' argued that the Council of Laodicea had failed to curtail observance of the seventh day and that in the time of Pope Gregory the Great there were still advocates of the old Sabbath, despite Gregory's strictures against them as being antichristian.[19] Even Ephraim Pagitt, the heresiographer, 'willingly' acknowledged that 'the Jewish Sabbath' had been observed by 'many primitive Christians', although he could not be persuaded that this included Gentiles.[20]

William Cave, the seventeenth-century patristic scholar and Canon of Windsor, summarized the understanding which seemed to prevail

---

[15] Peter Heylyn, *Respondet Petrus:* . . . (1658), 60–1. Cf. John Ley, *Sunday a Sabbath; or, a Preparative Discourse for Discussion of Sabbatory Doubts* (1641), 164, and *NPNF*, 2nd series, v. 547.

[16] Heylyn, *Respondet Petrus*, 61; *History*, 73–4.

[17] Edward Brerewood, *A Learned Treatise of the Sabaoth* (Oxford, 1630), 77, 101. Brerewood, of Gresham College, London, died in 1613. His work was published posthumously as part of the continuing Sabbatarian debate.

[18] Edmund Porter, *Sabbatum: The Mystery of the Sabbath Discovered* (1658), 32.

[19] John Ley, *Sunday a Sabbath* (1641), pref., 166. Cf. *NPNF*, 2nd series, xiii, pt. II, 92. Ley was regarded by Cox as one of the ablest exponents of Puritan Sabbatarianism.

[20] Ephraim Pagitt, *Heresiography, or a Description of the Heretics and Sectaries of these Latter Times* (6th edn. 1661), 173. The 6th edition contains considerably more information on Sabbatarians, particularly the Traskites, than the 1st edition of 1645.

generally in his day concerning the Sabbath in apostolic and post-apostolic centuries:

Next to the Lord's day, the Sabbath or Saturday (for so the word *sabbatum* is constantly used in the writings of the Fathers, when speaking of it as it relates to Christians) was held by them in great veneration, and especially in the Eastern parts honoured with all the public solemnities of religion. For which we are to know, that the gospel in those parts mainly prevailing amongst the Jews, they being generally the first converts to the Christian faith, they still retained a mighty reverence for the Mosaic institutions, and especially for the sabbath, as that which had been appointed by God himself (as the memorial of his rest from the work of Creation,) settled by their great master Moses, and celebrated by their ancestors for so many ages, as the solemn day of their public worship, and were therefore very loth that it should be wholly antiquated and laid aside. For this reason it seemed good to the prudence of those times (as in others of the Jewish rites, so in this,) to indulge the humour of that people, and to keep the sabbath as a day for religious offices. Hence they usually had most parts of divine service performed upon that day; they met together for public prayers, for reading the Scriptures, celebration of the sacraments, and such like duties. This is plain, not only from some passages in Ignatius and Clemens his Constitutions, but from writers of more unquestionable credit and authority. Athanasius, bishop of Alexandria tells us, that they assembled on Saturdays, not that they were infected with Judaism, but only to worship Jesus Christ, the Lord of the Sabbath; and Socrates, speaking of the usual times of their public meeting, calls the Sabbath and the Lord's day the weekly festivals, on which the congregation was wont to meet in the church for the performance of divine services. Therefore the Council of Laodicea amongst other things decreed, that upon Saturdays the gospels and other Scriptures should be read, that in Lent the Eucharist should not be celebrated but upon Saturday and the Lord's day, and upon those days only in the time of Lent it should be lawful to commemorate and rehearse the names of martyrs. Upon this day also, as well as upon Sunday, all fasts were severely prohibited (an infallible argument they counted it a festival day,) one Saturday in the year only excepted, viz. that before Easter-day, which was always observed as a solemn fast. Things so commonly known as to need no proof. But though the Church thought fit thus far to correspond with the Jewish converts, as solemnly to observe the sabbath; yet to take away all offence, and to vindicate themselves from compliance with Judaism, they openly declared, that they did it only in a Christian way, and kept it not as a Jewish sabbath, as is expressly affirmed by Athanasius, Nazianzen, and others; and the forementioned Laodicean synod has a canon to this purpose, that Christians should not Judaize, and rest from all labour on the sabbath, but follow their ordinary works, (i.e. so far as consisted with their attendance upon the public assemblies,) and should not entertain such thoughts of it, but that still they should prefer the Lord's day before it; and on that day rest as Christians: but if any were found to Judaize, they should be accursed.[21]

With a few reservations and amendments, most Seventh-day Men would have concurred. They would have preferred less emphasis on the dual role of the seventh day and the first day, particularly as a universal custom, and less emphasis on the concessionary nature of Seventh-day observance to Jewish converts. And they would perhaps have liked some specific indication that in parts of the Church at least the seventh day had stood on its own feet, an evident testimony to the apostolic faith which they believed it was their duty to restore.

THE CELTIC CHURCH

Various authorities over the past hundred years or so have consistently maintained that a Sabbatarian tradition persisted for several centuries in the Celtic Church. According to Skene, the Scottish historiographer, traces of observing both Saturday and Sunday in the early Irish Church were also found in Scotland, where they lasted until Margaret, in the eleventh century, reformed the Church according 'to the rules of the true faith (and) sacred customs of the universal church'.[22] Margaret's reforms were aimed, among other things, at prevailing attitudes to the Lord's day, for which she sought more recognition and more reverence.[23] Both Lang and Moffat refer specifically to the practice of observing the seventh day in the early Celtic Church. Moffat says that in keeping 'Saturday the Jewish Sabbath' the Celtic Church 'obeyed the fourth commandment literally upon the seventh day of the week'. This was 'customary in the Celtic church of early times, in Ireland as well as Scotland'.[24] Lang adds that Saturday was kept strictly 'in a sabbatical manner'.[25]

[21] William Cave, *Primitive Christianity: or the Religion of the Ancient Christians in the first Ages of the Gospel* (1673), 173–6.

[22] W.F. Skene, *Celtic Scotland: A History of Ancient Alban* (Edinburgh, 1877), ii. 346, 349, and W. Forbes-Leith (ed.), *The Life of St. Margaret, Queen of Scotland* (Edinburgh, 1896), 50–1.   [23] Skene, *Celtic Scotland*, 348–9.

[24] J.C. Moffat, *The Church in Scotland* (Philadelphia, 1882), 140.

[25] A. Lang, *A History of Scotland from the Roman Occupation* (Edinburgh, 1900), i. 96.

T. Ratcliffe Barnett noted that it was traditional in the ancient Irish Church to observe Saturday instead of Sunday as the day of rest,[26] and A.C. Flick points again to the custom of keeping the seventh day as a day of rest and of holding religious services on Sunday.[27]

More recent studies of the Celtic Church and relevant extant documents have tended to reinforce these earlier conclusions of nineteenth-century historians. In the 1961 edition of *Adomnan's Life of Columba*, edited by A.O. and M.O. Anderson, recognition of Saturday as the Sabbath, and the dual role of Saturday and Sunday in the life of the Celtic Church known to Adomnan are both noted. Adomnan referred to the first day of the week as 'Lord's day' ('dominica dies' or 'dies dominica') and called Saturday the Sabbath ('Sabbatum') or 'the day of Sabbath'.[28] Another more recent study points out that Adomnan invariably used the name Sabbatum when speaking of the seventh day, and always referred to the Sabbath 'in a manner betokening a respect which is not detected in writers two centuries later'.[29] This fits well with the thesis that the complete Romanizing of the Celtic Church occurred much later than it did in the British Church at large. According to Adomnan, Columba himself distinguished between the Sabbath and Sunday, although there is no clear evidence here that either Adomnan or Columba kept Saturday or Sunday exclusively.[30]

The deference given to both Sabbath and Sunday is apparent in Adomnan's reference to the Rule of Columcelle, where it is laid down that the allowance of food for Sabbath and Sunday are equal in amount 'because of the reverence paid to the Sabbath in the Old Testament'. The Sabbath differs from Sunday in respect of work only. Other regulations demonstrate further similarities between Sabbath and Sunday.[31] Hardinge cites instances from the *Mediaeval Handbook of Penance* and other contemporary sources which indicate a continuing tension between Saturday and Sunday, demonstrating perhaps a reluctance both to let go of the seventh day, and to take hold fully of the Lord's day with the rest of the Romanized Church in the British Isles.[32] That this was a period of transition is

[26] T.R. Barnett, *Margaret of Scotland: Queen and Saint* (Edinburgh, 1926), 97.
[27] A.C. Flick, *The Rise of the Mediaeval Church* (1909), 237.
[28] A.O. and M.O. Anderson (eds.), *Adomnan's Life of Columba* (1961), 120. On Adomnan, or Adamnan, Abbot of Iona, AD 679, see *DNB* and *ODCC*, s.v. Adamnan.
[29] L. Hardinge, *The Celtic Church in Britain* (1972), 84.
[30] Anderson, *Adomnan*, 25.   [31] Ibid. 120.
[32] Hardinge, *Celtic Church*, 84–5, and *passim*.

clear from Adomnan's reference to early Irish attempts 'to persuade Christians to observe Sunday as the Sabbath',[33] although the editors note that 'the sabbatical Sunday had not yet been accepted by Adomnan or in Iona at the time when Adomnan wrote'.[34]

This lingering ambivalence between Sabbath and Sunday, evident here in the Celtic Church and also at times in the post-apostolic Church at large, is perhaps one of the stronger evidences of an earlier commitment to the seventh day. Taken in context, and coupled with evidences of a sabbatizing process already begun, this dual recognition of Sabbath and Sunday suggests, as Hardinge remarks, 'that there was a gradual shift from the keeping of Saturday, the seventh day Sabbath, to the observance of both Saturday and Sunday and then to the celebration of Sunday exclusively'.[35]

Given the measure of respect for the Bible, particularly the Old Testament, which is evident in Celtic texts, it is not in the least surprising that observance of the seventh day is found in the Celtic Church. Patrick's allegiance to Scripture and his aversion to patristic and conciliar sources are well known.[36] According to one original source, the Bible was accorded paramount authority in Celtic theology and practice and was revered 'as the voice of the Holy Ghost addressing his people in the character of a king upon his throne'.[37] Laistner comments on 'the pre-occupation of Irish scholars with Biblical exegesis', often following a strictly literal hermeneutic.[38] It seems that particular respect was accorded to the Old Testament, in which connection the *Liber ex lege Moisi* played a prominent role. Patrick is said to have left a copy of 'the books of the Law, and of the book of the Gospel' wherever he established a church. The *Liber ex lege Moisi* is the only extant Celtic manuscript which fits this tradition.[39] Whether or not this is the case, the *Liber ex lege Moisi*

---

[33] Anderson, *Adomnan*, 27. The editors note that Adomnan wrote 'at a time when there was controversy over the question whether the ritual of the biblical Sabbath was to be transferred to the Christians Lord's-day', ibid. 25–6.

[34] Ibid. 29.   [35] Hardinge, *Celtic Church*, 89.

[36] e.g. W. Stokes, *The Tripartite Life of Patrick* (1887), ii. 567, and Hardinge, *Celtic Church*, 30.

[37] W. Stokes and J. Strachan, *Thesaurus Palaeohibernicus: A Collection of Old Irish Glosses* (Cambridge, 1901–10), i. 389, cited in Hardinge, *Celtic Church*, 32.

[38] M.L.W. Laistner, *Thought and Letters in Western Europe, AD 500 to 900* (1957), 146.

[39] Stokes, *Life of Patrick*, ii. 300 and J.F. Kenney, *The Sources for the Early History of Ireland*, i: *Ecclesiastical* (New York, 1929), 250, cited in Hardinge, *Celtic Church*, 50.

exerted a profound influence on Celtic thought. It is significant that the *Liber* commences with the Ten Commandments, and Hardinge is probably correct in asserting that the observance of the Sabbath of the Old Testament in the Celtic Church was a material outgrowth of an emphasis on Christian obedience inculcated through usage of the *Liber* in exegesis and pastoral instruction.[40]

The liturgical practices of the early Irish Church as reflected in the seventh-century *Antiphonary of Bangor* may also indicate a lingering devotion to the Sabbath. Hardinge records J.F. Kenney's observation that the *Antiphonary* is 'the only record surviving of the old Irish Church services unaffected by the Romanizing movement of the seventh and eighth centuries', and notes that included in it were suggestions for conducting the Divine Office at Easter, on Sabbaths, and Sunday in Eastertide, and on Sabbaths and Sundays throughout the year.[41] Hardinge's own conclusions, based on the Celtic regard for Scripture and the accompanying emphasis on the obedient life, are appropriate:

There was no Sabbatizing of Sunday during the Celtic period. The seventh day was kept from sunset on Friday until sunset on Saturday, and even until dawn on Sunday in some places. No work was done on it, as the laws of the *Liber ex lege Moisi* stipulate. While Sunday was also held to possess minor sanctity, and religious services were carried out on it, the daily chores, the gathering of food, the washing of hair and taking of baths, the going on journeys and carrying out of regular business transactions were all permitted on the first day.[42]

THE LOLLARDS

The most cursory survey of the geographical distribution of seventeenth-century Sabbatarian congregations would suggest an affinity with Lollardy. A Seventh-day presence was established in many areas which previously had been Lollard strongholds. London, East Anglia, Buckinghamshire and the Chilterns, the Severn Valley, particularly around Gloucester, Dorset, Wiltshire, and Hereford and the Welsh Borders may all be mentioned as typical in this respect. Since the Lollard movement persisted in some of these areas well

---

[40] Hardinge, *Celtic Church*, 210, 203.
[41] Kenney, *Sources*, 712; Hardinge, *Celtic Church*, 120–1.
[42] Ibid. 203.

into the sixteenth century,[43] there may have been a much stronger connection than is often granted between Lollard theology and that of the more radical anti-establishment groups which flourished in England during the seventeenth century. Claire Cross describes early Lollards as 'characterised first and foremost by their biblical fundamentalism',[44] and this, added to the rapid dissemination of Lollard ideas, the readiness with which they were received, the provision of the Bible or parts of it in the vernacular, and the persistence of a Lollard tradition in many parts of the country, is sufficient ground for concluding that Lollard influence may well have contributed to the later appearance of Seventh-day views.

This tentative conclusion is confirmed in the light of evidence from original sources. Once again it is reverence for the Old Testament and the Ten Commandments which initially delineates the Lollards as setting a precedent for later Sabbatarian theology. Wyclif himself had stressed the importance for Christians of obeying the Ten Commandments,[45] and although the Wycliffite *Lanterne of Light* may not have been his, it none the less may be taken as representative of Wyclif's thought. *The Lanterne of Light* is typical of Lollard commentaries on the Decalogue. It follows that form of the Ten Commandments used by the medieval Church, citing the third commandment as the Sabbath commandment, and speaking of the seventh day as the true Sabbath with the injunction: 'Have mind that thou hallow this holy day. In six days thou shalt work and do all thine own works, for so the seventh day is the sabbath of the Lord'. Several variations of this exhortation to observe the Sabbath

---

[43] G.F. Nuttall records continuity of the Lollard movement through the fifteenth and early sixteenth centuries, 'The Lollard Movement after 1384: Its Characteristics and Continuity', *TCHS* 12 (1935), 243–50. Cf. C. Cross, *Church and People, 1450–1660* (1976), where Lollardy is said to have survived, particularly in the south of England, where it had 'attracted new adherents', 53. A.G. Dickens notes Lollard survival in the sixteenth century in the Chiltern area of Buckinghamshire, in Essex, Berkshire, Kent, Yorkshire, and Nottinghamshire; A.G. Dickens, *The English Reformation* (1964), 26–33. Christopher Hill may not be completely accurate in concluding that 'the view that no day should be kept holy except Sunday goes back to the Lollards': C. Hill, *Society and Puritanism in Pre-Revolutionary England* (1969), 145. Dickens, *The English Reformation*, 22–37 and Cross, *Church and People*, 9–52, provide excellent summaries of Lollardy and its influence.

[44] Cross, *Church and People*, 16.

[45] See John Wyclif, *Select English Works of John Wyclif*, ed. T. Arnold (Oxford, 1869–71), iii. 82–92. Arnold states that Wyclif's tract on the Ten Commandments may have been based on an earlier commentary, ibid. 82. There is no hint of the Seventh-day Sabbath in this work.

are noted, with the gloss that it is the devil who leads men to break the Sabbath.[46] If the *Lanterne of Light* may be taken as typical of Lollard teaching, it is not difficult to perceive how reverence for the Sabbath would have arisen in Lollard communities.

Robert Pope of Amersham and Thomas Taylor of Newbury are both recorded as owning a suspect book containing the Ten Commandments.[47] Alice Collins, wife of a noted Lollard, and herself 'a famous woman among them', had memorized large portions of Scripture, and was often invited to recite the Ten Commandments, together with the Epistles of Peter and James, at conventicles in Burford *c.*1520.[48] In 1469 John Cornewe and John Breche, Lollards from Lydney, Gloucestershire, were called to abjure, among other opinions, the view that the authority of the Old Testament was preferable to that of the New Testament. 'Item quod auctoritas veteris testamenti preferenda et melior est novo testamento.'[49] According to Cross, as late as the early sixteenth century an Essex Lollard confessed to having taught others the Lord's Prayer and the Ten Commandments in English.[50]

The case of William Fuer of Gloucester is one of several specific instances now coming to light of Lollard Sabbatarianism. Fuer abjured under duress in 1448, saying that he derived his views from Bristol Lollards, including William Smith, one of the most noted Lollards of the day, who was eventually burnt for heresy. According to J.A.F. Thomson, who records Fuer's case, a considerable number of heresy trials had been conducted in the Severn Valley in the years preceding 1450, in which some of those tried revealed views more heretical than had previously been detected. Certainly extreme Sabbatarianism would have been so regarded, and Fuer confessed to holding such views, saying that the Sabbath should be observed as strictly as commanded in the Old Testament with the preparation of food as the only permissible activity.[51] It is not specifically clear

---

[46] L.M. Swinburn (ed.), *The Lanterne of Light* (1917), 90–1.

[47] Cross, *Church and People*, 33; J.A.F. Thomson, *The Later Lollards 1414–1520* (Oxford, 1965), 76.

[48] John Foxe, *The Actes and Monuments of John Foxe* (New York, 1965 edn.), iv. 238.

[49] A.T. Bannister (ed.), *The Register of John Stanbury, Bishop of Hereford 1453–1474* (1918), 119.

[50] Cross, *Church and People*, 38. Knowledge of the Ten Commandments was a frequent accusation brought against 'heretics' in the diocese of Lincoln in the early sixteenth century, Foxe, *Actes and Monuments*, iv. 223 ff.

[51] Thomson, *Later Lollards*, 36.

whether Fuer's Sabbatarianism extended to the seventh day, although given the general direction of Lollard theology, it is not impossible. A movement towards the stricter observance of Sunday appeared in England early in the fifteenth century,[52] arising in the main out of a growing Lollard conviction which could not overlook the injunctions of the fourth commandment. Gairdner and Spedding observed over a century ago that if Lollards had regarded the observance of Sunday as merely resting on the authority of the Church, they would have classed it with all other 'abuses of tradition . . . and other noxious superstitions which they were anxious should be thoroughly rooted out'.[53] William Fuer was clearly of that mind in maintaining a highly developed Sabbatarianism, and it is well within the limits of probability that his obdurate defence of the Old Testament Sabbath included the seventh day.

There is no such ambiguity in the earlier case of John Seygno of London, in the light of which perhaps Fuer's own views should be evaluated. In 1402, only a year after Parliament had assented to the anti-heresy Act, 'De haeretico comburendo', John Seygno and two others, Richard Herbert and Emmota Wylly, were brought before the courts on a heresy charge. Seygno had apparently been arraigned on a previous occasion at Canterbury, and having been convicted on charges similar to those now brought against him again, had sworn that he had never held views worthy of condemnation. Whether or not the earlier charges had included Sabbatarianism is not recorded, but now he admitted that the Sabbath was to be observed 'according to what was observed in the Old Testament'. Claiming that he wished to observe 'a Sabbath of this kind as described in the old law, that is according to the customs and rites of the Jews', he indicated that he intended to do so until he could be persuaded otherwise with sufficient reasons.[54] In the light of Henri Misson's account of later Seventh-day views, it is of more than passing interest that Seygno also held that swine's flesh should not be eaten because of its uncleanness.[55] On the strength

---

[52] Promoted initially by Thomas Arundel, Archbishop of Canterbury; H. Thurston, 'The Mediaeval Sunday', in *Nineteenth Century*, 46 (July 1899), 46, cited in Parker, *The English Sabbath*, 21.

[53] James Gairdner and James Spedding, *Studies in English History* (1881), 295–6.

[54] D. Wilkins, *Concilia Magnae Britanniae et Hiberniae ab Anno MCCCL ad Annum MDXLV* (1737), iii. 270–1.

[55] Ibid. Misson had observed that many Seventh-day Men in the latter half of the seventeenth century would not eat pork, *Memoirs*, 235.

of Seygno's case alone, it would seem incontrovertible that Seventh-day observance appeared among Lollards within twenty years of Wyclif's death and, moreover, that a direct connection between Lollardy and the Seventh-day Men is a distinct possibility.[56]

An early fifteenth-century manuscript, now in the British Library,[57] confirms that the Sabbath issue was debated in Lollard circles two centuries or so before observance of the seventh day was openly established in worshipping communities in England and Wales. The tract is described by one palaeographer as 'apparently directed against an aberration . . . that might be expected to follow from principles of Wycliffite scriptural interpretation'.[58] The author evidently felt the need to respond to those who questioned the change of the Sabbath from the seventh day to the first, as may be seen from the tract's title: 'A litil tretys agens ye opynyon of sum men yt seyn yat no man hath powr for to chaunge ye Saboth fro ye Satirday to ye Sonday. And here is pleynly proved ye contrarie, bi Holi Writt, and Doctouris sentence accordynge herwit.' The writer, most probably a priest, begins by referring to questions regarding the authority by which such a change in the day of worship could be made. Since there is no human authority which can change the law of God, some doubt had been cast on the validity of Sunday as a day of special significance: 'summen douten sith no man hath leeve for to chaunge ye ten comaundementis of God; how myghte we chaunge our Saboth fro ye Satirday to Sonday.'[59] The author explains that the law contains ceremonial as well as moral precepts, and that, since observance of the seventh day was ceremonial, it was no longer of binding force. Furthermore, the Church has authority to make what changes she deems necessary. In this instance Christ, who has power over all things, had appointed the Lord's day by His own actions.[60] The cases of John Seygno and William

---

[56] W.T. Whitley noted the influence of 'the Lollard element' on early General Baptists, particularly in Buckinghamshire and Berkshire; W.T. Whitley, *Minutes of the General Assembly of the General Baptist Churches in England* (1910), i, p. ix. This influence extended into the bordering areas of Hertfordshire and Oxfordshire.

[57] BL MS Harl. 2339.

[58] A.I. Doyle, 'A Treatise of the Three Estates', *Dominican Studies*, 3/4 (1950), 353.

[59] BL MS Harl. 2339 fo. 104ᵛ.

[60] Ibid., fos. 105ʳ–116ʳ. The arguments were essentially the same as would be brought against the Seventh-day Men in the seventeenth century. Bishop Reginald Pecock's views on the Ten Commandments may also be relevant: 'In particular he disputed the tendency to equate the Jewish Sabbath, the object of the third commandment, with the Christian Sunday. The commandment is no longer binding on Christians because it merely aims to maintain the Jewish Sabbath, and it is therefore

Fuer suggest that there were at least some in the Lollard fraternity who were not so persuaded.

CONTINENTAL SABBATARIANS

Well before the end of the sixteenth century references to Seventh-day observance had begun to appear in English Sabbatarian literature. In 1584, John Stockwood published *A Verie Profitable and Necessarie Discourse Concerning the observation and keeping of the Sabboth Day*, extracted from the earlier work of the German theologian Ursinus. Stockwood referred to Sabbatarians who 'obstinately and stiffly' upheld the 'ceremonial observation of the seventh day', which they regarded as immutable and completely binding.[61] In 1607 John Sprint noted the two extreme positions in the Sabbatarian controversy. At one end were those who maintained that no Sabbath at all was to be observed as such by Christians, while at the other end were those who held that 'the Jewish Sabbath of the seventh day' was to be kept 'being no less necessary for us to observe now, than it ever was for the Jews'.[62] Neither Stockwood nor Sprint state whether they refer to Seventh-day observance in England or not, although if the 1874 edition of *Chambers's Encyclopaedia* can be taken as a guide, it would have to be concluded that the seventh day had been observed in England widely from Elizabethan times.[63] If, on the other hand,

no more relevant to Christians than the command to eat the paschal lamb or to wear a cloth made of linen and wool, or the command not to use "an hors and asse couplid togider". The Christian Sunday does not commemorate the day on which God rested from the creation of the world, but the day of our Lord's resurrection. Neither reason nor history indicate that Christ translated the Jewish Sabbath into the Christian Sunday,' V.H.H. Green, *Bishop Reginald Pecock* (Cambridge, 1945), 181–2, citing Pecock's *Donet*, ed. E.V. Hitchcock (1921), 131, 148. Pecock was noted for his anti-Lollard views.

[61] John Stockwood (tr.), *A Verie Profitable and Necessarie Discourse Concerning the observation and keeping of the Sabboth Day* (1584), Ep. Ded. Aiii'. The running title reads 'An Exposition upon the fourth Commandment'. The original work of Ursinus was translated in its entirety in 1595 by Henry Parry under the title *The Summe of Christian Religion*. For Ursinus, who with other Continental Reformation theologians is frequently cited in the Sabbatarian literature, see J.D. Douglas (ed.), *The New International Dictionary of the Christian Church* (1974).

[62] John Sprint, *Propositions Tending to Prove the Necessary Use of the Christian Sabbath, or Lord's Day* (1607), 2. Sprint viewed observance of the seventh day as 'an unchristian opinion' and listed 'Sabbatary Christians' with Jews, Ebionites, Cerinthians, and Anabaptists, 3.

[63] 'In the reign of Elizabeth, it occurred to many conscientious and independent thinkers (as it had previously done to some Protestants in Bohemia), that the fourth

Stockwood and Sprint refer to Continental Sabbatarianism, then they were in good company, for both Erasmus and Luther had drawn attention to the Sabbatarian phenomenon on the Continent, Erasmus to Sabbatarians in Bohemia, 'a new kind of Jews',[64] and Luther to similar groups in Moravia and Austria, 'a foolish group of people who maintained the observance of the Sabbath according to Jewish manner and custom'.[65] Hospinian of Zurich likewise wrote against the Sabbatarians in 1592, demonstrating that the issue was alive on the Continent for much of the sixteenth century.[66]

In fact, the Continental Sabbatarian tradition went back considerably further, as was known to at least some English seventeenth-century Sabbatarian controversialists. John Prideaux, Rector of Exeter College, Oxford, and Vice-Chancellor of the University on three occasions during a distinguished career, maintained that in the twelfth century the neo-Ebionite Petrobusians, under their founder Peter de Bruis (or de Bruys), had been 'Jewish in this point'.[67] The eighteenth-century Church historian Mosheim mentions the Pasagini (or Pasagii) of Lombardy who were distinct on account of their teaching that the Law of Moses should be kept in all details except the offering of sacrifices, and their Arian views on the nature of Christ. With regard to the former, they were sometimes known as Circumcisii since they practised circumcision. Mosheim notes that they also abstained from unclean meats prohibited by the Mosaic Law.[68] The martyrs of Arras in 1420 were also reported to have kept 'the complete Law of the Jews' and to have 'observed Saturday instead of Sunday', and for this reason are said to have been marked with a yellow cross following the custom of designating Jews during the Middle Ages.[69] The charge of Judaizing, fairly or unfairly, was

commandment required of them the observance, not of the first, but of the specified seventh day of the week'. The Sabbatarians were 'numerous enough to make a considerable figure for more than a century', *Chambers's Encyclopaedia* (1874), viii. 402.

[64] Erasmus, *De amabili Ecclesiae concordia* (Antwerp, 1533), sig. F6ᵛ.

[65] *D. Martin Luthers Werke*, xlii (Weimar, 1911), 520.

[66] Rudolph Hospinian, *De Origine, Progressu, Ceremoniis, et Ritibus Festorum Dierum Judaeorum, Graecorum, Romanorum, et Turcarum* (Zurich, 1592), Ch. 3.

[67] Prideaux, *Doctrine of the Sabbath*, preface, A2ʳ.

[68] J.L. von Mosheim, *Institutes of Ecclesiastical History* (1841), ii. 510. On the Pasagini, or Pasagians, of the twelfth and early thirteenth centuries, see J.H. Blunt, *Dictionary of Sects, Heresies, Ecclesiastical Parties, and Schools of Religious Thought* (1886), s.v. Pasagians.

[69] P. Beuzart, *Les Hérésies pendant le Moyen Âge et la Réforme dans la région de Douai, d'Arras et au pays de l'Alleu* (Le Puy, 1912), 37–47. I am indebted to Dr J. Zurcher for this reference.

never far from the lips of those who opposed Seventh-day observance, and it persisted throughout the history of the English Seventh-day movement of the seventeenth and eighteenth centuries. George Huntston Williams records that an extreme movement of this nature arose *c.*1470 in the Kiev area of Russia, where it persisted well into the sixteenth century, making the Decalogue the basis of its religious life in much the same way as the later Pentateuchalists of Strasburg.[70] While many English Sabbatarians appear to have adopted Mosaic dietary laws, few would have rejected the Messiahship of Jesus or the authority of the New Testament as some of these extreme Continental groups are said to have done.[71]

With the sixteenth century there appeared in Europe a more coherent and widespread Sabbatarian movement, identifiable in the main with the Anabaptists of the Radical Reformation, although Luther himself had been embarrassed by the Sabbatarian inclinations of Carlstadt.[72] The year 1527/8 is the date usually given for the appearance of Sabbatarian Anabaptists in the Continental Reformation. At about this time Andreas Fischer adopted the Sabbatarian beliefs of Oswald Glait in Nikolsburg, Moravia, and became thenceforth Glait's principal co-labourer.[73] In 1528 they successfully propagated Sabbatarian views in Silesia, where they were opposed in public disputation and in print by Caspar Schwenckfeld. Glait shortly thereafter published *Buchlenn vom Sabbath*, to which both Schwenckfeld and Wolfgang Capito replied in print.[74] It is possible that Luther's own *Brief wider die Sabbather* (1538) may have been inspired, in part at least, by the Sabbatarians of Silesia and Moravia, since he had known of their existence from 1532, although he also notes the rise of Sabbatarians (Sabbather) in Austria during the same period.[75] The Moravian Sabbatarians were still noted in heresy lists in 1564 and 1589.[76]

English writers of the time, both religious and secular, were aware of other contemporary Saturday Sabbath-keeping movements, as

---

[70] G.H. Williams, *The Radical Reformation* (1962), 740, 835.

[71] Ibid. 252.

[72] References to Sabbatarian Anabaptism can be found in Williams, *Radical Reformation passim*. A more continuous account appears in G.F. Hasel, 'Sabbatarian Anabaptists of the Sixteenth Century', *Andrews University Seminary Studies*, 5/2 (1967), 101–21, and 6/1 (1968), 19–28.

[73] Williams, *Radical Reformation*, 410; cf. Hasel, *AUSS* 5/2: 107–15.

[74] Hasel, *AUSS* 5/2: 112.   [75] Ibid. 107.

[76] Ibid. 101–6; cf. Williams, *Radical Reformation*, 675, and H.A. De Wind, 'A Sixteenth Century Description of Religious Sects in Austerlitz, Moravia', *Mennonite Quarterly Review*, 29 (1955), 44–53.

Cox points out, and references may be found in several well-known seventeenth-century authorities. Samuel Purchas, chiefly known for his *Purchas his Pilgrims* of 1625, recorded that from the middle of the sixteenth century the Seventh-day Sabbath had been taught in Ethiopia,[77] a fact confirmed by Baratti's travels in that region, an account of which was published in an English translation in 1670. Baratti, an Italian gentleman, described how 'chaplains' at the Imperial Court expounded Scripture in the Emperor's presence 'on the Sabbath day . . . according to the ancient manner of the Jews'. Saturday, he explained, was the day appointed for public worship in Ethiopia 'because God on that day finished the great work of the creation of the world'.[78] In a note on the fly-leaf of his father's *The Insnared Taken in the Work of his Hands* (1677), Joseph Stennett referred to Baratti's account as evidence of contemporary Sabbath-keeping.[79] Stennett further cited Peter Heylyn's *Cosmography* in which the Melchites of Syria were also described as worshipping 'as solemnly on the Saturday as on the Sunday'.[80] These more remote and obscure observers of the seventh day would understandably have been of interest to a man of Stennett's learning and wide interests.

Other areas in which Seventh-day observance appeared in the sixteenth century include Poland, particularly Lithuania,[81] Bohemia (as noted by Erasmus),[82] and especially in Transylvania, where some Sabbatarians professed Unitarian views, and some adopted Mosaic dietary practices.[83] Williams notes that the Transylvanian Sabbatarians persisted at least until 1618, when they were formally excluded from the Unitarian fold.[84] A widespread Sabbatarian movement thus found expression across the European continent and beyond for much of the sixteenth century, and although a detailed survey of its

---

[77] Samuel Purchas, *Hakluytas Posthumus, or Purchas his Pilgrims* (1625), 1177.

[78] Giacomo Baratti, *The Late Travels of Giacomo Baratti, an Italian Gentleman, into the Remote Countries of the Abissins, or of Ethiopia, Interior,* tr. G.D. (1670), 46, 135.

[79] Stennett, *The Insnared Taken.* The BL copy (shelf-mark 1471 de 11) is one of the very few which have survived.

[80] Peter Heylyn, *Cosmography* (1674), book III, 40.

[81] Williams, *Radical Reformation,* 414, 686; Hasel, *AUSS* 6/1: 20–1.

[82] Hasel, *AUSS* 5/2: 106, 107, 114.

[83] Williams, *Radical Reformation* 730–2. On the Sabbatarian movement among Unitarians in the sixteenth and early seventeenth centuries, see E.M. Wilbur, *A History of Unitarianism: In Transylvania, England, and America* (Cambridge, Mass., 1952), 106–15.   [84] Williams, *Radical Reformation,* 732.

development and theology is beyond the scope of this work, it may be noted in passing that Glait and Fischer, its two most able proponents in central Europe, both emphasized in defence of their views the perpetuity of the moral law in the Decalogue, and the example of Christ, the apostles, and the early Church.[85] These were arguments well known to English Sabbatarians of the seventeenth century, as we shall see, and it is rather strange that there are so few references in the English Sabbatarian literature to this Continental movement. This may support the conclusion that the Seventh-day cause in England was spontaneous and self-contained, rather than being derived from Continental Anabaptism, as has sometimes been suggested, although East Anglia may have been susceptible to some Continental influence. It may also be indicative of a desire not to be too closely identified with a movement which, taken as a whole, was frequently characterized as legalistic, or Judaistic, or anti-trinitarian.[86]

THE SABBATARIAN CONTROVERSY

It was inevitable that the Sabbatarian controversy, 'peculiar to England of all Christendom' in the view of one contemporary,[87] should give rise to Seventh-day observance. This sixteenth- and seventeenth-century debate, frequently vigorous and occasionally acrimonious, continues to be a focus of scholarly attention, and although its broad features will be well known to most of those who read this study, it would hardly be conceivable to omit it entirely from any survey of Seventh-day antecedents. In the light of earlier observations on the Lollard tradition, it is significant to note, as a background to the defined Sabbatarian doctrine of Nicholas Bownd in 1595, a consistent emphasis on Sabbath observance, *per se*, from the early years of the English Reformation.[88] In 1548 John Hooper emphasized the Sabbath in *A Declaration of the Ten Holy Commaundements*, explaining that the fourth commandment was essentially moral like all the others, and therefore binding, rather than ceremonial,

---

[85] Hasel, *AUSS* 5/2: 116–21; 6/1: 22–7.

[86] Cf. Williams, *Radical Reformation*, 732, 835.

[87] Bodl. MS Rawl. D. 846 fo. 42ʳ.

[88] Parker's valuable study *The English Sabbath* does not exhaust the evidence for Sabbatarianism prior to the seventeenth century. Its most inexplicable omission is of any reference to the continuing Lollard or Wycliffite tradition.

although the specific day of rest had been changed.[89] In 1552 Hugh
Latimer reminded a congregation in Lincolnshire that 'God is and
remaineth still the old God: He will have us keep his Sabbath, as
well now as then.' The Sabbath day is 'God's ploughing day' when
the hearts of men are broken up to receive the seed of the gospel.[90]
Thomas Becon could be read for a thoroughgoing Puritan
Sabbatarian when he says that God's will is that men 'should sanctify
the Sabbath day' and upon it 'quietly meditate in God's law, read
the holy Scriptures, give themselves to divine contemplation, talk
of serious matters, pray to God for grace, give him thanks for his
benefits, visit the sick and comfortless, and continually be given to
the works of the Spirit'.[91]

Such views were readily incorporated into the doctrine of the
Elizabethan Church and found expression, for example, in the 1563
book of homilies which stated that:

God hath given express charge to all men, that upon the Sabbath day,
which is now our Sunday, they should cease from all weekly and work-
day labour, to the intent that like as God himself wrought six days, and
rested the seventh, and blessed and sanctified it, and consecrated it to
quietness and rest from labour, even so God's obedient people should use
the Sunday holily, and rest from their common and daily business, and also
give themselves wholly to heavenly exercises of God's true religion and
service.[92]

Parker says that this homily 'must be acknowledged as the primary
source of Sabbatarian teaching in the Elizabethan and early Stuart
period'.[93]

It was easy thenceforth for preachers and expositors alike to
uphold the ideal of the Sabbath, even though at the time its observance in practice might have left much to be desired. The Elizabethan 'merrie England' was so called largely on account of Sunday
diversions such as hunting, shooting, hawking, fencing, clowning,
and morris dancing, not to mention trading and other 'flagrant abuses

[89] John Hooper, *A Declaration of the Ten Holy Commaundements of almyghty
God* (1548), 341–2.
[90] Hugh Latimer, *The Works of Hugh Latimer*, ed. G.E. Corrie, i (Cambridge, 1844),
473.
[91] Thomas Becon, *The Early Works of Thomas Becon*, ed. J. Ayre (Cambridge,
1843), 38.
[92] *Certaine Sermons appoynted . . . to be declared and read . . . for the better understanding of the simple people* (1563), ii, fo. 138ʳ.
[93] Parker, *The English Sabbath*, 46.

of the Sabbath'.[94] Such laxness and obvious inconsistency with the professed doctrine of the Church gave rise to strictures such as those of Humphry Roberts, *An Earnest Complaint of divers Vain, Wicked and Abased Exercises Practiced on the Sabbath Day* (1572), and John Northbrooke, *A Treatise wherein Dicing, Dancing, Vain Plays or Interludes, with other idle Pastimes commonly used on the Sabbath are by the Word of God and ancient Writers reproved* (1579). In 1583 Gervase Babington, soon to become Bishop of Llandaff (later of Exeter, and finally Worcester), published his *Very Fruitfull Exposition of the Commandments*, one of a growing number of works intended to draw attention to the Sabbath problem, and to encourage more faithful observance of Sunday. In the same year the Puritan John Field took the occasion of an accident at the Paris Gardens near London to press home the gravity of Sabbath-breaking. Many had been killed and several injured in a large audience attending a bear-baiting on Sunday, and Field interpreted this as divine judgement on those concerned.[95] And in 1585 Lancelot Andrewes, later Bishop of Chichester (1603), Ely (1609), and Winchester (1619), delivered a series of lectures at Cambridge in which he expounded the doctrine that the Sabbath (Sunday) should be kept as a day of rest and worship on the grounds of the continuing morality of the fourth commandment.[96]

Thus Nicholas Bownd's *The Doctrine of the Sabbath* (1595), while a classic formulation of the Puritan concept and the immediate cause of the Sabbatarian debate, came from a well-established Sabbath tradition in English Reformation theology. Parker has pointed to a similar tradition in medieval and Catholic thought in a justifiable attempt to demonstrate that a Sabbath doctrine existed prior to Puritan Sabbatarianism. For all that, Bownd's work remains of significance, and his arguments and those of succeeding advocates of the Puritan view may be summarized as follows. The Sabbath was an ordinance instituted at Creation, and thus originated with Adam rather than with the Jews. The fourth commandment

[94] A phrase attributed to James Gilfillan, *The Sabbath Viewed in the Light of Reason, Revelation, and History* . . . (Edinburgh, 1861), 59. John Knewstub complained that 'the right use and end of the Sabbaothe' had been 'cleane altered', John Knewstub, *Lectures . . . upon the twentieth Chapter of Exodus* (1577), 73.

[95] John Field, *A godly exhortation, by occasion of the late judgement of God . . . concerning the keeping of the Sabboth day* (1583), *passim*.

[96] Lancelot Andrewes, *A Patterne of Catechisticall Doctrine* (1630), 234. 'The Decalogue is the law of nature revived, and the law of nature is the image of God.'

of the Decalogue was moral, in harmony with the rest of the Ten Commandments, and therefore perpetually binding. The Sabbath was also therefore moral and binding and was not ceremonial since it antedated all ceremonies. Christians were thus obliged to keep the Sabbath in the same way that the Jews had been obliged to keep the original seventh day, although now, under the New Testament, the Sabbath institution had been transferred from Saturday to Sunday. The change was justified on the grounds that the Sabbath commandment called for one day of rest after six days of labour. The actual day of rest could therefore be changed without affecting the inherent morality of the commandment. This had occurred under apostolic authority, hence the Sunday Sabbath was equally an institution of divine appointment and was to be observed for the entire twenty-four-hour period. The Sabbath was holy time, to be set aside for rest, worship, prayer, meditation, and all profitable spiritual exercises.[97]

Although no Puritan, Richard Hooker epitomizes that view of the Sabbath which, following the Puritan campaign launched with the Dedham classis and the publication of Bownd's book, came to prevail in English religious life for the better part of three centuries:

The moral law requiring therefore a seventh part throughout the age of the whole world to be that way employed, although with us the day be changed,

---

[97] Nicholas Bownde, *The Doctrine of the Sabbath* (1595), *passim*. The revised 1606 edition bore a lengthy title, of which the following is part: *Sabbatum Veteris et Novi Testamenti: or, The True Doctrine of the Sabbath, held and practised by the Church of God, both before and under the Law, and in the time of the Gospel* . . . (1606). Other notable works advocating the Puritan Sabbath include Richard Greenham, 'Of the Sabboth', in *The Workes of . . . Richard Greenham* (1601); Richard Bernard, *A Threefold Treatise of the Sabbath: distinctly divided into the Patriarchall, Mosaicall, and Christian Sabbath* . . . (1641); Ley, *Sunday a Sabbath;* John Owen, *Exercitations Concerning the Name, Original, Nature, Use, and Continuance of a Day of Sacred Rest. Wherein the Original of the Sabbath from the Foundation of the World, The Morality of the Fourth Commandment, with the Change of the Seventh Day are inquired into. Together with an Assertion of the Divine Institution of the Lord's Day, and Practical Directions for its due Observation* (1671). Other prominent Puritan advocates of the Sunday Sabbath include William Gouge, William Twisse, Richard Baxter, Nathaniel Homes, Daniel Cawdrey, and Herbert Palmer. Cawdrey and Palmer's *Sabbatum Redivivum, or the Christian Sabbath Vindicated: in a full Discourse concerning the Sabbath and the Lord's Day*, part I (1645), parts II, III, IV (1652) is described by R. Cox (*The Literature of the Sabbath Question*, ii (Edinburgh, 1865), 238) as 'the most elaborate defence ever published of the Sabbath doctrine'. The date of Owen's work is of interest, for he suggests that the observance of the seventh day might already have been more widespread than had hitherto been acknowledged, and notes the possibility that it might yet attract more adherents, *Exercitations*, 398.

in regard of a new revolution begun by our Saviour Christ; yet the same proportion of time continueth which was before, . . . we are bound to account the sanctification of one day in seven, a duty which God's immutable Law doth exact forever.[98]

To use Hooker's phrase, it was 'God's immutable Law' which gave the impetus to Puritan Sabbatarianism. As Patrick Collinson has aptly summarized it, the whole Sabbatarian controversy was based on 'the doctrinal assertion that the fourth commandment is not an obsolete ceremonial law of the Jews but a perpetual, moral law, binding on Christians'.[99] Sabbatarianism, and in particular Seventh-day Sabbatarianism, cannot be understood apart from its nexus in the Decalogue and the continuing authority of the Decalogue as it was perceived to exist in the New Testament. Bownd had emphasized the significance of the law in this respect and the Puritan writers who would follow him in asserting the necessity of the Sabbath would do likewise.

At the risk of being repetitive, some of the more salient aspects of the Puritan understanding of the law are essential to an adequate grasp of the wider Sabbatarian movement as well as of Seventh-day Sabbatarianism.[100] The moral law as set forth in the Ten Commandments was repeatedly emphasized by Sabbatarian writers as perpetually binding, an expression of the will of the divine Lawgiver himself. John White wrote, 'The Moral Law, seeing it sets down rules of governing a man as a man . . . is therefore universally and perpetually to be observed.'[101] The moral law was to be distinguished from the ceremonial law, which had been abrogated by the death of Christ. White says again, 'from the Ceremonial Law we are wholly freed by the coming of Christ into the world, who is the body of those shadows'.[102] The same was true, in general, of the judicial or social laws of the Old Testament, although some differences of opinion surfaced as to the continuing value for Christians of some aspects of this code.

---

[98] Richard Hooker, *The Lawes of Ecclesiasticall Politie* (Oxford, 1622), 378–9.

[99] P. Collinson, 'The Beginnings of English Sabbatarianism', *Studies in Church History*, 1 (1964), 207. Cf. id., *Godly People: Essays on English Protestantism and Puritanism* (1983), 429.

[100] E.F. Kevan's *The Grace of Law* (1964, repr. 1976) is a valuable more recent analysis of the Puritan understanding of Law in Scripture, and of the relationship between Law and gospel. Many of the following statements were noted by Kevan.

[101] John White, *A Way to the Tree of Life* (1647), 206.

[102] Ibid.

The moral law was effective in pointing out sin, and then of leading the penitent and believing soul to Christ. Samuel Bolton speaks of the law 'as a Reprover and Corrector of sin . . . not only to discover sin, but to make it appear exceeding sinful'.[103] And John Flavel, that powerful exponent of Puritan spirituality, admonishes: 'Learn hence the usefulness of the Law, to bring souls to Jesus Christ . . . It cannot relieve us or ease us, but it can, and doth awaken and rouse us: its a fair glass to shew us the face of sin; and till we have seen that, we cannot see the face of Jesus Christ.'[104]

The moral law was also the recognized measure of conduct and behaviour in the Christian life. John Ball, speaking of the covenant of faith, and the obedience required in a godly life, explains that 'they which believe God to be their God, must declare the same by obedience to his Commandments'. And further: 'This is an insepar-able consequent: that if we embrace God by faith, we must and ought to follow his Commandments by our deeds, and he that doth not this latter, bewrayeth that he hath not with a true heart and faith received the former.'[105]

The moral law, indeed, becomes internalized in the true Christian life, since it is written in the heart of the believer, tending to natural obedience. The law, which after man's sin was written on tables of stone, is 'turned to an internal law again' as God 'implants it on the heart as it was at first', and so becomes 'inbred' and 'effectual' once more.[106] Richard Sibbes explains that the dynamic of the new covenant 'is that we may expect from this Lordship of Christ, the performance of the covenant of grace in writing his law in our hearts'. Otherwise the 'covenant of grace should be frustrate as the first was'.[107]

And the moral law would be the standard by which all men, Christians included, would be measured in the last judgement. John Seagar states explicitly, 'the certainty of this world's dissolution should persuade us to be universal in our obedience', striving 'to practise every known duty prescribed in God's Word, after the example of Zacharias and Elisabeth his wife, who walked in all the

---

[103] Samuel Bolton, *The True Bounds of Christian Freedom* (1656), 119, 121.

[104] John Flavel, 'The Method of Grace', in *The Whole Workes of the Reverend Mr John Flavel* (1716), i. 278.

[105] John Ball, *A Treatise of Faith, divided into two Parts. The First shewing the Nature, the Second, the Life of Faith* (1632), 31–2.

[106] John Owen, *The Nature, Power, Deceit, and Prevalency of the Remainders of Indwelling Sin in Believers* (1668), 16, 17.

[107] Richard Sibbes, *Christs Exaltation Purchast by Humiliation* (1639), 145.

commandments of God blameless'.[108] Baxter says, 'Christ, at that great Assize, . . . as he governed by a Law, so will he judge by a Law, . . . and the equity of his judgement may be manifest to all'.[109] Such was the scope and strength of the Law in Puritan theology. As a *force majeure* in the emergence of sixteenth- and seventeenth-century Sabbatarianism it was quite irresistible. In retrospect, and given the immense respect for the Ten Commandments across all shades of opinion within the Anglican Church, to say nothing of the earlier and persisting Lollard tradition, it would have been remarkable indeed had the Sabbath not become a prominent issue. It was equally inevitable that, once the Sabbatarian debate had been joined, the question of the seventh day would sooner or later be raised. This possibility seems to have been inherent in an early seventeenth-century comment on the implications of the fourth commandment. 'Go through the whole commandment', say Dod and Cleaver in their popular *Exposition of the Ten Commandments* and 'what one word in all of it hath any note of ceremony? What reason savours of any special thing to the Jews that the commandment should be tied only to them?'[110] This was a rejoinder, in part at least, to those who had already begun to attack the Puritan Sabbatarian position as an unnecessarily extreme view of the Christian Sunday, the argument being that the ceremonial aspects of the fourth commandment applied only to the Jews. More directly, Bishop Francis White remarked that the 'errant' advocate of the seventh day, Theophilus Brabourne, had derived most of his arguments from 'Principles which the Sabbatarian Dogmatists had lent him'.[111] White even conceded that if the fourth commandment was indeed moral and perpetually binding 'then the Saturday Sabbath of every week must be observed by Christians, and not the Sunday or Lord's Day in the place thereof'.[112] It seems incontrovertible that there were precedents for the Seventh-day Men in Anglicanism and in Puritan Sabbatarianism, as there were also in other earlier and contemporary antecedents.

---

[108] John Seagar, *A Discoverie of the World to Come According to the Scriptures* (1650), 46–7.

[109] Richard Baxter, *Aphorismes of Justification, with their Explication Annexed* (1649), 318.

[110] John Dod and Robert Cleaver, *A Plaine and Familiar Exposition of the Ten Commandments* (1615), 126.   [111] White, *Treatise*, Ep. Ded., A2ᵛ.

[112] F. White, *An Examination and Confutation of a Lawlesse Pamphlet, Intituled, A Briefe Answer to a late Treatise of the Sabbath Day* (1637), 4.

2

John Traske and
Theophilus Brabourne

THE effect of British and Continental antecedents on the development of Seventh-day views in seventeenth-century England appears to have been more indirect than direct. Arguments in support of the seventh day which recur in the literature are generally theological and biblical, reinforcing the conclusion that the English Seventh-day movement was more a spontaneous response to the recovered authority of the Bible than a historically or geographically conditioned phenomenon, important as the antecedents undoubtedly were in themselves, or as incipient catalysts of a later reaction. If English Sabbatarian writers looked for clearly defined beginnings to the Seventh-day movement, they looked to more recent times, to the Puritan-Anglican Sabbatarian controversialists of the late sixteenth and early seventeenth centuries perhaps, and in particular to the first known Seventh-day Sabbatarians of any significance, John Traske and Theophilus Brabourne.

In 1636 Peter Heylyn observed that the opinions of Traske and Brabourne 'so far as it concerned the Sabbath were the very same'.[1] The reality, of course, was a little different. While there is some truth in the assertion that in contemporary minds the two men were inextricably linked,[2] contemporary minds also recognized some differences. Traske left behind him a movement, small, controversial, and proscribed, to perpetuate his opinions, while Brabourne left a literature, reasonably extensive, likewise controversial, but destined to exert considerable influence on the wider Seventh-day movement until at least the turn of the century. The Seventh-day Men themselves were much more comfortable with the latter than the former. There are few references to Traske in the Seventh-day

---

[1] Heylyn, *History*, ii. 259–60.
[2] Katz, *Sabbath and Sectarianism*, 16. Cox regarded Brabourne as 'the founder in England of the sect at first known as Sabbatarians'; Cox, *Literature of the Sabbath Question*, i. 157.

literature, while Brabourne's arguments are frequently cited or re-cast in support of Seventh-day theology. When the dust had settled, and it became apparent that observance of the seventh day was not something ephemeral, Brabourne was taken more seriously than Traske, by antagonists as well as protagonists of Seventh-day views. Archbishop Ussher noted Brabourne's part in the wider Sabbatarian debate, remarking that it was he who 'gave occasion to the raising up of these unhappy broils'.[3] Brabourne's arguments were likewise noted by Fuller, White, Heylyn, Ley, and Cawdrey and Palmer, *inter alios*, as serious propositions in the Sabbatarian debate.[4] Traske, on the other hand, is dismissed as a propagator of 'Jewish doctrines', 'a seducing imposter . . . and cunning deceiver', 'the father of the Jewish sect of the Traskites'.[5] Even when allowance is made for the strength of contemporary invective, the difference in attitude to Brabourne and Traske is quite evident, even though Brabourne is also on occasion called a Jew.[6] Heylyn was right to suggest that what linked Traske and Brabourne was their insistence that the seventh day should be observed as the Sabbath, but to associate them more closely, and to suggest that Brabourne was a Traskite,[7] is not warranted by the evidence. Regardless of all such differences, however, both Traske and Brabourne are legitimately regarded as seventeenth-century proto-Sabbatarians, whose work was funda-mental to the emergence and development of the Seventh-day move-ment as a whole.

JOHN TRASKE AND THE TRASKITES

The story of John Traske (Trask, Thraske, Trash, or Thrasco, 1585–1636) and his followers has been recounted, with varying detail

[3] Ussher to John Ley, cited in Nicholas Bernard, *The Judgement Of the Late Archbishop of Armagh, and Primate of Ireland . . . Of the Sabbath, and observation of the Lords Day . . .* (1657), 107.

[4] Thomas Fuller, *The Church-History of Britain, from the Birth of Jesus Christ until the year 1648* (1655), xi. 144; White, *Treatise, passim*; Ley, *Sunday a Sabbath, passim*, but esp. chs. 3 and 20; Cawdrey and Palmer, *Sabbatum Redivivum, passim*.

[5] Edward Norice, *The New Gospel not the True Gospel . . .* (1638), 1; *The History of King-Killers* (1719), 34.

[6] e.g. *CSPD* 1634–5, 126. White noted that 'this Jewish Sabbatarian finds already many idle and giddy-brained Christians to imbrace his book': White, *Examination . . . of a Lawlesse Pamphlet*, 3.

[7] *King-Killers*, 38; H.E. Phillips, 'An Early Stuart Judaising Sect', *TJHSE* 15 (1946), 65, 68.

and from various perspectives, on several previous occasions.[8] In view of its contextual significance for the development of Seventh-day Sabbatarianism, however, it must be repeated again, both to note its main features, and to emphasize aspects of Traske's work which warrant more attention. This is necessary even though Traske's Sabbatarianism was not typical of that which was to follow. Indeed, the continuing failure to note a distinction between the Traskites and the wider English Seventh-day movement is in itself sufficient justification for returning again to Traske and the early Jacobean Sabbatarians. It is imprecise to say, as D.S. Katz does, for example, that Traske was 'the first of a long line of seventeenth-century Judaisers and Saturday-Sabbatarians'.[9] Seventh-day Men may, or may not, have been among those whom K.L. Parker describes as 'judaising Christians who practised an extremely rigorous Sunday observance or reverenced Saturday instead of Sunday'.[10] The evidence from sources later in the seventeenth century indicates that while a few Seventh-day observers may have slipped back into Judaism the majority did not and were embarrassed and felt compromised by those who did. Traske himself was undoubtedly a Judaizer, at least during one period of his life, even though the charge may have been laboured by some of his enemies.[11]

Although the broad outline of Traske's life seems clear enough, the attempt to arrive at an accurate understanding of his theology and its development is complicated by two factors. In the first place, the contemporary evidence cannot always be relied upon as being objective. Of the five major seventeenth- and early eighteenth-century sources of information on Traske and the Traskites, four are to some degree evidently antagonistic or hostile.[12] B.R. White,

---

[8] White, *TCHS* 20/7: 223–33; D.S. Katz, *Philo-Semitism and the Readmission of the Jews to England, 1603–1655* (Oxford, 1982), 18–34; Parker, *The English Sabbath*, 161–4. See also W.B. Trask, *The Traske Family in England* (Boston, Mass., 1900).   [9] Katz, *Philo-Semitism*, 34.

[10] Parker, *The English Sabbath*, 169; cf. 'These judaizing Christians . . . observed Saturday according to the Jewish sabbath laws', 161.

[11] Cf. B.R. White's conclusion that 'Traske only held "Traskite" opinions, namely, that the Mosaic Law concerning foods and the Saturday Sabbath were binding upon Christians, during one brief period of his life in London'; White, *TCHS* 20/7: 223. This was a 'lapse into Judaism'. But these two doctrines of themselves may not be sufficient ground to sustain the charge. It would appear that Traske's Judaism consisted of more detailed observance of other Levitical laws.

[12] B.D. [John Falconer], *A Briefe Refutation of John Traskes Judaical and Novel Fancyes* (St Omer, 1618); Norice, *The New Gospel*; Pagitt, *Heresiography*; *King-Killers*; various references in *CSPD*, 1618 to 1639; cf. SM 581. In addition to the State

commenting on Traske's reported theology, fairly remarks, 'It is not clear how far such allegations were the garbled and inaccurate reports of enemies.'[13] All the more recent accounts of Traske's activity depend heavily on one or more of these early sources. This uncertainty impinges directly on the important matter of Traske's Sabbatarian theology and its origins. On the basis of these sources, Traske's Sabbatarian views have been traced traditionally to an esoteric experience of one of his disciples which Traske is alleged to have accepted somewhat credulously, and perhaps even without demanding the scriptural warrant he is reputed to have required for all doctrine and practice. Other evidence, as we shall see, suggests the equally plausible alternative that Traske may have advocated Sabbatarian views in various parts of the country before coming to London. Parker observes in this respect that he 'became notorious as a travelling preacher, spreading heterodox and judaical teaching'.[14]

Secondly, the attribution to Traske in the early literature of an extremely wide variety of unorthodox theological opinions must give rise to some caution. While it is impossible to ignore the early records, much of what they say of Traske's views and their impact would appear to be speculative, if not deliberately intended to paint a picture of the bizarre. Beyond the observance of Saturday and abstinence from the unclean meats of the Mosaic Law, themselves matters of heretical import as Traske discovered to his cost, he is also said to have maintained other views, which even by seventeenth-century standards would have to be regarded as extreme. According to one source, he held that a true minister of Christ could not teach error, and that to doubt the teaching of such a minister amounted to sin.[15] He is said to have regarded himself as the only 'Micaiah' beyond error, and Returne Hebdon, one of 'his distracted gang', as Antipas of the book of Revelation 'sent to discover Antichrist'.[16] Melchizedek was the Holy Spirit, and the resurrection of Christ should be celebrated annually on 'the fourteenth of March moon' to coincide with the Jewish Passover, and should

---

Papers, Falconer and Pagitt appear to be the most reliable. Evidence of the bias inherent in some of the sources is illustrated in the *King-Killers*, which includes Knox, Milton, Wyclif, and Hobbes among those worthy of condemnation, as well as John Owen, Obadiah Sedgwick, Nathaniel Homes, and Francis Rous.

[13] White, *TCHS* 20/7: 225.   [14] Parker, *The English Sabbath*, 162.
[15] Pagitt, *Heresiography*, 188.   [16] *King-Killers*, 35–7.

be followed by the eating of unleavened bread for seven days.[17] Some of Traske's followers were reported to wear sackcloth and ashes, and some to eat bread with 'quaking' and drink water with 'trembling' after a literal interpretation of Ezekiel 12: 18.[18] This would no doubt have been in the attempt to reach the state of 'Grace', since those who had attained such a state could not sin any more. Traskites were said to be involved with the daily observation of various aspects of Jewish law which they applied to such common-place activities as building, planting, weaving, and farming.[19] In complete contrast, the sources say that Traske eventually turned to Antinomianism and Familism,[20] thus repudiating the position he had taken after renouncing his 'Judaisme', and denounced preachers who 'made any use of the Law in their teaching . . . as legalists, justitiaries, messengers of Moses . . . and worse than Jews'.[21] To distinguish fact from fiction in relation to what Traske and his followers actually believed and practised is obviously not easy.

John Traske was born *c.*1585, in East Coker, Somerset.[22] Described later by a contemporary as 'a Puritan minister lately grown half a Jew', his first recorded occupation was that of schoolmaster.[23] It seems that he had been ordained *c.*1611 by the Bishop of Salisbury, after having earlier been refused by the Bishop of Bath and Wells on the grounds that he was unsuitable.[24] At one point he referred to himself as having been a preacher at Axminster in Devon, which must have been prior to 1615.[25] In these early years he had become known to the episcopal authorities in Devon, where he claimed to have lectured and preached extensively, as a purveyor of 'erroneous fancies'.[26] In 1615 he appeared in London, where he published his first book *A Pearle for a Prince, or a Princely Pearl* (1615), a moderate defence of paedobaptism, and where he was imprisoned briefly

---

[17] [Falconer], *Briefe Refutation*, 7, 57–8.   [18] Pagitt, *Heresiography*, 185.

[19] *King-Killers*, 36.

[20] Pagitt, *Heresiography*, 198; Norice, *The New Gospel*, 7.

[21] Norice, *The New Gospel*, 2.

[22] 1585 is preferable to the earlier date of 1583 sometimes suggested. A John Traske, son of Lionell Traske, was baptized on 15 Oct. 1585 at East Coker, and married in the same parish in 1606. This accords with information given by Traske when remarrying in London in 1617; see Katz, *Philo-Semitism*, 18.

[23] [Falconer], *Briefe Refutation*, 3, 9; Pagitt, *Heresiography*, 184.

[24] White, *TCHS* 20/7: 223, citing PRO, SP/16/72, fo. 45; cf. Fuller *Church-History*, x. 76.

[25] John Traske, *The Power of Preaching* (1623), title-page.

[26] [Falconer], *Briefe Refutation*, 10; *HMC*, Exeter (1916), 95.

in Newgate for 'going up and down as a wandering minister'.[27] The charge is significant.

In April 1616 William Cotton, Bishop of Exeter, refused to endorse the application of John Hazard as city lecturer because he had been 'a companion with Trasque' and had 'preached false doctrine'. Hazard protested, saying that at Lyme (Regis) he had twice publicly refuted 'the erroneous fancies of Trasque' and that the whole town could, if necessary, 'witness the same'.[28] Cotton had before this been concerned with evidence of 'Jewism' in the diocese, and a connection seems not impossible, particularly since Traske's London Judaizing may have included keeping the Passover.[29] Katz believes that a reference to Traske's 'aboad with Maister Drake in Devonshire'[30] alludes to this period in his life, and although direct evidence is lacking, it is certainly possible that the later, open appearance of Seventh-day views in Exeter and Tiverton may have stemmed from this period.[31]

Something similar may be said about events in the diocese of Ely. In 1614 several parishioners from five parishes were presented to the consistory courts for attending meetings held by 'a strange preacher, called Mr Traske' in Littleport, Chettisham, and Ely itself.[32] One reference in the diocesan records refers to a meeting at Littleport conducted by 'Mr Traske who had not a licence to preach'. Parishioners from Downham were also present at the meeting, and again it may be significant that Sabbatarianism was specified in Downham conventicles reported in 1669.[33] It may have been purely coincidental that it was the Bishop of Ely who was nominated by Charles I to produce an answer to Brabourne's second work advocating the seventh day, which he had boldly dedicated to the King.[34]

[27] W. Le Hardy (ed.), *Calendar to the Sessions Records (Middlesex)*, NS iii: *1615–1616* (1937), 107. Traske was detained by a warrant from the Archbishop of Canterbury and the Bishops of London, Ely, and Rochester.

[28] *HMC*, Exeter, 95–6.

[29] *HMC*, Salisbury, x (1904), 450–1; cf. Phillips, *TJHSE* 15, 65.

[30] Possibly John Drake of Musbury (d. 1628), or one of his sons, William Drake of Colyton (d. 1639), or Sir John Drake of Musbury (d. 1635), whose eighth daughter, Anne, was the third wife of Sir Richard Strode of Cattistock, Dorset, who later employed Traske as chaplain; see below, 150, 153.

[31] Katz, *Philo-Semitism*, 19; [Falconer], *Briefe Refutation*, 10. On Seventh-day views in Devon, see below, Ch. 4.   [32] EDR B/2/35, fos. 3r, 76v–78r, 113v, 114r, 190r.v.

[33] EDR B/2/35, fo. 62r; *OR* i. 35. Further details on Traske's work in the Ely diocese will be found in Ch. 9.

[34] F. White, *Treatise*, in reply to Theophilus Brabourne, *A Defence of that most Ancient, and Sacred ordinance of GODS, the Sabbath Day . . .* (1632).

By 1617 Traske had become established in London, where he gained a reputation for powerful preaching. 'He preached repentance so earnestly, that he caused many of his auditors to weep, yea to roar,' one account records.[35] Fuller remarked, somewhat uncharitably, that his voice had 'more strength than anything else he delivered'.[36] A key element in his work appears to have been that he adopted the practice of categorizing all men into one or the other of the three states of Nature, Repentance, and Grace. To recover the lost from the state of Nature, he preached Repentance, explaining that this condition was not to be maintained for the remainder of a believer's life, but only until the 'third estate was obtained . . . and that once gained, they . . . should have no more sorrow, but all Joy'.[37] Presumably this was because the third estate brought entrance 'into the Holy City' and a state of sinlessness.[38] The Calvinism implicit in Traske's theology is apparent here, and it is not difficult to see, given the general religious climate of the age, that he would have attracted a considerable following. From the meagre evidence that has survived it is impossible to determine precisely how large this following was, but the records that do exist suggest that Traskite congregations may soon have been established in several parts of the country. One contemporary account records that 'many people' had been 'confirmed' in Traske's 'Jewish opinions'.[39] At about this time, Traske selected four followers 'of the Third Estate' to assist him in his labours, and he ordained them by laying on of hands, 'in Wycliffe's style', to note the comment of one contemporary.[40] Three of the four were Hamlet Jackson, a tailor, Returne Hebdon (or Hebden), a 'gentleman's son', and Christopher Sands, whose name appears in most of the sources as having been instrumental in convincing others of Traskite views.[41]

Traske's determination to have scriptural authority for all doctrine and every aspect of daily life led him naturally enough to his

---

[35] Pagitt, *Heresiography*, 184.   [36] Fuller, *Church History*, x. 77.

[37] *King-Killers*, 34–5; cf. *Dissenters and Schismaticks Ex pos'd* (1715), 86.

[38] *King-Killers*, 34–5.

[39] [Falconer], *Briefe Refutation*, 3. In 1636 Traskites were still holding meetings in London and many other parts, *CSPD* 1635–6, 242–3; Bodl. MS Add. C.303, fo. 39.

[40] Pagitt, *Heresiography*, 190. According to Pagitt, Traske's mandate to his disciples included healing the sick by anointing with oil.

[41] Ibid. 189–90; *King-Killers*, 37–41. Cf. Returne Hebdon, *A Guide to the Godly* (1648), sig. A2. The name of Traske's fourth ordinand has not been preserved.

'singular opinion concerning the old Sabbath', as well as to the 'Mosaical difference of meats'.[42] It has generally been held that Traske came to a knowledge of the seventh day in 1617 through Hamlet Jackson, who is said to have been convinced himself as a result of seeing 'a shining light about him' while travelling in the country on a Saturday. Jackson, who had already been convinced of the seventh day in theory, was now constrained to observe it, and is said to have persuaded Traske likewise. The Traskites were at this time already observing Sunday in a 'Judaical' manner, according to one source, as well as practising other requirements of the Mosaic Law, and were soon persuaded by Traske to abandon the first day in favour of the seventh.[43] This unusual and in some respects doubtful series of events has been accepted uncritically by both contemporary and later historians of the Traskite movement.[44] It should, perhaps, be reconsidered in the light of Traske's activities in Devon and Cambridgeshire prior to his appearance in London in 1615. One less well-known account of the period suggests that Traske, 'a violent Sabbatarian', may have adopted Seventh-day beliefs before his ordination.[45]

Whatever the origin of Traske's Sabbatarianism, his settled reasons for observing the Saturday Sabbath were threefold, namely, that the Seventh-day Sabbath had been instituted at Creation, that it was required by the moral law of the Ten Commandments, and that it had not been abrogated by Christ in the New Testament.[46] The essence of this was that the fourth commandment specified that it was the seventh day of the week which was to be observed as the Sabbath, an injunction which Traske regarded as a law 'unrepealed by Christ and necessarily now to be observed by Christians'.[47] On this basis Traske and his followers adopted the seventh day, accepting the authority of the fourth commandment *in toto*, both in its command to observe the seventh day and in its direction to work on the remaining six days of the week, including the first.[48]

---

[42] [Falconer], *Briefe Refutation*, 3–4.

[43] Pagitt, *Heresiography*, 189–91; *King-Killers*, 37, 39, 40.

[44] Cf. White, *TCHS* 20/7: 225; Katz, *Philo-Semitism*, 21; Parker, *The English Sabbath*, 161–2.

[45] David Lloyd, *Memoires of the Lives, Actions, Sufferings & Deaths of those . . . Excellent Personages that Suffered . . . for the Protestant Religion* (1668), 164.

[46] Traske himself left no literature defending his Sabbatarian views. The information comes from [Falconer], *Briefe Refutation*, 21, 26.

[47] Ibid. 4.   [48] *King-Killers*, 37.

The Traskites were thus established as part of the fringe element of the English Jacobean religious scene. One contemporary says that Traske's opinions were shared 'by many other men and women',[49] and early in 1618 John Chamberlain wrote to Lord Carleton, noting the main Traskite doctrines of Saturday observance and abstinence from swine's flesh, and commenting: 'You will not think what a number of foolish followers he hath in this town, and in some other parts.'[50] Evidently within a year Traske and his disciples had been successful in propagating their views within the city of London and, although the evidence is tantalizingly scarce, beyond it as well.

The names of only a few of Traske's followers have survived. Hamlet Jackson, who is said to have been barely literate, appears to have been his chief aide. Jackson, as we shall see, seems to have been more inclined to Judaism than Traske himself.[51] Returne Hebdon came originally from Holmeshurst in Sussex, leaving a family inheritance 'for the commandment of God's sake, by his desiring to rest on the seventh day'.[52] Christopher Sands is said to have converted a minister, Mr Wright, and his wife, and also a Mary Chester.[53] As late as 1635 Sands appeared before the Court of High Commission on a charge of Judaizing.[54] Mary Chester also appears in the records in 1635 as a 'Jewess' imprisoned in Bridewell on account of her 'errors in holding certain Judaical tenets touching the Sabbath and distinction of meats'. In December of that year the Court of High Commission ordered her release on bond subject to her 'acknowledgement and recantation' of the said 'errors'.[55] It seems that she reverted to her 'heretical views' soon after being released.[56] A glazier, James Holly, appears as a Saturday-keeper in 1618,[57] and the anonymous author of the later *History of King-Killers* also mentions William Hilliard as a convert of Hamlet Jackson.[58] Edward Norice refers to a posthumous work by Traske published by Rice Boye, and John Taylor describes a widow Constable of Brentford 'turn'd from a Nonconformist to a Jew'.[59] Apart from a few incidental and unspecified references, this accounts for most of the Traskites currently known, with one exception.

---

[49] [Falconer], *Brief Refutation*, 3.   [50] *CSPD* 1611–18, 521.
[51] Pagitt, *Heresiography*, 189, 191.
[52] Hebdon, *A Guide to the Godly*, Ep. Ded., sig. A2ʳ.
[53] *King-Killers*, 41.   [54] *CSPD* 1635–6, 88.   [55] Ibid. 132.
[56] Pagitt, *Heresiography*, 195.   [57] *CSPD* 1611–18, 548.   [58] *King-Killers*, 41.
[59] Norice, *The New Gospel*, 4, 6, 50; John Taylor, *A Swarme of Sectaries and Schismatiques* (1641), 7. Norice also mentions a 'Mr G.', 7.

The best-known Traskite, apart from Traske himself, was his second wife. Traske had remarried in 1617 at the age of 'thirty-two or thereabouts'. His new wife was Dorothy Coome, of the same age and from the same city parish of St Sepulchre.[60] The marriage was to prove an important factor in the perpetuation of Seventh-day views. Dorothy Traske remained faithful to the seventh day to the end of her life, which came in 1645 after several years of harsh imprisonment. B.R. White comments: 'Her long and almost lonely obstinacy . . . has some significance for the history of the Seventh-Day Sabbath in puritan England since it virtually bridged the years between John Traske's congregation in 1617 and the years after 1648 when, once more, congregations were gathered to practise it.'[61] While it may not be accurate to imply that Dorothy Traske was virtually the sole remaining advocate of the seventh day in the pre-Commonwealth period, it is true that from the late 1640s, with the new religious liberty and freedom of expression and practice, the seventh day came into the open in a way previously unknown in England. Pagitt's observation in 1661 that Seventh-day views were 'lately much spreading' represents the growth of a religious conviction which Dorothy Traske had helped to sustain by refusing to recant or conform.[62]

That Traske and the Traskites were a topic of conversation at James I's dinner table is some measure of the attention they attracted.[63] It was not all to their good, however. By late 1617 Traske and some of his followers had been arrested. Traske was taken before the Court of High Commission which judged him 'worthy of very severe and exemplary punishment', and imprisoned him 'that he might not infect others'.[64] He remained in prison, on a diet of bread and water, until June 1618, when he appeared in the Star Chamber to receive what, by any standard, was a severe sentence. He was to be removed from the ministry, imprisoned for life, fined

---

[60] Guildhall Library, MS 10,091/6, fo. 26ᵛ, cited in Katz, *Philo-Semitism*, 18 n. 54. See also White, *TCHS* 20/7: 224.

[61] White, *TCHS* 20/7: 229. She spent the last fifteen years of her life in prison, adhering to a vegetarian diet, and refusing attempts to alleviate her poverty; *CSPD* 1639, 466, and White, *TCHS* 20/7: 228.

[62] Pagitt, *Heresiography*, Ep. Ded., sig. A3ʳ. Prior to her imprisonment Mrs. Traske had kept a school in which Pagitt's son had been a pupil. This may partially account for Pagitt's claim to have known Traske 'well', *Heresiography*, 161, 209.

[63] 'His majesty makes merry with the opinions of a new sect called Thrascists [sic]; their leader, Thrasco, is in prison', Nathaniel Brent to Lord Carleton, Feb. 1618, *CSPD* 1611–18, 524.   [64] Bodl. Add. MS C.303, fo. 39.

£1,000, whipped from the Fleet prison to Westminster and to
Cheapside, pilloried in both places, and branded in the forehead
with the letter J to signify that he had 'broached Jewish opinions'.[65]
How much of the sentence was in fact carried out is not clear, but
there is evidence that at least some of the physical punishment
was inflicted. Those of his followers who had also been imprisoned
appear to have fared better. Hamlet Jackson was released and,
accompanied by his wife, emigrated to Holland where he is said to
have become a full proselyte to Judaism.[66] Sands was also released,
although he appeared again before the Court of High Commission
in 1635 on a charge of Judaizing, some indication, perhaps, of a
continuance of Traskite views.[67] Hebdon died in prison in 1625,
and Dorothy Traske, as already noted, continued to live in confine-
ment until 1645.

That Traske himself did not suffer a similar fate is due to the fact
that by 1619 he had recanted of his 'Judaisme'. The term was his
own, and appeared in the title of a work intended to prove and
justify his changed views, which he published in 1620 as *A Treatise
of Libertie from Judaisme*, with the hope that he would now be 'as
resolute for Christ alone' as he had previously been 'for Moses and
Christ together'. Just how lasting Traske's recantation was has been
questioned, even though the work was dedicated to 'my holy and
tender mother, the Church of England', as a retraction of his 'foul
failings in . . . Judaisme'.[68] Although there is no clear evidence that
he reverted either to 'Judaisme' or to the observance of the seventh
day, he was again in trouble with the authorities in 1627, and the
Bishop of London wrote in that year of his intention to suspend
Traske, who is described as being 'a London clergyman', as 'an unworthy person and a Jew'.[69] Under examination Traske maintained

[65] Ibid., fo. 45. The sentence was imposed because Traske had written 'scandalous' letters to the King challenging the ruling of the Court of High Commission, in
addition to having attempted 'to divert his Majesties subjectes from theire obedience,
to followe him and his Jewish opynions'. Cf. 'Trask in the Star Chamber, 1619', *TBHS*
5: 10, and White, *TCHS* 20/7: 228. The date in the *TBHS* title was later amended to
1618, *TBHS* 5: 114.

[66] Pagitt, *Heresiography*, 180; Phillips, *TJHSE* 15: 70–1, where evidence for Jackson's
admission to the Jewish community in Amsterdam is considered.

[67] *CSPD* 1635–6, 88.

[68] John Traske, *A Treatise of Libertie from Judaisme* . . . (1620), 41; Ep. Ded., sigs.
3^r, 4^r. Traske argues principally against the Seventh-day Sabbath and abstention from
unclean meats, and hopes that 'if any have stumbled by my word or example' they
will not any longer 'be yoaked with that heavie yoak', ibid. 36.

[69] *CSPD* 1627–8, 278, 281, although the Bishop recognizes that Traske has a
faculty from a 'superior court'.

that he had not returned to keeping the seventh day, although he did admit that his wife still remained a Sabbatarian.[70] It appears that he was, in fact, suspended again, for in 1629 we read of his appeal to Laud, then Bishop of London, for reinstatement on the grounds of his known orthodoxy.[71]

Traske's tendency to itinerant preaching appears to have been sustained during his later years, despite the episcopal reluctance to sanction him. In 1623 he had described himself as a preacher at Tillingham in Essex, and the 1627 episode had been occasioned, in part at least, by invitations to preach in London.[72] During the years between his formal 'recantation of Judaisme' and this last clash with the authorities, he is reported to have exercised an acceptable ministry, though not without further breaches of ecclesiastical discipline.[73] At some point during the 1620s Traske had returned to the west country, where Sir Richard Strode of Cattistock, Dorset, had engaged him as chaplain. In this capacity he preached in the Strode household and also at other places to which Sir Richard had 'carried him . . . abroad with him into the country to preach'.[74] For this indiscretion Sir Richard was later admonished by the Court of High Commission to have nothing further to do with 'irregular ministers'.[75] Just when it was that Traske served in the Strode household, or, for that matter, precisely when he was connected with 'Maister Drake in Devonshire', is to some extent of secondary significance as far as any possible connection with later Sabbatarianism is concerned. But it is worth noting that Cattistock was situated in that area of Dorset where Seventh-day views later flourished, almost as the hub of a wheel between Dorchester, Beaminster, Sherborne, and Sturminster Newton, where Seventh-day congregations were gathered when conditions were more favourable.[76] It may not be amiss to note again that similar congregations appeared in at least three localities in which Traske appeared as a preacher, here in his own home territory of Dorset, in neighbouring East Devon, and in the Isle of Ely.

The records of Traske's later life are even scarcer than those relating to his more active years, and all that can be said with some

---

[70] Ibid. 289.   [71] *CSPD* 1628–9, 576.

[72] Traske, *The Power of Preaching*, title-page; PRO, SP 16/73/64, cited in White, *TCHS* 20/7: 231.   [73] PRO, SP 16/72/45, cited in White, *TCHS* 20/7: 230.

[74] PRO, SP 16/261/55ᵛ, 56ʳ, cited in White, *TCHS* 20/7: 232.

[75] *CSPD* 1634–5, 121.

[76] On Seventh-day congregations in Dorset, see below, Ch. 5.

certainty is that at some time in the late 1620s or early 1630s he again returned to London, to end his spiritual pilgrimage in the fellowship of the semi-separatist 'Jacob–Lathrop' congregation.[77] The last reference to Traske, in 1636, recounts how he was once more arrested, following a Court of High Commission order to seek out 'sectaries' (including specifically 'Thraskists'), and committed to the Poultry Counter for ten days. His health was failing, however, and he was released on bail, and 'shortly after translated'.[78] He was taken to his grave in Lambeth churchyard from the house of one of the members of the Lathrop congregation, and buried 'contrary to the manner that other men are, with the heels the way that the heads of other men lie'.[79] Fuller later described Traske as one of the principal 'broakers of Judaisme',[80] and there can be little doubt either that the doctrines of his earlier years justified the charge or that he is remembered principally in theological terms as 'a man contrary to all men', 'a Jewish Christian', 'the Father of the Jewish sect of the Traskites'.[81]

As far as the sect itself was concerned, the records suggest a history somewhat longer than that conceded by Pagitt. He had concluded that the Traskites had died out with Dorothy Traske 'in less than half a generation' from their inception.[82] This would have been in 1645 or shortly thereafter. In 1636, the year of John Traske's death, Traskites were reported as holding meetings 'in London and in many other parts',[83] which would account for the order in that year to arraign 'Thraskites' among other sectaries. In 1641 *The Brownists Conventicle* complained that 'novellists', including 'Thraskites or Sabbatarians', pervaded almost 'every diocesan parish'.[84] In the 1645 edition of his *Heresiography* Pagitt himself had noted an important distinction between Sabbatarians and Traskites, the former 'affirming the old Jewish Sabbath to be kept', the latter

---

[77] But not as a Baptist, as Katz, *Philo-Semitism*, 32. The Jacob–Lathrop congregation which Traske joined under the ministry of Lathrop did not consider the question of baptism until after Traske's death, and although Henry Jessey became its pastor in 1637 it was only slowly that he moved to an antipaedobaptist position: White, *English Baptists*, 59–60. Had Traske wished to identify with Baptist views, he would probably have joined the group which seceded from the Jacob–Lathrop congregation in 1633 over the baptismal issue, *TBHS* 1 (1908–9), 255; B. Stinton, 'A Repository of Divers Historical Matters relating to the English Antipedobaptists' (1712), 6, AL, MS F.P.C.c.8.   [78] *CSPD* 1635–6, 242; Stinton, 'Repository', 7.

[79] *King-Killers*, 38; Pagitt, *Heresiography*, 196.

[80] Fuller, *Church History*, x. 76.   [81] *CSPD* 1611–18, 521; *King-Killers*, 34.

[82] Pagitt, *Heresiography*, 197.   [83] *CSPD* 1635–6, 243.

[84] *The Brownists Conventicle* (1641), 2.

'who would have us observe many Jewish ceremonies'. Although it is probable that this distinction was not always drawn by other contemporaries it was clearly maintained by Pagitt in 1661,[85] and it is therefore conceivable that, as C.E. Whiting believed, the Traskites continued as a separate sect well into the eighteenth century.[86] Certainly they were noted by Alexander Ross in 1683.[87] In view of Traske's own theological extremism, to say nothing of his widely reported recantation, lack of any evidence that he ever opposed infant baptism, and the fact that he ended his days in fellowship with a non-Traskite congregation when Traskites were still active and meeting in London, it seems a little surprising that Seventh Day Baptists have claimed him as their earliest exponent.[88] Certainly, a direct connection between Traske and the later Mill Yard congregation cannot be sustained. Even at the loss of thirty years or so, the pedigree of the wider Seventh-day movement without the Judaizing element would appear to be more attractive.

THEOPHILUS BRABOURNE AND A THEOLOGY OF THE SABBATH

Theophilus Brabourne (Braborne, or Bradbourne, 1590–1662) appears in the *Concise Dictionary of National Biography* simply as a 'divine', a 'minister of Norwich', whose claim for attention was that his *Discourse upon the Sabbath Day* (1628) and *Defence of . . . the Sabbath* (1632) argued the observance of the Saturday Sabbath.[89] Brabourne is also noted by Fuller, Wood, and Brook *et al.*, and more recently by Hill, Parker, and Katz, and appears in the *Oxford Dictionary of the Christian Church*.[90] A revision of the *DNB*

---

[85] Pagitt, *Heresiography*, sig. A3ʳ.

[86] Whiting, *Studies in English Puritanism*, 316, although Whiting's use of original sources here is difficult to substantiate, and the distinction he makes between Traskites and Sabbatarians (319) is not altogether convincing.

[87] Alexander Ross, Πανσεβεια: *or, A View of all Religions in the World* (6th edn. 1683), 376. This 'enlarged and Perfected' edition shows no change from the 1st edition of 1653 as far as Traskites are concerned. The 20th edition of Edward Chamberlayne's *Angliae Notitia* (1702) noted 'Traskitts [*sic*] now called Seventh-day-men, who keep the Jewish Sabbath', 258.

[88] *SDBEA* 1 (1910), pp. xxiii, 41. A recent view indicates a more moderate understanding of Traske's relationship to Seventh Day Baptists, although the author does not mention that Traske never formally renounced infant baptism: Sanford, *A Choosing People*, 51.

[89] *The Concise Dictionary of National Biography*, s.v. Brabourne.

[90] Fuller, *Church History*, xi. 144; Anthony Wood, *Athenae Oxonienses* (1691–2), ii. 541; Benjamin Brook, *The Lives of the Puritans* (1813), ii. 362 ff.; Hill, *Society and Puritanism*, 174, 197, 362; Parker, *The English Sabbath*, 198–9, 201; Katz, *Philo-Semitism*. 34–8; *ODCC*, s.v. Brabourne.

entry by its author, Alexander Gordon, in an 1887 edition of the
Sabbath Memorial provides a fuller and mainly reliable account of
Brabourne's life and work.[91] Denounced in 1634 as a Jew, a heretic,
and a schismatic, there is little doubt that Brabourne remained
at heart a loyal Anglican throughout his life, eschewing fellowship
with separatist or Sabbatarian congregations. There is equally little
doubt that his Seventh-day views were seminal to the seventeenth-
century Sabbatarian movement as it was being formed and as it
developed in England and Wales, and later in North America.

Brabourne was the elder of two sons of Henry Brabourne, a
Norwich hosier with strong Puritan sympathies, who wanted
Theophilus to 'prove a godly minister'. He attended the Free School
in Norwich until he was 15 and then, instead of matriculating at
Cambridge, was sent, rather surprisingly, by his father to London,
*c.*1605, to sell hosiery in the family business. This was because
the bishops had begun 'to silence godly ministers' of the Puritan
sort, and Henry Brabourne reasoned that under these circumstances
Theophilus would suffer such a fate if he was to take priest's
orders. Brabourne remained in London for several years until he
married Abigail Galliard, whereupon he returned to Norwich, *c.*1618/
19, and, with a renewed interest in the ministry, proceeded MA
prior to being ordained in 1621 by Thomas Dove, Bishop of Peterborough.[92] What happened between his ordination and the publication of his first book in 1628 is not clear, although he was licensed
for the diocese of Norwich in 1622 and is noted as curate of Catton
in 1630.[93]

Two theories have been advanced for the development of
Brabourne's belief in the seventh day. Gordon says that Brabourne's
attention was drawn to the Sabbath question by the publication in
1621 of Thomas Broad's *Three Questions Answered*, concerning the
obligations of the fourth commandment.[94] Broad, an anti-Sabbatarian,

---

[91] Alexander Gordon, 'Theophilus Brabourne, M.A.', in *SM* 49–50 (1887), 565–70.

[92] Ibid. 566; Theophilus Brabourne, *A Reply to the Indoctus Doctor Edoctus* (1654),
94. Abigail Galliard was the daughter of Roger and Joane Galliard of Ashwell Thorpe.
By this marriage Brabourne became brother-in-law to Benjamin Fairfax, who was
ejected from Rumburgh, Suffolk, in 1662, and who married Abigail's sister Sarah.
Brabourne was also brother-in-law to Roger Galliard, rector of Kenninghall, and
William Galliard, schoolmaster at Fundenhall, *SM* 49–50: 566.

[93] Gordon, *SM* 49–50: 566.

[94] *DNB*, s.v. Brabourne. Broad was rector of Rendcomb, Glos., Parker, *The
English Sabbath*, 165; cf. 199.

denies a pre-Mosaic or morally binding Sabbath, saying that the Lord's day is to be kept according to the custom of the primitive Church and in harmony with the constitution of the Church of England. Broad's *Three Questions* was a direct response to 'the Sabbatharies' who wanted Christians to 'observe the Jewes Sabbath',[95] and a connection is not impossible even though Brabourne clearly would not have derived a belief in the seventh day from this source. A second suggestion links Brabourne with Traske. Broad had noted that 'many' were inclined to 'the seventh day for Sabbath',[96] and W.T. Whitley, the Baptist historian, thought that the 1627 proceedings against Traske had interested Brabourne, even though at the time he appears to have been living in Norfolk.[97] He had possibly been in London at the time of Traske's earlier trial in 1618 and is not likely to have remained unaware of Traske's activities and the attention the trial brought to the early London Sabbatarians. Yet Brabourne seldom mentions Traske in any of his numerous publications. While Brabourne may have been led to consider the issue by both Broad and Traske, a more probable explanation for his Sabbatarianism is to be found in his own evident respect for the authority of Scripture, leavened perhaps by the 'Sabbatarian dogmatists' of the time.[98] This is more reasonably interpreted as referring to Sabbatarian controversialists such as Dod, Bound, and Sprint, or Greenham, Ames, and Perkins, many of whom Brabourne specifically mentions, than to anti-Sabbatarians or proscribed or incarcerated Traskite sympathizers.[99] Heylyn remarked that advocates of the seventh day build squarely on the foundations laid by Puritan Sabbatarians and that they 'ploughed with no other than their heifers',[100] and it is probable that he had Brabourne in mind.

---

[95] Thomas Broad, *Three Questions Answered* (1621), 3.

[96] Ibid., Ep. Ded. See Bodl. MS Bodley 538, for three later pieces by Broad *contra* Brabourne: 'Concerning the Sabbath' (1632); 'A confutation of Mr. Brabourn's Sabbath-doctrine, which is, that we Christians ought to keep holy the Jewes Sabbath, or Saterday' (n.d.); 'Two Treatises: The one Concerninge the Sabbaoth or Seventh day, The other Concerninge the Lords day or first day of the weeke' (n.d.).

[97] W.T. Whitley, 'Men of the Seventh Day', unpublished MS, Angus Library, Regent's Park College, Oxford, MS 41.e.1., Ch. 3, 2; cf. Katz, *Philo-Semitism*, 37.

[98] Brabourne, *Discourse, passim*. Brabourne's opening comment 'To the godly and well-affected Reader' is that 'all who are truly Gods' have 'a propensity and holy inclination . . . unto all God's Commandments', Ep. Ded., sig. *2ʳ; cf. White, *Treatise*, Ep. Ded., sig. A2ᵛ.

[99] Brabourne, *Discourse*, 122, 174, 218; cf. Katz, *Philo-Semitism*, 38.

[100] Cited in Cox, *Literature of the Sabbath Question*, i. 158.

The appearance of Brabourne's *Discourse upon the Sabbath Day* in 1628 was a watershed in the development of Seventh-day belief and practice in seventeenth- and eighteenth-century England. It was the first printed work in the English language to advocate the religious observance of Saturday, and represents a remarkably well-matured Seventh-day theology. The general thrust of Brabourne's arguments, both here and later, is apparent in the title: *A Discourse upon the Sabbath Day; wherein are handled these particulars ensuing;— 1. That the Lord's Day is not Sabbath Day by Divine institution. 2. An exposition of the iiii Commandment . . . and particularly here it is shown at what time the Sabbath day should begin and end . . . 3. That the Seventh-day Sabbath is not abolished. 4. That the Seventh-day Sabbath is now still in force. 5. The author's Exhortation and reasons, that nevertheless there be no Rent from our Church as touching practice.*[101]

Besides confirming a chronological link with earlier Puritan Sabbatarian argument, Brabourne's title emphasizes the foundation of Seventh-day beliefs in the Decalogue, thereby also confirming a theological link with earlier Wycliffite Sabbatarian thought. Although Brabourne made it clear from the beginning that he wanted no division in the Church 'as touching practice' he nevertheless made it equally clear that the matter contained important consequences and that his readers would ultimately have to make a decision between Saturday and the Lord's day:

And now let me propound unto your choice, these two days: the Sabbath day on Saturday, or the Lords day on Sunday; and keep whither of the twain you shall in conscience find the more safe. If you keep the Lords day, but prophane the Sabbath day, you walk in great danger and peril (to say the least) of transgressing one of Gods eternal and inviolable Laws, the 4th Com(mandment): but on the other side, if you keep the Sabbath day, though you prophane the Lords day, you are out of all gunshot and danger,

---

[101] The *Discourse* is thorough and well argued, but poorly printed, and contains many typographical errors. Brabourne explains that owing to 'troubles raised up against' both himself and his book, he was unable to 'be present at the press, to peruse, correct, and amend the faults therein', *Discourse*: sig. *4ʳ. The thoroughness of the work suggests that Brabourne might have been convinced of the seventh day some time before the *Discourse* appeared in print. Whitley confuses the *Discourse* with Brabourne's second work *A Defence of . . . the Sabbath Day* (1632), which was not merely a 'corrected and amended' edition of the *Discourse*; W.T. Whitley, *A Baptist Bibliography*, i (1916), 9.

for so you transgress no Law at all, since Christ nor his Apostles did ever leave any Law for it.[102]

Brabourne apparently saw no conflict between this somewhat pointed advice and the hope he had earlier expressed that there would be no disharmony in the Church resulting from the advancement of Seventh-day views. It seems that he rather naïvely hoped, at this point at least, that the Anglican establishment as a whole might turn to the seventh day.[103]

As might have been anticipated, others were not as sanguine. In 1632 Brabourne's second book, *A Defence of . . . the Sabbath Day*, appeared as an undertaking 'against all Anti-Sabbatharians both of Protestants, Papists, Antinomians, and Anabaptists', and specifically in response to ten clergymen who had opposed the Seventh-day views put forward in the *Discourse*.[104] In the interim Brabourne had discussed the issue at length with the antagonists named on the title-page of the *Defence*, but without any satisfactory resolution.[105] By 1632 the climate had changed perceptibly, and whereas the *Discourse* had been published in 'a time of peace', the *Defence* now appeared at 'a time of war', to use Brabourne's own words,[106] and

---

[102] Brabourne, *Discourse*, 220.

[103] 'How were it to be lamented . . . to see a few keep Saturday for Sabbath, and a multitude to keep Sunday Sabbath, what a confusion and what an heart-burning it may breed. I beseech God for special wisdom and prudence therefore in this point, that nothing be done rashly, but also as may be for the edification of the Church of God, and for every members particular comfort', *Discourse*, 229.

[104] Brabourne, *A Defence of that most Ancient, and Sacred ordinance of GODS, the Sabbath Day. Consequently, and together with it, 2. A Defence of the iiijth Commandement: 3. A Defence of the integrity and perfection of the Decalogue, Morall Law, or X Commandements. 4. A Defence also, of the whole and intire worship of God, in all the partes thereof, as it is prescribed, in the first Table of the Decalogue. 5. A Discovery of the Superstition, impurity and corruption of Gods worship; yea, and Idolatry, committed by multitudes, in sanctifying the Lords Day for a Sabbath Day, by the iiijth Commandement . . .* (1632). It is almost certain that there was not a 1631 edition, *Defence*, sig. c4ᵛ. The ten clergymen were named on the title-page, without initials, as Greenwood, Hutchinson, Furnace, Benton, Gallard, Yates, Chappel, Stinnet, Johnson, and Warde. Alexander Gordon identified Hutchinson as John Hutchinson of Trinity College, Cambridge, later a Baptist; Benton as Thomas Benton, ejected from Pulham; Gallard as Brabourne's brother-in-law Roger; Yates as John Yates of St Andrew's, Norwich; Warde as John Ward of St. Michael's at Plea, Norwich, later an Independent; and Johnson possibly as Nathanael Johnston, MD, who in 1659 wrote against the Socinian view of the Sabbath, *SM* 49–50: 569. Gordon incorrectly designates Stinnet as Edward Stennett of Abingdon, rather than William Stinnett of Norwich, for which suggestion I am indebted to Mr Oscar Burdick.

[105] Brabourne, *Defence*, sig. C2ᵛ.   [106] Ibid., sig. C4ᵛ.

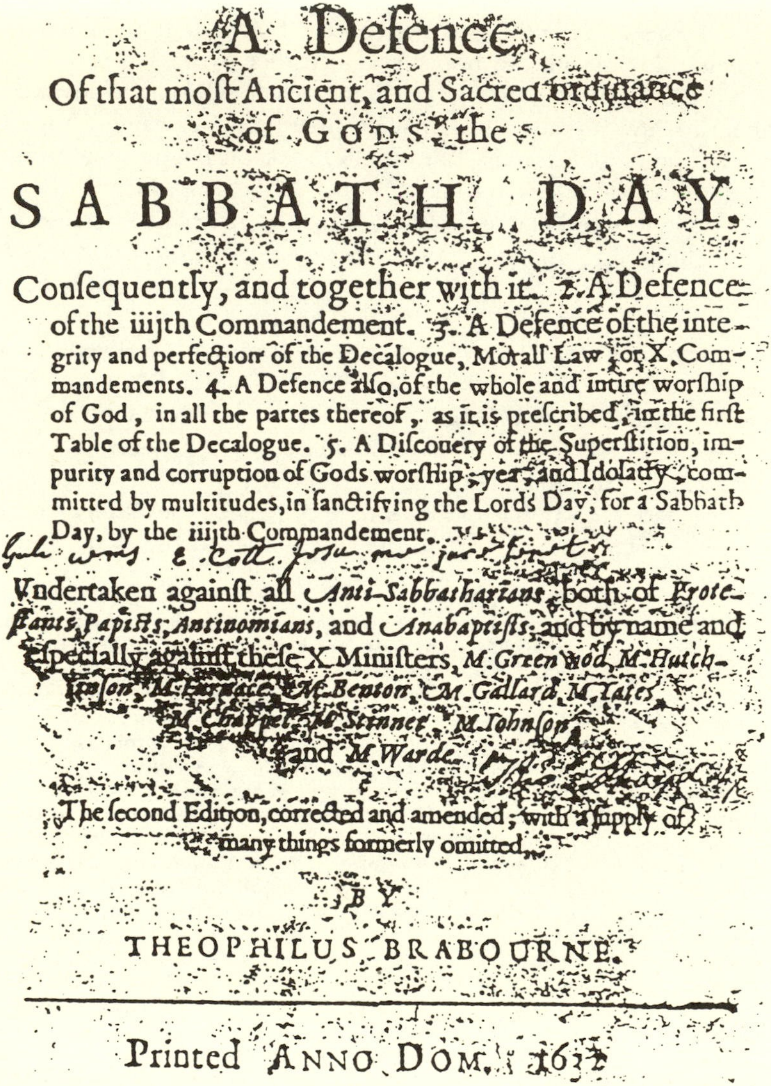

A Defence

Of that most Ancient, and Sacred ordinance of G o d s the

SABBATH DAY.

Confequently, and together with it. 2. A Defence of the iiijth Commandement. 3. A Defence of the integrity and perfection of the Decalogue, Morall Law, or X. Commandements. 4. A Defence alfo, of the whole and intire worfhip of God, in all the partes thereof, as it is prefcribed, in the firft Table of the Decalogue. 5. A Difcouery of the Superftition, impurity and corruption of Gods worfhip; yea, and Idolatry, committed by multitudes, in fanctifying the Lords Day, for a Sabbath Day, by the iiijth Commandement.

Vndertaken againft all *Anti-Sabbatharians* both of Proteftants, Papifts, Antinomians, and *Anabaptifts*, and by name and efpecially againft thefe X Minifters, M. Greenwood, M. Hutchinfon, M. Barnet, M. Benton, M. Gallard, M. Tates, M. Chappell, M. Stinnet, M. Johnfon, and M. Warde.

The fecond Edition, corrected and amended, with a fupply of many things formerly omitted.

BY

THEOPHILUS BRABOVRNE.

Printed ANNO DOM. 1632

FIG. 2 Title-page of Theophilus Brabourne's *A Defence...of...the Sabbath Day*, 1632

the enterprise required assistance. Although the *Defence* was issued as a 'second edition', it was in fact an extensive revision of the 1628 *Discourse* 'with a supply of many things formerly omitted'. It reiterated and expanded the basic arguments of the *Discourse*, maintaining that the seventh day should be kept holy on the grounds of the perpetual morality of the Decalogue and the lack of divine authority for transferring the Sabbath institution from the seventh to the first day of the week. The *Defence* was boldly dedicated to Charles I in the hope that the King would undertake Sabbath reformation similar to that initiated by Old Testament kings such as Hezekiah and Josiah, and also to the archbishops and bishops of the realm, from all of which it might be concluded that Brabourne had thought the matter through with much care.[107] 'The soundness and clearness of my cause giveth me good hope,' he wrote, and sent the *Defence* on its way, aware of the possible consequences and prepared to defend it wherever necessary, but at the same time quoting Esther, 'and if I perish, I perish'.[108]

That which Brabourne appears to have anticipated soon became a reality. By early 1634 he was imprisoned in the Gatehouse, pending proceedings in the Court of High Commission in which he was to answer the charge of holding and disseminating 'erroneous, heretical and judaical opinions'.[109] In April and early June he made two brief appearances in court, before finally being examined concerning his views on 26 June in the presence of a hundred or so clergymen and several hundred lay onlookers.[110] These proceedings alone were sufficient to ensure that news of Brabourne's Sabbatarian beliefs was carried far and wide across London and probably well beyond. In court, Brabourne acknowledged that he was the author of the *Defence*, and admitted that he was a Sabbatarian 'as much bound to keep the Saturday Sabbath as the Jews were before the coming of Christ'. Taken out of context, and without reference to his other arguments, this would have been sufficient to brand him a Judaizer, which quite clearly he was not. The court had heard all it needed, however, and he was declared a Jew, a heretic, and a schismatic, 'worthy to be severely punished'. Accordingly it was ordered that he be deposed from all ministerial office, excommunicated, fined £1,000 and expenses, ordered to make a public retraction of his

[107] Ibid., sigs. A2–4. [108] Ibid., sig. C3ᵛ.
[109] *CSPD* 1634–5, 126. [110] *CSPD* 1633–4, 579; 1634–5, 108.

views, and remanded in custody to appear again at a later date, presumably to make the required recantation. A week later, 'for maintaining and publishing heretical and judaical opinions touching the Sabbath' the fine was reimposed, and he was ordered to appear before the Bishop of Ely, although the sentence, including the fine, was suspended pro tem.[111]

It is not entirely clear if this constituted a second appearance before Bishop White. The State Papers indicate that between July and October of 1634 the keeper of the Gatehouse prison was authorized to allow Brabourne liberty to visit the Bishop of Ely 'and go elsewhere', although another source suggests that the conferences between Brabourne and the Bishop preceded the High Commission proceedings.[112] Brabourne later remembered these meetings as lasting 'many days, an hour or two in a day' and including at least one session with Archbishop Laud,[113] but does not indicate at which point in the trial they occurred, nor the exact purpose they served, since the court had already passed sentence. Be that as it may, Brabourne appeared again in late October with a printed recantation of his 'errors', which, for some reason, the court declined to accept. Instead, it ordered a form of abjuration to be prepared through which Brabourne would make an acceptable public renunciation of his 'Judaical and erroneous opinions'. Over the next six months he was in and out of court on several occasions 'perfecting' his statement, until finally on 30 April 1635, the court accepted his submission as an appropriate recantation.[114] Just when Brabourne was released is not clear, although he appears to have returned to Norwich during 1635 to continue his ministry, having spent at least eighteen months in prison amongst 'rogues, lousie felons, and cheaters'. Even then, the matter dragged on until February 1636, when the £1,000 fine, originally imposed in 1633 it seems, and then reimposed and suspended from time to time during 1634 and 1635, was finally remitted.[115]

The length of the proceedings against Brabourne may have been due in part to the difficulty in reaching agreement on the form of

---

[111] *CSPD* 1634–5, 126, 127, 176; Gordon, *SM* 49–50: 567. Cf. W.H. Hart, *Index expurgatorius Anglicanus*, iii (1873), 75.

[112] *CSPD* 1634–35, 176, 258; cf. Gordon, *SM* 49–50: 566.

[113] Brabourne, *Indoctus Doctor*, 74.

[114] *CSPD* 1634–5, 273, 493, 533, 542, 549; 1635, 180, 190, 196.

[115] Gordon, *SM* 49–50: 567; Brabourne, *Indoctus Doctor*, 101; *CSPD* 1635, 230.

words to be used in his abjuration. Bishop White, who had been commissioned by Charles I to prepare a reply to Brabourne's publications, maintained that Brabourne made a 'voluntary and humble submission' before 'a public and honourable audience' thereby becoming 'an unfeined convert' to his mother Church, in short, a complete and acceptable recantation.[116] Brabourne viewed matters differently. 'I did not recant one tittle of what I wrote against it [Sunday]. I only wrote that I confessed it [Sunday] to be a holy day of the Church, and so much I might have said of Christmas Day also.'[117] The argument over Brabourne's recantation seems to have revolved ultimately around the word 'necessarily', i.e. whether or not Saturday should 'necessarily' be observed as the Sabbath. Brabourne had apparently conceded the necessity, this being his 'recantation of a rash word, not of the matter', and he stoutly maintained to the end that he had not retracted anything of substance concerning the seventh day.[118]

It is difficult at a distance of more than 350 years to ascertain precisely what was said throughout these lengthy proceedings, let alone to determine what was meant. Perhaps Brabourne did recant, at least momentarily, or partially. Certainly the Court of High Commission was satisfied. And if he did, in a form acceptable both to himself as well as his prosecutors, that was hardly a culpable act, particularly in view of the fact that one of his judges, Sir Henry Marten, had moved during the trial that the ancient anti-Lollard legislation 'De haeretico comburendo' should be brought against him.[119] It is of more significance that, after keeping an appropriately low profile for several years, Brabourne, in 1654, returned to advocating the seventh day openly. Between then and his death in 1662[120] he published at least seven further works which in part or in whole defended his position on the Saturday Sabbath. *In toto*, and including the earlier *Discourse* and *Defence*, Brabourne's works unquestionably provided a theological base sufficiently strong to sustain through nearly four centuries a religious conviction which at that time and since has attracted considerable opposition from

---

[116] White, *Treatise*, 305.   [117] Brabourne, *Indoctus Doctor*, 101.

[118] Ibid. 100. Brabourne also maintained that the suggestion of a full recantation had first been canvassed by John Collings, who so virulently opposed him in the mid-1650s as a former 'Boltpoak, Weaver, Hostler, and Maltster, now a nonsensical scribbler'; Collings, *A New Lesson for the Indoctus Doctor* (1654), title-page. Cf. Brabourne, *Indoctus Doctor*, 101; *DNB* s.v. Brabourne.

[119] PRO, SP/16/261, fos. 68ʳ, 103ᵛ, 181ᵛ.   [120] NRO, NCC Wills 1662, OW80.

all points of the ecclesiastical spectrum.[121] Perhaps it is a mark of the man's moderation as well as his conviction that, shortly after returning to the propagation of Seventh-day views, he could say: 'I could above five years ago have made a schism in the church about the Sabbath day, and given more strength of reason and scripture for it, than any sect in our time can for their separations, had I not known schism to be a sin against God and a sin against authority.'[122] Six years later, and still from within the Anglican fold, Brabourne could argue that the Sabbath question was 'now the Highest Controversy in the Church of England', a view which was shortly reinforced by John Owen's fear that many might yet turn to the seventh day.[123] All of Brabourne's later works were written as a layman, since he relinquished his orders in 1648 on inheriting property from his brother. Most of these latter years were spent in writing and publishing, for in addition to a considerable contribution to the Sabbath literature between 1654 and 1660, he produced several further works, largely on the questions of church government and discipline. During these years, he appears to have resided in Norwich, where he died in 1662, leaving £10 in his will for 'the poor Sabbath-keepers in Norwich', to be distributed by Christopher Pooley and his elders.[124]

In total, Brabourne produced more than 1,000 pages in support of the Saturday Sabbath, covering in great detail the whole range of arguments for the seventh day, as well as dealing with the objections commonly brought against Seventh-day observance, and the arguments in favour of the Lord's day. It was by any standard

---

[121] Several incomplete or incorrectly cited lists of Brabourne's works on the Sabbath have been published, e.g. Cox, *Literature of the Sabbath Question*, i. 73, 80, 443–4; *TBHS* 2 (1910–11), 55; *SM* 49–50: 569–70. The following would appear to include all his published works dealing in whole or in part with the seventh day (short titles only; see Appendix IV for full titles): *A Discourse upon the Sabbath Day*, 1628; *A Defence of . . . the Sabbath Day*, 1632; *Of the changing of Church-Discipline*, 1653; *The Second Part of the Change of Church Discipline*, 1654; *A Reply to the Indoctus Doctor Edoctus*, 1654; *The Second Vindication of my first Book of the Change of Discipline*, 1654; *A Reply to Mr Collings Provocator Provocatus*, 1654; *An Answer to M. Cawdry's two Books of the Sabbath*, 1654; *An Answer to Two Books on the Sabbath . . . Mr Ives . . . Mr Warren . . .*, 1659; *Of the Sabbath Day*, 1660. There is also an unpublished MS, *c.*1631, 'An answer to Mr Burton on the Lords Day Sabbath', Bodl. MS Bodley 538, fos. 11–40. The only known copy of *Of the Sabbath Day* (*BB*, i. 91–660) is currently missing from the shelves at Dr Williams's Library.

[122] Brabourne, *The Second Part of the Change of Church Discipline* (1654), 56.

[123] Brabourne, *Of the Sabbath Day* (1660), title-page; Owen, *Exercitations*, 399.

[124] NRO, NCC Wills 1662, OW 80. On Pooley, see Chs. 9 and 10.

an impressive output, giving evidence throughout of a keen mind and a thorough grasp of the biblical and historical material involved. To reduce it all to a sentence or two is probably unfair, yet Brabourne himself might not have objected had he been told that his Sabbatarian theology was, in effect, contained in two principles, the general principle of the authority of Scripture and the corollary to that of the authority of moral law as expressed in the perpetually binding Ten Commandments. While later Sabbatarian writers would return frequently to those two fundamentals it was indisputably Brabourne who first laid them down in the seventeenth century as the basis for a revived theology of the seventh day.

An unequivocal respect for the authority of Scripture recurs in Brabourne's writings. His basic argument, as well as the incipient relationship of moral law to Scripture, appears in this statement from the *Discourse*: 'When it can be shown me, that in Scriptures account any day of the week save Saturday, the last day of the week, was called the seventh day, then may I be brought to think the Fourth Comm[andment] may be understood of some other seventh day besides Saturday, and not till then.'[125] It is the scriptural 'account', the authority of divine revelation in the Word, which alone will persuade Brabourne. This is, of course, a thoroughly Puritan outlook, shared by Brabourne with his antagonists, and is applicable to every aspect of doctrine and at all times in the experience of true believers and the true Church. Thus, the Sabbath was instituted at Creation and is therefore applicable to both Jews and Gentiles, the latter being able to 'make sense of it' when they 'have the light of Scripture'.[126] Those who claim that Christ changed the Sabbath from the seventh to the first day are admonished to 'search the Scripture'.[127] Edward VI, his bishops, and Parliament conceded 'that they knew no Scripture for the Lord's day or Sunday more than for Christmas day and the other holy days of the Church'.[128] Similarly, the Dutch Anabaptists 'hold that there is no Scripture for the Lord's day and say there is more to be said for the Seventh-day Sabbath than the Lord's day'.[129] And likewise, the 'Lords day is called in Scripture the first day of the week'.[130] Only that which Scripture commands and clarifies in respect of the Sabbath has been acceptable to the faithful body of Christ in ages past, hence Brabourne

---

[125] Brabourne, *Discourse*, 75.   [126] Brabourne, *Of the Sabbath Day*, 8.
[127] Ibid. 28.   [128] Ibid. 69.   [129] Ibid. 3, 4.
[130] Brabourne, *Answer to Cawdry*, 12.

is able to ask one of his adversaries, 'Shall the words in the Scripture be thought to change their sense with the times? Shall they have one sense today, and another tomorrow?'[131] And again, to another opponent, 'Do you think the sense of Scripture, or exposition of it, doth change with the times? Mens opinions in these days do change with the times, today one thing, tomorrow another: and will you have the sense of Scripture changeable too? Then the Scriptures are a Nose of wax to bow them which way men list.'[132] The issue is fundamentally one of revelation and authority and of willingness to be subject to Scripture correctly interpreted, and Brabourne, at all times unambiguous, presses the point with characteristic frankness:

> I care not whether you keep Saturday-Sabbath, Sunday-Sabbath, or Monday-Sabbath . . . but if we have respect to God or to his Scriptures, let us give him the day of his own choice, not another; let us not so shamefully and abominably corrupt his Scriptures by notorious false expositions. It were far better for the Church and State to have no Scriptures, than to have Scriptures falsely expounded to the people.[133]

It was precisely because this was happening in the churches, in Brabourne's view, that he began the *Discourse* on this very note. To the detriment of the general populace's spiritual understanding, the first day of the week was widely referred to as the Sabbath, 'promiscuously, and altogether without warrant of holy Scriptures', whereas in fact Scripture designated the seventh day as the Sabbath.[134] The widespread ignorance of the true biblical Sabbath was 'of dangerous consequence amongst the common people', who when they heard the fourth commandment referred to, naturally understood it to mean Sunday.[135] Brabourne wanted the true identity of the Sabbath made known, as well as the real import of the fourth commandment and the fact that observance of the Lord's day rested on ecclesiastical law rather than on divine law as revealed in the Word of God. 'The raising up this new Sabbath, which hath no Com[mandment] for it, from Christ or his Apostles, makes way for the throwing down the old Sabbath, which stands by an express Com[mandment] from God.' The real danger lay in the substitution of human authority for divine authority, the tendency to 'lean more to our human reasons . . . than to God's express Fourth

---

[131] Ibid. 92.   [132] Brabourne, *Answer to Two Books*, 4, 5.
[133] Brabourne, *Answer to Cawdry*, 94.
[134] Brabourne, *Discourse*, 1.   [135] Ibid. 1–2.

Com[mandment]'.[136] Brabourne wanted reason to be 'subservient, the handmaid to the Holy Scriptures',[137] emphasizing that observance of the Lord's day elevated human authority above that of Scripture and the Decalogue.

There is not in all the New nor Old Testaments any commandment to set up any other Sabbath than the seventh day from the creation . . . It is not by any express command from Christ or his Apostles, but by an ordinance of the Church, as is the doctrine of many great divines, and of our church in the book of Homilies, that we sanctify the Lord's day, rather than any other day of the week.[138]

That Brabourne remained firm to this basic position is clear from a statement in his 1660 *Of the Sabbath Day* where he again contrasts the official ecclesiastical position with that of Scripture: 'Our clergy say, Christ altered and changed the Sabbath from the seventh to the first day. But this is a notorious slander raised against Christ, for search the Scripture and you shall nowhere find that Christ spake one word against the Sabbath, or about altering and changing it.' In Brabourne's view the Sabbath had not been changed, but remained 'a perpetual ordinance', applicable to Christians in all ages.[139] In view of the prevailing confusion, he therefore castigates those 'blind guides of our time' who lead the people to believe 'that the Lord's Day is the Sabbath day, and not the seventh day',[140] thus perverting the intended sense of Scripture.

It was only a short step from arguing the authority of Scripture in general to arguing the authority of the Moral Law in particular. In Brabourne's thought, as the preceding paragraphs will have shown, the two were inextricably linked. In stressing the Ten Commandments as an expression of divine will for human conduct, especially for the conduct of those within the body of Christ, Brabourne shared a viewpoint held by most of his Anglican contemporaries of whatever shade of opinion. He differed from the majority of them only in taking the argument to its logical conclusion. 'The Moral Law or Decalogue, spoken by God, and wrote by His Finger in Tables of Stone, is still in force,' he asserted. And, citing Matthew 5: 17, 18, he continued, 'In these words Christ doth ratify the law, in every jot and tittle of it to the World's end, or until

---

[136] Ibid. 10–11.   [137] Ibid. 56.   [138] Ibid. 38, 59.
[139] Brabourne, *Of the Sabbath Day*, 28.
[140] Brabourne, *Reply to Collings*, 61.

Heaven and Earth perish.'[141] It was sound doctrine, and few would
have disagreed. But the logical conclusion was a different matter
altogether:

Consequently the Seventh-day Sabbath, which is part of this law, is also in
force . . . hence it clearly follows, that if not a jot or tittle must be taken
from the Law, then the Seventh day Sabbath in that Law must still be in
force, and untaken away. You may as well take away the third or fifth
Commandment, as the fourth Commandment, or any part of it.[142]

Brabourne is arguing here not only for the authority of the law, but
also for its unity. The binding obligation of the moral law extended
in his view to the whole law, for which he finds support in the
Epistle of James. Citing James 2: 8–12 Brabourne reminds us that
James uses two of the Ten Commandments to illustrate the essential unity of the Decalogue. To break the law against murder or
adultery is to break the whole law, since each individual law is a
part of the whole for the good of mankind, and an expression of
the mind of the Lawgiver. 'He that said or spake one law . . . said
or spake another.' Brabourne concluded, 'So reason I; He that said
or spake the nine commandments, He said or spake the Ten Commandments. Now if St. James logical reasoning be good, mine cannot
be bad, and therefore the ten do bind as well as the nine.'[143]

Clearly akin to the unity of the Law was its universality. In commenting on this aspect of the Decalogue, Brabourne responds to
an objection frequently brought against the seventh day, namely,
that the Sabbath was a Jewish institution, and thus not obligatory
for Christians to observe. Brabourne had several answers to this,
the first emerging from the essential unity of the Decalogue. If the
fourth commandment had been given to the Jews only, then so
were the other nine intended for the Jews. It did not seem consistent to Brabourne to single out one of the Ten Commandments and
give it a special and limited jurisdiction peculiar to itself and distinct
from the other requirements of the Decalogue. Either the Ten Commandments in their entirety were universally applicable, or they
were all limited in their jurisdiction to the Jews. Common practice
argued the point well enough, since Christians regarded the other
nine commandments as to be observed without question.[144] Turning

---

[141] Brabourne, *Of the Sabbath Day*, 3–4.   [142] Ibid. 4.
[143] Brabourne, *Answer to Two Books*, 12–13.
[144] Brabourne, *Of the Sabbath Day*, 56–7.

to the New Testament, Brabourne appealed to Mark 2: 27, 28 and Christ's statement that the Sabbath was made at Creation for man. This was 'before there was any distinction of Jew and Gentile', Brabourne noted. The antiquity of the Sabbath and its purpose in Creation therefore testified to its universality, its relevance to 'all men, not only Jews'.[145] Moreover, the entire Christian revelation had been given initially to the descendants of Abraham, and Brabourne asks, 'And will you reject the Gospel because it was first given to Jews?'[146] To exclude Gentiles from the jurisdiction of the Sabbath commandment is to change the plain intent of Scripture, and Brabourne complains, 'Never was any of God's Ten Commandments so wrested and abused in exposition as this fourth Commandment, unless it be the second Commandment by the Papists.'[147]

A further twist to the 'Jewish' argument against the seventh day was that the fourth commandment was partly ceremonial, and in that respect limited to the pre-Christian dispensation. Brabourne had little difficulty in dealing with this line of reasoning, which he called a 'monstrous . . . hotch-potch', 'a confusion and jumbling together' of things obviously intended to be kept separate. If, in fact, the fourth commandment did contain ceremonial elements, then it was the only one of the Ten Commandments to differ 'so far in kind from its fellows', 'as if God had wrote morals and ceremonials both upon the same Table . . . and twisted in one commandment something perpetual, some other thing temporary'. This was inconceivable, since the Ten Commandments had all been written by God himself on tables of stone 'which no ceremony was', and it would mean that only part of one commandment of the whole law was ceremonial. To grant this would be 'to suppose our God to plough in his field with an ox and ass yoked together,' or 'to sow it with seeds of divers kinds'. From another standpoint, if the Ten Commandments did represent a combination of moral and ceremonial elements, if Moses had 'jumbled things unskillfully together', then the implications were almost too disturbing to contemplate. 'Which of the Ten Com[mandments] may not suffer violence, laying out such parcels of them as disconceit [*sic*] us, and letting stand still what fancy us?'[148] It was much more prudent, to say nothing

---

[145] Brabourne, *Answer to Two Books*, 8, 10.
[146] Brabourne, *Of the Sabbath Day*, 57.
[147] Brabourne, *Answer to Two Books*, 5.
[148] Brabourne, *Discourse*, 100–2.

of theological and exegetical exactness, to avoid ceremonials altogether and accept the Decalogue as it had always been accepted prior to arguments about the seventh day, as a unified and universal moral law.

The crux of this Saturday–Sunday debate lay in the identity of the seventh day, in the exactness with which the day could be determined, and whether or not 'a' seventh was as acceptable as 'the' seventh. The clear wording of the fourth commandment said, 'The seventh day is the Sabbath'. Brabourne's argument here is that 'seventh' is an ordinal number defining the position of the seventh day in a succession of days, 'the seventh which follows the sixth in order before it'. Thus 'by the seventh year of the King's reign is not understood one of the seven year indefinitely, but the last year of the seven definitely and precisely'.[149] Likewise, 'a bond to be paid the seventh of March is not to be paid upon one of the seven days of March indefinitely . . . but definitely upon the seventh day from the first day of March'.[150] Hence 'this word seventh in the Fourth Commandment is not a cardinal but an ordinal number, notifying not any one of the seven days, but the seventh and last day of the seven, which is our Saturday'.[151] The original text of the fourth commandment confirmed this explanation, since the Hebrew words for Sabbath and seventh carried the definite article prefix signifying something definite and certain, not something indefinite and uncertain.[152] Brabourne himself is therefore able to be definite and certain: 'When the Fourth Commandment binds to the seventh and last day of the week, it cannot bind to the first day.' And 'the Jews were not left at random, as not knowing which day of the seven God meant, for they knew it well, like as if God should say, "Remember Saturday".'[153] It all seemed so clear to Brabourne, and if at times he appears a little impatient, we should remember that for him the quest for reformation of the Sabbath was a quest for honest and faithful interpretation of the biblical text. When applied to the fourth commandment this meant that the seventh day of the week could only be Saturday:

That one word in diverse texts may signify diverse things is nothing strange, but that one and the same word in one and the same text, the Fourth

---

[149] Brabourne, *Answer to Cawdry*, 64–5.   [150] Ibid. 33.
[151] Ibid. 65.   [152] Brabourne, *Of the Sabbath Day*, 32.
[153] Brabourne, *Answer to Cawdry*, 28; *Discourse*, 72.

Commandment, should signify anciently one thing and in our days another thing, this is an absurdity matchless. That by Sabbath and seventh day the Fourth Commandment should enjoin the Saturday to the Jews, and the Sunday to the Gentiles, the Saturday for thousands of years unto Christ and the Sunday for ever after Christ, this may well be called the Queen of absurdities.[154]

Thus, 'the Fourth Commandment is for the seventh and last day of the week', the Lord's day being unknown 'when the Fourth Commandment was given on Mt. Sinai'.[155]

There is much more that Brabourne says about the Sabbath in the context of moral law, and more again on other elements in his Sabbatarian theology. Indeed, there are few aspects of the Seventh-day debate which he does not at some point address, and a summary of his theology, based on a survey of all his major works, indicates the following reasons for his support of the Seventh-day Sabbath and his rejection of the Lord's day:

The seventh day is specified in the perpetually binding moral law of the Ten Commandments.

The Sabbath is a memorial of Creation, instituted for man's good at Creation.

The seventh day was observed by Christ and his apostles.

The seventh day was not abrogated or changed by Christ or his apostles.

The seventh day was observed by the post-apostolic Church for several centuries.

The Sabbath is a sign and a means of the believer's sanctification.

The Lord's day was not commanded or substituted for the seventh day by divine authority.

The observance of the Lord's day is based on canon law and ecclesiastical decree only.

The New Testament texts used to support Sunday observance are incorrectly so interpreted.

The change from Sabbath observance to Sunday observance was instituted by the post-apostolic Church.

This change was predicted in prophecy as a work of the 'little horn' of Daniel 7.

Most of these arguments, if not all of them, were picked up and recast and developed by later Sabbatarian apologists, many of whom

---

[154] Brabourne, *Answer to Cawdry*, 92–3.   [155] Ibid. 12.

will be noted subsequently. The preceding pages have concentrated on Brabourne's argument from the perpetuity of the moral law in the Decalogue, because this is clearly the basic element in his Sabbath doctrine. Much of his *Answer to Cawdry* is a defence of the seventh day in relation to moral law and detailed discussion of interpretation of the fourth commandment in relation to the seventh day of the week. The centrality of the Decalogue and the fourth commandment is readily apparent throughout the *Discourse* and the *Defence*. Something similar may be said of many of the succeeding Seventh-day writers. The fourth commandment looks back to Creation and the institution of the Sabbath, and the moral law as a whole is taken by New Testament writers as being fundamental to the life and practice of believers in Christ. This is not to imply that Christian observance of the moral law is in any way legalistic or Judaistic, as Seventh-day apologists were frequently called on to reiterate.

Most of the other arguments in favour of the seventh day put forward by Brabourne and his successors were in some way derived from or related to the argument from the Ten Commandments and Brabourne's continuing emphasis on the fourth commandment as being central to a sound Sabbath doctrine is legitimate and unavoidable. So, again, 'The Moral law, or Decalogue, spoken by God, and wrote by His Finger in Tables of Stone, is still in force', 'The Fourth commandment saith the seventh day is the Sabbath', 'And now let me propound unto your choice these two days, The Sabbath day on Saturday, or the Lord's Day on Sunday.'[156] The dilemma thus posed, and argued by Brabourne or deduced from the reading of Scripture itself, lay at the heart of the Seventh-day movement as it developed in England and Wales over the next century and a half.

[156] Brabourne, *Of the Sabbath Day*, 3; *Answer to Cawdry*, 28; *Discourse*, 220.

3

The Mill Yard Church

THE identity of the first seventeenth-century Sabbatarian, and the location and origin of the first Seventh-day congregation may never definitely be established. Almost certainly it was not Robert Dogs,[1] and it may not have been John Traske or one of his disciples. It may not even have been in London that the seventh day was first publicly observed, although many of the pre-1650 references to Seventh-day observance assume or indicate a London connection. In 1618 Thomas Coo wrote accusingly to James Holly from Newgate gaol, concluding the letter 'Saturday, your Sabbath'.[2] In a lecture at Oxford in 1622 John Prideaux noted, probably with reference to the London Traskites, that some had proceeded 'to bring in again the Jewish Sabbath'.[3] In 1636 Margaret Former was arraigned for being a Sabbatarian and keeping Saturday as the Sabbath,[4] and ten years later Thomas Edwards, the author of *Gangraena*, an intemperate catalogue of 'Errours, Heresies, Blasphemies, and pernicious Practices', cited a letter which reported, 'Last Saturday the Jewish Sabbath was kept again.' Edwards's correspondent noted that observance of the seventh day had spread to 'other parts', and that even some magistrates approved, hoping that soon the seventh day would be kept 'here as at Amsterdam'.[5] *The Brownists Conventicle*, published in London in 1641, specified 'Thraskites or Sabbaterians' as one of the contemporary sects holding private meetings for

---

[1] As suggested by L. Magalotti, *The Travels of Cosmo the Third, Grand Duke of Tuscany, through England . . . in 1669* (1821), 445; cf. Hill, *Society and Puritanism*, 196. But Magalotti tends to distort, reporting without qualification that Puritans considered themselves 'free from all sin', that polygamy was an Anabaptist tenet 'allowed among Christians', that at Independent worship services 'every member of the sect made a speech, according to his caprice', and that James Nayler was the founder of the Quakers: *Travels*, 426, 433, 437, 447. The name of Robert Dogs does not appear elsewhere in the contemporary literature.

[2] *CSPD* 1611–18, 584.   [3] Prideaux, *Doctrine of the Sabbath*, sig. Ci[r].

[4] Ley, *Sunday a Sabbath*, 123–4.

[5] Thomas Edwards, *Gangraena: or A Catalogue and Discovery of many of the Errours, Heresies, Blasphemies and pernicious Practices of the Sectaries of this time . . .* (1646), 95.

worship.[6] Well before the end of the sixteenth century the visitation articles for the Archdeaconry of Middlesex had asked for information about 'secret conventicles', specifically enquiring whether any parishioners were suspected of being 'Papists, Anabaptists, Libertines, or of the detestable sect of the Family of Love, or any other notable heresy'.[7] London, apparently, had an established inclination to Nonconformity as the seventeenth century began, a fact clearly demonstrated in the early appearance of Independent and Baptist congregations. It is not surprising, then, either that John Traske's Sabbatarian views found ready acceptance in the metropolis, or that by the early eighteenth century London should have become home to four, perhaps five, Seventh-day congregations.

ORIGINS AND THE PRE-RESTORATION YEARS

The beginnings of the General Seventh-day Baptist congregation which later came to be known as the Mill Yard church are best described as obscure.[8] A church book which begins in 1673 and extends to 1840 refers to a 'former book' which has not survived.[9] Seventh Day Baptists, and others, have claimed that the Mill Yard church originated with John Traske, and although the connection has not been proved, it is not impossible.[10] It is more likely, however, that Mill Yard's roots are to be traced to the Fifth Monarchist John More and the celebrated court physician Dr Peter Chamberlen, or to William Saller and the congregation he may have led in the early to mid-1650s. More and Chamberlen were both openly Sabbatarian at a later date and members of Mill Yard, and were consecutively leaders of the Lothbury Square congregation, 1652–54, whose views regarding the seventh day have been a continuing subject of discussion.[11]

---

[6] *Brownists Conventicle*, 2. Banisterians, Brownists, Anabaptists, and Familists were the other sects mentioned by this author.

[7] *Articles to be Enquired of by the Churchwardens and Swornmen within the Archdeaconry of Middlesex* (1582), no. 14.

[8] *TBHS* 2: 247. On Mill Yard see W.H. Black, 'The Mill Yard Seventh-Day Baptist Church', *SR* 14/32 (1858), 126; Micklewright, *Notes and Queries*, 191: 95–9, 137–40, 161–3, 185–9; W.T. Whitley, *The Baptists of London* (1928), 111–12, and 'Men of the Seventh Day', Ch. 6; [Joseph Davis], *The Last Legacy of Mr. Joseph Davis, Senr.* (1707); MYM 1673–1840, *passim*; *BQ* 1: 87; *SDBEA* 1 (1910), 39–44. This last source is not always reliable.   [9] MYM 7, 81, 123.

[10] *SDBEA* 1: 39, 41; Thirtle, *TBHS* 3: 183.

[11] On Chamberlen (or Chamberlain) see *DNB*, s.v. Chamberlen; Thirtle, *TBHS* 2: 9–30: 110–17; J.H. Aveling, *The Chamberlens and the Midwifery Forceps* (1882); *FMM*

Whether or not this Baptist–Fifth Monarchy congregation, which practised believer's baptism by immersion, the laying on of hands, and foot-washing, had corporately adopted the seventh day before its disintegration in 1654 is to some extent immaterial. Besides More and Chamberlen, its membership included another Fifth Monarchist, more prominent than either of them in that respect, John Spittlehouse,[12] who by 1656 was writing in favour of the seventh day, after having previously published *A Vindication of the Royal Law of Jehovah . . . the Decalogue* in 1653[13] while a member of the More–Chamberlen church. Spittlehouse shortly joined forces with William Saller (or Sellars), later to appear as elder at Mill Yard, to publish *An Appeal To the Consciences of the chief Magistrates of this Commonwealth, touching the Sabbath-day* (1657), 'in the behalf of themselves and several others who think themselves obliged to observe the seventh day of the week for the Lord's holy Sabbath'.[14] More himself, in *A Generall Exhortation to the World* (1652), had contended that a true Christian is known by his observance of all the Ten Commandments and that a believer's allegiance to Christ

244–5; Katz, *Sabbath and Sectarianism*, 48–89; *BDBR* i. 133–5. On More, see *FMM* 256; *BDBR* ii. 248. On Chamberlen, More, and the Lothbury Square Church, see Bodl. MS Rawl. D.828; C. Burrage, 'A True and Short Declaration . . .', *TBHS* 2 (1910–11), 129–60; [W.T. Whitley], 'Chamberlen's First-Day Church', *TBHS* 2 (1910–11), 190–2; Thirtle, *TBHS* 3: 176–89; Katz, *Sabbath and Sectarianism*, 57–70.

[12] On Spittlehouse, see *FMM* 263; *BDBR* iii. 194–5. Seven members of the Lothbury Square congregation, including Chamberlen and Spittlehouse, signed the Fifth Monarchist *A Declaration of several of the Churches of Christ . . . Concerning the Kingly Interest of Christ, and The present Suffrings of His Cause and Saints in England*, in June 1654. The other signatories were John Light, John Davies, Richard Ellis, Richard Smith, and Robert Feak, all signing 'in the name of the whole Church that walks with Dr Chamberlain'. More and Dr Theodore Naudin had by this time 'fallen away'. More's Fifth Monarchist interests had been made plain in *A Trumpet Sounded: or The Great Mystery of the two Little Horns Unfolded* (1654), which attacked Cromwell. Capp says he was only known as a Fifth Monarchist until 1654, *FMM* 256. Naudin had been reported for plotting against the Protectorate, and had been imprisoned in the Tower, charged with high treason, but subsequently released, see *FMM* 256.

[13] Cf. this with the title of Edward Stennett's openly Sabbatarian treatise of 1658, *The Royal Law contended for* (for full title see Bibliography).

[14] Saller and Spittlehouse, *An Appeal*, title-page. Saller was also known as Sallers, Seller, Sellars, and Salter. The *Appeal* was expanded and reprinted in 1679, after both Spittlehouse (1659) and Saller (1678) had died, with the complaint that in 1657 it had been 'deceitfully turned off and never examined by some that the Parliament had called to do it', *An Appeal* (1679), sig. A2ʳ. The *Appeal* was an important, if abortive, document in the consolidation of the Seventh-day movement. Addressed to the House of Commons, it openly argued the Seventh-day case, urging the government to establish the true Sabbath since, *inter alia*, it would expedite the conversion of the Jews: *An Appeal*, 13.

Die Veneris, 8 Martii, 1649.

M r. *Millington* Reports from the Committee of Plundred Minifters, the matter of Fact touching the Book entituled, *The Doctrine of the Fourth Commandment deformed by Popery, reformed and reftored to its Primitive Purity,* &c. And the examination of *Auguftine Nicholas,* Servant to *Gartrude Dawfon,* Printer of the faid Book for *James Oakeford*; and the examination of *John Hide.*

Refolved by the Parliament,

That this Book (entituled, *The Doctrine of the Fourth Commandment deformed by Popery, reformed and reftored to its Primitive Purity, &c.*) afcerting the obfervation of the Iewifh Sabbath, and condemning the obfervation of the Lords day as the Chriftian Sabbath, is Erroneous, Scandalous and Prophane, contrary to the practice of the Apoftles, and of all the Chriftian Churches.

Refolved by the Parliament,

That all the Printed Copies of the faid Books be burnt; And that the Marthal be required to do the fame at the Exchange and in Cheap-fide.

Refolved by the Parliament,

That all Printed Copies of the faid Book, wherefoever they fhall be found in *England* or *Wales,* fhall be brought to the Chief Magiftrate of the place where the fame fhall be found, who is hereby required and enjoyned to caufe the fame to be burnt accordingly.

Hen: Scobell, Cleric. Parliamenti.

London, Printed by *Edward Husband* and *Iohn Field,* Printers to the Parliament of *England,* 1 6 4 9.

F IG. 3 The Parliamentary Resolution of 1650 (new style) ordering the burning of James Ockford's *The Doctrine of the Fourth Commandement* was 'not to consist of one, or two, or three, or four particulars, but in the observing of all the commandments . . . and every particular thereof'.[15] A John Moore appears as one of the trustees of Mill Yard at a later date, and when Chamberlen and his wife Anne were excluded from Mill Yard in 1675, they pursued their Sabbatarian convictions in fellowship with the Bell Lane congregation.[16]

Chamberlen had adopted the seventh day himself in 1651, and it is conceivable that he could have led the Lothbury Square congregation in First-day worship while privately observing the seventh day. Similar instances of individuals personally inclined to the seventh day but in fellowship with First-day congregations were not unknown as the Seventh-day movement developed,[17] and the attitude of the government at the time to Seventh-day Sabbatarianism would have made this a prudent course for Chamberlen to take.[18] On the other hand, there are some similarities between the membership roll of Lothbury Square in 1653 and that of Mill Yard in 1673, and it is quite possible that the More–Chamberlen congregation was Seventh-day from the time its records begin in 1652, or earlier,[19] placing little emphasis on its Sabbatarian stance for the sake of expediency, or simply because it was not regarded as a matter of great consequence. It is also possible, of course, that Lothbury Square was a mixed congregation at this point, in the process of evolution to being completely Seventh-day. This would also have been in keeping with the experience of other congregations as Seventh-day views were canvassed around the country. Chamberlen was already Seventh-day, and More had written strongly in favour of observing the whole Decalogue in 1652, the year in which the anonymous pro-Seventh-day *The Moralitie of the Fourth*

[15] John More, *A Generall Exhortation to the World* (1652), 6, 7.

[16] W.H. Black (ed.), *The Last Legacy of Joseph Davis, Snr.* (1869), 77; MYM 11, 131 and *TBHS* 3: 186–8.

[17] e.g. Joseph Stennett II, who ministered at Little Wild Street, 1737–58, while remaining Sabbatarian himself: Whitley, *Baptists of London*, 125; *TBHS* 3: 177; and John Maulden, who remained for a time at Rupert Street, after accepting the seventh day and before joining Mill Yard: see below, 157.

[18] In 1650 a Parliamentary committee had ordered that all copies of James Ockford's *The Doctrine of the Fourth Commandement* should be publicly burnt and its printer apprehended for examination. The *Publick Intelligencer* for 21–8 Feb. 1659 reported that the House of Commons had appointed a committee 'to consider how to suppress the meetings of Quakers, Papists . . . and the setters up of the Jewish worship'.

[19] On the nature of the Lothbury Square congregation, and the possibility of its being Sabbatarian, see Appendix III, 'The More–Chamberlen Church Reconsidered'.

Commandement had appeared in London. Spittlehouse, as we have noted, published in defence of the Decalogue in the following year. Whatever the situation might have been at Lothbury Square, the troubled congregation came to an abrupt and untimely end in May 1654, and Chamberlen soon appears in association with a Seventh-day group meeting in Whitechapel, quickly assuming a prominent role as he had when he had joined John More's church.[20]

It is not entirely clear whether a Seventh-day congregation including some of the Lothbury Square members gathered around Chamberlen at this time, or whether he joined a group already observing the seventh day. He later claimed to have been 'the first that endeavoured to rescue that commandment (i.e. the Fourth) from the Triple-crowned-little Horn's changes of Times and Laws',[21] but that might have been prompted by failing memory or wishful thinking, although one source does state that Mill Yard was founded by Chamberlen 'somewhere about 1654'.[22] Spittlehouse, formerly of Chamberlen's Lothbury Square congregation, reported in 1656 that some were observing the seventh day, and William Saller, who published with Spittlehouse in 1657, is noted in that year as being a Seventh-day preacher in London, although he does not appear clearly as elder of Mill Yard until 1673.[23]

The Saller connection is, in fact, an important one. He had come out strongly in favour of the seventh day as early as 1653 with a short but incisive piece entitled *Sundry Queries Tendred to . . . Ministers of Jesus Christ, for clearing the Doctrine of the Fourth Commandement, And the Lords Sabbath Day.* This publication, it appears, had been circulated to London clergy, 'both Parish-Preachers, and Pastors of the Congregated Churches', in the hope that it would rally support for the seventh day. When that did not eventuate, Saller reissued it *c.*1660 for 'the consideration of all men', hoping that it would lead those who read it to be of 'one mind' with him concerning the seventh day.[24] It would seem from all this

---

[20] Katz, *Sabbath and Sectarianism*, 71.

[21] Peter Chamberlen, *The Sons of the East* (1682), bds.   [22] Cf. *SO* 1: 84–5.

[23] John Spittlehouse, *A Manifestation of sundry gross absurdities . . . in reference to the abrogating of the seventh-day-Sabbath . . .* (1657), 6; Tillam, *Seventh-Day Sabbath*, 50–1; MYM, p. i. Saller is somewhat elusive prior to 1673. Whitley confuses him with a son of the same name also in fellowship with Mill Yard from 1673–4, *BB* i. 227, s.v. Saller.

[24] W[illiam] S[alter] [Saller], *Sundry Queries formerly tendred to the Ministers of London, for clearing the Doctrine of the fourth Commandement, and the Lord's* SABBATH-DAY, *but now tendred to the Consideration of all Men* (1660), 1, 2. See *STC* for publication date. Isaac Penington provided a Quaker response to Saller's wish

that Saller had adopted Seventh-day views by 1653, if not earlier, although he does not appear as a member of the More–Chamberlen church. Since Saller later served as elder at Mill Yard, it must be concluded that at this time he could have been associated with a Sabbatarian congregation quite distinct from the Chamberlen church and which in its own right could claim ancestry of Mill Yard.

Chamberlen himself appeared as one of the contenders for the seventh day, together with Thomas Tillam and Matthew Coppinger, in a debate over the Sabbath which lasted for four days in the Stone Chapel, St Paul's, in 1658 in which he was opposed by Jeremiah Ives.[25] Ives subsequently published an account of these proceedings, *Saturday No Sabbath* (1659), in which he referred to the church 'whereof Mr Chamberlain is a member'.[26] It would seem that Whitley was essentially correct in maintaining that some continuity between the More–Chamberlen congregation of 1652–4 and Mill Yard had been reasonably established,[27] as it would also appear correct that others not directly connected with Chamberlen had been observing the seventh day from early in the 1650s. Chamberlen himself seems to have receded from prominence by the end of the decade, although his influence continued throughout his lifetime. In 1683, a Sabbatarian who was arrested and questioned regarding suspected implication in a plot against the King said that he 'owned the Sabbath day' and was 'of Dr Chamberlaine's religion'.[28]

An identifiable Seventh-day congregation first comes into the light with the arrest and execution of its elder, John James, in October– November 1661. This series of events can only properly be understood in the context of the Fifth Monarchy movement. In January of that year Thomas Venner, a Fifth Monarchist desperado, had led

'to enforce upon Christians the observation of the Jewish Sabbath', with *The New-Covenant of the Gospel Distinguished from the Old Covenant of the Law* . . . (1660) and a broadsheet *An Epistle to all such as observe the Seventh-day of the Week for a Sabbath to the Lord* (1660). See also his *To the Jews Natural and to the Jews Spiritual* (1677).

[25] Ives is noted by Whitley as a keen debater against Seventh-day views. The Stone Chapel had been let in 1653 to accommodate a General Baptist congregation led by Edmund Chillenden, another strong opponent of the Saturday Sabbath, Whitley, *Baptists of London*, 113.

[26] *TBHS* 3: 246; Jeremiah Ives, *Saturday No Sabbath: Or, the Seventh-Day Sabbath proved To be of no force to the Beleeving Gentiles in the times of the Gospel* (1659), sig. A2ʳ, 35, 62–3. In 1654 a church had 'walked with' Chamberlen. Under the circumstances Ives would not have been reluctant to note any change of status affecting Chamberlen, had such a change taken place.

[27] W.T. Whitley, 'A Century of Sabbath Doctrine, 1595–1695', 140, in C.H. Green's copy, notebook 10, SDBHS library.   [28] *CSPD* July–Sept. 1683, 4.

an abortive uprising against the government of Charles II, for which he had been tried and executed.[29] The basis of Fifth Monarchist activism was an interpretation of the prophecies of Daniel and Revelation which held that the final kingdom in the succession of earthly powers delineated in Daniel chapters 2 and 7 was that of Christ Himself, and a conviction that His followers on earth were required to assist in its establishment, using force if necessary. The Fifth Monarchy movement had been growing since the mid-1640s, and by the 1650s the idea of actively hastening the kingdom of God on earth had become increasingly attractive to many. Venner himself had been involved in earlier abortive plots to overthrow the government, for which he had been imprisoned.[30] Although many Fifth Monarchists were not as radical as Venner and his immediate followers, the government was understandably suspicious of any Fifth Monarchy tendencies, and a large group of Seventh-day Men was arrested and imprisoned as late as 1671 on account of being suspected Fifth Monarchy sympathizers.[31] It has been suggested elsewhere that it was possible in the mid-seventeenth century to believe in the coming 'Fifth Monarchy' and use Fifth Monarchist terminology without espousing military or political ambitions at all.[32] When James replied to the lieutenant who arrested him that he 'did own the Fifth Kingdom which must come',[33] it can readily be perceived why this should have been construed in the worst light, even though it is extremely doubtful that James was anything but an ardent millenarian hoping for the expected early return of Christ.

In the event, James was arrested while preaching to a congregation of about forty in Bull-Stake Alley, on Saturday, 19 October.[34] Spittlehouse may well have been a member of this congregation prior to his death in 1659 and, if so, would have contributed to its image as a Fifth Monarchist conventicle. Various accounts of this incident have been given, and we do not need to linger over details that can readily be ascertained elsewhere. James was tried, convicted of treason, and beheaded, and, presumably as a warning to the members of his congregation, his head was displayed on a pole

---

[29] *FMM* 117–20, 199.   [30] Ibid. 81, 267.

[31] J.C. Jeaffreson (ed.), *Middlesex County Records,* iv (1892), 29–30. Capp has identified the Seventh-day Men involved, and gives a brief description of each in *FMM* 239–70.   [32] See Ball, *A Great Expectation,* 181–92.

[33] T.B. Howell (ed.), *Cobbett's Complete Collection of State Trials,* vi (1810), 72, and *passim* for an account of the arrest, trial, and execution of James.

[34] See *A Narrative of the Apprehending, Committment, Arraignment, Condemnation, and Execution of John James* (1662), *passim*; *BDBR* ii. 138; *FMM* 253.

outside the meeting-place where he had been arrested. His essentially apolitical position, as well as his intense Sabbatarianism, are evident in the speech he gave at Tyburn prior to his execution: 'I do own the Commandments of God, the Ten Commandments as they are expressed in the 20th of Exodus. I do here, as before the Lord, testify I durst not . . . willingly break the least of those Commandments to save my life.' And although in some way he seems to have felt that his observance of the seventh day had led to his present predicament, he went on, 'I do own the Lord's holy Sabbath, the seventh day of the week to be the Lord's Sabbath; you know the commandment, "Remember that thou keep holy the seventh day".'[35] This assumption might not have been altogether wrong, for the authorities at this time tended not to make too great a distinction between Seventh-day Men and Fifth Monarchy Men. For how long James's congregation had been gathered, or what happened to it subsequently, is not clear, although it is generally agreed that James was one of the first known pastors of the Mill Yard congregation. Some continuity throughout the 1660s seems fairly certain, since the Mill Yard church book records the dates at which some of its older members joined: 'Sister Soursby' in 1664, 'Sister Davis' in 1665, 'Bro. Mayo' in 1668, and 'Sister Tucker' in 1669.[36] A Mrs (Elizabeth) James appears in the 1674 list of members. When the Mill Yard congregation reappears in 1673 it is with William Saller, Sen., as elder, and with a membership of more than seventy. In that year the congregation moved from Whitechapel to East Smithfield, where it remained until 1689, first under Saller's leadership and then from 1675 onwards with Henry Soursby as elder.[37]

TO THE TURN OF THE CENTURY

Just when Saller had assumed leadership at Mill Yard is not clear, though by tradition he appears to have succeeded John James in 1661 or shortly thereafter. It is also possible, as has already been suggested, that he led this congregation or an earlier one before this date. Whatever the precise chronology of Mill Yard or Saller himself, the establishment of the Seventh-day movement in London in the mid-1650s and 1660s was probably due as much to him as to any other individual. In addition to his *Sundry Queries*, published

[35] Howell (ed.), *State Trials*, vi. 98–9.   [36] MYM, p. lxvii.
[37] MYM, pp. i, 5; Whitley, *The Baptists of London*, 111. Soursby was also known as Sowersby, Souersby, or Scrosby.

with Henry Jessey's help *c*.1653,[38] and his *Appeal To the Consciences of the chief Magistrates*, published jointly with John Spittlehouse in 1657, Saller sent forth a steady stream of Sabbatarian and general devotional literature between 1658 and 1671 which undoubtedly strengthened the claim of the Seventh-day Men to be part of the orthodox Christian tradition. His *Means to Prevent Perishing* (1658), a series of sermons on John 17: 3 outlining the way of salvation and emphasizing a true knowledge of God, compares well with any of the recognized spiritual guides of the seventeenth century. It also indicates that Saller by this time had become established in pastoral preaching. In 1660, or thereabouts, he added *An Appendix* to Spittlehouse's *The Unchangeable Morality of the Seventh-day Sabbath*, and followed this with *A Preservative against Atheism* (1664), and *The Seventh-day Sabbath no Ceremony* (1667), a reply to Thomas Grantham's *The Seventh-Day Sabbath Ceased as Ceremonial* . . . (1667).

Perhaps Saller's most significant contribution to the Sabbatarian debate was his *An Examination of a late Book published by Dr Owen, Concerning a Sacred Day of Rest*, which appeared in 1671 in reply to John Owen's influential *Exercitations Concerning . . . a Day of Sacred Rest* (1671). It is perhaps here that Saller's grasp of the fundamental character of Seventh-day theology and his exposition of it is most plain. The Sabbath was instituted at Creation and therefore 'hath its place by birthright in the Decalogue' thus being 'naturally moral', i.e. arguable from the standpoint of natural law as well as moral law. It is, moreover, impossible that it should ever lose its constituent 'naturalness'.[39] This is an extension of the argument from moral law which previous Seventh-day writers had seen as fundamental to their case. In response to Owen's charge that the law leads to bondage, Saller argues, 'It is trusting to the works of the law for righteousness that genders to bondage, through man's error and corruption.'[40] The law itself does not precipitate bondage, any more than it inheres to legalism or Judaism, a charge that was laid at the Sabbatarians' door with regular frequency. Few answered it more precisely than Saller in responding again to Owen:

---

[38] An introduction to the 2nd edition of *Sundry Queries* states that the piece was originally published 'about the year 1653, with the advice and assistance of that Reverend Minister of Christ, Mr H. Jesse, whose the last two Queries be'.

[39] William Sellars [Saller], *An Examination of a late Book published by Dr. Owen, Concerning a Sacred Day of Rest* . . . (1671), 13.   [40] Ibid. 19.

Let him not slander Christ whatever he casts upon the Sabbath-keepers. But this I shall say for my brethren as well as for myself, we are all of us of the Apostles mind, quite dead to the Law, not having the least hope or expectation to bring forth any acceptable fruit unto God by virtue of it. We look not at all to receive grace or strength from the Law, to sanctify us no more than to justify us.[41]

Succeeding generations of Seventh-day Men would be grateful to Saller for this early and quite explicit attempt to argue the validity of the Seventh-day Sabbath from the context of an orthodox soteriology.

Saller was succeeded in the Mill Yard eldership in 1678 by Henry Soursby, who had been a member of the congregation at least since 1674 and probably earlier.[42] Soursby led the church for the next thirty-three years until he died in 1711. Under his pastorate Mill Yard saw consolidation and steady, if not spectacular, growth. It was said to be flourishing in 1682, with a membership of approximately eighty.[43] By 1689 it was reported as meeting at Peacock Court until 1691, when the beneficence of one of its members, Joseph Davis, sen., enabled the purchase of a property in Mill Yard, Goodman's Fields. In 1700 the building was conveyed by Davis to nine trustees for the use of the congregation and became its permanent home until destroyed by fire in 1790, whereupon it was rebuilt.[44] The Mill Yard premises included a meeting-place, almshouses, and a burial ground. By a further deed executed in 1706 Mill Yard trustees were required to make an annuity of £5 from the Davis estate to the ministers of Seventh-day congregations in North Walsham, Woodbridge, Braintree, Chertsey, Wallingford, Tewkesbury, Salisbury, Sherborne, and in Buckinghamshire.[45] It could be said, perhaps,

[41] Ibid. 30.

[42] A 'sister Soursby' is recorded as a Mill Yard member in 1664, MYM, p. lxvii. Whitley gives Soursby as elder at Mill Yard 1678–1711, *BB* i. 228.

[43] W.H. Black, in *SR* 14/32: 126; Whitley, *Baptists of London*, 111.

[44] In 1705 Davis purchased the manor at Little Maplestead in Essex. His entire estate eventually passed to Mill Yard after the death, without heir, of his son Joseph Davis, Jun., in 1731; William Wallen, *The History and Antiquities of the Round Church at Little Maplestead, Essex* (1836), 137–8.

[45] Black (ed.), *The Last Legacy*, p. xii; *Reports from the Commissioners for Charities*, xix (1840), part 1, 870–3. For comments on the apparent discrepancies in the Charities Commissioners' list, see Appendix II, 'Notes on Supposed Sabbatarian Congregations, 1650–1750', particularly n. 17. The Commissioners also noted that while Davis in 1706 had designated specific congregations to benefit from his will, there were at the time other Sabbatarian churches in London and the country: Commissioners for Charities, MS 210274/A/3.

that under Soursby's ministry Mill Yard moved in status from being
a continuation or an outgrowth of a Commonwealth or early Restoration sect of dubious ancestry, to being a more settled, if somewhat extreme, wing of the General Baptist Church.

Soursby also contributed to the Seventh-day literature when, in
1683, in conjunction with Mehetabel Smith, one of his congregation, he published *A Discourse of the Sabbath: or The Controversies
about the Sabbath Stated and Examined, with Reference unto the
Law of Nature, the Law of Moses, and the Law of Christ*. Developing
the idea argued by Saller concerning natural law, Soursby and Smith
reasoned that the institution of the Sabbath in Eden before the fall
must mean that the Sabbath was part of the 'Law of nature' since
it had been established 'before sin entered, and so before the shadows of Christ' (the ceremonial law), and since 'Adam knew by
nature what corrupt men now do not'. Indeed, the Ten Commandments were 'the great transcript of the Law of Nature', and hence
observance of the seventh day was grounded in natural law as well
as moral law.[46] This also precluded the Sabbath from being ceremonial since it could not be both ceremonial and moral at the
same time. 'Either it must be an Universal and Perpetual Law,
or . . . be supposed Ceremonial.' Further, the antiquity of the Sabbath and its 'place in Paradise' exclude it from ceremonial law since
'ceremonies in their original institution had relation to Christ the
Redeemer from sin', and since the seventh day was a Paradise-
institution, 'it clears it from the imputation of ceremonial'.[47] Those
who debated the Seventh-day issue with advocates like Soursby
and Smith might not have agreed with their conclusions, but they
would hardly have denied that the Seventh-day Men had considered the matter, or claimed that their theology was superficial.

THE HIGH YEARS

Soursby died in 1711 and was followed by John Maulden and John
Savage as joint elders.[48] Savage had been a member at Mill Yard
since 1657 and a trustee since 1700, and Maulden, a shoemaker,
had been elder at Rupert Street General Baptist church prior to

---

[46] Henry Soursby and Mehetabel Smith, *A Discourse of the Sabbath: or The Controversies about the Sabbath Stated and Examined, with Reference unto the Law
of Nature, the Law of Moses, and the Law of Christ* (1683), 3, 5.
[47] Ibid. 93.   [48] Whitley, *Baptists of London*, 111.

joining Mill Yard in 1710.[49] Maulden died in 1715, though not before making a noteworthy contribution to the Sabbatarian cause. In 1708, under the pseudonym of Philotheos, he published *A Threefold Dialogue, Concerning the Three Chief Points in Controversy amongst Protestants in our Days*. The matters at issue were free will, infant baptism, and 'whether the Seventh, or First Day of the week, be the Sabbath of the Lord'.[50] Maulden's answer was a moderate, well-reasoned defence of the seventh day, indicating that he must have adopted the Saturday Sabbath some time before leaving Rupert Street. The *Threefold Dialogue* was republished under Maulden's name in 1728, although his most persuasive apology for the seventh day appeared, also posthumously, in 1724 as *The Ancient and Honourable Way and Truth of God's Sacred Rest of the Seventh-Day Sabbath*, which included a critical examination of the so-called Sunday texts and of the argument that the day of rest had been changed to the first day in honour of the Resurrection. Perhaps these posthumous publications were part of a concerted and sustained effort by the Mill Yard congregation to further the Seventh-day cause. Under John Savage a special day of fasting and prayer had been set aside in March 1717, 'that God will be pleased to raise up more faithful labourers to plead for and support his despised truth'. Savage had been appointed to write to all Seventh-day congregations in England, inviting them to participate in this day of intercession.[51] An interesting sidelight on the Maulden–Savage pastorate, and the attitude of the church to joint eldership, is that while Maulden believed in foot-washing, Savage did not, holding moreover that communion should be celebrated only once a year. The church permitted both views of foot-washing, and the members were given freedom to adopt whichever view they preferred.[52] This potential source of division would soon have been forgotten after Maulden's death, although a possibly greater cause for disharmony came shortly after Savage's death in 1720, when the Calvinistic Seventh-day church which had once been under Joseph Stennett's care joined Mill Yard for regular Sabbath worship.[53]

[49] Ibid. 109. Rupert Street was also known as Goodman's Fields General Baptist.

[50] Philotheos [John Maulden], *A Threefold Dialogue, Concerning the Three Chief Points in Controversy amongst Protestants in our Days* ... (1708), title-page.

[51] MYM 228.   [52] SO 1: 109.

[53] SO 3/46 (6 May 1847), 182. Some sources say that the Pinners' Hall congregation merely shared a building with Mill Yard, e.g. Whitley, *Baptists of London*, 119; *TBHS* 5: 78. But cf. *TBHS* 5: 109. The inference that the two congregations began

Mill Yard remained without pastoral leadership until 1727, when Robert Cornthwaite accepted the call to eldership. Cornthwaite, born at Bolton, and one of eight children of a mother who was widowed relatively early in life, came to Mill Yard from Boston, where he had briefly led a First-day congregation until accepting the Seventh-day Sabbath. As a young man he had been a Presbyterian, but had become Baptist and a minister at Chesham prior to his Boston pastorate. He began to preach at Mill Yard in 1724, became a member in 1725, and was ordained as elder the following year.[54] Cornthwaite's arrival marked the beginning of an important era in Mill Yard's history, for although upon his appointment the Pinners' Hall Calvinists withdrew from joint worship on account of his alleged Socinian leanings,[55] Mill Yard flourished under his ministry. Whereas a day of intercession for new leadership and the Seventh-day cause in general had been observed in 1717, already by 1730, the year in which Peter Russell was appointed as Cornthwaite's assistant, the Mill Yard records show that a day of prayer and thanksgiving was held to mark renewed interest in the seventh day in various places around the country as well as at Mill Yard itself.[56] The Sabbatarian cause was further strengthened over the next decade or two, largely as a result of Cornthwaite's publications. Cox described Cornthwaite as 'one of the ablest defenders' of the Seventh-day position,[57] and between 1730 and 1745 he produced a series of works on the Sabbath, of which his *Essay on the Sabbath* (1740) was of most significance. The *Essay* was essentially a response to recent works advocating observance of the Lord's day by Joseph Hallett, Alexander Jephson, Thomas Chubb, Grantham Killingworth, Daniel Dobel, and Isaac Watts.[58] It would hardly have

to worship together immediately after Stennett's death in 1713 cannot be substantiated, *SO* 1: 116. The Mill Yard records show that in Mar. 1720 an invitation was sent to Joseph Stennett II, then at Leominster, to preach at Mill Yard since 'it might be useful for the promotion of the Sabbath'. The church agreed 'to invite him in love, trusting to his moderation, he knowing our principles about ye General point', MYM 234. On Joseph Stennett II, see *DNB* and below, 157–8, 235–6.

[54] *SO* 1: 117; *PDM* 6 (1799), 1–3; *BQ* 1: 135.
[55] *MGA* ii (1910), 49.   [56] MYM 247–8, 256.
[57] Cox, *Literature of the Sabbath Question*, ii. 198. There were fifty-three members at Mill Yard in 1737, *SO* 1: 117.
[58] Joseph Hallett, *A Free and Impartial Study of the Holy Scriptures recommended* (1729), and *A Third Volume of Notes on Several Texts of Scripture* (1736); Alexander Jephson, *A Discourse Concerning the Religious Observation of the Lord's Day* (1737); Thomas Chubb, *Dissertation concerning the Time for Keeping a Sabbath*

been possible to assemble a more heterogeneous company than this, ranging from Jephson, the Anglican traditionalist, Hallett the Arian, Chubb the Deist, Watts the classical Independent, to the Baptists Killingworth and Dobel. In the mid-eighteenth century the Sabbath issue was clearly not dead. Although Dobel has been described as 'a man of little culture',[59] he is of some interest in terms of Sabbatarian activity. A member of the General Baptist church at Cranbrook, Kent, and later to be its elder,[60] he had in 1737 replied to Maulden's *Ancient and Honourable Way* with *The Seventh-Day Sabbath not obligatory on Christians*. Two years later he published again against the seventh day with . . . *an Examination of Mr Elwall's chief Argument for the Continuation of the Seventh-day Sabbath* . . . (1739). Sir William Tempest of Cranbrook had joined Mill Yard in 1732, and one wonders if Dobel's concern is any indication of a wider interest in the seventh day on the part of General Baptists in Kent.

Cornthwaite was the last of the seventeenth- and eighteenth-century defenders of the seventh day, and possibly the most logical and lucid apologist which the English Seventh-day movement had produced to date. He brought together the arguments which had given rise to the Sabbatarian cause early in the seventeenth century, sustained it during times of opposition and persecution, and given it new life in the mid-eighteenth century. Cornthwaite believed that the observance of the seventh day had been laid down in Paradise for Adam and all his posterity; that inclusion of the requirement to observe the seventh day in the moral law given at Sinai was a renewal of the Edenic institution; and that Christ and the apostles, far from having indicated any intention of changing the day of rest to the first day of the week, had given clear indications by word and example that the original seventh day should

---

(1737); Grantham Killingworth, *A Supplement to the Sermons . . . at Salters-Hall against Popery . . . with the Appendix: concerning the First Day of the Week* . . . (1738); Daniel Dobel, *The Seventh-Day Sabbath not obligatory on Christians* (Canterbury, 1739); Isaac Watts, *The Holiness of Times, Places, and People under the Jewish and Christian Dispensations Considered and Compared* (1738). On Hallett, Dissenting minister at Exeter, see *DNB*, sv. Joseph Hallett III; on Jephson, rector of Craike, Co. Durham, see Cox, *Literature of the Sabbath Question*, ii. 191; on Chubb and Killingworth, see *DNB*; on Dobel, see *BB* i. 215. Caleb Fleming also entered the debate with *The Fourth Commandment Abrogated by the Gospel* (1736), and *A Plain and Rational Account of the Law of the Sabbath* (1736).

[59] Cox, *Literature of the Sabbath Question*, ii. 464.   [60] *BB* i. 215.

and would be kept by their followers. Even if such guidance had not been given by the founder of the Christian Church and his disciples, the reasons for which observance of the seventh day was required in Paradise and at Sinai would have made its continuing observance as incumbent on later generations as on the patriarchs and the Jews. 'We want the same rest and refreshment as they did, and the commemoration of the works of creation is perhaps more reasonable and necessary . . . at this distance of time from the creation than in the early ages of the world.' Hence for Cornthwaite there seemed to be no necessity for a specific restatement of the obligation to keep the Sabbath, for neither Jesus nor any of the disciples had had the least thought of making any alteration to that which had been laid down in Eden for the benefit of mankind in general. There was thus 'no foundation in reason for any formal renewal of the command of the Sabbath under the Christian dispensation'.[61]

Although reason is important to Cornthwaite, particularly in evaluating the biblical and historical evidence for the Sabbath, and in correctly interpreting the biblical text, the Sabbath itself is not grounded in reason, but in revelation. While a regular period of rest from labour is obviously necessary for man, the time and nature of that rest cannot be determined merely through rational thought. 'There is nothing in reason which will oblige us to fix upon one hour, day, week, or month in five, seven, ten, twenty or any one determinate number of hours, days, weeks, or months, for a Sabbath.'[62] The Sabbath and its identity can only be known through revelation, from Scripture. The title of Cornthwaite's *Essay on the Sabbath* required 'a plain, scriptural resolution' of the questions involved. Indeed, the Sabbath issue was of critical significance in the continuing debate with Rome over authority in the Church. Protestants of all persuasions claimed that 'the Bible and the Bible only' was the 'rule of faith and practice', yet in reality were 'sadly hampered' in the argument with Rome because the claim to total allegiance to Scripture fell to the ground in the matter of the day of rest and worship. 'If therefore we desire to persuade the Papists that we are in earnest in our Reformation . . . it is undoubtedly our incumbent duty honestly to give up those points which we cannot

---

[61] Robert Cornthwaite, *An Essay on the Sabbath* . . . (1740), 81.
[62] Ibid. 4–5.

fairly defend.'[63] There are echoes here of Brabourne, who had noted 'the continual warfare, battling with Romish doctrine' and had called for a completion of the Reformation with respect to the Sabbath, urging Protestants to 'imitate the more pure primitive churches, from whom the church of Rome is fled in practise of the Sabbath day, than the corrupted Romish church, from whom we sucked this evil milk'.[64] Protestants in general would have concurred about the Reformation, but demurred when it came to the Sabbath.

Cornthwaite placed much emphasis on Christ's attitude to the Sabbath, and that of the apostles and the early Christian Church and the continuity of Seventh-day observance in the early centuries. The Sabbath which Christ Himself had kept had been the same Sabbath observed by the Jews since Sinai, 'the very same day of the week which was at first set apart'.[65] This day was 'unrepealed by Christ'. The same day had been observed in the Christian era from the day following the Crucifixion, and it had still been in force at the time of the destruction of Jerusalem. 'Christ and his apostles not only kept the seventh-day Sabbath, but also never said a word that we can find, either that it should be abrogated or changed for another.'[66] With reference to Christ's meeting with the disciples on the first day, and to the coming of the Holy Spirit on the Day of Pentecost, incidents frequently cited as evidence in support of First-day observance, Cornthwaite asked, 'But what relation have any of these actions to a Sabbath? Where have we any intimation that any or all of these taken together, should constitute that day of the week on which they should happen, the Christian Sabbath?'[67] Cornthwaite further pointed out that there was not the slightest evidence in the biblical record of any accusation brought by the Jews of the first century that an attempt had been made by early Christians to set aside the Sabbath in favour of the first day. Had such an attempt been made, it would certainly have attracted the attention of the hostile Jewish authorities. 'Tis not to be supposed the Jews would ever suffer the Sabbath to be changed, the due observation of which they justly imagined to be the very foundation, as it were, of all religion, without making any opposition, when they so long made such a stir and bustle about things of a much inferior kind.'[68] The general witness of the New Testament

---

[63] Ibid., pp. iii–iv.　　[64] Brabourne, *Discourse*, 225–6.
[65] Cornthwaite, *Essay*, 10.　　[66] Ibid. 32, 42.
[67] Ibid. 56.　　[68] Ibid. 44.

argued strongly against any change in the original day of worship. Commenting on Paul's 'silence' on any change of the Sabbath and the fact that it was 'the constant practice' of the apostles to observe the seventh day, Cornthwaite says that these two facts are 'arguments of such force and weight' when duly considered, that they alone 'are sufficient to refute all the arguments . . . that the religious observation of the first day is of divine institution'.[69] He concludes:

We may strongly infer that no abrogation or change of the Sabbath was ever intended under the Christian dispensation; for, if neither Christ, who was faithful as a son, and who assured His disciples that He had made known to them all things that He had heard from His Father—nor St. Paul, the great apostle of the Gentile world, who appeals to others that he had not kept back anything useful from them, nor shunned to declare to them all the counsel of God—have signified anything concerning either the abrogation or change of the Sabbath, it is a strong indication that such an abrogation or change was no part of the will of God, which was to take place under the Christian dispensation.[70]

A passing glance at Mill Yard's membership during Cornthwaite's pastorate reveals something of the Seventh-day movement in general, as well as of the Mill Yard congregation itself. Nathaniel (or Nathan) Bailey, the lexicographer, had joined the Mill Yard fellowship in 1691, and remained as a member until his death in 1742, despite having been censured in 1711 for 'frequent light and low conversation with two single women, he being a single man and a high professor, and they in principle and practice being so unfit company for his diversion and pleasure'.[71] It is as likely as not that this 'diversion' represented or grew out of Bailey's work as a schoolmaster or lexicographer. He kept a successful boarding academy at Stepney, and over a period of several years published numerous philological, etymological, and historical works, the most significant of which was *An Universal Etymological English Dictionary* (1721), which went to thirty editions by 1802, and formed the basis of Dr Samuel Johnson's celebrated English dictionary.

George Carlow had joined Mill Yard from Woodbridge in Suffolk in 1706, and remained a transient member until his death in 1748,

---

[69] Robert Cornthwaite, *Reflections on Dr Wright's Treatise on the Religious Observation of the Lord's Day* . . . ([1731]), 15. Samuel Wright, DD, had published in 1726 *A Treatise on the Religious Observation of the Lord's Day, according to the express Words of the Fourth Commandment.*   [70] Cornthwaite, *Essay*, 43.
[71] MYM 195. On Bailey, see *DNB*, and *BQ* 6: 134.

even though a Seventh-day congregation persisted at Woodbridge for much of the eighteenth century, with Carlow one of its leading members.[72] In 1724 Carlow replied to an attack on the Sabbatarian position by Henry Ward of Woodbridge with *Truth Defended*, another of the many apologies for the seventh day which issued from Mill Yard during the first half of the eighteenth century. Carlow's own literary inclinations were apparently encouraged by his association with Mill Yard, for he subsequently produced at least two further works in defence of the Saturday Sabbath.[73] It seems that at one point he was even considered as elder of the Mill Yard congregation.

One of the most colourful Mill Yard members during these years was undoubtedly Edward Elwall of Dudley, who became a Sabbatarian in 1719 and joined Mill Yard the following year, remaining a transient member until his death in 1744.[74] Elwall was in reality a unique combination of Sabbatarian, Baptist, Quaker, and Unitarian, who had been baptized in the River Severn near Bristol at some point prior to being convinced of the seventh day. *The Dictionary of National Biography* describes him as an Ebionite, and whether or not this is wholly justified, his Unitarian views are clearly evident in many of his somewhat eccentric works advocating the seventh day which appeared between 1724 and 1744. Elwall had been unsuccessfully prosecuted for blasphemy at Stafford in 1726, and an account of the trial by Elwall himself[75] drew the following comment from Joseph Priestley: 'It is impossible for an unprejudiced person to read this account, which is written with so much true simplicity, perspicuity, and strength of evidence, without feeling the greatest veneration for the writer, the fullest conviction and love of the truth, and a proportional zeal in maintaining it.'[76]

---

[72] For Woodbridge, see below Ch. 9.

[73] See Appendix IV, under 1729 and 1733, for details of these two rare works by 'G.C.', attributed to Carlow by W.H. Black. I am indebted to Mr Oscar Burdick for this information.

[74] On Elwall, see *DNB*; *TBHS* 7: 200; MYM 231–2; C.J.L. Elwell, *The Iron Elwells* (1964).

[75] The fourth edition of Elwall's *A Declaration Against all the Kings and Temporal Powers under Heaven* . . . (1741) included 'An Account of the Author's Trial and Prosecution at Stafford Assizes'.

[76] Joseph Priestley, *An Appeal to the Serious and Candid Professors of Christianity* (1791), 59. Priestley's tract included a reprint of Elwall's own account of his trial. The piece had been published by Priestley in 1771 under the title *The Triumph of Truth*.

The most prominent Mill Yard member during the eighteenth century, and perhaps at any time, was undoubtedly the barrister Sir William Tempest, of Cranbrook, Kent. Following membership of the Inner Temple in 1692, and of the Middle Temple in 1706, Tempest was made a baronet, and was elected a member of the Royal Society in 1712. He was reputedly a personal friend of Dr Samuel Clarke the Cambridge metaphysician and Dr Benjamin Hoadly, successively Bishop of Bangor, Hereford, Salisbury, and Winchester. Having become increasingly concerned over the invalidity of infant baptism, Tempest was baptized at his house at Cranbrook in 1725, and admitted to fellowship at Mill Yard, on recommendation of the Baptist church at Cranbrook, by prayer and the laying on of hands.[77] Such a distinguished member would have graced any Baptist congregation in the eighteenth century, and Tempest was frequently called on to fill the Mill Yard pulpit, to the satisfaction, it is said, of both congregation and preacher.

INTO DECLINE

On Cornthwaite's death in 1754, Daniel Noble was appointed elder at Mill Yard,[78] with Peter Russell still assistant. Noble had been born at Whitechapel in 1729 and educated at Cornthwaite's school[79] until he was 16, before attending Rotheram's academy at Kendal and then Glasgow University. He had shown great promise at school, quickly mastering grammar and language and outstripping all the other students at Cornthwaite's school to become proficient in Latin, Greek, and French.[80] From an early age he had felt a conviction about the ministry and was diligent in searching for truth 'as for hid treasure', with the result that he came to believe firmly in the doctrines of general redemption, adult baptism, and the perpetuity of the Seventh-day Sabbath.[81] He was baptized by Cornthwaite in 1743, and shortly after returning to London in 1752 began to preach at Mill Yard, prior to succeeding Cornthwaite in 1754. In many respects Noble was Mill Yard's most eminent minister, and the

[77] Micklewright, 'A Mill Yard Layman', *Notes and Queries*, 192 (1947), 514.
[78] On Noble, see *PDM* 5 (1798), 441–7; *SR* 3/2: 5; *BQ* 1: 135–8.
[79] The tradition at Mill Yard was for a self-supporting ministry. Cornthwaite, and several other incumbents, ran a school during the week to earn a living. Noble also was a schoolmaster.   [80] *PDM* 5: 447; *SR* 3/2: 5.
[81] *PDM* 5: 442. Noble is elsewhere described as 'a lifelong Sabbatarian', *Notes and Queries*, 191: 162.

prospects for him and his congregation looked good. Within a century this mother church of the Seventh-day movement had moved from being a suspect congregation of artisans under the pastoral care of a barely literate ribbon-weaver, to one which attracted the fashionable and well educated under the care of an able and talented minister, a situation which Noble could have consolidated to the lasting benefit of the Seventh-day cause at Mill Yard and throughout the country. In the event, precisely the opposite took place and Mill Yard's decline began within a few years of his appointment.

A major reason for this change of course seems to have been the fact that in 1766, when Mill Yard was at the height of prosperity, Noble accepted the pastorate of the First-day church in Paul's Alley in addition to his Mill Yard responsibilities. Within a few years Paul's Alley had merged with Glasshouse Street Baptist church, and Noble continued in this dual role until his death in 1783.[82] Whether or not to avoid giving offence to his Sunday-keeping flock, Noble never published anything in favour of the seventh day as most of his predecessors at Mill Yard had done, although he was eminently qualified to do so. Neither did he engage in any form of public advocacy of the seventh day, as far as can be ascertained. Correctly or incorrectly, Mill Yard's decline, and with it the decline of the Seventh-day movement elsewhere in the country, has been attributed to this strange ambivalence, all the more unaccountable in view of his reputed fidelity and diligence in the discharge of his ministerial responsibilities.[83]

Mill Yard's changing fortunes might also have been due, at least in part, to a tendency to Unitarianism. It has been said that by the mid-eighteenth century Mill Yard had in fact become Unitarian,[84] and if this was so, it would inevitably have put the Seventh-day cause a step further away from orthodoxy. On Cornthwaite's appointment in 1726 the Calvinistic Sabbatarians had withdrawn from joint worship at Mill Yard in protest at his supposed Socinian views, which were known to have been shared by Noble, his successor. Even before this, there were indications of a tendency to Unitarianism under John Savage. He had declined to subscribe to a Trinitarian statement of belief which had been prepared at the 1719 conference of Baptist

---

[82] *PDM* 5: 445; Whitley, *Baptists of London*, 114.
[83] *SO* 1: 124; *PDM* 5: 443.
[84] Micklewright, *Notes and Queries*, 191: 97.

churches called to settle the Trinitarian–Unitarian dispute.[85] Edward Elwall, of course, had felt quite comfortable at Mill Yard for two decades between 1724 and 1744, during which time he had issued a number of publications in defence of the seventh day, but which also gave evidence of an Arian Christology and a Unitarian view of the Godhead. For well over half a century, then, Mill Yard's Sabbatarianism had been tinged with a growing anti-Trinitarianism which culminated in Noble's thirty-year ministry.[86] It could hardly have made the difficult task of proclaiming the doctrine of the seventh day any easier.

Mill Yard was the only Sabbatarian church in the country which maintained an unbroken witness for more than three centuries, and although its later history strictly falls outside the scope of this study, a brief survey of its last one hundred years will not be out of place. In 1760, shortly after Noble succeeded Cornthwaite, Mill Yard's membership stood at eighty-seven,[87] and it had not grown by his death in 1783, when he was followed by William Slater. Six years later Peter Russell, who had assisted Cornthwaite, Noble, and Slater for fifty-nine years, also died, leaving Slater to keep the cause alive single-handed for more than thirty years, until he too passed away in 1819.[88] Slater's years at Mill Yard were marked by a series of unfortunate occurrences from which it would have been difficult for any congregation to recover. In 1790 the church premises were burnt down, and although subsequently rebuilt, they became a source of contention among the remaining members, some of whom objected to a proposal that they be used by the Curriers' Hall Sabbatarians. The number of male members declined drastically, one source says to nil, worship was discontinued for a period, and the church was involved in lengthy and costly lawsuits which further tarnished its waning image.[89]

No minister could be found to succeed Slater, and the pastorate remained vacant until 1840, when the eminent antiquarian and assistant keeper at the Public Record Office, W.H. Black, took

---

[85] *SO* 1: 109.

[86] W.H. Black, the nineteenth-century Mill Yard minister, and Mill Yard itself, were both listed as Unitarian in 1846: J.R. Beard, *Unitarianism Exhibited in its Actual Condition* (1846), 333.   [87] *BQ* 1: 136.

[88] MYM, p. lxxxiv. On Mill Yard's history from the nineteenth century, see Micklewright, *Notes and Queries*, 191: 139–40, 185–8.

[89] Whitley, *Baptists of London*, 111–12.

charge.[90] He was succeeded in turn in 1872 by an American, Dr William Mead Jones, Black's son-in-law and a distinguished Orientalist. Under Black the church was affiliated in 1843 to the American Seventh Day Baptist Conference, and also to the General Baptist Assembly, from which it withdrew again in 1869.[91] If Mill Yard stood any chance at all of revival it would have been under Black and Jones, who came unexpectedly late to a cause that would have benefited from their efforts at least half a century earlier. But by the mid-nineteenth century matters had already gone too far, the membership having diminished to six by 1855 and to three by the time Jones arrived. In 1885 the Mill Yard premises were requisitioned for the development of the railway system, a further blow to any hopes of renewal. Mill Yard continued in name well into the twentieth century, first under W.C. Daland, another American,[92] and then under Col. T.W. Richardson, who reorganized the congregation in 1905, holding meetings in his own house at Wood Green and then in a hired hall in Canonbury.[93] After Richardson's death in 1920, services were conducted by a retired Baptist minister until James McGeachy, a former Seventh-day Adventist, joined the fellowship in 1927, becoming its pastor in 1928. McGeachy remained in charge until his retirement in 1966, after leading worship since 1939 for a small congregation in a room in the Upper Holloway Baptist Church.[94]

The remnant at Mill Yard had survived for considerably longer than could have been anticipated, owing to a succession of laudable attempts to keep alive a flame that by the time of McGeachy's retirement had burned for more than 300 years. But although the Sabbatarian cause among Arminian Baptists was thus represented at Mill Yard for a century and a half beyond Noble's death in 1783, it was never again marked by the appeal it had enjoyed under Cornthwaite, or by the urgency and vigour which had characterized its establishment and growth in the earlier years of the seventeenth century.

[90] On Black, see *DNB*, and INB, in *TBHS* 7: 187–8, which records that he left two daughters and a deacon as the only members of the church.

[91] Whitley, *Baptists of London*, 112; INB, *TBHS* 7: 188, which points out that Mead Jones was editor of the *Sabbath Memorial* from 1875: p. 212. See also E.A. Wallis Budge, *By Nile and Tigris* (1920), i. 51–3.

[92] *SO* 1: 219. After four years at Mill Yard, Daland returned to North America to become president of Milton College, Wisc.

[93] Whitley, *Baptists of London*, 112.   [94] *BQ* 14: 163.

A HUGUENOT SABBATARIAN CONGREGATION

Before leaving the Mill Yard church and its wider influence, we must return to the later years of the seventeenth century to note an extension of the Mill Yard interest, concerning which there is unfortunately only the barest information. In recounting the history of London Sabbatarianism in the seventeenth and eighteenth centuries, F.H. Micklewright noted 'a fascination' in the Mill Yard congregation 'for Huguenot refugees who came to England after the revocation of the edict of Nantes, in 1685'.[95] It is not clear whether this is a reference to the Huguenot congregation, evidently Seventh-day, which met in Mill Yard early in the eighteenth century, and possibly even before that, though apparently not in the Mill Yard premises. Robert Burnside of Curriers' Hall noted in 1825 that there had been Sabbatarians among the refugees who had come to England from France, but failed to give a date.[96] Daniel Noble is said to have descended from a family of French refugees,[97] and at least three prominent seventeenth-century English Sabbatarians, Theophilus Brabourne, Peter Chamberlen, and Joseph Stennett, had Huguenot connections. Brabourne married Abigail Galliard; Chamberlen was descended from a Huguenot family through his grandfather William, who had sought refuge in England in 1569, settling in Southampton, and his mother was a Huguenot, Sarah de Laune; and in 1688 Stennett married Susannah Guill, the daughter of a Huguenot refugee.[98] It is possible that there may have been a connection between Susannah and the congregation which applied for a licence to meet in the new house of widow Suffish (?) in Mill Yard in 1708.

By 1700 there were twenty-four or twenty-five French congregations meeting regularly in London and Westminster and the existence of a Seventh-day group among them is not entirely surprising.[99] The licence is typical of applications approved by the authorities in respect of Dissenting meeting-houses:

[95] Micklewright, *Notes and Queries*, 191: 188; *BQ* 14: 164.

[96] Burnside, *Remarks*, 113.   [97] Ivimey, *History*, iv. 236.

[98] *TBHS* 2: 10; *PDM* 1: 92.

[99] G. Beeman, 'Notes on the Sites and History of the French Churches in London', *Proceedings of the Huguenot Society of London*, 8/1: 16, although Beeman does not mention a Sabbatarian congregation in 1700. Henri Misson, who travelled widely in England at the end of the seventeenth century, counted twenty-two French-speaking churches in London in 1698, and noted Sabbatarians as one of the chief sects in England, regarding them as distinct from 'the several sorts of Anabaptists present in the country'; Ozell (tr.), *Misson's Memoirs*, 232–5.

These are to certifie to whom it may concern, that we whose names are hereunder written, being Protestant Dissenters from the Church of England distinguished by the name of Baptists or Sabbath-day men, do intend to hold a place for Religious Worship, in our way of Baptists or Sabbath-day men, in the new house in Mill Yard, in Goodman's Fields, in the county of Middx. which said new house is now in the occupation of the widow Suffish (?) and others.

In witness whereof we have hereunto set our hands, the 7th day of July, 1708,

Pierre Rousset, Ml. Grimault, Nicolas Dubuisson, Aienne Galet.[100]

A similar application on behalf of the Mill Yard congregation itself is filed for 1709, signed by John Savage, Thomas Slater, and Thomas Rowe. It describes the Mill Yard members likewise as 'Protestant Dissenters from the Church of England commonly distinguished by the name of Baptists, or Seventh-day people'.[101]

Mill Yard's interest in the Huguenot cause at this time is clear from the Mill Yard minutes. In 1707 five French believers are recorded requesting baptism but not membership at Mill Yard, and in the following year Henry Soursby and another member were asked by the church to speak with 'Bro. Dugas' regarding his 'communicating with his French Brethren without giving notice to the church'.[102] These records appear to confirm the existence of an established Huguenot congregation in loose association with Mill Yard early in the eighteenth century.

There is no indication of the size or composition of this Huguenot group, or of its ministry, or why it should apply for a licence to meet in a private house when Mill Yard was virtually next door. We must leave unanswered for the present these and a number of other questions concerning this congregation and its relationship to Mill Yard, and to Pinners' Hall, and to the English Seventh-day movement in general. By the turn of the century, even without the Huguenot strand, the movement was firmly established in London as part of the accepted Dissenting tradition. Yet, while Mill Yard and Pinners' Hall would remain at the hub of the English Seventh-day tradition for the best part of two more centuries, theirs were by no means the only voices raised in defence of the Saturday Sabbath, as we shall see.

---

[100] Guildhall Library, MS 9579.   [101] Ibid.   [102] MYM 176, 181.

4

The London Calvinistic
Sabbatarian Churches

THE differences between General Baptists and Particular Baptists
were significant enough, in their own eyes at least, to keep them
separate for most of three centuries. Those who understand the
strength of early Nonconformist conviction that all doctrine and
practice were to be regulated according to the clear teaching of
Scripture will appreciate the basis of this separation much more
readily than those who do not. The General Baptists, the older of
the two groups, were so called because they believed in general,
or universal, redemption, i.e. that Christ died for the sins of all,
and consequently in man's free will. The Particular Baptists, who
began to appear in England from 1640 onwards, believed that Christ
died only for the elect, and were accordingly Calvinistic and
predestinarian in their theology.[1] While there were, of course, many
points of agreement between these two wings of the English Baptist
movement,[2] there were also other differences. Thus, one would
have been more likely to find imposition of hands for the Holy
Spirit, the practice of foot-washing, refusal to eat blood, and perhaps adherence to other elements of the Mosaic dietary laws, and
anointing for the sick, among General Baptists than among Particulars.[3] While both groups insisted on believer's baptism, some
Baptist historians have thought that General Baptists placed more
emphasis on the life of the believer subsequent to baptism, requiring
consistent and continuing submission to the will of God, and evident
holiness of life.[4]

---

[1] Whitley, *British Baptists*, 66; White, *English Baptists*, 7.
[2] See e.g. E.A. Payne, *The Baptists of Berkshire through Three Centuries* (1951),
15.   [3] *MGA* i, p. xxi.
[4] Whitley held that for General Baptists, the doctrine of believer's baptism was
not primary, but that they stressed more the doctrine of salvation by the imitation
of Christ, rejecting, and sometimes opposing, the Lutheran doctrine of Justification
by Faith. This would have been a natural corollary to their doctrine of the Church
and their dissatisfaction with the Anglican position that all, regardless of their way
of life, were members of the body of Christ, ibid., pp. xii, xxi.

It might be expected, therefore, that Saturday Sabbatarianism would have been stronger among General Baptists. Yet, while many Seventh-day Baptist groups were undoubtedly of this mind, particularly in the earlier years,[5] there were also many Particular Baptists who adopted the seventh day.[6] Nowhere was this more apparent than in London, where two of the three major Seventh-day congregations were strongly Calvinistic, and another, the Sabbatarian group led by Henry Jessey, leaned that way rather than towards the universalism and free will of the General Baptists. Reminders of the fundamental theological difference between the General and Particular Baptists regarding the efficacy of the Atonement and man's free will occurred from time to time in the relationship between the Mill Yard and Pinners' Hall churches and can be seen in their minute books. There is no evidence, however, that the Calvinism of either Pinners' Hall or Bell Lane reached the extremes that it did in some Baptist churches, especially in the eighteenth century. To say that some London churches were Calvinistic is not to imply that they were rigid or exclusive, as may be seen from the fact that John Belcher and Joseph Stennett were usually pleased to preach wherever they were invited.

BELL LANE

A congregation of Particular, Calvinistic Seventh-day Sabbatarians appeared in London between 1661–2 under the leadership of John Belcher,[7] and although in its relatively brief existence it worshipped at several different locations, it has come to be known as the Bell Lane church.[8] Two theories have been suggested for the origin of Bell Lane as a congregation worshipping on the seventh day but distinct from Mill Yard. One suggestion sees Bell Lane arising as the result of a withdrawal from Mill Yard on account of dissatisfaction with Peter Chamberlen, and a fear of further government reprisals following the trial and execution of John James.[9] This theory

---

[5] But cf. the following General Baptist opinion on the Sabbath which, in 1795, was still said to be 'various and unsettled', although the majority 'in general think that the Jewish Sabbath is abolished', *A Comprehensive Account of the General Baptists with respect to Principle and Practice* (Coventry, 1795), 125.

[6] Cf. White, *English Baptists*, 8.

[7] On Belcher (or Bellchar), d. 1695, see *BDBR* i. 52–3; *FMM* 242, and below, 176–7.

[8] On Bell Lane, see Whitley, *Baptists of London*, 114, reading Wentford Street for Windford Street, and Simon for James Brunt; cf. *BB* i. 234, and *FMM* 243.

[9] Katz, *Sabbath and Sectarianism*, 78, 83.

assumes that Chamberlen exercised some influence at Mill Yard following the death of James, which may or may not have been the case, but more importantly, it fails to explain how a significant number of presumably convinced Arminians could so quickly have adopted a Calvinistic theology. A more likely suggestion seems to be that Bell Lane arose from a Fifth Monarchy congregation which had met in Coleman Street under Belcher in the early 1660s.[10] Certainly Bell Lane retained a predisposition to Fifth Monarchist thought for at least another decade, and Belcher's known activities at this time appear to corroborate this explanation. He was first known in London in 1658 when he was arrested with John Canne and Wentworth Day and other Fifth Monarchists at a meeting in Swan Alley. Capp suggests that at this point he was already Seventh-day, although this is doubtful.[11] In September 1661 he was reported as a leading Fifth Monarchy agent and an itinerant preacher travelling from 'county to county'.[12] He had appeared at Stow-on-the-Wold and elsewhere in Gloucestershire in 1660 in association with the spread of Sabbatarian views, and was back in London in 1661 as the chief preacher at a conventicle in Coleman Street.[13] Whatever the actual course of events that led to the formation of Bell Lane, the date usually given of 1662 is reasonable enough, with Belcher as elder, and Richard Parnham, a London silversmith and former quartermaster in Colonel Ireton's regiment, his assistant within a few years of its establishment.[14]

The fortunes of Bell Lane were so bound up with those of John Belcher, who led the congregation for thirty-three of its forty or forty-one years, that a few further details of his career will be appropriate. Although known principally as a London bricklayer, Belcher had in fact come originally from Oxfordshire, being described in one source as 'once an Oxfordshire yeoman'.[15] A John Belcher represented the Kingston Blount Baptist church as Messenger at a meeting of the Abingdon Association at Tetsworth in 1656,

[10] W.T. Whitley, 'A Century of Sabbath Doctrine, 1595–1695', in C.H. Green's copy of Whitley's MS, notebook 10, p. 159, SDBHS Library, Janesville, Wis. Green dates the MS 1911, and notes that it was rejected by the American Sabbath Tract Society. This MS differs in some respects in both structure and detail from the Whitley MS 'Men of the Seventh Day', in the Angus Library, Regent's Park College, Oxford.
[11] *FMM* 121.   [12] *BDBR* i. 52; *CSPD* 1661–2, 98, 161.
[13] *Strange and True Newes from Glocester* (1660), 5; Robert Clark, *The Lying-Wonders* (1660), 5, 16; *BDBR* i. 52.
[14] *SO* 2: 156. On Parnham, see *FMM* 257.   [15] *BDBR* i. 52.

which shortly considered whether or not the seventh day was to be observed as the Sabbath 'under the Gospel'.[16] By 1660 the churches in the Association were being warned that Belcher had been excommunicated from Abingdon and advised not to invite him to preach. This may lend support to the suggestion that he had been converted to the seventh day by Edward Stennett of Abingdon, although Whitley also suggests that he had adopted the Saturday Sabbath following the 1658 Stone Chapel debate between Chamberlen, Tillam, and Ives.[17] 'One Belcher', a 'foreigner', appeared again in Kingston Blount in 1669 as preacher to a mixed congregation of 'Presbyterians, Independents, Quakers, and Sabbatarians'.[18] There is undoubtedly some connection between this, and the fact that much later, in 1687, in addition to his pastoral duties at Bell Lane, Belcher is noted as a member of the Seventh-day church at Wallingford, which is requested to authorize him as an occasional preacher at Pinners' Hall. At about the same time he is also recorded in the Pinners' Hall minutes as a 'public messenger to all the churches', with specific mention of those in Oxfordshire and Gloucestershire.[19]

Certainly in its early years Bell Lane continued to entertain Fifth Monarchy hopes, and even if they were tempered somewhat by expediency and perhaps, as time passed, by a mellowing theology, there is still some justification for Katz's conclusion that it was 'the most radical of the Saturday-Sabbatarian gathered churches'.[20] Perhaps to avoid government harassment, or on account of it, the congregation moved at frequent intervals during these early years. Belcher had been at Coleman Street and Limehouse in 1661, and Bell Lane itself was meeting at Brick Lane by 1664, and then Bell Lane in 1665, and again at Fenchurch Street by 1677, after the meeting-place in Bell Lane had been destroyed in 1671.[21] Matters had come to a head in June of that year, when informants reported

---

[16] B.R. White (ed.), *Association Records of the Particular Baptists of England, Wales and Ireland to 1660*, iii (1974), 145, 158, 211.

[17] Ibid. 205, 211; Whitley, *Baptists of London*, 114.   [18] *OR* iii. 824.

[19] PHCB 11–12. The records of the Pinners' Hall/Curriers' Hall Seventh-day Baptist church are catalogued at Dr Williams's Library as 'Francis Bampfield Seventh Day Baptist Congregation (Curriers' Hall, and elsewhere). Records of the congregation, 1686–1843'. They are referred to here and throughout as the Pinners' Hall church book. The records begin at the time the church was reconstituted in 1686, two years after Bampfield's death.   [20] Katz, *Sabbath and Sectarianism*, 105.

[21] Whitley, *Baptists of London*, 114; cf. *BB* i. 234, where the congregation is at Brick Lane by 1661; *BQ* 14: 162.

that they had heard Belcher, 'a Sabbatarian or Fifth Monarchy Man', preach to 'an unlawful assembly' in Bell Lane, on the Song of Solomon 1: 12. The text referred to the King sitting at his table, and in its exposition Belcher had cited Isaiah 52: 1, 2 (reported, it is clear, with some licence), 'Arise, O Jerusalem, and shake off thy dust, and then sit down in peace'. Belcher, it was further stated, had interpreted this to mean that the saints were to arise 'and obey neither prince nor prelate, but shake off thy dust 'till thou sit down in peace'. On the strength of this report twenty-seven men, the greater part of Bell Lane's male membership, were arrested and committed to Newgate gaol, and four others, presumably those regarded as the leaders, were sent to the Tower. They were John Belcher, 'a notorious knave out of Oxfordshire', Richard Goodgroom, 'formerly committed by the Lord General for a dangerous person', John James, 'a dangerous person', and Arthur Squibb, who had been MP for Middlesex in the Barebones Parliament and was later to be licensed as a 'Baptist' preacher in Surrey.[22] Sir John Robinson shortly wrote to Joseph Williamson, Lord Arlington's secretary, that he had brought to the Bench 'the twenty-seven Sabbatarians or Fifth Monarchy Men', and had offered them the oath of allegiance. When they had refused, they had been indicted, found guilty, and were ordered to be imprisoned at the King's pleasure. Similar proceedings were taken against the four held in the Tower for being 'dangerous and seditious persons against the Peace, owning themselves to be of the sect of Sabbatarians or Fifth Monarchy Men', refusing to take the oath of allegiance and refusing to promise that they would not take arms against the King.[23] Nothing further is recorded of these events, and it must be assumed that all were released, although in March 1672 the Bell Lane church wrote apprehensively to the church at Newport, Rhode Island, about the future of those who had recently been released, who 'tho' not now in hold, yet stand prisoners, and us know not what the issue will be'.[24] Capp says that Belcher was not heard of after this as a Fifth Monarchy Man,[25] and although this was also true for most of the

---

[22] *CSPD* 1671, 356–7; PRO SP 29/291/112. Details of all thirty-one are given in *FMM*, appendix I, 239–70.

[23] *CSPD* 1671, 386; Jeaffreson, *Middlesex County Records*, iv. 29–30.

[24] Bell Lane to Newport, Rhode Island, 24 Mar. 1672, in 'Samuel Hubbard's Journal, c.1633–1686', 68, SDBHS, Janesville, Wis., MS 194x.6, p. 68.

[25] *FMM* 242.

others concerned, the stigma of radical millenarianism would never wholly leave the Seventh-day movement.

Perhaps Bell Lane's chief claim to recognition is the role it played in establishing belief in the Seventh-day Sabbath in New England. Through the influence of Stephen Mumford, who in 1664 brought Seventh-day convictions with him from Bell Lane to Newport, Rhode Island, the London congregation became known as the mother church of Seventh Day Baptists in North America. Isaac Backus, in his *Church History of New-England*, succinctly summarizes Mumford's part in this event, and the basis of Seventh-day observance in the American colonies:

Stephen Mumford came over from London in 1664, and brought the opinion with him, that the whole of the ten commandments, as they were delivered from mount Sinai, were moral and immutable, and that it was the antichristian power, which thought to change times and laws, that changed the Sabbath from the seventh to the first day of the week. Several members of the first church in Newport embraced this sentiment, and yet continued with the church for some years.[26]

The New England Sabbatarians kept up a correspondence with the brethren in England which proved to be an important factor in maintaining the Seventh-day cause in North America. Over the next twenty years or so, while the fledgling company in Newport struggled for survival against severe trials and difficulties, the church at Bell Lane kept in contact at regular intervals with letters of encouragement and exhortation.

The first such recorded letter, sent in March 1668, was signed by John Labourn, Edward Fox, William Gibson, Aaron Squibb, John

---

[26] Isaac Backus, *A Church History of New-England . . . With a Particular History of the Baptist Churches*, iii (Boston, Mass., 1796), 232. It is more likely that Mumford emigrated to avoid persecution, as did many of his contemporaries, than as the result of a congregational decision at Bell Lane to send him as a missionary to Rhode Island (as Katz, *Sabbath and Sectarianism*, 135). In 1663 Mumford was recorded as a member of the Tewkesbury Baptist church, which at that point seems to have been mixed-communion. Although he may have left for America from Tewkesbury, this does not necessarily mean that the traditional view of his having been a member at Bell Lane prior to his departure needs to be revised. He did not arrive in New England until early in 1665, which allows sufficient time for him to have moved to London, *BQ* 10: 288; *70th Annual Report of the Seventh Day Baptist Historical Society* (1986), document E, 5, 6. In any case, instances of Sabbatarians holding dual membership were not uncommon in the seventeenth century: John Belcher was a member at Bell Lane and Wallingford, Edward Stennett at Wallingford and Bell Lane and, presumably, Pinners' Hall, and George Carlow at Woodbridge with transient membership at Mill Yard.

Belcher, Robert Woods, Robert Hopkin, John Jones, Christian Williams, Samuel Clarke, and Richard Parnham,[27] on behalf of 'The Church of Christ meeting in Bell Lane, London, upon the Lord's holy Sabbath, desirous to keep the commandments of God and the testimonies of Jesus'. It sent greetings to 'a remnant of the Lord's Sabbath-keepers' in and around Newport,[28] and besides laying a foundation for cordial relations between the Sabbatarians of Old and New England, also gave evidence of a mature, thriving, and well-ordered congregation at Bell Lane within only a few years of its own establishment. This, of course, was before the traumatic events of 1671, which might have decimated a weaker congregation, and the letter's eschatological emphasis is accordingly still overt and strong. It admonished the Newport Sabbatarians to be 'steadfast and immovable', to be 'abounding in the work of the Lord, looking for the blessed hope and glorious appearance of the great God, and our Saviour Jesus Christ'. Coming events would reveal the true King, the 'only Potentate', the end of 'anti-Christian darkness', and the identity of God's real saints. They were to rejoice in the knowledge that God was 'further revealing his truth', especially the truth concerning his holy law and the Sabbath, which would be 'revealed more and more' as the time drew near for the destruction of the 'fourth monarchy' and the 'mother of harlots' and 'the beast that carries her' who had 'changed times and laws'. 'The nearer we come to the promised glory, the more will the mysteries of God be opened to us'. All this would culminate in the great 'blessing of Sabbath-keepers, when they shall be exalted to ride upon the high places of the earth, and have dignity and prosperity, temporal and spiritual'. The believers at Bell Lane assured those at

---

[27] Bell Lane to Newport, 26 Mar. 1668, cited in *SDBM* 1/1 (Jan. 1852), 24–6. Ten of the eleven signatories were among those arrested in 1671, and are cited in *FMM*, appendix I: Labourn as Labory; Woods as Woodward. Aaron Squibb is usually known as Arthur Squibb, who held several important offices in the 1640s and early 1650s, prior to becoming a Fifth Monarchist; see also *BDBR* iii. 199–200. Edward Fox is Edmond. Whitley says that not all resided in London, i.e. some were transient members of Bell Lane. This might have been true at least of Woods, who is usually connected with East Anglia, *BB* i. 231, although Capp lists him as a London labourer, *FMM* 269; cf. Whitley, 'Men of the Seventh Day', 7/6. Cf. also the letter from Bell Lane to Newport, 22 Aug. 1685, signed by John Belcher, Henry Cooke, Robert Hopkins, John Waters, Joseph Parkham, Giles Ray, Simon Blunt, John Labourn, and Christopher Williams, SDBHS, MS 194x.6, pp. 141–2.

[28] Bell Lane to Newport, 26 Mar. 1668, *SDBM* 1/1: 24.

Newport of their continuing prayers, as 'fellow heirs of the Kingdom of our Lord, which is now hastening upon us'.[29]

Subsequent letters addressed matters of more immediate concern
in the life of both churches: advice on relationships with those who
had withdrawn from fellowship and abandoned the Sabbath, concern
over Bell Lane's own future in the aftermath of the 1671 arrests, and
the need for constant care in maintaining the standards of the church
above reproach, since the cause had suffered much on account of
'some men of bad practices'.[30] Stephen Mumford returned to London for a brief visit in 1675, where he was 'received of the brethren
with much joy' and 'a great desire to know of our place and people'. He reported back to Newport that Mill Yard under William
Saller was 'a thriving hopeful people', that Francis Bampfield,[31] who
preached to Sabbatarians in London was 'renowned throughout the
city', and that some of the Bell Lane people were talking of returning with him to Rhode Island. As things turned out, William Gibson,
one of the signatories to the 1668 letter and a Bell Lane stalwart,
joined the Newport church with his family that same year, and later
became its second pastor.[32]

Bell Lane appears to have remained active and prosperous
throughout the joint eldership of Belcher and Parnham. This may
have been due, in part at least, to the moderating influence of the
Stennett family, for from quite early in its history, Bell Lane seems
to have enjoyed a reciprocal relationship with the Stennetts, both
with Edward Stennett and his Wallingford congregation and later
with Joseph Stennett.[33] Belcher's link with Wallingford in 1687 has
already been noted, and it has been suggested that as early as

[29] Ibid. 27–8.
[30] Bell Lane to Newport, 27 Feb. 1670; 24 Mar. 1672; 17 Sept. 1674, in the Hubbard
Journal, SDBHS, MS 194x.6, pp. 59–60, 68, 73, respectively. The 'men of bad practices' almost certainly included Thomas Tillam whose Judaizing activities on the
Continent had recently brought discredit upon the Sabbatarian movement in England. Tillam was also reported to Newport by Joseph Davis as 'a very great blemish
to the truth', Joseph Davis to Newport, 5 Aug. 1674, SDBHS, MS 194x.6, p. 76.
[31] Francis Bampfield had come to London from the West Country in 1673, and
preached both at Mill Yard and Bell Lane before establishing his own Sabbath-
keeping congregation in 1674. On Bampfield (or Bamfield, or Bampfylde) see *DNB*,
s.v. Bampfield, and *BDBR* i. 33–4, and below, Ch. 5.
[32] Stephen Mumford to Newport, 14 Apr. 1675, SDBHS, MS 194x.6, pp. 78–82.
[33] On Joseph Stennett I (1663–1713), see *DNB*; W. Wilson, *The History and Antiquities of Dissenting Churches and Meeting Houses in London, Westminster and
Southwark*, ii (1808), 595–605; *PDM* 1 (1794), 91–5, 129–36; and *SDBM*1/1: 26.

THE
ROYAL LAW
Contended for.

OR,

Some brief Grounds ſerving to prove
that the *Ten Commandments* are yet in *full force*, and
ſhall *ſo remain*, till Heaven and Earth paſs away.

ALSO,

The SEVENTH-DAY-SABBATH proved from
the *Beginning*, from *the Law*, from *the Prophets*,
from CHRIST, from his *Apoſtles*, to be a
duty yet incumbent upon *all men*.

By a Lover of Peace with Truth, *Edward Stennet*.

The Second Edition, Corrected and amended.

Whereunto is added,

A faithful Teſtimony againſt the Teachers of *Circumciſion*, and
the *Legal Ceremonies* ; who are lately gone into *Germany*.

*They that forſake the Law, praiſe the Wicked : but ſuch as keep the Law,
contend with them.* Prov. 28. 4.
*Let us hear the concluſion of the whole matter; Fear God, and keep his Com-
mandments : for this is the whole duty of man.* Eccleſ. 12. 13.
*The Sabbath was made for man, and not man for the Sabbath : Therefore
the Son of Man is Lord even of the Sabbath.* Mark 2. 27, 28.
Then ſhall I not be aſhamed, when I have reſpect to all thy Commandments,
Pſal. 119. 6.

LONDON, Printed in the Year, 1667.

FIG. 4 Title-page of Edward Stennett's *The Royal Law Contended for*, 1667
edn., including the *A Faithful Testimony* of the same date against Thomas
Tillam and Christopher Pooley

1667–8 Edward Stennett held membership with Bell Lane.[34] Belcher's only known literary contribution to the Seventh-day cause came in 1664 when he provided the preface to Stennett's *The Seventh Day is the Sabbath of the Lord*, although in 1667, together with Stennett and three more of his congregation, he signed the *Faithful Testimony Against The Teachers of Circumcision and the Legal Ceremonies*.[35] Parnham similarly wrote an introduction to the second edition of Stennett's *Royal Law Contended for* in 1667. In 1683 the congregation moved yet again, to Wentford Street, before finally settling at Pinners' Hall, which it shared with Joseph Stennett from 1690.[36]

Bell Lane's later years were characterized by a deepening relationship, not always easy, with the Pinners' Hall church. Since 1674, when Francis Bampfield had drawn off some of the Bell Lane members, the two congregations had been in contention over the right of individuals to move from one Sabbath-keeping congregation to another.[37] The problem was illustrated by the case of John Jones. He had originally been a member at Bell Lane, had subsequently transferred to Pinners' Hall, and then had returned to Belcher's congregation.[38] Bell Lane claimed that Jones had not been recommended by them to Pinners' Hall and that he should therefore still be a member with them. There were others who seemed to move between Bell Lane and Pinners' Hall, usually in that direction, with no good reason, unless it was related to a preference for preachers, which in the seventeenth century was not an acceptable reason for transferring membership from one congregation to another. A letter from Pinners' Hall to Bell Lane, recorded in the Pinners' Hall church book in 1686, mentions the alienation this matter had caused, and proposed that the rift should be healed.[39]

---

[34] Whitley, 'A Century of Sabbath Doctrine', 160, presumably on the assumption that Stennett's signature to the 1667 *Faithful Testimony* indicated transient membership at Bell Lane.

[35] *Contra* Thomas Tillam and Christopher Pooley, principally. On Pooley see *BDBR* iii. 49–50, and *FMM* 258. The other known Bell Lane signatories, besides Stennett, were Squibb, Parnham, and Woods, with George Eve and John Gardner completing the list. Gardner may also have been at Bell Lane since he proclaimed Fifth Monarchy views in the 1650s in London, although his name is not among those arrested in 1671, cf. *FMM* 116, 135. A George Eve preached at Watford in the early days of the Baptist cause, *c.*1650: *BQ* 26: 206, and may have represented a non-London interest in the protest against Tillam, as Woods and Stennett may also have done.

[36] Whitley, *Baptists of London*, 114.   [37] PHCB 11.   [38] Ibid. 10, 15.

[39] Ibid. 4–5. A similar problem arose later between Pinners' Hall and Mill Yard over the admission of members under censure. A joint letter was drawn up in 1711,

The problem was eventually resolved in 1689, after more than three years of negotiation and only after it had been referred to the Messengers of the 'Baptised Churches in London', including Hanserd Knollys, Isaac Lamb, and Benjamin Keach.[40] The ordination of Joseph Stennett to the Pinners' Hall eldership in 1690, at which Belcher, Knollys, and Lamb officiated, probably helped matters, and henceforth Belcher's congregation met at Pinners' Hall on Saturday afternoon, while Stennett's people worshipped in the morning, with the understanding that each congregation should support the services of the other. Even so, the pathway was not always smooth, and in 1692 several Bell Lane members complained that the preaching of John Piggott was unacceptable at joint meetings on account of his Arminianism.[41]

These were to be the final years of the Bell Lane church. Parnham had died in 1681 and when Belcher also died in 1695, Henry Cooke and Simon Brunt were appointed as joint elders.[42] Brunt, who had been in fellowship with Bell Lane since before 1671, and who had been imprisoned in 1685 as a supporter of Monmouth, is said virtually to have led the congregation after Belcher's death.[43] If Henry Cooke, who is otherwise unidentifiable, was the Henry Cock who had led a Buckinghamshire Sabbatarian–Fifth Monarchy congregation since the mid-1660s, Brunt's prominence at Bell Lane may have been overstated.[44] This, however, is unlikely. In any case Cooke appears quite clearly as the minister of Bell Lane in records for 1695, and together with Brunt, was one of fifty Baptist signatories to a loyal declaration to the King in 1696.[45] The end, however, was near. The Pinners' Hall records show that Bell Lane was in strife and dissension from the end of 1701, allegedly over the defection

---

signed by Henry Soursby for Mill Yard and Joseph Stennett for Pinners' Hall, outlining the basis for future procedures, and suggesting that past differences should 'be buried in oblivion', MYM 193.

[40] PHCB 15.

[41] According to the Bell Lane messengers who raised the matter with Pinners' Hall, Piggott 'did not frequent Sabbath meetings, tho' he professed to keep ye 7th day Sabbath', PHCB 18, 24; see also *BB* i. 234, *TBHS* 5: 78. On Piggott see *BB* i. 225 and Wilson, *Dissenting Churches* iv. 13–14.

[42] *BB* i. 234; *SO* 2: 173. Belcher's funeral sermon was preached by Joseph Stennett, and published as *The Groans of a Saint under the Burden of a Mortal Body* (1695), Wilson, *Dissenting Churches*, ii. 585, 605; *BB* i. 17–695.

[43] *FMM* 245; *TBHS* 4: 28.

[44] On Henry Cock, of Chalfont St Giles, see *FMM* 246.

[45] PHCB 44; *TBHS* 6: 184–5.

of Cooke over the seventh day. Whether or not this was the case, is difficult to substantiate. He had been a relative late-comer to the Bell Lane fellowship, although it is said that at one time he had preached regularly at Mill Yard. Early in January, nine members from Bell Lane requested membership at Pinners' Hall, on grounds of dissatisfaction with the ministry at their own church. Cooke died shortly thereafter, and by June, under Brunt's guidance, the congregation was dissolved, thirty-three members in all joining Pinners' Hall and a few going to Mill Yard, including Peter Chamberlen's widow, Anne.[46] It seems rather a drastic step to have taken when other congregations persevered with far fewer members, but perhaps the competition at Pinners' Hall under Joseph Stennett was too strong. The Bell Lane members themselves, with the benefit of hindsight, might have said that their work was done, the seeds of Sabbath doctrine having been planted firmly in American soil, there to ensure the endurance of Seventh-day observance for generations to come.

PINNERS' HALL

A second Calvinistic Seventh-day church was founded in London in 1675 by Francis Bampfield, who had arrived in the city *c.*1673 from Dorset where, despite frequent and lengthy imprisonment, he had already materially helped to establish the Sabbatarian cause.[47] During these early months in London he forged links between both existing Seventh-day congregations. The Mill Yard records show that soon after his arrival he was married to Damaris Town, the ceremony being witnessed by four Mill Yard members, including William Saller and Henry Soursby. His reputation as one of the best preachers in the West of England had evidently preceded him, and he was invited to preach at both Mill Yard and Bell Lane.[48] By 1674 he had attracted sufficient following to hold regular meetings for worship at his home in Bethnal Green, and a church was formed in March 1676, when nine members signed the covenant on behalf of a congregation of forty-three, comprising sixteen men and twenty-seven

---

[46] *SO* 2: 173; PHCB 84–92.

[47] Francis Bampfield, *A Name, an After One, or, A Name, a New One . . . or An Historical Declaration of the Life of Shem Acher* (1681), 26. On Bampfield's earlier work in Dorset and Wiltshire, see below, Ch. 5.

[48] MYM 3; Ivimey, *History*, ii. 480; Bampfield, *A Name*, 27.

women.[49] The simple covenant did not even make a direct reference to the congregation's Sabbatarian principles:

We own the Lord Jesus Christ to be the One and Only Lord and Lawgiver to our Souls and Consciences. And we own the Holy Scriptures of Truth as ye One and only Rule of Faith, Worship and Life, According to which we are to Judge of all our Cases.

It was signed by Francis Bampfield, Thomas Pierce, William Mercer, William Toovy, James Warner, James Humber, John Belcher, jun., Andrew Geddes, and Samuel Thompson.[50] Although Bampfield is sometimes charged with having drawn off members from Bell Lane and Mill Yard, none of these names appears in extant contemporary lists from either of the other two churches. The congregation continued to meet in Bampfield's house for the next five years, first at Bethnal Green and then at Great Moorfields, and it was during this period that he was authorized by the church to visit the Seventh-day churches in Wiltshire, Hampshire, Dorset, Gloucestershire, and Berkshire.[51] It may be assumed that he had previously had contact with most if not all of these congregations. In 1681 Bampfield hired Pinners' Hall, where the church was to meet for worship for the next forty years, and from which it took its name. Pinners' Hall has been described as a church 'of considerable strength and reputation', attracting adherents 'of a superior social class', and this was without doubt due to the calibre and renown of its first three ministers, Bampfield, and Edward and Joseph Stennett.[52]

Bampfield again illustrates the link between a strong church and a strong apologetic. In the period between 1672 and 1681, Bampfield wrote several major works advocating the seventh day, all of which were published during his years at Pinners' Hall.[53] While they are not on the whole as easy to read as many of the other Seventh-day

---

[49] Bampfield, *A Name*, 26; PHCB, p. 'e'; Wilson, *Dissenting Churches*, ii. 585.
[50] PHCB, p. 'e'.
[51] Bampfield, *A Name*, 7; *SDBEA* 1: 53. Some sources indicate that worship was conducted at Devonshire Square during this period, e.g. Wilson, *Dissenting Churches*, ii. 589.   [52] *TBHS* 5: 78; Whitley, *Baptists of London*, 119, 134.
[53] *The Judgment of Mr Francis Bampfield . . . for the Observation of the Jewish or Seventh Day Sabboth . . .* (1672), published by William Benn, *BB* i. 2–672; *DNB*, s.v. Benn. *All in One. All Useful Sciences and Profitable Arts in One Book of Jehovah Aelohim . . .* (1677); *Septima dies, Dies Desiderabilis, Sabbatum Jehovae. The Seventh-Day-Sabbath the Desirable Day . . .* (1677); *A Name, an After-One* (1681); *The House of Wisdom* (1681). *All in One* and *Septima Dies* are described on respective title-pages as parts one and two of the same work.

works which had previously appeared, and at times revealed a mild eccentricity, they would certainly have influenced the more educated mind, and may have engendered the interest which this type of person showed in Pinners' Hall for much of its history.[54] Bampfield's two major works were published in 1677. From them it can be seen that his fundamental arguments for the seventh day were its foundation in Creation and its foundation in Christ, 'Creation-work and Redemption-work' to use his own words, both issuing from 'Jehovah-Christ', who as the 'All in All' and the 'All-in-One', was both Creator and Redeemer.[55] It behoved believers, therefore, to consider carefully Creation-work and Redemption-work, since from them both the Seventh-day Sabbath could be derived, justified, and celebrated.[56] Of the three London Seventh-day churches, Pinners' Hall would have been seen as the most representative of Calvinistic Reformed theology and Bampfield's strong Christological and soteriological emphasis undoubtedly would have contributed to this perception.

The doctrine of Creation was crucial to a true and adequate understanding of the Sabbath and its purpose in the divine will. The 'God of Infallible Veracity' had given a 'most faithful, punctual record' of the work of Creation, from which the Seventh-day Sabbath followed logically and inevitably:

The day on which this world began to be created, was properly one day. . . . There was not at that time any other day that had actual existence. Those days of this one created week, which did follow in the same week, were ordinal, and successive, and numerable. . . . There was one day which was the beginning of days . . . And this and other distinct days in this week of the Creation, are properly a distinct enumeration of distinct days. . . . The evening and the morning of every day were a distinct day, and were distinct parts of every day. The one day was before the second, and the third day was after the second, the fourth followed the third, and the fifth was after the fourth, the sixth succeeded the fifth, and the seventh which

---

[54] Whitley, after Wilson (*Dissenting Churches,* ii. 591), thought that Bampfield prefigured Hutchinsonianism and the theories of Thomas Burnet and John Woodward: *British Baptists,* 134. Cf. Katz, *Sabbath and Sectarianism,* 131–2, 181–97, where Burnet is strangely missing. On Burnet and Woodward, see *DNB.* See also R.L. Greaves, 'Francis Bampfield (1615–1684): Eccentric Hebraist and Humanitarian', *Bulletin of the Institute of Historical Research,* 44 (Nov. 1971), 224–8.

[55] Bampfield, *Seventh-Day-Sabbath,* 39. There is no evidence that either Bampfield's followers or his opponents regarded this as a step towards Unitarianism or Sabellianism. [56] Ibid.

is the last day of the week, was the Holy close of that week. There is but one seventh day in the week. No other day in this, or in any following week, is properly the seventh day of the week in the weekly revolution.[57]

This argument from the sequential succession of days at Creation had an important corollary. The week itself, as a unit of time, testified to the identity and perpetuity of the Sabbath:

There were seven distinct days severally created in order of time, and no more, which being ended, another week begins. An whole full complete week doth consist of seven days, not of six or fewer days, not of eight or more days . . . a week in its successive returns has a natural existence, a created being, which doth unchangably establish the six foregoing days of every week to be working days, and the seventh, the last, the closing day of every week, to be the weekly Sabbath-day, or day of Rest.[58]

Merging this into the argument from natural law, Bampfield maintains that Creation had 'a natural order'. The works of Creation, accomplished in six successive days, inherently carry in them that 'which would convince a natural conscience, exercising right reason, especially when the true information and clear discovery thereof is brought unto him by Scripture revelation'. The completed order of Creation was 'pure' and 'natural', a 'created state', and therefore 'the created order of the seven days of that one work' must still retain their inherent 'naturalness'. Thus, 'the last day of the week, and no other, is alone the seventh day and the Sabbath day'.[59] The 'real intent', the 'designed purport', of the Sabbath thus instituted was to enable man to reflect on his divine origin, to meditate on the implications of Creation, to commune with the Creator, in sum to provide the believer with everything necessary 'for the feeding of his thoughts, the nourishing of his soul, the satisfaction of his spirit, the strengthing [sic] of his heart, and the inlightning of his mind'. The transference of the weekly Sabbath to another day had 'wholly inverted this established order'.[60]

The foundation of the Sabbath in Christ was of yet greater importance for the true believer, since he was the 'First-seventh-day-Sabbath-Observer', and 'the great Exemplary Pattern for his Disciples to imitate and follow . . . in all Acts of Decalogical obedience'.[61] He who was Redeemer had been 'Creator too', for interpreted in the light of other biblical texts 'Jehovah Christ' was the divine agent

---

[57] *All in One*, 65, 93.   [58] Ibid. 96, 98.   [59] *Seventh-Day-Sabbath*, 21.
[60] *All in One*, 45.   [61] *Seventh-Day-Sabbath*, 8; *A Name*, 13.

active in the Creation of the world and of man. 'It was he that rested from his works of Creation, blessing, sanctifying, and keeping the Seventh-day Sabbath'. Moreover, it was 'Jehovah-Christ as Mediator', who at Mt. Sinai had proclaimed the 'Law of the Ten Words', 'the Seventh-day God' himself who rested 'from all his works', and who 'in the days of his flesh . . . through the weeks of his life yielded obedience unto this Command by keeping the Seventh day as the weekly Sabbath.'[62]

This had a consequence of immense proportions for Bampfield, and for all like him who were concerned with the Protestant soteriological formula of justification and sanctification. Christ's obedience, which included obedience to the fourth commandment, was a constituent element in the justification which could be obtained from him in the removal of sin and guilt, and of the sanctification which was required by him in the consequent Christian life. Bampfield explained it more fully thus:

The Lord Christs Obedience unto this fourth Word, in observing in his life time the Seventh day as a Weekly Sabbath day . . . is a part of that perfect Righteousness which every sound believer doth apply to himself in order to his being justified in the sight of God; and every such person is to conform unto Christ in all the acts of his Obedience to the Ten Words. . . . And whither shall we go to get ourselves clothed with Sabbath righteousness, but unto him, putting on this Lord Jesus, and making this Jehovah to be our righteousness? How can there be such an apt, proper, distinct, suitable Sabbath-righteousness from Christ applied to the soul, but by those who make out after that weekly seventh-day-Sabbath-righteousness, which was in its perfection in Christ? . . . He has left us an example, a pattern, a copy, such as Writing-masters do leave to their scholars, that we should follow his steps. He that saith he abideth in Christ, ought himself to walk even as he walked.[63]

This, in essence, was Redemption-work, and Bampfield summed it up neatly: 'Christ Himself hath put the crown upon the head of the seventh day'. 'Sabbath day and seventh day are connatural and reciprocal'. The Sabbath had 'a primitive constitution that must stand firm'. Observance of the seventh day, then, was bound up with man's very nature and destiny. Man and the Sabbath 'will be coeval whilst weeks do last'. 'They will live and stand together,' man the

---

[62] *Seventh-Day-Sabbath*, 7–8.
[63] Benn, *The Judgment of Mr Francis Bampfield*, fos. 7ᵛʳ (the second so numbered); *Seventh-Day-Sabbath*, 8.

crowning glory of Creation and the object of saving grace, the Sabbath a sign and a means of his sanctification.[64]

Early in 1679, shortly after the settling of Pinners' Hall, Bampfield proposed an association of Seventh-day churches, which had it succeeded would undoubtedly have changed the course of the Seventh-day movement in England and Wales and possibly in America as well. This proposal, sent to congregations in England, Holland, and New England,[65] and motivated by a conviction that the truth of the seventh day would enjoy a revival 'a little before the Coming and Appearing of our Lord Jesus Christ in glory', suggested an annual or more frequent meeting of Messengers from each church, with a letter from congregations unable to send representatives. Precisely why this idea did not meet with a warmer response, at least from the English churches, is difficult to say, for it was imaginative, in harmony with movements in the Baptist churches at large, and founded on arguments which ought to have convinced the most hesitant of its necessity and timeliness. Bampfield maintained that an association would:

1. Strengthen ties between Seventh-day congregations.
2. Promote growth, and a better understanding of Scripture.
3. Help to answer queries and resolve problems which churches might have.
4. Encourage the training of suitable candidates for ministry.
5. Embark on the preparation of a more accurate translation of the Bible.
6. Work for the better education of children and young people.
7. Foster poor relief and the welfare of needy members.
8. Expedite the conversion of the Jews.[66]

Bampfield was evidently a man of vision, and the very breadth of these proposals might have seemed too daunting to many in the ranks of the relatively small and scattered Seventh-day congregations. Nothing resulted from this suggestion, however, and it must be concluded that the Seventh-day movement was stifled and stunted by its own lack of response to a proposition which almost certainly would have ensured its stability and growth.[67]

---

[64] *Seventh-Day-Sabbath*, 22.

[65] SDBHS, MS 194x.6, p. 102. The proposition was supported by Edward Stennett.

[66] *A Name*, 24–5.

[67] An association of Seventh-day churches was inaugurated in Rhode Island in 1696, only twenty years or so after the seventh day was first observed in New England.

The times, of course, were not immediately propitious for many of Bampfield's suggestions, as he was shortly to be reminded. He had already served more than his fair share of time in prison, ten years in all, but more was to come. The renewed persecution of Dissenters in the early 1680s was the background against which Bampfield spent the last years of his life. While preaching at Pinners' Hall on 17 February 1683 he was arrested, with six others, taken before the Lord Mayor, and fined £10. The following week, while preaching as usual to his congregation at Pinners' Hall, he was arrested again, taken to the Old Bailey and offered the oath of allegiance which, on conscientious grounds, he refused. Thereupon he was taken to Newgate, where he remained until October when he again appeared at the Old Bailey, and was offered the oath once more. On refusing, he was returned to Newgate, where he died on 16 February, almost a year to the day from his first arrest. Bampfield's death brought to a close the first chapter in Pinners' Hall's history, the congregation dispersing to meet in private houses until it was reconstituted in 1686.[68]

In that year the church wrote to Edward Stennett 'pastor of the congregation of Sabbath-keepers in and about Wallingford', inviting him to conduct ordinances for them, which he did on 25 October, the first time that the Lord's Supper had been celebrated at Pinners' Hall since Bampfield's death. That day thirty-six members signed a new covenant, including two of Stennett's sons, Jehudah and Benjamin, with a further six members being added by baptism and transfer from Wallingford, including Joseph Stennett, who was shortly to become Pinners' Hall's most illustrious minister. In response to a letter from Pinners' Hall to Wallingford, Edward Stennett agreed to be their pastor on the understanding that he would come 'sometimes' to labour amongst them, and that he could 'promise nothing for length of time'.[69] Thus, while retaining the Wallingford pastorate, he served in a similar capacity at Pinners' Hall until 1689, with Jehudah Stennett and William Mercer as ruling elders, and with the occasional assistance of John Belcher, sen., who had also been asked through Wallingford and the churches in Gloucestershire to

[68] Francis Bampfield, *The Lords Free Prisoner* (1683), 3. 4; G.M. Pike, *Ancient Meeting Houses* (1870), 166–8; Ivimey, *History*, ii. 479–80; *CR* 26; Wilson, *Dissenting Churches*, ii. 589, where some of the apparently conflicting dates can be reconciled by adopting the new style.

[69] PHCB 6. On Edward Stennett's earlier career and his ministry at Wallingford and in neighbouring localities, see below, Ch. 6.

preach and administer the ordinances. Belcher had agreed to preach, but not to officiate at the Lord's Supper, since some in his London congregation had been offended at the transfer of John Jones. When the latter was suspended from preaching at Pinners' Hall in 1688 on the grounds that he had attempted unlawfully to influence the election of candidates to Parliament, Jehudah and Joseph Stennett were appointed to preach when Edward Stennett and John Belcher were unavailable. Jehudah shortly returned to live in the country, and thereafter the preaching was shared between Joseph Stennett and John Jones, who had been reinstated after making an apology for his misdemeanours.[70]

Although these arrangements suggest some instability in the newly reorganized church, Pinners' Hall began to grow, with further transfers from Wallingford and from First-day congregations in London, as well as by baptisms. Mary Pert, a member of Henry Danvers's Baptist church, had been convinced of the seventh day and asked for membership at Pinners' Hall, although her own congregation refused to recommend her. Mary Weaver from Isaac Lamb's church was similarly convinced, although there is no record in her case of opposition. Both were received into fellowship at Pinners' Hall.[71] A degree of catholicity, not always evident in the Seventh-day churches, can be seen under Stennett's pastoral oversight. As has already been noted, Pinners' Hall sought to strengthen ties with Bell Lane, as well as to maintain good relationships with other Baptist congregations. John Belcher, Hanserd Knollys, and Isaac Lamb officiated at the ordination of Joseph Stennett,[72] and Edward Stennett conducted the Lord's Supper at Pinners' Hall on a Sunday on at least one occasion. The laying on of hands was practised, and although it is not clear whether under Edward Stennett it was for all new members or only for those who requested it, later it became a condition of membership for all newly baptized believers. Within a few years the church was evidently beginning to prosper again and Stennett decided to withdraw. In 1689 the congregation called his son, Joseph, to be 'teaching elder', and he was duly ordained, Belcher, Knollys, and Lamb officiating, on 4 March of the following year.[73] The brightest days at Pinners' Hall were about to begin.

Joseph Stennett I, variously described as 'distinguished', 'eminent',

---

[70] PHCB 12–13.   [71] Ibid. 5, 6.
[72] Wilson, *Dissenting Churches*, ii. 597.   [73] PHCB 10, 15, 18–19.

'learned and pious', was by common consent one of the leading Nonconformist ministers of his day. Perhaps the most telling comment on his standing and ability was that of an Anglican prelate who is reported to have said that if Stennett would only conform and be reconciled to the Establishment, no preferment within it would have been considered above his merit.[74] Joseph was born in Abingdon in 1663, the second son of Edward, and educated at Wallingford Grammar School where, in addition to a thorough grounding in philosophy and church history, he became fluent in French and Italian and proficient in Hebrew, Greek, and other Oriental languages. It is said that the Bible had been his constant study from a child, as a consequence of which 'he was not ashamed of any notion in religion because it was grown out of fashion'. He had been brought up 'with a true sense of the value of English liberty', and had early seen the effect of religious bigotry and intolerance which had resulted in the imprisonment of his father. Besides being widely known as a fluent preacher with a masterly command of the English language, Stennett was also a poet and a hymn-writer and some of his hymns are still sung today.[75] In 1688 he married Susanna Guill, the daughter of a French Huguenot refugee, thereby becoming related by marriage to Daniel Williams the Presbyterian divine and benefactor, and the founder of Dr Williams's Library in London.[76] Joseph Stennett was well prepared for ministry in the Dissenting tradition and it is not surprising that under his care Pinners' Hall flourished.

Until 1703, the Pinners' Hall church book was kept by Stennett himself. It shows that between his ordination in 1690 and 1702, thirty-seven men and seventy-eight women were added to the membership, bringing the total on the church roll at the end of 1702 to 176. While more than thirty had come from the now defunct Bell Lane church, the record shows that many new members were baptized by Stennett during these years.[77] Some also came by

---

[74] *PDM* 1: 132.

[75] Ibid. 91–2; Joseph Stennett, *Works* (1732), i. 7–36. *The New Advent Hymnal* (1952) includes Stennett's 'Another six days work is done, Another Sabbath has begun; Return, my soul, enjoy thy rest, Improve the day that God has blessed,' etc., by which it has been said that he will be best remembered as one of the early Baptist hymn-writers: *BQ* 8: 261.

[76] On Williams, see *DNB*. Susanna was sister of Williams's second wife.

[77] PHCB 18–92; *TBHS* 3: 93.

transfer from other Baptist churches in London. Thus in 1695, for example, five members were added from five different Baptist congregations, clear evidence that the Sabbath issue was still being discussed in the wider Baptist fraternity.[78] Indeed, Stennett's prominence among Baptists would of itself have kept the matter to the fore, and his ministry at Pinners' Hall was undoubtedly strengthened by his standing in the Baptist community. In 1696 he was appointed to represent the Baptist churches in preparing and presenting a loyal address to William III, and was introduced to the King by the Earl of Peterborough. Thereafter he frequently represented the Baptist denomination on similar public occasions. In 1704, although by nature averse to disputation, he was prevailed upon by his Baptist colleagues to reply to David Russen's *Fundamentals without Foundation, or, a True Picture of the Anabaptists* . . . , a work which was generally thought to be unfair and tendentious, and which Stennett is said to have answered 'with so much learning and solid reasoning, that his antagonist never thought fit to make any reply'.[79] In 1706 he represented the Protestant Dissenting ministers of London in preparing an address for presentation to the Queen at Windsor.[80] Two years earlier, unknown to him, a copy of his thanksgiving sermon for the victory at the battle of Hochstadt was given to Queen Anne, who rewarded him with a gratuity from the Privy Purse.[81] It was no mean thing to be a Sabbatarian and a member of Pinners' Hall while Stennett continued as minister.

This is all the more remarkable since Stennett continued to command this respect while attracting members from other Baptist churches. The most notable example was that of Benjamin Keach's church at Horsleydown. One of the five members who had joined Pinners' Hall in 1695 was Elizabeth King, a member of Keach's congregation. She was the first of many from that church to migrate to Pinners' Hall over the next five years. The Pinners' Hall records show that between 1695 and 1700 at least fifteen Horsleydown members joined Pinners' Hall, including Hannah Green, Keach's

[78] PHCB 39–43. The churches concerned were those of Elias Keach, Benjamin Keach, John Piggott, 'Mr Learner' (Richard), and a 'Baptist church in Southwark'.
[79] *PDM* 1: 94, 130; Stennett, *Works,* i. 23.
[80] *PDM* 1: 132, possibly at the request of the General Body of Protestant Dissenting Ministers of the Three Denominations, which had functioned since 1702; see G.F. Nuttall, *The General Body of the Three Denominations: A Historical Sketch* (1955), 2.   [81] *PDM* 1: 132.

daughter.[82] Matters came to a head in 1699–1700, when Keach found it necessary to preach and publish against the seventh day in an attempt to stem the tide. Keach himself said that the Sabbath issue at Horsleydown had 'almost put the whole congregation into a flame'. He delivered a series of sermons, shortly afterwards published under the title *The Jewish Sabbath Abrogated, or The Saturday Sabbatarians Confuted* (1700), which he believed contained 'many new arguments, not found in former authors', and by which he endeavoured to persuade those in his congregation who had already begun to observe the seventh day, and the 'several that were wavering', that the old Sabbath had been superseded by the Lord's day. Keach explained that his intent was 'to convince them by Scripture and by solid arguments'. The Pinners' Hall minutes paint a slightly different picture, revealing that those who had joined Pinners' Hall from Horsleydown 'and some of the church to which they belonged' had been 'severely berated by Mr Keach . . . for keeping the seventh-day Sabbath'.[83] Stennett does not appear to have responded to Keach's efforts against the seventh day, and the two continued to respect each other, with no evidence of a rift between them.[84]

Other London churches might well have viewed these events with some alarm, had Stennett not been well known and respected in the wider Baptist community. In 1703, or thereabouts, he accepted an invitation to minister to the First-day General Baptist church at Paul's Alley in the Barbican[85] where he had already served as occasional preacher, and which Whitley says was by far the wealthiest Baptist congregation at the time. This apparent compromise was probably motivated by necessity, since the relatively small Pinners' Hall congregation could not adequately support Stennett and his large family.[86] Wilson comments that this was only one

---

[82] PHCB 46, 58, 75, 79–81. Hannah Green was dismissed from Pinners' Hall within a year for 'opening shop to trade on the seventh day', and for entertaining Quaker ideas, ibid. 53. Apparently she eventually became a Quaker: AL, MS 36 G.A.e. 10, fo. 94r.

[83] Benjamin Keach, *The Jewish Sabbath Abrogated, or The Saturday Sabbatarians Confuted* (1700), Ep. Ded., sig. A2r; PHCB 75.

[84] *TBHS* 3: 94. Keach later asked Stennett to preach his funeral sermon: Ivimey, *History*, ii. 377.

[85] *TBHS* 3: 93. A note in the Paul's Alley church book for 22 May 1695 records that 'Bro. Joseph Stennett be continued in the ministry', *TBHS* 4: 46.

[86] Wilson, *Dissenting Churches*, ii. 597; iii. 234, 236; Whitley, *Baptists of London*, 112; *PDM* 1: 93.

instance of Stennett's wider ministry in London, and that 'being of
a liberal spirit, he preached constantly on the first day', not confin-
ing his labours to congregations which agreed with him in every
detail.[87] He continued to minister to the Pinners' Hall Sabbatarians,
and although in 1706 he was 'respectfully dismissed' from Paul's
Alley on account of his Calvinistic views, it appears that the work
at Pinners' Hall suffered as a result of his divided attention.[88] The
minute book which had been kept by Stennett until 1703 suddenly
discontinues detailed entries at that point, and whereas in the
period 1690–1703 114 members had been added, between 1703
and 1713 only twenty-eight were received into the Pinners' Hall
fellowship. Whitley comments, 'We are loath to believe that Stennett,
who had been invited to help the ordinary First-day church at
Barbican, neglected this church henceforward.'[89] There were, of
course, no mass accessions from Bell Lane or Horsleydown during
this latter period, but the evidence none the less seems to substantiate a principle that Stennett should have known from the outset,
that no man could serve two, or more, masters.

A more lenient judgement could be derived from what, after all,
might well have been one of Stennett's most important contributions to the Seventh-day movement, his desire to keep it firmly
within mainstream Nonconformist tradition. In 1693 Mary Monk
had been excommunicated from Pinners' Hall, and in 1698 Joseph
Clement and Benjamin Johnson had been admonished personally
by Stennett, all for heterodox views on the nature of Christ.[90] In 1704,
as we have already noted, at the request of several leading Baptists,
Stennett published his only major work, a reply to David Russen's
attack on the Baptist movement which had occasioned much ill-
will on account of its tone and perceived lack of objectivity.[91] Baptists

---

[87] Wilson, *Dissenting Churches*, ii. 597.   [88] *MGA* i. 66.
[89] PHCB 93 ff.; *TBHS* 3: 93.   [90] PHCB 29, 30, 62–4.
[91] David Russen, *Fundamentals without Foundation, or, a True Picture of the
Anabaptists in their Rise, Progress and Practice. Written for the use of such as take
'em for saints, when they are not so much as Christians* (1703). Joseph Stennett, *An
Answer to Mr David Russen's book Entituled, Fundamentals Without a Foundation*
(1704). Stennett did not publish on the seventh day, although he preached a series
of sermons on the subject at Pinners' Hall, which drew a response from Edward
Elliott, *Plain Scripture-Proof that the Christian Church in under no obligation to
keep any of the Jewish Sabbaths* (1708). Stennett's Sabbatarianism was not always
regarded with indifference. Some churches had objected to the inclusion of Pinners'
Hall in the revived London Association in 1704, Brown, *English Baptists*, 41.

were openly indebted to Stennett for this thorough and fair piece of work, as they, and others, were also indebted to him for the advice and encouragement he frequently gave in a less conspicuous way to young ministers and candidates for the Nonconformist ministry in general.[92] A further evidence of his ecumenicity may be seen in his involvement in the establishment in 1708 of a church, presumably First-day, at Colnbrook in Buckinghamshire.[93] Earlier, while convalescing from illness at Tonbridge in 1700, he had preached regularly on the first day for several weeks. He had also wanted to write a complete history of the English Baptist movement and had gathered material for this purpose.[94] Although the task was never completed due to his untimely death at the age of 49, it may be taken as further evidence of a broad-mindedness which earned him and his Sabbatarian cause a respect which a narrow sectarianism would never have realised.[95] By the time of his death on 11 July 1713, after a ministry of twenty-three years, almost 150 members had been added to Pinners' Hall, and the total membership had more than tripled since the reorganization under his father in 1686. A question remains, however, regarding his latitudinarianism, and that of his son, and grandson, as to whether in the end it was a help or a hindrance to the long-term interests of the Sabbatarians.

Stennett's death brought a decided change in Pinners' Hall's fortunes. No pastor could be found to succeed him, and for the next fourteen years the church remained without a minister, with preachers supplied, often from Mill Yard. In 1721, as we have seen, the congregation moved to Mill Yard, where it shared Sabbath worship until 1727, when Edmund Townsend was called from Aston-upon-Carrant in Gloucestershire.[96] Townsend had been minister of the Aston[97] (or Ashchurch) Seventh-day church since 1720, and had been ordained in 1722 'that he might minister the ordinances ... and preach to other churches in want'. He had supplied Mill Yard and Pinners' Hall for about four years during the time of their

---

[92] *PDM* 1: 134.   [93] Whitley, *Baptists of London*, 127.   [94] *PDM* 1: 130.

[95] Although it is recorded that he was engaged in controversies with Penn the Quaker and with the Socinians Hedworth and Emms, 'Some Account of the Life of . . . Joseph Stennett', 23, in *Works*, i (1732).

[96] Whitley, *Baptists of London*, 119; *SDBEA* 1: 54; *TBHS* 5: 109. The suggestion that the decline of Pinners' Hall may have been due to the fact that 'it never plucked up heart to own a building' is not without point, *TBHS* 5: 78.

[97] Aston-upon-Carron (Carrant), Glos., *TBHS* 2: 99.

combined services, and had apparently lived in London for a period while still retaining pastoral responsibility for Ashchurch.[98] It was easy for him, therefore, to accept the call to Pinners' Hall in 1727. The days of Sabbatarian worship at Pinners' Hall were, in fact, over, for with Townsend's appointment the congregation moved to Curriers' Hall in Cripplegate, and henceforth it was known also as the Curriers' Hall, or Cripplegate, Seventh-day church. Townsend remained at Curriers' Hall for thirty-six years until his death in 1763. Although Ivimey describes him as a worthy and respectable man and 'a useful minister, greatly esteemed in his day', Pinners' Hall never returned to its former glory, and the slow decline which had set in after Stennett's death and the long interim without a minister continued.[99]

Townsend was the last minister of any real consequence at Curriers' Hall, and after his death the church survived without pastoral care once again, this time for four years, until Thomas Whitewood[100] arrived in 1767. He preached only three times and administered the Lord's Supper once before dying later that same year.[101] Dr Samuel Stennett, grandson of Joseph Stennett I and senior minister at Little Wild Street, and one of the most renowned Baptist ministers of the eighteenth century, who had supplied Curriers' Hall during the interim following Townsend's death, was now called to the pastoral office. Although he never formally accepted the call, he preached in the morning[102] and administered the Lord's Supper for several years, and for that reason is sometimes listed as having been the minister at Curriers' Hall between 1767 and 1780. His interests, however, clearly lay with Little Wild Street, and there is no evidence that he was seriously interested in a

---

[98] *SDBEA* 1: 44–5; *SO* 1: 116–17.

[99] Whitley, *Baptists of London*, 119; Ivimey, *History*, iii. 407. From 1724 Townsend served as a member of the Baptist Board, *TBHS* 5: 100, and he and Robert Cornthwaite of Mill Yard are both listed as belonging to the General Body of Protestant Dissenting Ministers of the Three Denominations: *TBHS* 5: 107–8.

[100] At Reading, not Seventh-day, 1749–67.   [101] *SR* 3/46: 182.

[102] The afternoon service was taken by Samuel Burford until 1768, and then in rotation by him and Macgowan of Devonshire Square until 1774, then by John Rippon, Reynolds of Cripplegate, Clarke of Unicorn Yard, and Dr Jenkins, who later moved into the country and was succeeded by Thomas Dawson. The latter 'afterwards renounced his Sabbatarian notions' and preached to a First-day congregation in Surrey Road: Wilson, *Dissenting Churches*, ii. 607.

revival of the Sabbatarian cause at Curriers' Hall.[103] Robert Burnside, who supplied in the afternoons from 1780, was appointed pastor in 1785 and remained as such until 1826, but he spent most of his time and energy in teaching. G.M. Pike noted that Burnside was held in 'high esteem in the Three Denominations', but that during his ministry there were 'few, or no accessions to the number of his followers'.[104] In 1799 the church moved from Curriers' Hall to Red Cross Street and in 1812 to Devonshire Square. By the time that J.B. Shenstone was appointed to succeed Burnside in 1826, the church had dwindled to five resident members and, though after his demise in 1844 worship was conducted for a few years more by W.H. Murch, the end was in sight. Services came to an end in 1849, and the last member died in 1863.[105] Pinners' Hall had survived for nearly two centuries, and in that time, under a succession of distinguished preachers, had received into its fellowship several hundred new members.

THE HENRY JESSEY GROUP

On account both of his links with Independent and Baptist churches and their leaders, and his own extensive ministry, Henry Jessey is rightly regarded as one of the influential moderate figures in pre-Restoration Nonconformity.[106] He is usually associated with the early London Jacob–Lathrop Independent congregation, with a branch of which he remained in fellowhship until his death in 1663. What is not widely known is that he became convinced of the seventh day at some point in the mid- to late 1640s, and that as a consequence,

---

[103] *SR* 3/46: 182; Wilson, *Dissenting Churches*, ii. 607. See also *DNB*. Samuel Stennett is said to have observed the seventh day at home with his family. John Rippon and Joseph Jenkins are also said to have supplied Curriers' Hall during the earlier 'Stennett years'. See also Ch. 5 n. 107.

[104] Pike, *Ancient Meeting Houses*, 189–90.

[105] Whitley, *Baptists of London*, 119; *TBHS* 5: 82; *BQ* 6: 180. At Burnside's ordination in 1785, the congregation consisted of twenty-one members, sixteen 'in town', and five 'in the country', PHCB 130; Wilson, *Dissenting Churches*, ii. 608.

[106] On Jessey (1601–63), see *DNB*; *BDBR* ii. 140; B.R. White, 'Henry Jessey, a Pastor in Politics', *BQ* 25 (1973–4), 98–110, and 'Henry Jessey in the Great Rebellion', in R. Buick Knox (ed.), *Reformation, Conformity and Dissent* (1977), 132–53. White has rescued Jessey from an undeserved obscurity; see also G.F. Nuttall for the significance of his moderating influence, *Visible Saints: The Congregational Way 1640–1660* (Oxford, 1957), 119–20.

at an undetermined date, probably between 1647 and 1653, he began to worship with a small group on Saturday in his own house.[107] The main evidence for Jessey's Sabbatarianism is a reference in his biography in 1671,[108] but a careful reading of his published works provides additional information concerning his Sabbatarian views.

Prior to becoming pastor of a congregation derived from the old Jacob–Lathrop church in London in 1637, Jessey had taken Anglican orders and had served as curate and tutor at Assington, Suffolk, 1627–33, and vicar at Aughton in Yorkshire, before going to London in 1635. Jessey was a graduate of St John's, Cambridge, and a distinguished Hebrew and rabbinical scholar, with a corresponding reverence for the authority of the Bible and a deep attachment to the Judaeo-Christian tradition.[109] Although usually described as a Baptist, Jessey was not at the heart of that movement, and certainly was not 'the most influential founder of the English Baptists'.[110] His congregation remained mixed-communion until his death after the Restoration, and included some who maintained the validity of infant baptism. White thus remarks that Jessey 'always remained outside the mainstream of Calvinistic Baptists'.[111] Although ultimately he received believer's baptism at the hands of Hanserd Knollys, who was a thoroughgoing Baptist, Jessey is probably best described simply as an Independent, with strong leanings to Baptist, and Sabbatarian, principles. His biographer states that while the two major points of difference between him and his congregation were baptism and the Sabbath, his tolerant broad-mindedness and fear of division led him not to make an issue of either.[112]

The date at which Jessey began to observe the seventh day with a small group of fellow believers, perhaps, but not necessarily, from his own congregation, has usually been put at a point in the early to mid-1650s. His biographer records that in his later years he

---

[107] Jessey's Sabbatarianism merits more comment than White's passing reference in Knox, *Reformation, Conformity and Dissent*, 151, but was not as crucial to the development of the Seventh-day movement as implied by Katz, *Sabbath and Sectarianism*, 20–1.

[108] [Edward Whiston], *The Life and Death of Mr Henry Jessey* (1671), 87.

[109] [Whiston], *Life of Jessey*, 1–10; White in Knox, *Reformation, Conformity and Dissent*, 132–3. See also Benjamin Stinton, 'An Account of Some of the Most Eminent and Leading Men among the English Antipaedobaptists', AL, MS 36 G.A.e.10, pp. 29–36.

[110] e.g. *DNB* and *BDBR* ii. 140; Katz, *Sabbath and Sectarianism*, 21; *TCHS* 3: 88.

[111] White in Knox, *Reformation, Conformity and Dissent*, 137.

[112] [Whiston], *Life of Jessey*, 87–8.

kept the Sabbath 'in his own chamber, with only four or five more of the same mind', and that he did so only after having been convinced for some two years that the seventh day should 'be kept by Christians evangelically'.[113] By early 1657 Jessey was regarded by Spittlehouse as a suitable defender of the seventh day against John Simpson, probably because it was known in Sabbatarian circles that he had contributed to William Saller's *Sundry Queries* in 1653.[114] It has even been suggested that the anonymous *Moralitie of the Fourth Commandement* (1652) was Jessey's, although in view of his desire to avoid 'offence' and 'breaches' on account of the seventh day this seems unlikely, though not impossible. The inference that he was Seventh-day at the time of accepting the Jacob–Lathrop pastorate or soon thereafter is quite untenable.[115]

It may be more profitable to seek for clues in another direction. Beginning in 1645, Jessey published annually a scriptural almanac, giving basic solar, lunar, and tidal information, as well as items of historical or biblical significance. From this first edition the name of the last day of the week was explained as 'Saturni=Saturn's day=Seventh or Sabbath'.[116] The 1647 version went much further, on the basis of purporting to explain the significance of the number seven in Scripture, and the nearness of the Fifth Monarchy of Daniel. Jessey noted the repeated occurrence of the number seven in the Bible as a designation of completeness, and explained that seven thus used was a type of the Sabbath, signifying the rest and fullness inherent in the day, and the 'glorious liberty that believers and all have in Jesus . . . as Himself witnesseth, Luke 4: 18–22; Col. 2: 14–17; Heb. 4: 3, 9–11'.[117] Of the women who came to anoint the body of Jesus after the crucifixion, Jessey commented, 'the Sabbath night coming on they rested, according to the Command[ment], Luke 23: 53–56,' adding that Christ rose from the tomb 'early the third day, the first of the Sabb[ath]'. Jessey's point seems unmistakably clear, yet for those who might still have missed it, he explained

---

[113] Ibid. 87.

[114] Spittlehouse, *A Manifestation of sundry gross absurdities*, 8; William Saller, *Sundry Queries* (1660), 1, 2.

[115] Burdick, SDB Bibliography, 12; [Whiston], *Life of Jessey*, 87; Katz, *Sabbath and Sectarianism*, 20–1.

[116] H[enry] J[essey], *A Calculation for this present year, 1645* ([1645]), sig. A2^r.

[117] H[enry] J[essey], *A Scripture Almanack, or, A Calculation for the year 1647* (1647), sig. B8^r. See White, *BQ* 25: 98–110 for Jessey's Fifth Monarchist leanings and his belief that 'the coming kingdom required obedience now'.

that of the many laws Jehovah had appointed 'typing Christ our fulness', the seventh day was 'his sabbath . . . which he blessed and sanctified'.[118] It would seem, then, that Jessey was sharing his Sabbatarian views by the mid-1640s and if, indeed, 'he kept his opinion much to himself' for two years or so prior to gathering a group for Sabbath worship, the Jessey congregation might well have begun Seventh-day observance c.1646 or 1647. Certainly 1653 would seem rather late.

Jessey was a man of broad vision, and at least two of his three major concerns had Sabbatarian connotations. Like many of his contemporaries, Jessey was deeply interested in the conversion of the Jews, and in their readmission to England, which was under official consideration in the 1650s.[119] Jessey published several pieces during these years related to the Jewish question, including *The Glory and Salvation of Jehudah and Israel; a Treatise to reconcile Jews and Christians in the Faith of the Messiah* (1650). Although there is little in any of these publications explicitly relating to the seventh day, the Sabbath was none the less an obvious link between Jews and Sabbatarian Christians, and it is reasonable to suppose that in Jessey's thinking observance of the original Sabbath would facilitate the great work of bringing the Jews to faith in Christ. Jessey's other major concern, besides the production of a new version of the Bible based on a corrected text, was the establishment of Independent congregations in as many parts of the country as possible.[120] To this end he was engaged in at least four extended preaching tours intended to strengthen existing congregations and to encourage the formation of others. In 1639 he was sent to Wales by his London church to assist in the gathering of the first Independent congregation in Wales at Llanvaches. In 1653 he visited more than thirty churches in East Anglia, mainly in Essex, Norfolk, and Suffolk; in the following year he went north; and in 1655 he toured in the south and south-west among churches in Hampshire, Wiltshire, Dorset, Somerset, and Devon.[121] It may be

---

[118] J[essey], *A Scripture Almanack*, sigs. A5ʳ, B8ʳ.

[119] [Whiston], *Life of Jessey*, 83–4.

[120] Ibid. Cf. AL, MS 36 G.A.e.10, where Benjamin Stinton records that the scheme for a new translation of the Bible, which had attracted eminent scholars of different nationalities, was thwarted by the events which followed the Restoration, fos. 31ᵛ, 32ʳ.

[121] [Whiston], *Life of Jessey*, 83–4; White in Knox, *Reformation, Conformity and Dissent*, 140–1; *TBHS* 2: 240; *BQ* 26: 349.

merely coincidence that nascent Sabbatarian groups existed in many of these areas at the time of Jessey's visits, or were then in the process of forming. Whitley believed that Jessey's western itinerary at least persuaded some to consider the Sabbath question.[122] In 1653 Jessey had urged Thomas Tillam, who had recently been in communication with Peter Chamberlen, to go to East Anglia where a Sabbatarian cause had existed at least since 1647.[123] All this merely demonstrates a possible link between Jessey and the developing Sabbatarian movement during the 1650s, and the view that Jessey, together with Francis Bampfield and Peter Chamberlen demonstrated 'the essentially respectable quality of extreme Sabbatarianism', while true, needs to be tempered by the knowledge that he proceeded down the Sabbatarian path 'with great caution, that there might be no offence or breaches among professors'.[124]

Although Jessey's later years involved him in religio-political activities which eventually brought him to prison,[125] his small Sabbatarian congregation appears to have continued to meet at least until his death in 1663. His own settled views on the matter are reflected in the posthumous *Miscellanea Sacra, or Diverse Necessary Truths* (1665), in which he argued that believing Christians 'should seek the communion of saints, and should have respect to all the Ten Commandments of the Law'. Given the background, the message is unmistakable, and it may be assumed that many of the several thousand who paid Jessey their last respects at his funeral were aware of his Sabbatarianism, as they were of his Baptist principles.[126] Despite his reluctance to make an issue of the seventh day, or of believer's baptism, there were no doubt many Sabbatarians who felt as the Baptists did: 'It proved no small honour and advantage to the Antipaedobaptists to have a man of such extraordinary piety and substantial learning amongst them.'[127]

[122] Whitley, 'A Century of Sabbath Doctrine', 167.
[123] Whitley, 'Men of the Seventh Day', 4/3, 4.
[124] Katz, *Sabbath and Sectarianism*, 91; [Whiston], *Life of Jessey*, 87.
[125] White, in Knox, *Reformation, Conformity and Dissent*, 148–52. Together with Hanserd Knollys and John Simpson, Jessey was suspected of seditious preaching, and of training others for similar purposes. In 1661 they were assisted occasionally by John James, *TBHS* 3: 126.
[126] Henry Jessey, *Miscellanea Sacra, or Diverse Necessary Truths* (1665), 173; cf. 71, 86; [Whiston], *Life of Jessey*, 94.   [127] AL, MS 36. G.A.e.10, fol. 31^r.

5

The South and South-West

THE Seventh-day Men were well represented in the southern and south-western counties of England for more than two centuries. W.E. Mellone, writing in the *Jewish Quarterly Review* at the end of the nineteenth century, claimed that at least seventeen 'comparatively large and flourishing' Seventh-day congregations had met regularly for worship and instruction in Commonwealth and Stuart times, and that Sabbatarian churches had begun to appear in some western and south-western counties during, or soon after, the imprisonment of Dorothy Traske.[1] This would put the first appearance of Seventh-day views in the south of England in the early 1640s or even in the late 1630s. The evidence seems to confirm such relatively early beginnings in Salisbury, and perhaps also in Exeter, and Tiverton. It also demonstrates that before the disappearance of a Sabbatarian presence in Salisbury in the middle of the nineteenth century, the cause had been established in Surrey, Hampshire, Wiltshire, Dorset, Devon, and well represented in Somerset. Mellone's figure of seventeen major Seventh-day congregations in London and the rest of the country is almost certainly an underestimate by any count, for there were at least nine groups in the six counties named. Sabbatarians also lived in villages near to towns where congregations were established. Thus Sabbatarians at Holnest and Castleton in Dorset in the 1670s and 1680s were probably members of the Sherborne congregation, although it is quite possible that they met locally for worship on occasion rather than travelling into Sherborne itself.[2] The tenacity with which many clung to the seventh day in isolation and frequently in the face of

---

[1] W.E. Mellone, 'Seventh-Day Christians', *JQR* 10 (1898), 405–6, 418.
[2] The final tally of Seventh-day churches depends on whether identifiable groups in a given area are regarded as part of one church or as congregations in their own right. While Sabbatarians at Holnest and Castleton would seem to have belonged to the Sherborne congregation, the same would not have been true of those at Beaminster, which was much further in distance from Sherborne and more of a distinct community. The Llanwenarth record suggests that in 1690 all the Dorset groups were part of one church.

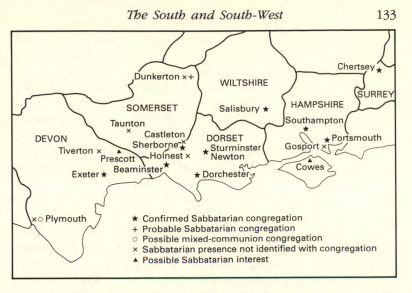

MAP 2 Locations in southern and south-western counties associated with seventeenth- and eighteenth-century Sabbatarianism

calumny or even persecution, particularly in some parts of the south-west was no doubt due to what in their minds was, as Mellone observed, a 'perfectly logical and . . . impregnable' conviction.[3]

CHERTSEY

The Seventh-day congregation which worshipped in Chertsey, Surrey, first appeared with any clarity in 1668, and persisted at least until the middle of the eighteenth century, or even later. For most of its life in the seventeenth century, this church centred around two prominent individuals, Arthur Squibb and William Burnet, and although never large, maintained a steady presence for most of its life, due principally to the foundation laid in its early years by Squibb and Burnet.

Arthur Squibb was a man of some standing in the 1640s and 1650s who had gathered a separatist church in his own house by 1649. It would seem that his conversion to Independent, and perhaps Baptist, principles had occurred only a short time before, for

[3] Mellone, in *JQR* 10: 407.

in 1646 he was employed as receiver of revenues for the Archbishop of Canterbury. By 1653 he was a Justice of the Peace at Westminster, and in that same year he sat as Member for Middlesex in the Nominated Parliament.[4] Precisely when he adopted the Seventh-day Sabbath is not known,[5] but in 1668 he signed a letter to the church in Newport, Rhode Island on behalf of the Bell Lane church, and in 1667 he added his name to the *Faithful Testimony* against Thomas Tillam and the other 'teachers of circumcision and the legal ceremonies'.[6] In 1670 he was indicted for refusing to take the oath of allegiance, and in the following year was arrested, along with several others, mainly from Bell Lane church, as a Fifth Monarchist and Seventh-day Man.[7] In 1672, he was licensed as an 'Anabaptist' to preach in his own house in Chertsey, as was the other key figure in Chertsey's early history, William Burnet, who was also licensed for the house of William Longust, or Longhurst.[8] The Chertsey Sabbatarians were probably meeting before this, and the mid-1660s seems a reasonable point from which to date the beginnings of this congregation.[9] It may well have begun earlier than that.

Burnet is first known as the author of *The Capital Principles of . . . Quakers Discovered* (1668), written as 'an exhortation to keep close to the scriptures'. Burnet was concerned that the Quaker emphasis on 'the light and life of Christ within' implicitly undermined the fundamental truths of historic Christianity regarding the nature of Christ and the completed Atonement on the cross, since those who claimed to have the 'light within' were tempted to believe that salvation could come from obedience to that inner light, rather than from a completed and sufficient act of grace in history.[10] Moreover, the doctrine of 'the light within' as a final authority encouraged rejection of the external authority of Scripture. Burnet undoubtedly spoke for many beyond the ranks of Sabbatarians in

---

[4] *FMM* 263; Whitley, 'Men of the Seventh Day', 7/6; *BDBR* iii. 199–200.

[5] Squibb was named as an elder of a Presbyterian classis in Godalming, Surrey, in 1648: W.A. Shaw, *A History of the English Church . . . 1640–1660*, ii (1900), 433.

[6] The 'Aaron Squibb' of the Bell Lane letters to Newport, Rhode Island, can be identified as Arthur Squibb, see above, 108, n. 27.

[7] *CSPD* 1671, 356–7. Squibb may, or may not, have been a member of Bell Lane at this time. He was regarded as one of the leaders of the group arrested and, together with John Belcher, Richard Goodgroome, and John Jones, was sent to the Tower.

[8] *OR* i. 323, 471.   [9] *SO* 2: 212.

[10] William Burnet, *The Capital Principles of the People called Quakers Discovered and Stated out of their own Writings* (1668), 3, 27, 34 ff.

attempting to defend the incarnate Word and the written Word against the Quakers. He had also observed what he felt was a fanatical exhibitionism in many Quakers, resulting in behaviour unbecoming those who professed the gospel, and deriving, in his view, from their rejection of any external constraints on doctrine or decorum.[11]

The Quaker, George Whitehead, replied to Burnet with *The Light and Life of Christ within* (1668), noting the conflicts over free will, predestination, and redemption then prevalent in Baptist churches, and pointing out that 'several of their teachers', including Burnet, upheld the seventh day and had 'preached, writ and printed for the imposing of it on Christians' generally.[12] Burnet, in fact, had not mentioned the Sabbath at all in his attack on the Quakers, which had somewhat disappointed Whitehead, who, it seems, had hoped to score some additional points against Burnet on that issue. Whitehead had to content himself with charging Burnet with being 'an envious and persecuting spirit', and with bracketing him with Thomas Tillam 'their great Seventh-day-Sabbath man'.[13]

Both Squibb and Burnet had accepted the seventh day some years before they were licensed to preach in their own houses in Chertsey in 1672, and it seems more reasonable to conclude that the Chertsey Sabbatarians met in both houses, than to suppose that there were two Seventh-day groups active in this locality at the same time. It is also possible that Chertsey, like other congregations with Seventh-day interests, was a mixed congregation in its earlier years, since Whitehead, while singling out Burnet of Chertsey as a Baptist, was also responding to Baptist attacks on Quakerism in Buckinghamshire and Sussex, and stated that only 'some hearers' among the Baptists he knew were of Seventh-day convictions.[14]

Although nothing further is heard directly of the Seventh-day cause in Chertsey until 1690, the Compton census gives thirty Nonconformists active in the town in 1676. That this Sabbatarian

---

[11] Ibid. 7, 19, 24.

[12] George Whitehead, *The Light and Life of Christ within* (1668), preface, A2^r.

[13] Ibid., A2^v. Whitehead continued the controversy with Burnet and other Baptists in *The Christian Quaker and his Divine Testimony Vindicated*, part II (1673), noting again divisions among Baptists, 'some preaching up a personal Election, others general Redemption; some for Christ's dying for all, others for his dying but for a few; some for the Jews Seventh Day Sabbath, others opposing it', (p. 87) and attacking Burnet, particularly for his belief in the resurrection of the body, 138–45.

[14] Ibid., A2^r.

congregation continued through these difficult years seems certain from the Llanwenarth record which states that in 1690 William Burnet was elder of a Seventh-day congregation at 'Cherssey', with Thomas Stickland, or Strickland, as a 'ministering brother'.[15] Squibb had died in 1680, and although little else is known of Strickland, he appears to have served the congregation well in succession to Squibb. In 1698 Chertsey is noted as 'flourishing' under Burnet's care,[16] although Strickland is mentioned again in 1707 when he was relieved of a debt to the London Sabbatarian, Joseph Davis, by the provisions of the latter's will.[17] It may be some indication of Chertsey's relative strength throughout these years, that in the Llanwenarth record it is not listed as a 'remnant' as were so many of the Seventh-day groups recorded there as having survived the traumatic times of exclusion and persecution. The last mention of Burnet comes in 1699, when Rebekah Humber was recommended from Pinners' Hall to the Seventh-day church at 'Chersey walking with Mr Wm. Burnet'.[18] His ministry of over thirty years was unquestionably crucial to Chertsey's survival, and remains as a reminder of the argument that continuity of able pastoral care is an essential element in congregational stability.

Chertsey continued to maintain a witness to the seventh day well into the eighteenth century. The Joseph Davis charity instituted in 1706, by which £5 per annum was to be given to the 'teachers' of nine Seventh-day congregations outside of London, included Chertsey.[19] Although no recognizable minister or elder is known after Burnet, the congregation was still in existence in 1716, and in the previous year a 'Mr Turner' had received £1 from the estate of Mary Hall of Pinners' Hall, 'for use in Chertsey'. In 1744 Pinners' Hall agreed to receive Thomas Major into fellowship after correspondence with 'our Sabbath-keeping friends at Chertsey', and at some point subsequent to 1755 Mary Major, who in that year joined Pinners' Hall, was recorded as being 'at Chertsey'. This is the last known mention of the Chertsey Sabbatarians, who elsewhere are said to have become extinct by 1780.[20] The picture thus remaining

---

[15] William Salt Library, S. MS 33; NLW, Deposit 409 B, which is reproduced in *BQ* 14: 165. Probably Thomas Strickland, who in 1672 was licensed as a Baptist for William Wilkinson's house in Effingham, *OR* i. 570; 2: 1017.
[16] *SO* 2: 205.   [17] Black (ed.), *Last Legacy*, 47.   [18] PHCB 71
[19] *Reports from the Commissioners for Charities*, xix, pt. I, 871.
[20] *TBHS* 3: 91; PHCB 117, 126, 18 (the second so numbered); *SO* 2: 212.

of the Seventh-day church at Chertsey is of a small, solid congregation, loyal to its convictions through trial and difficulty, generally keeping a low profile, and remaining in touch with one of the larger London churches for the better part of one hundred years. In these respects Chertsey was typical of many similar Seventh-day congregations across the country.

SALISBURY

Salisbury was also named in the Joseph Davis bequest in 1706, but its origins go back well before that, as also its later history continued for a century or more after Davis had designated the congregations which were to benefit from his charity. The Salisbury congregation proved to be one of the longest surviving Seventh-day churches in the country, sustaining a Sabbatarian presence in Wiltshire for some two centuries. Its history may conservatively be commenced with the appearance of James Ockford's *The Doctrine of the Fourth Commandement*, published in 1650, and evidently intended to be distributed widely in Salisbury, as in other places. The full title of the book claimed that the fourth commandment had been 'Deformed by Popery' and that it was now to be 'Reformed and Restored to its Primitive purity'.[21] In all probability Ockford knew that even in the new religious climate his sentiments would be likely to revive .the fears of Judaizing which had followed Traske and Brabourne, and that the authorities might act accordingly. He was probably not in the least surprised when they did.

In February 1650, Francis Dove, Mayor of Salisbury, notified Parliament in London that a hundred copies of Ockford's book had been seized in the city, and enclosed a copy for their examination. The matter was referred to the committee for plundered ministers, which was asked to consider the book and report to the House of Commons within a week. On 8 March the House resolved that Ockford's book, 'asserting the observation of the Jewish Sabbath and condemning the observation of the Lord's day', was 'erroneous,

---

[21] Ockford (Oakeford, or Okeford), originally from Salisbury, has been identified with John Oakford of East Rudham, Norfolk, fl. 1657 (Whitley, *BB* i. 67), whom Whitley elsewhere calls James: ibid. 41. Ockford is not heard of again in Salisbury after the publication of his book. His second work was published in Amsterdam as *The Tryal of the Truth;, or, rather the Law is the Truth* (Amsterdam, 1656). Cf. *TBHS* 7: 222, where he is again named John, and is said also to have written, in 1657, on baptism.

scandalous and prophane, contrary to the practice of the Apostles, and of all the Christian churches,' and ordered all copies in England and Wales to be surrendered and publicly burnt, and its author to be arrested and imprisoned.[22] Although it is doubtful that this latter injunction was ever carried out, the destruction of the book was evidently thorough. Only one copy is known to have survived.[23] A parliamentary proclamation confirming the decision and ordering the burning of the book throughout the realm was issued that day, signed by Henry Scobell, clerk to the Parliament.

The Doctrine of the Fourth Commandement was the first English book to advocate the seventh day since Brabourne's *Discourse* and *Defence*, and the first book by a Baptist to do so. It may not, however, be an accurate indication of the origin of Seventh-day observance in Salisbury. Beginning in 1631, and then regularly through the 1630s, James Oakeford was presented by the church-wardens of St Thomas's, together with Abraham Cade and Joan Slowe, as an 'Anabaptist recusant', absenting himself from his parish church and failing to pay his parish dues. In 1633 he was also presented for not having his child baptized according to Anglican practice. By 1637 all three were noted as 'separated and excommunicated', Cade by this time also having refused to have his children baptized.[24] Similar records exist for the Salisbury parish of St Martin's. In 1632 Elizabeth Townsend and Margaret Unquarry were presented 'for working upon the Sabbath day' (i.e. Sunday), and in the next few years several parishioners, including John Everard and his wife, Thomas Hoare and his wife, a Mr Newman, and William Ball the younger, were presented variously for 'absenting themselves from church on Sundays and holy days', 'working ordinarily on the Lord's day' or 'the Sabbath day', and failing to have their children baptized. In 1639 George Tennon was presented for allowing his wife and daughters to sew and knit on 'the Sabbath day'.[25]

Whether or not these records represent the beginnings of a Seventh-day congregation in Salisbury is not entirely clear, but Ockford's early adoption of Baptist views is hardly in doubt. The

---

[22] Bodl. MS Tanner 56, fo. 176; *Journals of the House of Commons*, vi, 2 Sept. 1648–14 Aug. 1651, 374, 378.

[23] The existing copy, now in the library at Christ Church, Oxford, once belonged to William Wake, Archbishop of Canterbury, and bears his autograph. Cox refers to a copy belonging to Samuel Gilfillan, see *Literature of the Sabbath Question*, i. 479.

[24] WRO, D4/10.   [25] Ibid.

names differ from those in the Salisbury group in the old Porton church book which records the beginnings of the Baptist cause in Salisbury. It has, in fact, been suggested that Sabbatarian principles appeared early in Salisbury in the context of a General Baptist church, and Marjorie Reeves places their origin 'a little later' than 1630–2.[26] A manuscript in the records of Brown Street Baptist church in Salisbury suggests that the congregation had its beginnings in an affiliation with a General Baptist church in Amsterdam 'probably holding Sabbatarian views'.[27] Whatever the precise circumstances in which Seventh-day observance took root here, it may be argued that only a well-established congregation would be able to help forward the circulation of a large consignment of a book that was sure to be viewed with suspicion by the authorities. 1640 seems a very reasonable date for the beginnings of the Seventh-day movement in Salisbury.

The diocesan records for Salisbury break off in 1639 and do not recommence until after the Restoration, when a somewhat different picture emerges, without Ockford. In 1674 twenty parishioners from St Thomas's were presented for non-attendance, including John Laws and his wife, Sir John Penruddock and his wife, and a Mrs Strickland.[28] Penruddock had been presented in 1664 for the same reason, and John Laws is known to have been one of two 'ministering brethren' in the Seventh-day church at Salisbury by 1690. A Thomas Strickland, as we have already noted, ministered to the Seventh-day people at Chertsey in 1690.[29] Similar presentments were made throughout the 1660s and the early 1670s in the other Salisbury parishes of St Martin's and St Edmund's, although in 1674 the churchwardens at St Edmund's took the unusual step of requesting further time to enquire into the identity of those neglecting to receive the sacrament in the parish church.[30] Michael Aldridge, who lived at Southampton, was named in the Llanwenarth record as

---

[26] *SO* 3: 12; *VCH* Wilts., iii. 101.

[27] N. Carter, 'Wiltshire Nonconformity', MS in the Salisbury, Brown Street, church records, J5. On the early Salisbury–Amsterdam connection see 'Salisbury and Tiverton about 1630', *TBHS* 3: 1–7.

[28] WRO, D1/54. Penruddock, probably of Compton Chamberlayne, and son of John Penruddock, executed at Exeter in 1655 for complicity in a Royalist plot, and grandson of Sir John Penruddock, High Sheriff of Wiltshire 1643–4, *DNB*. A John Strickland, rector of St Edmund's, Salisbury, ejected in 1662, was still preaching in the parish in 1669, where he was buried in 1670, *CR* 467.

[29] WRO, D4/10; *BQ* 14: 165.   [30] WRO, D1/54; D4/10.

elder at Salisbury in 1690; he first appears in 1672, licensed as a
Baptist for West Cowes in the Isle of Wight together with James
Wise, who in 1672 was also licensed for the house of Thomas Batt
(or Ball?) in Salisbury.[31] John Hall was the second ministering
brother at Salisbury by 1690, and he may have been the son or
brother of William Hall who was, with others, presented at St
Edmund's in 1670 and again in 1681 for non-attendance and for not
having their children baptized.[32] The records of all three Salisbury
parishes show *omnia bene* after 1688, but that would in all likeli-
hood not have been the case had the stringent regulations of the
1660s and 1670s, particularly as enforced by Seth Ward, Bishop of
Salisbury from 1667, been continued. These fleeting glimpses of the
Seventh-day cause at Salisbury during the difficult post-Restoration
years, are amplified and confirmed by the knowledge that Francis
Bampfield preached there to a Sabbatarian church in 1675. His stay
was probably longer than intended, since he was arrested and
imprisoned in Salisbury gaol, as he had been some four years earlier in 1671, prior to moving to London.[33]

As was the case with many Independent and Baptist congregations in the latter half of the seventeenth century, a much more
stable situation prevailed for Seventh-day churches from 1689 onwards, and names were more freely cited. In 1695 and 1698 respectively Elizabeth Bagg and Mary Batt were admitted to Pinners' Hall
on recommendation from Salisbury. A more expected link, on
account of Salisbury's General Baptist leanings, was with Mill Yard
in 1706, when the teacher of the Sabbatarian congregation in Salisbury was named as one of the beneficiaries of Joseph Davis's will.[34]
Thereafter the references to Salisbury in any form are scarce, and
it seems that, as with so many other Seventh-day congregations in
the early eighteenth century, this one too was slipping into slow
and irreversible decline. In 1749 Thomas Whitewood was called
from Salisbury to the Baptist church in Reading, although he was
known to be a Sabbatarian. Reading had been without a minister
for several months, and Salisbury, weakened by the death of some
of its more wealthy members, was no longer able to support a
permanent ministry. Salisbury reluctantly agreed to the call, and
Whitewood accepted it on the clear understanding that he would

---

[31] *BQ* 14: 165; *OR* ii. 1051, 1075; WRO, D1/27.   [32] WRO, D4/10.
[33] Salisbury, Brown Street, church records, J5; Bampfield, *A Name*, 7.
[34] PHCB 41, 69; cf. Cox, *Literature of the Sabbath Question*, ii. 81.

not make the Sabbath an issue at Reading.[35] Were it not for a somewhat unusual line of evidence, it would have to be concluded that Whitewood's departure marked the end of any significant Sabbatarian witness in Salisbury.

That this did not occur, however, is plain from the records pertaining to the present Baptist church in Salisbury. A deed relating to the Brown Street building in 1734 gives a list of the trustees, describing them as 'persons entrusted for the congregations meeting in Sarum called Baptists of the First Day and Seventh Day's persuasions, who are distinguished by that name for dissenting from the Established church upon the account of their baptizing adult persons only by way of dipping'. The trustees included John Sutten of Winterbourne, who, in 1731, together with several other Seventh-day Men, had benefited from the estate of Joseph Davis, jun., of Mill Yard.[36] Similar deeds were drawn up in 1748, 1774, and 1795, all using the same wording to indicate that Brown Street was for the shared use of 'Baptists of the first day and seventh day's persuasions'. In 1795 the trustees included Joseph Stennett (IV), and Robert Burnside, the latter then being the minister at Curriers' Hall.[37] While mixed-communion congregations are often encountered in seventeenth-century Independent and Baptist records, the Salisbury arrangement was unusual, if not unique. It seems to have worked smoothly for several decades, each congregation respecting the other's separate and doctrinal identity. The opening entry in the Brown Street First-day church book commencing in 1766 reads, 'This book belongs to the Baptist congregation of the Calvinist perswation [sic], who keep the first day of the week for their Christian Sabbath.'[38] The words are obviously carefully chosen, and it is only necessary to read between these lines to perceive with equal clarity the identity of the other congregation which used Brown Street. They were General Baptists of Arminian persuasion, keeping the seventh day of the week, which in the minds of some of the Salisbury Particulars at least had about it a touch of the old Jewish

[35] C.A. Davis, *History of the Baptist Church, Kings Road, Reading* (Reading, 1891), 30. On Whitewood, see *BQ* 1: 143 and Wilson, *Dissenting Churches*, ii 2: 607; *TBHS* 6: 143.

[36] Black (ed.), *Last Legacy*, 72; G.A. Moore, *The Story of Brown St. Baptist Church, Salisbury* (n.d.), 12.

[37] Moore, *Brown St. Baptist Church*, 12, 17. The original deeds, deposited at Baptist Church House, confirm this account.

[38] Brown Street church book, 1766–82, 1.

Sabbath. An indenture dated 1829 does not mention the Seventh-day people, and it may be concluded that at some point early in the nineteenth century, Saturday Sabbatarians ceased to exist in Salisbury as a worshipping congregation.

A note in the Pinners' Hall church book in 1844 serves as an epitaph for the Seventh-day cause in Salisbury. In that year the last Salisbury Sabbatarian, Sarah Blake (neé Major) died, aged 88. She had lived at Salisbury for most of her life, although in 1771 as a young woman she had joined Pinners' Hall, where her parents were members, and had remained in fellowship with the London church thereafter. Whether it was the memory of having been baptized by the renowned Dr Samuel Stennett or simply her own Calvinistic leanings, her ties with Pinners' Hall transcended even local family connections, for her grandfather had ministered to the Salisbury Seventh-day congregation during the latter years of the eighteenth century. Whatever the reasons, and whether or not she actually worshipped with the Salisbury Sabbatarians, the record states that she maintained 'a strict observance of the holy Sabbath until her death'.[39] With that event, the Sabbatarian witness in Salisbury also came to an end.

HAMPSHIRE

In 1675 Francis Bampfield was sent by his London congregation as a special messenger to the Seventh-day churches in Wiltshire, Hampshire, Dorset, Gloucestershire, and Berkshire. The locations of congregations in all these counties are readily identifiable, with the exception of the Hampshire group. Little evidence remains of what once was clearly an active fellowship, beyond the fact that it existed and was visited by Bampfield.[40] The few clues that do remain point generally in the Southampton–Portsmouth direction, with the possibility of a connection in the Isle of Wight, but reveal little of the beginning or the end of this elusive congregation. The exclusion of any reference to a Hampshire church in the Llanwenarth record could be taken to indicate that it had dissolved or gone to ground before 1690.

The diocesan records for Hampshire for the seventeenth century

---

[39] PHCB 170–1. Joshua Toulmin conducted the funeral of a William Blake in 1799.   [40] Bampfield, *A Name*, 7.

differ in one noteworthy respect from those extant in other dioceses. Whereas in most instances references to Sabbatarians, or
Seventh-day Men, or even 'Jews', are fairly frequent for localities
where a Seventh-day congregation existed, the Hampshire records,
although extensive and in many respects full of detail, referring
frequently to Quakers, Presbyterians, Papists, and Anabaptists, make
no reference to Sabbatarians as such.[41] It may be that Sabbatarians
in Hampshire were classified as a matter of course as Anabaptists,
or even Baptists, for both Michael Aldridge and James Wise were
so described in the licences issued in 1672, and similar classifica-
tions are found regularly in other areas.[42] Aldridge, as we have seen,
appeared later as elder at Salisbury while living at Southampton,
and was licensed for West Cowes in the Isle of Wight in 1672,
together with James Wise, who was also licensed for Thomas Batt's
house in Salisbury.[43] Wise had previously been reported as the leader
and chief preacher of one of three conventicles described as Fifth
Monarchist in Southampton in 1669.[44] It is quite possible that a group
such as this, at this period, was Sabbatarian without being openly
so classified.

An undated mid-seventeenth-century presentment in the diocesan records suggests that Portsmouth at that time provided an
ideal context for the establishment and development of Nonconformist congregations. 'Our town abounds with sectaries of all sorts,'
the churchwardens reported, explaining that a large population
and the constant influx of strangers and foreigners 'discapacitated'
them from 'truly knowing how many they are or what assemblies
they keep'. Another report referred in general terms to the presence
in Portsmouth of Presbyterians, Quakers, and Anabaptists.[45]

A much later link with Portsmouth comes with Thomas Whitewood, known successively as the minister of Salisbury, Reading
(First-day), and Curriers' Hall, from the mid-1740s to 1767. W.T.
Whitley and E.A. Payne were both aware of his Sabbatarian convictions, but although Payne states that he came from Salisbury,
where he is first known as a Sabbatarian, Whitley traces him back

---

[41] HRO, Winchester Diocesan records, *passim.*

[42] e.g. Arthur Squibb at Chertsey, in 1672, see above, 106.

[43] *OR* ii. 1051, 1075. In 1670, John More, earlier connected with Peter Chamberlen
and London Sabbatarianism, published *Moses Revived; or a Vindication of an ancient Law of God* . . . from New Chapel, Cowes. The tract argued the 'Unlawfulness
of eating blood'.

[44] *OR* i. 143.   [45] HRO, B/3/A/Box 3, Portsmouth.

to Portsmouth.[46] It is not known how long he was at Salisbury before moving to Reading in 1749, but if his stay there followed the pattern of most known Seventh-day pastorates it would have been of several years' duration. Assuming that Whitley's ascription is correct, Whitewood would probably have come to Salisbury from Portsmouth at some point in the first quarter of the eighteenth century, and although this of itself would not be proof of a Seventh-day congregation then in existence, it might be an indication of a past or languishing cause. In fact, the clearest single piece of evidence of a lingering Sabbatarian interest in Hampshire is dated 1715, when Thomas Green was admitted to membership at Mill Yard on the recommendation of the church at Gosport, signed by the minister, Mr Kelley (or Kelloy), and several other members.[47] This would suggest a link with Salisbury on account of the General Baptist principles involved, and would thus tend to confirm the Aldridge–Wise connection between Salisbury and the Southampton–Portsmouth area.

While much of this is somewhat speculative, the existence of a Hampshire Seventh-day congregation is indisputable, and the available facts suggest that Seventh-day views may have persisted longer in this area than has hitherto been supposed.

DORCHESTER, SHERBORNE, AND STURMINSTER NEWTON

The Sabbatarian movement in Dorset surfaced later than in almost any other part of the country, coming to light as a recognizable strand in Dorset Nonconformity only after the Restoration. It is difficult to ascertain whether or not an unidentified Sabbatarianism prevailed here before this, although with nearby Salisbury having entertained Seventh-day views for the previous twenty years or so, and Henry Jessey having visited the area in 1655, the possibility cannot be dismissed. Whitley suggested that Jessey's West Country tour may have drawn attention to the Sabbath issue in Salisbury and Dorchester.[48] Further west, in Exeter, as we shall see, the seventh day had been openly celebrated well before its first known observance in Dorchester and Sherborne and even before Jessey's visit. It is also possible that John Traske's earlier connections with

---

[46] Payne, *The Baptists of Berkshire*, 90; *BB* i. 183.   [47] MYM 221.
[48] Whitley, 'A Century of Sabbath Doctrine', 167. Cf. Ivimey, *History*, ii. 521.

south-west Dorset may have prompted an interest in the Beaminster district, so perhaps some seeds had taken root in Dorset which only required more favourable conditions in which to germinate. Such a climate was provided during the years Francis Bampfield spent in Dorset, first as rector of Rampisham, then as vicar of Sherborne, and finally as a Nonconformist, active principally in Sherborne and the north of the county. It was undoubtedly from him more than any other individual that the Seventh-day cause in Dorset initially drew its strength.

Bampfield himself was relatively a late-comer to Seventh-day observance. As the scion of two notable Devonshire families and the son of John Bampfylde of Poltimore, sheriff of Devon, and descended from the family of Sir Francis Drake, Bampfield was destined for a career in the Church of England.[49] In 1640, after graduating from Wadham College, Oxford, he had been presented to the living at Rampisham in west Dorset by his father, where he remained until 1653, when he removed to Sherborne to become vicar.[50] The Rampisham years had marked him as a man of great integrity and ability as well as a distinguished preacher, 'the most celebrated preacher in the West of England', and his induction at Sherborne is said to have been witnessed by 2,000 parishioners. While at Sherborne he preached regularly to large congregations drawn by his eloquence, learning, and pastoral concern. He was a noted Hebraist, and is said to have regularly read the Old Testament from the Hebrew text, as well as the New Testament from the Greek. Densham and Ogle describe him as 'one of the most remarkable men of his time, a time when remarkable men were not scarce'.[51] His theological journey was described with rather less respect by Anthony Wood, who observed, 'He was first a Churchman, then a Presbyterian, afterwards an Independent, an Anabaptist, and at length almost a complete Jew and what not.'[52] It was that progression, which occurred gradually but with increasing

---

[49] Bampfield's mother, formerly Elizabeth Drake of Buckland Monachorum, Devon, was daughter of Thomas Drake, Sir Francis Drake's brother.

[50] Bampfield, *A Name*, 2; *DNB*; W. Densham and J. Ogle, *The Story of the Congregational Churches of Dorset* (Bournemouth, 1899), 245. *Reports and Transactions of the Devonshire Association*, 67 (1935), 320.

[51] Densham and Ogle, *Congregational Churches*, 245–6; Mellone, *JQR* 10: 426. See also Crosby, i. 363–9. Ivimey described him as 'a zealous loyalist [Royalist] and a zealous conformist' who conformed longer than any other minister in Dorset, *History*, ii. 476–7.   [52] *Athenae Oxonienses*, ii (1691), 571.

momentum between 1650 or thereabouts, while he was still at Rampisham, and the mid-1660s which led him and many others in Dorchester, Sherborne, and the surrounding area to the Saturday Sabbath.

After his ejection from Sherborne in 1662, Bampfield began to preach in his own house, but within a month was arrested and imprisoned briefly before being released with a caution. In 1663, while preaching at a Nonconformist meeting in Shaftesbury, he was again arrested and committed to Dorchester gaol, where he remained for almost nine years until released by special warrant from Lord Arlington to the high sheriff of Dorset in May 1672.[53] Bampfield himself tells us that it was during this long imprisonment that he first began to observe the seventh day, in 1665, although there is some evidence that he had been convinced on the matter as early as 1662-3. Bampfield also resolves the question of the existence of a Seventh-day congregation in Dorchester gaol during these years, stating that five or six others were also convinced, and observed the seventh day with him.[54] Proof is lacking for the assertion that a separate Seventh-day congregation had existed in Dorchester since the mid-1650s, but it is not impossible, and would have provided a more logical source for the Dorchester Seventh-day people who were still in evidence in 1690. Most of Bampfield's fellow-prisoners are likely to have come from well beyond Dorchester itself and would have left the town with their convictions when released. It is certain that at least one of Bampfield's fellow Sabbatarians in gaol was from the Sherborne district.[55]

It was while still in prison that Bampfield first wrote in favour of the seventh day in an exchange with William Benn, the ejected minister of All Saints, Dorchester, who published Bampfield's views, together with his own reply, in 1672 under the title, *The Judgment of Mr. Francis Bampfield . . . for the Observation of the Jewish or*

---

[53] Densham and Ogle, *Congregational Churches*, 228, 247; Ivimey, *History*, ii. 477-8; *CSPD* 1671-2, 597.

[54] Bampfield, *A Name*, 7, 12; Densham and Ogle, *Congregational Churches*, 251; see also, G.F. Nuttall (ed.), *Letters of John Pinney 1679-1699* (Oxford, 1939), 2, 3 for a letter from Isaac Clifford to Pinney, *c.*1666, from Dorchester gaol confirming Bampfield's Sabbatarianism. It was here also that Bampfield became convinced of believer's baptism, later baptizing himself in the river at Salisbury, *A Name*, 14. It is unlikely, therefore, that Bampfield was minister of the Dorchester Baptist church in 1662, as in D. Jackman, *300 Years of Baptist Witness in Dorchester, 1645-1945* (Dorchester, 1945), 4, 16. [55] *SO* 1: 85, 93; *CSPD* 1671-2, 597.

Seventh Day Sabbath. Benn may have wished to counter a growing interest in the seventh day in Dorchester and Dorset, although by the time Bampfield was released later that year observance of the Saturday Sabbath was well established in several Dorset localities.[56] The publication by Benn of Bampfield's arguments may have done more to advance his cause than contain it, particularly in an area which seems to have been predisposed to Nonconformity and the plain preaching of the Bible. In that context, Bampfield's reasons for keeping the seventh day would have sounded reasonable enough: the sufficiency of Scripture for all doctrine, the completeness of the Ten Commandments as a rule for daily living, the necessity for a Sabbath, or day of rest, the seventh day as the only day to be observed by divine command, and the example of Christ in keeping the seventh day. This latter point was the crowning argument to Bampfield for a Christian observance of the seventh day, since every true believer was to be conformed to Christ 'in all the acts of his Obedience'.[57]

Shortly after his release from prison in May 1672, Bampfield was issued with a general licence to preach and conduct services in any place licensed for Nonconformist worship.[58] It was a *carte blanche* given to relatively few Nonconformists, and Bampfield made the most of it in consolidating an already thriving Seventh-day work in Sherborne before he left for London in 1673. The house of Elizabeth Cooth was licensed for unspecified Nonconformist worship in 1672, and had in all probability been used as the venue for unauthorized conventicles for some time previously. In 1673 a congregation was reported as meeting there attended by 'several persons rebaptized by Francis Bampfield', who was also named as the preacher.[59] Elizabeth Cooth had been reported regularly from 1666

---

[56] Benn published 'for the satisfaction of divers friends in the West of England', title-page. The work was reprinted in 1677. According to Benn, Bampfield's acceptance of the Saturday Sabbath was 'the discourse of many, the wonder of not a few, and the grief of some'. Benn's allusion to the Seventh-day people as 'the Jewish sect' (sig. A2ʳ), probably indicates a Sabbatarian congregation in Dorchester.

[57] Benn, *The Judgment of Mr Francis Bampfield*, fos. 3–7. The Dorset–Wiltshire area may also have been predisposed to Nonconformity and a literal interpretation of the Bible from Lollard activity. Professor Claire Cross cites the case of William Ramsbury, who claimed to have visited more than twenty towns and villages in Dorset and Wiltshire on the premiss that it was 'of greater merit for priests to go through the countryside with a Bible under their arm, preaching to the people, than to say matins, or celebrate masses'; Cross, *Church and People*, 21.

[58] *OR* i. 523; iii: 263; *CSPD* May–Sept. 1672, 292.　　　　[59] *OR* i. 573; WRO, D5/28.

onwards, together with many other Sherborne parishioners, for being absent from church and for failing to receive the sacrament. It cannot be assumed that all who were named in these presentments were Sabbatarians, although some clearly were. Christopher Sport was first presented in 1668 for not paying his church rates and 'for saying he would not conforme to Sunday worship'. Gyles Richmond, Thomas Burroughes, and Mary Sterne were listed in 1671 as 'Sabbatarians . . . keeping the Jewish Sabbath', and Joshua Brooke from nearby Castleton was presented in 1668 'for not coming to church, denying the Lord's day, and keeping the Jewish Sabbath'.[60] This particular piece of information is rather confusing, since the State Papers record that Brooke had been imprisoned with Bampfield at Dorchester between 1663 and 1672. Brooke's presentment in 1668 may have been 'in absentia', so to speak, reflecting a known or reputed Sabbatarian practice prior to his imprisonment. From 1673 he was presented with monotonous regularity for a variety of typical Nonconformist 'offences', including non-attendance, living with his 'reputed wife . . . without lawful marriage', and for allowing his family and servants to follow 'their bodily and ordinary labours in trade' on the Lord's day. This is the picture of a thoroughgoing Sabbatarian Nonconformist, and it is not surprising that in 1684 he was finally noted as excommunicate.[61]

The case of Ann Stroud of Holnest is further evidence of the spread of Seventh-day views into the country areas around Sherborne. It was reported in 1670, 'she doth keep Saturday for her Sabbath, and doth sell her wares upon Sundays and doth not come to Divine Service nor receive the Sacrament'. Ann, 'a reputed Jew', was also presented variously by the Holnest churchwardens over the next fifteen years as a 'Nonconformist' and 'Sabbatarian' working on the Lord's day, and together with her husband William, refusing to have their children baptized 'by a lawful minister'.[62] The Strouds, of course, would have recognized the legitimacy of a Nonconformist ministry, in the same way that Joshua Brooke and his wife would have been legally married, in their eyes, according to

[60] WRO, D5/18, 19, 28, 44.
[61] WRO, D5/28; *CSPD*, 1671–2, 597, where it was stated that Francis Bampfield, 'clerk', John Leach, 'tanner', and Joshua Brooke had been convicted 'almost nine years since' on a charge of 'unlawful assembly in Shaftesbury'.
[62] WRO, D5/18, 28.

Nonconformist practice.[63] When the requirements for reporting on the religious practices of Nonconformists were relaxed, a major source of information on Sabbatarian activity in the mid- to late seventeenth century disappeared, and nothing further is heard of either Joshua Brooke or Ann Stroud.

As far as Sherborne is concerned, it continued as a centre of Sabbatarian activity well into the eighteenth century. In 1694, Mary Parmiter (or Parminter) was recommended to Pinners' Hall by the 'church of Baptised persons keeping the Seventh-day Sabbath in and about Sherborne in Dorsetshire'. Evidently the Sherborne congregation was recognized as extending beyond the town itself, although in 1690 it did not appear to have any precedence over Dorchester, Beaminster, or Sturminster Newton.[64] The Sabbatarians at Sturminster remain difficult to identify, probably on account of the fire which destroyed a large part of the diocesan records at Blandford in 1731. The work in Dorset seems to have coalesced gradually around Sherborne, for this was one of the churches specified in 1706 to receive help from the Joseph Davis charity, suggesting that a reasonably strong cause existed there at that time. The last mention of the Sabbatarian believers in Dorset in encouraging. Mill Yard received a letter in 1717 'from the Sabbath-keeping church in Dorsetshire' requesting John Savage to visit them that summer to baptize 'several persons' and 'put them into some gospel order' by the ordination of local elders who would be capable of administering 'the ordinances . . . for time to come'.[65] On that evidence alone, it may be concluded that some years of life yet remained for the Seventh-day Men in Dorset.

BEAMINSTER

Beaminster was known as a seat of dissent and sectarian activity from early in the seventeenth century. A hint of what was to come was offered in 1606 when the churchwardens reported that the

---

[63] How far Brooke represented Nonconformist practice in 'burying a child in his garden contrary to law and decency', is another matter (WRO, D5/28), although the practice was not unknown among Quakers, see e.g. HWRO, 807/2289/20, where John and Elizabeth Allibon were presented at Treddington, Worcs., for using their garden as a burial ground.

[64] PHCB 34; *BQ* 14: 165.   [65] MYM 226.

communion table in the parish church was not placed in the chancel, but stood 'in the midde allie of our church to the good liking of all the parishioners'.[66] In 1634 a churchwarden, John Hillary, reported during the archiepiscopal visitation of William Laud, that 'one Thomas Conway of Beaminster doth keep, and to his house doth frequent private congregations tending to Conventicles'.[67] One record says that during the reign of Charles I all the religious sects which characterized that age were represented in Beaminster.[68] If true, this would mean that Sabbatarians, or even Traskites, were known there as early as at any place in the country. The Strode family was prominent in Beaminster from early in the seventeenth century through Sir John Strode,[69] and Cattistock, home of Sir Richard Strode who had employed John Traske in the late 1620s or early 1630s and who had taken Traske to preach in neighbouring localities, was not far away. The Axminster–Lyme Regis area, where Traske had been known for preaching unorthodox doctrine prior to going to London in 1615, was nearby to the south-west.[70] In 1634, Hillary had also charged the curate, Thomas Spratt, with allowing an unlicensed minister to preach,[71] and Joseph Crabb, a later incumbent at Beaminster, was accused of having 'poisoned' his parishioners with 'factious & Schismatical Sermons & discourses'.[72] All this was fertile soil in which sectarian seeds of every sort would easily grow, and although Crabb was ejected following the Restoration,[73] Beaminster by then had been ready for thoroughgoing Nonconformity for some time.

All the licences issued in 1672 in respect of Beaminster, either to individuals or for places of worship, were designated as Presbyterian. While it might be too much to expect a licence with a Sabbatarian designation, given Beaminster's previous history Baptists or Anabaptists might well have been represented as they were at several other locations in the county. The house of Lancelot Cox

---

[66] WRO, Dean of Sarum, churchwarden's presentments, 1606–8, cited in M. Eedle, *A History of Beaminster* (1984), 60.　　　　　[67] Ibid. 61.

[68] R. Hine, *The History of Beaminster* (Taunton, 1914), 88.

[69] Eedle, *History of Beaminster*, 62.　　　[70] Cf. above, 50.

[71] WRO, Dean of Sarum, churchwarden's presentments, 1634, cited in Eedle, *History of Beaminster*, 61.

[72] Cited in R.L. Greaves, *Deliver us from Evil: The Radical Underground in Britain, 1660–1663* (New York, 1986), 98.

[73] Crabb, vicar of Netherbury with Beaminster, and ejected 1661, was installed vicar of Axminster, Devon, 1662 but was regarded as having Nonconformist sympathies, *CR* 139–40.

was accordingly licensed in 1672 as a Presbyterian meeting-place, as also was the house of John Locke, as well as the room beneath the Market House.[74] Whether or not all three locations in fact were Presbyterian meeting-places is an open question, since the official descriptions may not have been entirely accurate in any case.[75] In 1669, three years before the Declaration of Indulgence, a conventicle of about a hundred had been reported at Cox's house including 'people unknown, from London and places distant'.[76] When Sabbatarianism did eventually come into the open at about this time, there were hints of connections with earlier Sabbatarians elsewhere. The house in East Street which belonged to Cox was later used by Thomas Hoare, an Independent minister, and his wife. A Thomas Hoare and his wife had been presented at Salisbury in 1634 for non-attendance at the time of James Ockford's adoption of Baptist, and perhaps Sabbatarian, views.[77] Joseph Newman, who was known at Beaminster from 1679 and who, according to the Llanwenarth record, was the leader of Dorset Sabbatarians in 1690, may have been related to a Dorset or Wiltshire Anabaptist family of that name. A 'Mr. Newman' had been presented for non-attendance in Salisbury at the same time as Thomas Hoare, James Ockford, and others.[78] James Daniel, who was to survive as the most influential Sabbatarian in Beaminster, had been mentioned in the diocesan reports for Sherborne in 1670, again as a non-attender.[79] The house of one Thomas Ball was licensed for Anabaptist meetings at Tarrant Keynston in 1672, and William Ball had been presented at Salisbury, again with Thomas Hoare and Mr Newman, for absenting themselves from their parish church and not receiving 'the Holy Sacrament of the Lord's Supper'.[80] Individually the links are tenuous, but collectively they suggest the possibility that Sabbatarianism may have been known at Beaminster before it was first revealed in the official records of 1668.

In that year James Daniell, jun., attorney, was presented to the Dean as an absentee from worship in the parish church, with a note that almost appears as a justification, 'But [he] doth keep Saturday

---

[74] *OR* ii. 1135.

[75] According to Turner, Francis Bampfield was reported as a Presbyterian in 1672: *OR* ii. 1132.

[76] Cited in Eedle, *History of Beaminster*, 61.   [77] Ibid. 62; WRO, D4/10.

[78] *BQ* 14: 165; WRO, D5/28; D4/10.   [79] WRO, D5/28.

[80] WRO, D4/10; *OR* ii. 1143 where Bull is an alternative for Ball.

the Jewish Sabbath.'[81] Daniel, as Newman, was a well-known
Beaminster family name of long-standing Nonconformist convictions,
and James, by the time his name begins to appear in the ecclesiastical records, was the senior surviving family representative in the
town.[82] He was presented again, with others, in 1674, 1679, 1682,
1684, and finally in 1685 when he was described as an 'excommunicate person'. In 1679 he was presented with Joseph Newman,
and in 1684 with John Daniel and James Daniel, jun., and in 1686
with his wife, Susannah.[83] During these years many others were
presented with him, but none of them, including any of his family,
was specifically designated as Sabbatarian, although it is probable
that some of them at least shared his Seventh-day views. Daniel
died in 1711 at the age of 100, and according to his wish, was
buried at a spot where he believed he had been preserved from
death by divine providence some years before. During the
Monmouth rebellion he was reported to have fled from Sedgemoor
and hidden under some straw at his farm, where the pursuing
soldiers failed to discover him. It was there that he was buried, as
were a number of his descendants.[84] How many of them were
Sabbatarians is unknown, but if, as is probable, James Daniel remained a Sabbatarian to his death, he at least ensured the survival
of Seventh-day views in Beaminster until 1711.

Other evidence suggests that, in fact, early eighteenth-century
Sabbatarianism in Beaminster was stronger than that. In 1710 the
Beaminster believers had written to Mill Yard querying the propri-
ety of the ordinances being administered by someone from without
the immediate congregation. Mill Yard had replied to the effect that
'a private brother approved by the generality of the congregation
may administer ordinances',[85] and presumably this is what occurred
for the next few years in the absence of a duly ordained elder. In
1727, as we have already seen, John Savage was authorized by Mill
Yard to visit the Seventh-day churches in Dorset in order to baptize
'several persons', ordain local elders, and 'administer the ordinances'.[86] It may be assumed that Beaminster was included, for the
Sabbatarian cause appears to have continued here for some time
yet. In 1731 Thomas Bousher of Beaminster was named as one
of many beneficiaries from the will of Joseph Davis, jun., who

---

[81] WRO, D5/18.   [82] Eedle, *History of Beaminster*, 62–3.
[83] WRO, D5/18, 28.   [84] Eedle, *History of Beaminster*, 65.
[85] MYM 189.   [86] Ibid. 226.

bequeathed generous sums to several known Sabbatarians, many of them ministers of Seventh-day congregations extant at the time.[87] The tradition that the Seventh-day church in Beaminster became extinct *c*.1710 may need revising.

EXETER, TIVERTON, AND PLYMOUTH

John Traske's early career in Devon has already been alluded to, particularly the concern it caused the Bishop of Exeter, William Cotton, in 1616, who by then was aware of Traske's part in the dissemination of doctrinal views which the Bishop regarded as false. Traske was reported to have preached widely in Devon before going to London *c*.1615, and this was probably the period of his 'aboad with Maister Drake' and the time at which he earned the reputation for preaching 'erroneous fancies', chiefly in the eastern part of the diocese.[88]

As early as 1600 Cotton had reported a high level of sectarian activity in the city of Exeter itself, with as many as twenty different 'factions' and 'many conventicles in gardens and fields'. At one of these meetings it had been intended to celebrate 'a passover', but the intervention of the authorities had ensured that it did not take place.[89] It may, or may not, be significant that Traske's later London Sabbatarianism included the observance of the Passover as well as other elements of an almost complete retrogression to Judaism.[90] Traske returned for a time to the West Country after his well-publicized excursion into Judaizing Sabbatarianism in London, and although he had 'recanted' by then, his earlier 'erroneous opinions' were known to Sir Richard Strode, who employed him as chaplain,[91]

---

[87] Black (ed.) *Last Legacy*, 72. Other beneficiaries, besides John Sutten, noted earlier, included Joseph Stennett II 'of Exeter', Edmund Townsend 'of Mill Yard', Philip Jones 'of Cheltenham', John Ridley 'late of Plymouth', and Daniel Wright 'of Colchester'. Stennett's congregation was not Seventh-day. Townsend was by this time of Pinners' Hall, although he retained connections with Mill Yard, Ridley was minister of the Seventh-day church in Woodbridge, Suffolk and Jones of the Ashchurch–Natton congregation, Gloucestershire. In 1742 a Thomas Bosher resigned from Milborne Port where he had been minister of the Baptist church since at least 1715: *TBHS* 2: 105, *BQ* 3: 258. Bosher, a General Baptist, was known at Loughwood in 1756 as an advocate of Arian and Unitarian views, *TBHS* 4: 141. The theological link between Bosher and Mill Yard is strong, and Bousher and Bosher may well be the same.   [88] On Traske's early activities in Devon, see above, 50–1.
[89] *HMC* Salisbury, x. 451.   [90] Phillips, *TJHSE* 15: 65.
[91] PRO, SP 16/261, fos. 55ᵛ, 56ʳ, cited in White, *TCHS* 20/7: 232.

as presumably they were also to many other people. One could hardly have been a figure of some recent notoriety, albeit briefly, to say nothing of carrying a brandmark in the forehead, without attracting some attention, and Traske's presence in the Strode household in the late 1620s or early 1630s must have reminded many of his earlier views, if nothing more. Beyond that, Strode's custom of taking Traske 'into the country to preach in other places'[92] would have revived old memories for some and provided food for thought for others. The development of Seventh-day Sabbatarianism in east Devon and west Dorset cannot be divorced entirely from any link with one of its first and best-known advocates. The broader Puritan Sabbatarianism of the age also provided a congenial climate for the emergence of Saturday Sabbatarianism, and the complaint of an Anglican official from Exeter, in 1618, against the Puritans' 'too strict observance of Sabbath' may not be without its significance.[93]

The eventual appearance of a Seventh-day group in Exeter in the 1650s may, however, have been due to other influences altogether. A General Baptist church had existed in Tiverton from early in the seventeenth century, with connections with Salisbury and Amsterdam. Tiverton was then the centre of the wool trade in the west of England, and in 1612 had a population of approximately 8,000, which included a number of Flemish weavers from the Netherlands who had been encouraged as immigrants since the later years of Elizabeth's reign. Many of these were Anabaptists, and some of the early correspondence between Tiverton and the other early English Baptist congregations and the mother church in Amsterdam is preserved in that church's archives.[94] By 1628, Anabaptists with very English names were being fined for absenting themselves from the parish church, and by the late 1630s 'advocates of Seventh-day Baptist and Fifth Monarchy views' had appeared in Tiverton as well as Salisbury.[95] While Whitley's thesis that the Seventh-day movement emerged as disillusioned Fifth Monarchists adopted more

---

[92] Ibid.   [93] *CSPD* 1611–18, 526.

[94] White, *English Baptists*, 28–9; C. Pattenden, *Tiverton Baptist Church* (n.d.), 3. See also Whitley, *British Baptists*, 53–4.

[95] 'Salisbury and Tiverton about 1630', *TBHS* 3: 3; *VCH* Wilts., iii. 101. It is worth noting that Stephen Coven, ejected in 1660 from Sampford Peverell, six miles from Tiverton, and in 1665 called 'a wandering Seditious Seminary', should turn up in 1672 licensed as an Independent in the Watlington–Warborough area of Oxfordshire, a centre of Sabbatarian activity; M. Clapinson (ed.), *Bishop Fell and Nonconformity*, Oxfordshire Record Society 52 (Oxford, 1980), 7, 52.

pacifist Seventh-day opinions does not stand up to close investigation,[96] it is clear none the less that in some areas Fifth Monarchists were also Seventh-day Men. The Tiverton people could be early examples of this relationship. Already in 1631 a Tiverton Baptist, James Toppe, had voiced strong millenarian views, and there is ample evidence that the Fifth Monarchy Men were well established in Tiverton by the middle of the century.[97]

It may, then, have been this Fifth Monarchy connection which precipitated the first appearance of Saturday Sabbatarianism in Exeter. Devon was an important *locus* for Fifth Monarchy activity in the 1650s and by 1653 expressions of faith in the dawning fifth kingdom were coming from a congregation in Exeter. This church was said to consist mainly of weavers and worsted-combers, and as such would have enjoyed a practical relationship with Tiverton, as well as a common hope.[98] Henry Jessey had been expressing Fifth Monarchy views in London since 1647, and by the early 1650s was openly engaged in moderate Fifth Monarchist activity.[99] Naturally enough, he included Exeter when in 1655 he visited other Baptist or Independent congregations in the west and south-west, including Lyme Regis, Honiton, and Plymouth. As has already been pointed out, this tour came after he had adopted Seventh-day views himself. The Lyme–Axminster–Honiton area had been worked much earlier by Traske, and Plymouth was to reveal unexpectedly late traces of an interest in the seventh day. The identification of Fifth Monarchy Men with Seventh-day Men in this area seems reasonably well grounded.[100]

---

[96] Whitley, 'A Century of Sabbath Doctrine', 112 and *British Baptists*, 86. Cf. E.A. Payne, 'More about the Sabbatarian Baptists', *BQ* 14: 161–6; *FMM* 224. Any theological transformation that took place is more likely to have been from a militant Fifth Monarchism to a quieter millenarianism. Capp's point that Seventh-day views in many cases were held in addition to Fifth Monarchist beliefs is well made. Cf. G.F. Nuttall's observation that both Fifth Monarchist and Seventh-day views arose from 'a close attention to Scripture', in a review of Capp's book in *Journal of Theological Studies*, 24 (1973), 312.

[97] James Toppe, 'Christs Monarchicall and personall Reigne upon Earth over all the Kingdoms of this world', BL, Sloane MS 63; *FMM* 125, 132. On Toppe, see also W.H. Burgess, 'James Toppe and the Tiverton Anabaptists', *TBHS* 3 (1912–13), 193–211.

[98] *FMM* 76, 67, 85.   [99] Ibid. 22, 39, 59, 81.

[100] Allan Brockett notes that Exeter Baptists, who met in Deanery Hall between 1649 and 1654, were at first tinged with Fifth Monarchist doctrine. He also notes 'Sabbatarian Baptists' as a seventeenth-century sect of some significance, apparently without being aware of the presence of Seventh-day views in Exeter: Allan Brockett, *Nonconformity in Exeter, 1650–1875* (Manchester, 1962), 6, 14–15.

Whatever its origins, and regardless of how long the seeds had lain dormant or partially germinated, Seventh-day observance came into the open in Exeter in 1651 with the appearance of a functioning congregation. In October a report was published in London confirming that 'several' citizens of Exeter 'openly profess the Jewish opinion, and keep Saturday Sabbath', working normally on the Lord's day without interference from the authorities.[101] This may not have been completely accurate, since at about the same time another report reached London stating that the Mayor of Exeter, with a view to prosecution, had examined a man for working on the Lord's day, but had been informed that Saturday was the man's Sabbath, 'which day according to the religion of the Jews' he had declared he would always observe. The accused was spared from the penalty required by Act of Parliament for non-observance of the Lord's day by the payment of a forfeit by 'some that were of the Jewish opinion'.[102] Presumably some of his brothers in the faith had come to the rescue.

A Fifth Monarchy emphasis appears to have been sustained here throughout the 1650s, and may even have been the reason for John Belcher's visit to Devon in 1661. Belcher, who had adopted the seventh day by 1660, was regarded in official circles by the following year as one of the leading itinerant Fifth Monarchy preachers, travelling around the country in an attempt to sustain the Fifth Monarchist cause.[103] Although he is recorded only in general terms to have visited Devon, it would have been strange had he not included Exeter. Long after he had abandoned aggressive Fifth Monarchy doctrine Belcher was regarded as 'a public messenger to all churches keeping the Seventh-day Sabbath',[104] an assignment which again may have taken him to the West Country, even though there are no known records revealing that the Saturday Sabbath still persisted in Exeter in 1687, the year in which Belcher visited the Sabbatarian churches.

However, before concluding that all interest here in the seventh day was completely dead before the end of the seventeenth century,

---

[101] W. Birchley, *The Christian Moderator* (1652), 21, citing 'a weekly pamphlet', dated 6 Oct. 1651.   [102] *Diary*, 3 Oct. 1651.

[103] *BDBR* i. 52–3; *FMM* 207; Clark, *The Lying-Wonders*, 5.

[104] In 1687 Pinners' Hall wrote to Edward Stennett's church in Wallingford and Thomas Hitchman's church in Gloucestershire, requesting them both to urge Belcher to include Pinners' Hall in part of his general ministry as 'public messenger', PHCB 11–12.

mention must be made of Joseph Stennett II. In 1721 Stennett accepted a call to minister to the South Street Particular Baptist church in Exeter, after having previously declined an invitation to Mill Yard in London.[105] Stennett at this time was in fellowship with Leominster, although he had lived at Abergavenny before that, having married a daughter of Nathaniel Morgan of Usk.[106] Stennett remained loyal to the Seventh-day convictions of his father and grandfather throughout his life, observing the Saturday Sabbath at home with his family even after leaving Exeter in 1737 to become the minister of the influential church at Little Wild Street in London.[107] Morgan was also a Seventh-day Man, and Seventh-day convictions had persisted at both Leominster and Abergavenny and in neighbouring areas throughout the latter part of the seventeenth century, and perhaps even longer.[108] Stennett thus came to Exeter having maintained an unbroken contact with the Seventh-day movement from birth, and having preached at Leominster and Abergavenny at the beginning of his ministry.[109] Given his own predisposition to Seventh-day observance it is not unreasonable to assume that he might have been attracted to Exeter by the prospect of being able to remain in touch with both First-day and Seventh-day believers as he had at Leominster and Abergavenny, and as his

---

[105] Joseph Stennett II (1692–1758) is mentioned briefly in the *DNB*. The date of his call to Exeter has been variously given as 1718, 1719, 1720, and 1721. The last date seems to be correct from two letters from Exeter to Leominster, the first in Mar. 1721 (NLW MS 11095E), the second dated July and signed by nineteen members of the Exeter congregation, Burnet Morris Index, s.v. Stennett, Westcountry Studies Library, Exeter. One of the signatories is W. Newman, the only name to correspond with that of any known West Country Sabbatarian.

[106] Joshua Thomas, BBC, MS G 98a(1), 120.

[107] Crosby, *History*, iv. 322; *BQ* 5: 85. But not as minister of a Seventh-day church in Little Wild Street, as *BQ* 8: 302. He was assisted and later succeeded at Little Wild Street by his son Samuel (1727–95). Both men were eminent among Baptists and in wider circles. Joseph was known personally to Edmund Gibson, Bishop of London, and was said to be highly regarded by George III. He was one of the founders of SPCK. Samuel, 'a man of broad views and considerable public influence' (*DNB*), was also a Sabbatarian by conviction and private practice: Wilson, *Dissenting Churches*, ii. 607.

[108] *TBHS* 6: 176. On Leominster and the Abergavenny–Llanwenarth district, see below, Ch. 8, *passim*.

[109] A Stennett is said to have preached at Abergavenny about 1706 (*BQ* 14: 164), but this could hardly have been Joseph II. Joshua Thomas suggested that Joseph II began to preach at Abergavenny *c.*1714, and that he may have been assistant to Thomas Holder at Leominster. The March 1721 letter from Exeter to Leominster requested Holder's assistance at Stennett's ordination, BBC, MS G 98a(1), 120; NLW, MS 11095E.

father had done while minister of Pinners' Hall. Although there is
nothing to suggest that Exeter South Street was anything but First-
day, other Baptist congregations in the eighteenth century admitted
Seventh-day believers to fellowship,[110] besides which Seventh-day
congregations outside of London had generally kept a low profile,
maintaining a small and silent witness unknown to the authorities
and to most of the local populace. The possibility of a lingering
Seventh-day interest in Exeter cannot therefore be dismissed.

Perhaps Stennett's greatest contribution to Baptist life in the West
was his long-standing involvement with the revived Western Association, particularly in its stance against Arianism and Arminianism
in the 1720s and 1730s, and its fundamental commitment 'to ensure
the promotion of biblical truth'.[111] There may be a hint of an accommodation of Sabbatarian views in the life of the Association at
this period, perhaps in deference to Stennett's own convictions.
The Association was reformed in 1732 on the understanding that
associating churches subscribed to the 1689 Confession of Faith.[112]
It was, however, noted that 'they who differ from the Confession of
Faith with respect to the time in which the Sabbath is to be observed are not to be understood by their subscription to contradict
their particular judgement in this matter'.[113] A similar latitudinarian
position will be noted later on the part of the Northamptonshire
Association in 1786.[114] During these years Stennett preached at
meetings of the Association and served as its Moderator, and hence
came into contact regularly with the messengers of other churches
in the Association. Thus he could be expected to have been aware
of any interest in the seventh day at Plymouth, even though there
is no evidence of a distinct Seventh-day congregation having been
gathered there. In 1731 John Ridley, who had recently accepted a
call to the Woodbridge Seventh-day church in Suffolk, via Pinners'
Hall, was described as 'late of Plymouth', and in 1748 his daughter

[110] e.g. Horsley and Hillesley in Gloucestershire, see below, Ch. 7.

[111] Brown, *English Baptists*, 85–6; A. Gabb, *A History of Baptist Beginnings, with
an Account of the Rise of the Baptist Witness in Exeter and the Founding of the
South Street Church* (Exeter, 1954), 35.

[112] The 1689 General Assembly of Particular Baptists had thoroughly discussed
the Sabbath issue, deciding that it was the 'duty' of all Christians and churches
'religiously to observe the Lord's day, or first day of the week'. Ivimey gives the
reasons for this decision, *History*, i. 479–99.

[113] R. Hayden, 'The Particular Baptist Confession 1689 and Baptists Today', *BQ* 32:
406, citing Caleb Evans's MS 'Records of the Western Association'.

[114] See Ch. 10 n. 6.

married Benjamin Stennett, minister of the Seventh-day people at Ingham and Joseph Stennett's brother.[115] Ridley was a thoroughly convinced Sabbatarian, and is hardly likely to have adopted such views in order merely to accept the Woodbridge invitation. The inference is that he followed his Sabbatarian convictions at Plymouth before being called to Suffolk. In 1761 Pinners' Hall wrote to the Baptist church in Plymouth enquiring after the welfare of a Mr Remlatt who had been dismissed from them to the West Country,[116] and in the following year Peter Rendall was admitted to full fellowship at Mill Yard from Plymouth 'having been a transient member . . . for about a twelve month'.[117]

While the evidence is patchy, what can be said with some certainty is that a Seventh-day congregation worshipped in Exeter in the mid-seventeenth century, and that Seventh-day views may have continued there, and may have been present in Plymouth and in other parts of Devon until the middle of the next century.[118] The Saturday Sabbath was also observed at Taunton, midway between Exeter and Dunkerton, and near enough to Sherborne to suggest that the influence of the Bampfield family and their followers may have extended into Somerset from Dorset and East Devon.[119]

DUNKERTON

Dunkerton's chief claim for attention as a focus of Sabbatarian activity in the mid- to late seventeenth century is its connection with the

---

[115] Black (ed.), *Last Legacy*, 72; *SO* 2: 44. A.J. Klaiber, *The Story of the Suffolk Baptists* (1931), 33–4. Ridley had been ordained at Plymouth in 1726, Stennett and Isaac Hann officiating, *SO* 2: 44.

[116] PHCB 127.   [117] MYM 287.

[118] Joseph Alsop, who came to Bristol Academy *c.*1771 from the Natton Seventh-day church and went to Prescott, Devon, in 1773, may privately have maintained Sabbatarian views. He was one of three signatories to the letter of dismission for William Hitchman from Natton to Hillesley in 1762; Hillesley church book, 2, GRO, D2869. The Alsop family continued to be represented at Natton during this period and later. In 1801, Ann Alsop replied to an attack on the Seventh-day interpretation of the fourth commandment by Thomas Edmonds of Upton, with *Remarks on the Rev. T. Edmond's pamphlet . . . and an attempt to vindicate their conduct who observe the Seventh-day Sabbath . . .* (1801). It is not impossible that Joseph Alsop followed the example of Joseph Stennett II in ministering to a First-day congregation while observing the seventh day privately, *BQ* 5: 266; *SDBEA* 1: 63. Thomas Hiller and William Hitchman, both from Natton, also ministered to First-day congregations, see Ch. 7.

[119] A member was transferred from Taunton to Pinners' Hall in 1687, PHCB 111. Henry Jessey had visited Taunton in 1655.

Bampfield family, and in particular with Thomas Bampfield, who settled there c.1660 after a distinguished political career in London and Devon.[120] Thomas was a younger brother of Francis Bampfield and, according to his own testimony, had adopted the Saturday Sabbath by 1667.[121] Francis had visited Dunkerton and preached there between his ejection from Sherborne in 1662 and his imprisonment at Dorchester in the following year, probably late in 1662.[122] Whitley states that both Francis and Thomas exerted an influence for the seventh day 'near Bath' from 1660 onwards, although since Francis moved to London shortly after his release from prison, the influence of Thomas is likely to have been the greater. He is said to have sheltered various ejected ministers at Dunkerton, and encouraged conventicles.[123] Humphrey Philips, who had been assistant to Francis at Sherborne and ejected with him in 1662 for refusing to conform, was named as the principal teacher at a conventicle of 300 which was reported in 1669 as meeting in William Clement's 'sheep house' in Dunkerton.[124] Apart from this early connection with Sherborne, and a visit to Dorchester by Thomas Bampfield in 1671,[125] Dunkerton appears to have remained isolated from the mainstream of the Seventh-day movement, and probably would not have merited more than passing comment were it not for Bampfield's personal standing and his later contribution to the Seventh-day literature.

Thomas, the youngest son of Sir John Bampfylde of Poltimore, near Exeter, had been trained as a lawyer, and admitted to the Middle Temple in 1642. He soon rose to prominence in his home town of Exeter, and was elected Member of Parliament for the Exeter constituency in the four successive Parliaments of 1654, 1656, 1658, and 1660. In 1656 he was appointed Recorder of Exeter and a commissioner for taxes in Devon. Bampfield had been present at Cromwell's installation, and had risen to what under other circumstances might have been regarded as one of the most prominent

---

[120] On the Bampfield family, see *DNB*.

[121] Thomas Bampfield, *A Reply to Doctor Wallis, his Discourse Concerning the Christian Sabbath* (1693), 18.

[122] Densham and Ogle, *Congregational Churches*, 248.

[123] Whitley, 'Men of the Seventh Day', 9/4; 8/2.

[124] Densham and Ogle, *Congregational Churches*, 247; *OR* i. 11. Philips was chaplain to Thomas Bampfield at Dunkerton at about this time, but Calamy indicates that their relationship cooled over the Sabbath issue, *CR* 388. Subsequently Philips preached widely in Somerset and Wiltshire, before being licensed in 1672 as a Presbyterian for his own house at Priston, Somerset, as well as for Dunkerton and other places, *OR* ii. 1080–2.   [125] *CSPD* 1671, 362.

positions in the land, Speaker of the House of Commons.[126] But in Richard Cromwell's short-lived Parliament between January and April 1659 neither members nor Speaker had much opportunity to shine. Bampfield's legal judgement, and perhaps also his religious interests, were recognized in 1656 when he was appointed to chair the Parliamentary committee which investigated the case of the Quaker James Nayler, after his pseudo-Messianic entry into Bristol, riding on an ass.[127] Although Bampfield's career came to an abrupt end with the Restoration he remained highly respected in his former constituency, and in 1687, somewhat surprisingly, was appointed a member of the Presbyterian Committee of Thirteen in Exeter, and in 1688 Deputy-Lieutenant of Devon.[128] All in all, the Sabbatarians could claim few men who had risen as high as Thomas Bampfield.

Dunkerton remained the Bampfield family seat for several generations, and it is likely that Thomas entered the Sabbatarian debate from there in 1692 with a work whose title was reminiscent of his brother's theology. Bampfield's *An Enquiry Whether the Lord Jesus Christ made the World, and be Jehovah, and gave the Moral Law? And Whether the Fourth Command be Repealed or Altered?* (1692) drew three replies, one of which came from the learned mathematician and theologian John Wallis. His *A Defence of the Christian Sabbath* (1692) was a lucid, erudite, and well-reasoned attack on the Seventh-day position. Bampfield's *A Reply to Doctor Wallis* (1693) drew from Wallis the second part of his *Defence* (1694), but this well-informed and important exchange was terminated by Bampfield's death in 1693. Isaac Marlow joined in with *A Tract on the Sabbath Day* (1694), a defence of the older Puritan Sunday Sabbath directed to 'Jewish Saturday-Sabbatharians and others',[129] and evidence

---

[126] *DNB*; Densham and Ogle, *Congregational Churches*, 245.

[127] Whitley, 'Men of the Seventh Day', 9/2. On the Nayler episode and its implications, see H. Barbour, *The Quakers in Puritan England* (1964), 62–4; I. Roots, *The Great Rebellion 1642–1660* (1966), 205–9.

[128] *TUHS* 11: 129, 144; *CSPD* 1687–9, 199. Although Whitley claimed him as a Baptist, a more recent study concludes that Bampfield was an 'active Presbyterian until his death', *BQ* 28: 254. The possibility of a Presbyterian Sabbatarian is intriguing. Densham and Ogle record that Francis Bampfield, prior to adopting Baptist and Sabbatarian views, had been inclined to Presbyterianism through Richard Baxter: *Congregational Churches*, 245.

[129] Isaac Marlow, *A Tract on the Sabbath Day. Wherein the keeping of the First Day of the Week a Sabbath is justified by a Divine Command and a Double Example contained in the Old and New Testament. With Answers to the chiefest Objections made by the Jewish Seventh-day Sabbatharians and others* (1694).

perhaps that the original Sabbatarian debate had not yet been satis-
factorily concluded. Certainly it indicates that the Seventh-day cause
was not, at the end of the seventeenth century, on the point of
extinction, as has sometimes been suggested.[130]

As a lawyer, Bampfield was understandably concerned with
authority, and in matters of faith and practice the authority by which
the Christian life should be regulated. To Bampfield, the dual authority of Christ and Scripture must be final, taking precedence
over any pretended authority of the Church even though that authority was argued from the standpoint of the ultimate authority of
God himself. 'If the Church had such power as some pretend, there
being such variety of churches, which of the churches shall give the
world a rule in this [the Sabbath]?'[131] It was a fair question, asked
repeatedly by those with a genuine concern over the Sabbath issue,
and one which Bampfield believed had remained unanswered for
a hundred years or more. The question, in fact, presupposed the
very argument which Bampfield sought to challenge. The answer
to the Sabbath question should not be sought from the Church, but
from the explicit word of Scripture and from the example of Christ.
Bampfield's study of the Bible led him to conclude that Christ had
not only kept the seventh day 'constantly . . . as his custom was'
throughout his earthly life but, as the title of the *Enquiry* indicated,
had, as Creator instituted the Sabbath at the beginning and as
Jehovah had enshrined it in the moral law delivered at Sinai.[132]
Since 'man's glory in the world lies in his conformity to Christ', and
since 'our conformity to him lies in our keeping all his commands',
and since 'the Ten Commands are absolutely confirmed by Christ',
that is by his own giving of the Moral Law and his own obedience
to it, Bampfield concluded that the Decalogue was the 'settled
standing rule of our obedience to the end of the world.'[133] The
authority of the moral law, of the Ten Commandments, is the authority of Christ and Scripture together and in sum.

For Bampfield, the question of authority extended to the attempt
to change the Sabbath from the seventh day of the week to the first.
Since 'no law can be dispensed with, or altered, in any point, by
any authority, but that which is equal to that which enacted it,' and
since 'no pope, or other men on earth can pretend to an authority

---

[130] e.g. Whitley, 'Men of the Seventh Day', 10/1; D. Coomer, *English Dissent under
the Early Hanoverians* (1946), 26. But cf. Brown, *English Baptists*, 46.
[131] Bampfield, *An Enquiry*, 2.   [132] Ibid. 39, 5–18.   [133] Ibid. 5.

equal to the authority of God,' and since there was 'no divine precept for any other than the seventh day,' it alone was unarguably and for ever the true, biblical Sabbath instituted at Creation and extending to the end of time.[134] 'The law to alter the seventh day to the first' was introduced by a spurious authority, Bampfield argued, 'by the bishops of Rome, who though they pretended to dispense with the laws of the church, could not alter or dispense with the laws of God'.[135] If this suggests the legal mind of the lawyer, it was balanced by the obedient mind of an honest disciple of Christ. 'I think we may be sufficiently certain which is the seventh day in the weekly circulation, and am willing to observe that blessed and sanctified day . . . which I think is the Lord's day, and not changed.'[136] This, in a sentence, expressed the sentiments of the Seventh-day Men as they recovered from the times of persecution and hardship, and faced the challenge of a new century.

[134] Ibid. 135.   [135] Ibid.   [136] Bampfield, *Reply to Wallis*, 3.

6

The Chilterns and
the Thames Valley

THE doctrine of the Seventh-day Sabbath found ready acceptance in a number of towns and villages in Berkshire, Oxfordshire, and Buckinghamshire, notably in the region where these three counties converge at the western end of the Chilterns, overlooking the Vale of Oxford. The Seventh-day Men also obtained a foothold at Watford in Hertfordshire, and between there and Oxford several Seventh-day congregations flourished from the late 1650s until the middle of the eighteenth century and, in one instance at least, later than that. Seventh-day churches, or mixed-communion churches including Sabbatarians, can be identified at Wallingford in Berkshire, Kingston Blount, Watlington, Warborough, and Berrick Salome in Oxfordshire, and Bledlow, Amersham, Chorley Wood, and Chalfont St Giles in Buckinghamshire. Seventh-day views persisted in at least one of these groups, Watlington, until the beginning of the nineteenth century. Sabbatarians were also reported in many other localities in these counties, sometimes as isolated representatives of the Seventh-day movement and sometimes in fellowship with predominantly Sunday-keeping congregations. Thus, in 1659, the messenger of the Baptist church at Oxford reported at the Association meeting that two were observing the seventh day but keeping fellowship with the church,[1] while at Lewknor in 1682 an unnamed couple, one of them a 'Satturday Sabbatarian', were reported to the Bishop of Oxford as having vacated their house and left the district in order to avoid the consequences of legislation against Dissenters.[2] The late attachment to Lollard views in this whole area has already been noted,[3] and even if no direct continuity between a

---

[1] White, *Association Records*, iii. 191.

[2] An 'Anababtist [*sic*] and his wife, a Satturday Sabbatarian, have put a Tenant into their concerns . . . and are gone aside to avoyd ye penal Lawes, declaring this to be the persecuted Shire of England, and this place hereabouts . . . to be ye warmest corner in it', John Bushell to Bishop Fell, July 1682; ORO, MS Oxf. Dioc. c.430, fo. 27.　　　　　　　　　　　　　　　　　　　　　　　　　[3] See above, 30–2.

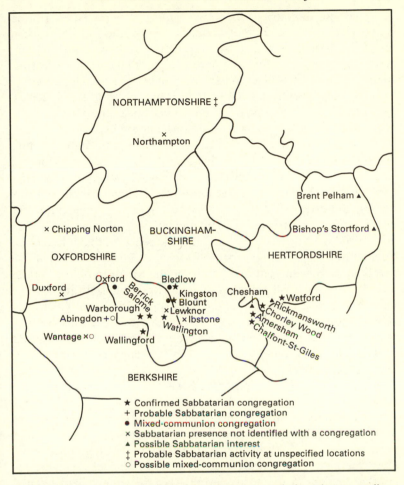

NORTHAMPTONSHIRE ‡

× Northampton

Brent Pelham ▲

× Chipping Norton

BUCKINGHAM-
SHIRE

Bishop's Stortford ▲

OXFORDSHIRE

HERTFORDSHIRE

Oxford   Bledlow
Duxford   ×   ● ★   Kingston   Chesham   ★ Watford
  Berrick   ★ Blount   ▲ ★ Rickmansworth
  Salome   × Lewknor   ★ Chorley Wood
Warborough   ★ ★   ★ \ × Ibstone   ★ Amersham
Abingdon + ○   Watlington   ★ Chalfont-St-Giles
Wantage × ○   ★
  Wallingford

BERKSHIRE

★ Confirmed Sabbatarian congregation
+ Probable Sabbatarian congregation
● Mixed-communion congregation
× Sabbatarian presence not identified with a congregation
▲ Possible Sabbatarian interest
‡ Probable Sabbatarian activity at unspecified locations
○ Possible mixed-communion congregation

MAP 3 Locations in counties in the Chilterns and the Thames Valley, Hertfordshire, and Northamptonshire associated with seventeenth- and eighteenth-century Sabbatarianism

possible Lollard Sabbatarianism and that of the seventeenth century can be established, the tendency to a thoroughly biblical faith may well have predisposed the region to an extensive and lingering attachment to the Sabbatarian views of the Seventh-day movement.

The Seventh-day Sabbath first came into the open in this region at the fourteenth meeting of the Abingdon Association of Baptist

churches[4] in May 1656, when two questions were raised by the
messengers of the church at Oxford. They wanted to know, first,
'what the beast is which is spoken of in the Revelation of John,
what is his image, and what it is to worship him and to receive his
mark upon the forehead or in their right hand' and, secondly,
'whether the Seventh-day Sabbath, as it was given in Exod. 20: 10,
be in force to be observed by the saints under the Gospel'. The
Association records leave both questions unanswered, although they
were formally referred to all the churches represented at the meeting
for serious consideration 'in the fear of the Lord' and 'for the
knowledge of his mind and will'.[5] It may be concluded that the
Sabbath issue had come to the fore in the Baptist churches of this
area by the early 1650s, and that by 1656 it had assumed sufficient
significance to be treated as a matter of general concern. At the
1659 meeting of the Association, Wantage reported that it had been
kept 'from the spreading errors of the times', Quakerism and 'those
that hold the Seventh-day Sabbath',[6] and the Kingston Blount church
asked for advice on whether it and two neighbouring Baptist
churches should continue in fellowship with Bledlow, which was
now predominantly Sabbatarian.[7] Wantage did, in fact, lose one or
two to the seventh day, and a year later Kingston Blount reported
further defections, a regular group of Sabbatarians having now been
established at Watlington.[8]

A precise date for the origin of Seventh-day observance in this
region is, once again, difficult to establish, although it is clear that
Edward Stennett[9] played a major role in establishing the cause at
Wallingford and perhaps also at other neighbouring localities. There
are also some Fifth Monarchy connections in this region of Berkshire. Stennett, a physician, and soon to be one of the most respected leaders in the early Seventh-day movement, had been a
chaplain in the Parliamentary army during the Civil War, and by the
mid-1650s was a member of the Abingdon Baptist church founded

---

[4] Also known as the Berkshire Association.

[5] White, *Association Records*, iii. 158.

[6] Ibid. 190–1.   [7] Ibid. 195; cf. *BQ* 26: 20.

[8] In 1674 a John Belcher, probably John Belcher, jun., later a member at Pinners'
Hall, married Mary Wilson of Wantage. Cf. G.F. Nuttall, 'Association Records of the
Particular Baptists', *BQ* 26: 20.

[9] On Stennett, fl. 1654–1705, the first of four generations of eminent Sabbatarian
Baptist ministers, see *PDM* 1: 89–90; *FMM* 263; Crosby, *History*, i. 368–73; Wilson,
Dissenting Churches, ii. 592–5.

by John Pendarves.[10] Pendarves, an Oxford graduate, had resigned the living of St Helen's, Abingdon, in 1649 to become rector of Wantage, prior to founding the Abingdon Baptist congregation *c*.1650.[11] By 1655 Pendarves was known as a leading Fifth Monarchist, and a great rally of Fifth Monarchists and Baptists from all over the country gathered at his funeral at Abingdon in 1656, at which Stennett was present.[12] Pendarves had been active in the Pyrton–Chinnor area of Oxfordshire in the early 1650s, and had been involved in a public debate over baptism in the Pyrton parish church in 1652. Shortly thereafter, Baptist congregations had appeared in Watlington, Kingston Blount, and Bledlow.[13] Whether this is enough to substantiate Whitley's claim that the Seventh-day movement in this region was the result of a general evolution of Fifth Monarchists to Sabbatarians[14] is doubtful, although Stennett's Sabbatarianism was marked by a strong eschatological hope and he may have entertained mild Fifth Monarchy views for a brief period between 1655 and 1658.[15]

There can be no such ambiguity about Stennett's acceptance of the seventh day or his influence in establishing the Sabbatarian cause in east Berkshire and across the Thames in south Oxfordshire. As a member of the Abingdon Baptist church his attention may have been drawn to the seventh day by the questions referred to the churches at the 1656 Association meeting. At some point prior to 1658 or early that year, he became convinced of the Saturday Sabbath, and published *The Royal Law Contended for* (1658), the first of several works in favour of the seventh day which came from his pen, and which Whitley concluded had exerted much influence, particularly in the immediate locality.[16] This suggestion seems to be supported by the fact that John Hanson of Abingdon replied immediately with *A short Treatise shewing the Sabbatharians*

---

[10] *BDBR* iii. 204. See also *DNB*.

[11] *FMM* 258; *BDBR* iii. 20. See also *DNB*.

[12] *FMM* 107, 132–3, 263.

[13] White, *Association Records*, iii. 139, 195; cf. Payne, *The Baptists of Berkshire*, 149. Bledlow does not appear to have been represented at any of the early Association meetings, perhaps on account of its Sabbatarianism.

[14] Whitley, 'Men of the Seventh Day', 4/8.

[15] *FMM* 263. Cf. Stennett's letter to Rhode Island, 1670, where he describes himself as a 'waiter for the consolation of Israel in the return of the latter day glory, and perfect restoring of all the Lord's good old ways'; Stennett to Newport, 6 Mar. 1670, in 'The Hubbard Journal', SDBHS, MS 194x.6, 56.

[16] Whitley, 'Men of the Seventh Day', 7/2.

confuted by the new Covenant (1658), a work which Hanson said
had been precipitated by the proclamation of the Seventh-day
Sabbath in Berkshire. Hanson refers to Edward Stannett (*sic*), 'a
Sabbatharian of Abingdon', and records that a sermon in favour of
the seventh day had recently been preached at midday 'in a town
in Barkshire', and that a citizen of Abingdon regularly opened shop
on the first day.[17] Whitley also maintained that the discontinuance
of the Association meetings in 1658 was due to the turmoil created
in the Baptist churches by the publication of Stennett's *Royal Law*,
although this does not now seem to have been the case.[18] Certainly
discussion of the Sabbath continued among believers, and eventually
Seventh-day congregations appeared at Wallingford under Stennett's
leadership, and elsewhere at nearby Watlington, Warborough,
Kingston Blount, and Berrick Salome, all maintaining connections
with Stennett or Wallingford while that congregation continued to
exist.

EDWARD STENNETT: ABINGDON AND WALLINGFORD

Stennett's Seventh-day church at Wallingford is a classic example of
a congregation whose history cannot adequately be reconstructed
on account of insufficient, and at times conflicting, evidence. This
is particularly true of any attempt to determine its origin. Although
Wallingford was to become an influential centre of Seventh-day
activity in the late seventeenth- and early eighteenth centuries, the
evidence that has survived suggests that this congregation did not
come together before the early 1670s, a date later than any of the
other Seventh-day congregations in the area. This anomaly can
only be resolved by accepting that Stennett directed the growing
work from Abingdon until he moved to Wallingford *c.*1671.[19] Although it is feasible that he could have ministered to a church in
Wallingford from Abingdon, there is no direct evidence for such a
congregation until 1672, when Stennett was licensed, as a Baptist,
to conduct services in his own home in the remains of Wallingford

---

[17] John Hanson, *A short Treatise shewing the Sabbatharians confuted by the new
Covenant* (1658), 3, 34.
[18] Whitley, 'Men of the Seventh Day', 7/3. Cf. White, *Association Records*, iii.
185 ff.
[19] Stennett to Newport, 9 Apr. 1671, SDBHS, MS 194x.6, 67. This letter was written
by Stennett from Wallingford, where, he says, 'I now live'.

Castle.[20] Indeed, there is more evidence, meagre as it is, for Sabbatarian activity in Abingdon and emanating from there in the late 1650s than there is for Sabbatarianism at Wallingford at any time prior to 1672. Unless further evidence comes to light we may have to be content with assuming that for twelve years or so after his adoption of the seventh day Edward Stennett remained at Abingdon nurturing the Seventh-day cause in Berkshire and Oxfordshire and elsewhere by his writings, and ministering to an unidentified congregation, perhaps at Wallingford, but more probably at Abingdon.[21] This conclusion need not undermine the traditional understanding that Wallingford was the mother church to several other Seventh-day congregations across the Thames in Oxfordshire and Buckinghamshire.

The foregoing uncertainty should not be allowed to detract from Stennett's stature in the Seventh-day movement, or his contribution to its stability at a time when it was under increasing pressure from Baptist and other Dissenting traditions, as well as from government legislation. This period can be put between the late 1650s and the early 1670s, a time of growth for the Seventh-day movement, but also of renewed controversy over the Saturday Sabbath,[22] and of difficulty for those who sought to observe it. *The Royal Law Contended for*, which included a second part entitled *The Seventh Day Sabbath proved from the Beginning*, was reprinted in 1667, and may be seen primarily as a straightforward attempt to advance the Seventh-day cause at a time when it was already gaining momentum in several parts of the country. Stennett's *The Seventh Day is the Sabbath of the Lord* (1664), with a preface by John Belcher, was more of a defence against William Russell's *No Seventh-Day-Sabbath*

[20] *OR* i. 543.

[21] In 1707 a Mr Fowler 'of Oxfordshire near Abington' was baptized at Mill Yard. He is referred to again in the Mill Yard Minutes in 1722: MYM 178, 239.

[22] William Aspinwall's *The Abrogation of the Jewish Sabbath* (1657) was one of the first works in England directed specifically against Seventh-day observance. Aspinwall was followed in the next fifteen years or so by a number of influential opponents of the seventh day, including Thomas Collier, *The Seventh Day Sabbath Opened and Discovered* (1658); Edmund Warren, *The Jews Sabbath Antiquated* (1659); Jeremiah Ives, *Saturday No Sabbath* (1659); William Russel[l], *No Seventh-Day-Sabbath Commanded by Jesus Christ in the New-Testament* (1663); Thomas Grantham, *The Seventh-Day Sabbath Ceased as Ceremonial . . .* (1667); Richard Baxter, *The Divine Appointment of the Lords Day Proved . . . And consequently the Cessation of the Seventh day Sabbath* (1671), and John Owen, *Exercitations* (1671). Other later seventeenth-century writers of note against the seventh day included Nathaniel Homes, John Bunyan, John Wallis, and Isaac Marlow.

Commanded by Jesus Christ in the New-Testament (1663) and Jeremiah Ives's *Saturday No Sabbath* (1659), both typical of a steady stream of anti-Seventh-day literature which first appeared in 1657 and continued through to the middle of the following century. Stennett's signature to the *Faithful Testimony Against The Teachers of Circumcision* (1667), and his *The Insnared Taken in the Work of his Hands* (1677), were both intended to counteract developments within the Seventh-day movement itself tending to undermine its credibility. The former was directed against the Judaizing innovations of Thomas Tillam and Christopher Pooley in East Anglia,[23] the latter a response to John Cowell of Tewkesbury, who had left the Seventh-day people, largely on account of Tillam and Pooley, and who had published his reasons for so doing in a well-argued apology entitled *The Snare Broken* (1677). Cowell had also been upset by a certain rigour he had detected in Stennett's *The Seventh Day is the Sabbath*, which he felt maintained that the death penalty was still in force, as in Old Testament times, for profanation of the Sabbath.[24] Cowell was one of the very few who wrote against the seventh day after having previously written for it. His influence, perhaps a little surprisingly, appears to have been negligible, even in his own immediate locality.

During these years Stennett also wrote several letters to the recently founded Seventh-day church in Rhode Island, 'that little remnant of the woman's seed that keep the commandments of God and the faith of Jesus'.[25] This correspondence gives a cameo of the English Seventh-day movement in the late 1660s and the early 1670s and, among other things, confirms that Wallingford first appeared as an identifiable congregation *c*.1671.[26] In 1668 Stennett reported from Abingdon that there were in England 'about nine or ten churches that keep the Sabbath, besides many scattered disciples, . . . many once eminent churches [having] been shattered in pieces'.[27]

---

[23] On Tillam and Pooley in East Anglia, see below Ch. 9.

[24] John Cowell, *The Snare Broken: Being a true and faithful account of the Authors Grounds for his leaving off the observation of the Sabbath of the First or Old Covenant . . .* (1677), 33–4, citing Stennett, *The Seventh Day is the Sabbath . . .* (1664), 52. On Cowell and the Ashchurch Seventh-day church, see below, Ch. 7.

[25] Stennett to Newport, 6 Apr. 1670, SDBHS, MS 194x.6, 56.

[26] Stennett to Newport, Apr. 1671, ibid. 67–8.

[27] Stennett to Newport, Feb. 1668, *SDBM* 1/1: 27. Stennett may not have known of all the Seventh-day churches in existence at this time, for even if he considered all the groups and congregations in a county or similar geographical region as one church, there were more than ten in existence in 1668.

This was after the initial thrust of post-Restoration repression. He was able to add, without foreknowledge of events that lay ahead, that although the believers in England had 'passed through great opposition for this truth's sake . . . the opposers of truth seem much withered, and at present the opposition seems to be declining away'.[28] Shortly, however, and still from Abingdon, he spoke of opposition coming now from professed believers, 'the spirit of Antichrist and opposition against ye truth . . . as really . . . as ever I saw it in the parish', with some having 'set themselves against the Lord's Sabbath', being bound by 'a new law, which Christ never was made under, nor never suffered the curse of'.[29] This is the nearest we get to any clear indication of a rift in the Abingdon Baptist church over the seventh day. It may be significant that Stennett's next letter to Newport was written from his new home in Wallingford.

By 1671 the times had changed again, and Stennett wrote from Wallingford of 'thick clouds and darkness', and of the saints 'much spoiled in their estates for meeting together to worship the Lord, and in . . . jeopardy every hour'.[30] This may even indicate that meetings were suspended for a time prior to the licensing of Stennett's home in 1672. Even so the settlement of the east Berkshire congregation of Sabbatarians in Wallingford Castle gave it much-needed stability, and despite the oppressive atmosphere Stennett had reported in 1671 the church seems to have come through these trials and difficulties relatively unscathed. In 1674 Stennett reported, 'The little flock over which I watch through the grace of God are generally well, and our number hath increased.' Nine had been added to the fellowship 'and more baptised' since his last letter, and Stennett was now again full of hope. 'The Lord is at work here . . . let us cry night and day unto the Lord to send faithful labourers into his harvest, for the harvest is white in many places.'[31] We do not know how far afield Stennett was looking when he made this statement, but nearby, in many little towns and villages to the east of Wallingford, the harvest was already being gathered.

Perhaps as a direct result of Stennett's broad vision and concern

---

[28] Ibid. 26.

[29] Stennett to Newport, 6 Apr. 1670, SDBHS, MS 194x.6, 56–7. Stennett advised the Newport church to withdraw from sinful and disorderly persons 'that are drawn back from ye sabbath to prophaneness after light and establishment therein'.

[30] Stennett to Newport, 9 Apr. 1671, SDBHS, MS 194x.6, 67–8.

[31] Stennett to Newport, 15 Aug. 1674, ibid. 72–3.

for the Seventh-day cause beyond his own immediate locality, the church in Wallingford became the centre of Sabbatarian activity in the east Berkshire–south Oxfordshire area for half a century or more. In 1682 Richard Manning, the Anglican incumbent of the Oxfordshire parish of Chalgrove, reported to the Bishop of Oxford that one of three known Dissenters in the neighbouring village of Berrick Salome[32] was Joseph Wise, 'who holds the Jewish Sabbath, and is against infant baptism, being of one Stannett's [*sic*] church, living in Wallingford Castle'.[33] Wise applied for a licence for his own house in Berrick Salome in 1700, and Sabbatarians from surrounding villages were still meeting there in 1738.[34] Wallingford, meanwhile, continued as the mother church of the Seventh-day movement in the region, supporting other congregations besides that at Berrick Salome. Stennett preached at Watlington in the 1680s and 1690s and in 1690 was recorded as elder there.[35] Watlington and Warborough are said to have originated as a result of the Wallingford witness,[36] and although this might be an argument for an earlier beginning there, it is more likely that Wallingford is used loosely for the Sabbatarian cause in east Berkshire as a whole before it was settled at Wallingford. In 1669, one Stamp, a brazier from Abingdon, was reported as one of the principal teachers at Warborough.[37]

Wallingford also maintained a link with Pinners' Hall in London, several members transferring from the Berkshire congregation to Pinners' Hall between 1688 and 1700.[38] As previously noted, John Belcher of Bell Lane was recorded as a member at Wallingford in 1687. Wallingford was also mentioned in both the Llanwenarth record of 1690, and in Joseph Davis's will of 1706,[39] thus establishing it as a recognized centre of the Seventh-day movement at the turn of the century. In 1707 Joseph Stennett wrote from London to his wife in Wallingford, acknowledging a letter from her, and speaking of his joy at learning of new converts at Wallingford

---

[32] A chapelry in the Chalgrove parish.
[33] ORO, MS Oxf. Dioc. c.430, fo. 7.
[34] Clapinson (ed.), *Bishop Fell*, 52 n. 51.
[35] *VCH* Oxon., viii. 246; *BQ* 14: 165.
[36] Clapinson (ed.), *Bishop Fell*, pp. xxi, 7, 52.
[37] Lambeth MS 952/1, fo. 112, cited in Clapinson (ed.), *Bishop Fell*, 43.
[38] e.g. PHCB 13, 17, 22–3, 74. Hannah Harding transferred to Pinners' Hall from Wallingford in 1699, and back again to Wallingford in 1700, 74, 77.
[39] *BQ* 14: 165; *Reports from the Commissioners for Charities*, xix, pt. I, 871.

'convinced of Baptism' and about to join the fellowship there.[40] In 1715 Wallingford received £5 from the estate of Mary Hall of Pinners' Hall, a bequest which was designated 'for Edward Stennetts youse'.[41] Although Stennett had been dead for ten years, this and the foregoing fragments provide adequate evidence that the Wallingford church did not become extinct immediately after Stennett's death, even though some members were reported to have joined Richard Comyn's Presbyterian congregation at this point.[42] Hereafter references to the Seventh-day cause in Berkshire or Wallingford are scarce, and the centre of gravity seems to have been transferred across the Thames to Watlington, where it remained until the Seventh-day movement finally disappeared from this region nearly a century later.

BLEDLOW AND KINGSTON BLOUNT

In 1659 it was reported that most of the Baptists in Bledlow 'do now hold the Seventh-day Sabbath'.[43] Bledlow had emerged as a Baptist congregation in the early 1650s, soon after John Pendarves's efforts in nearby Pyrton across the Oxfordshire border. In 1662 thirty-seven persons were listed in the archdeaconry visitation records for refusing to attend services in the parish church,[44] and although none was at this point identified by persuasion, several soon appeared in subsequent records as Baptists, and many as Sabbatarians. Those listed in 1662 had included Nathaniel Costard and Edward Stevens and their wives, and Phyllis Costard (widow), and Hannah her daughter, and John Sullins. In October of that year, and again in 1664, further reports named the same group for refusing to have their children baptized, and for non-attendance at

---

[40] NLW, MS 11095E. This letter contains the original of the famous epitaph Joseph Stennett composed for his parents, as inscribed on their tombstone in St Peter's churchyard, Wallingford.

[41] *TBHS* 3: 90. The money was sent via 'Mr Batt'. There may be a link with Salisbury here, for Mary Batt had earlier joined Pinners' Hall from Salisbury: ibid. 93.

[42] W.H. Summers, *History of the Congregational Churches in the Berkshire, South Oxon, and South Bucks Association* (Newbury, 1905), 289. Comyn himself died a few months later. According to Calamy, Stennett, 'a lay preacher', had alternated on the Lord's day with Comyn at Wallingford for some time previously, Edmund Calamy, *A Continuation of the Account of the Ministers . . . Ejected . . .* (1727), i. 133. On Comyn, see *CR.*   [43] White, *Association Records*, iii. 195.

[44] BRO, D/A/V 6, fos. 31^v–33^r.

the parish church 'on Sundays as is by the state required'.[45] Sullins was described in the returns as 'head of the observers of the Saturday Sabbath', and Stevens 'the laceman', who was Sullins's father-in-law, Costard 'yeoman', Richard Sale 'yeoman', and Edward Sleeves 'weaver', were specified with him as Sabbatarians.[46] Three conventicles were reported in Bledlow in 1669, one of them in the house of Edward Stevens as having been held there for at least the previous five years.[47] Costard, Stevens, Sale, and Sullins were all presented regularly from 1662 onwards, and it seems beyond doubt that this group represents the nucleus of the Bledlow Sabbatarians who had adopted the Seventh-day Sabbath by 1659.

The 1669 episcopal returns which had reported a conventicle of some twenty persons meeting in the house of Edward Stevens also designated John Sullins as teacher. Sullins was described as a lacemaker, 'a seller of small wares', and a 'constant observer of the Jewish Sabbath'. He was also noted to be 'of quality'. Apart from Sullins and Stevens, Costard, Sale, and Sleeve, the rest of the group were described as 'mostly of the female sect [sic]'.[48] An interesting comment on the Bledlow Sabbatarians was that they 'do frequently resort to the conventicles of the Presbyterians'.[49] This is probably a reference to the group which met in the house of John Coldham, one of the two other conventicles reported in Bledlow in 1669, which may have attracted the Sabbatarians because the eminent ejected minister George Swinnock preached there from time to time.[50] The willingness of the Sabbatarians to mix with the Presbyterians may throw a little light on the nature of the Kingston Blount congregation, as well as on the relationship between the Dissenting congregations in Bledlow itself. The Bledlow Sabbatarians were also reported to be in contact with those at Amersham in 1669, and Robert Turner, a 'deacon' from the Bledlow church, appears to have been the first person to have been buried in the new burial ground of the Amersham Baptists in 1677.[51] Despite the question

---

[45] BRO, D/A/V7, fos. 45ʳ–46ᵛ.   [46] LAO, Diss. 1/8, 6.

[47] Ibid.   [48] Ibid.; *OR* i. 78.   [49] LAO, Diss. 1/8, 7.

[50] Swinnock, who after his ejection in 1662 served as chaplain to the Hampden family in Great Hampden, also preached to a large conventicle of 200 Presbyterians and Anabaptists in Thame, and to one composed of 'separatists of all sorts' in Bicester: Lambeth MS 951/1, fo. 112ʳ, ᵛ; Clapinson (ed.), *Bishop Fell*, pp. xvi, xvii. On Swinnock, see *DNB* and *CR*.

[51] *BQ* 17: 85; W.T. Whitley (ed.), *The Church Books of Ford or Cuddington and Amersham* (1912), 210.

raised by the Kingston Blount church at the 1656 Association meeting concerning continuing fellowship with the Bledlow Sabbatarians, the latter evidently cultivated good relationships with fellow Baptists and others in the Dissenting tradition.

John Sullins's name does not appear in the extant records after 1669, and we hear nothing more of Costard until 1682 or of Stevens until 1685. In 1682 Costard was indicted for negligence 'in office' and fined £2 10s. for disobeying an order of the justices, and in 1685 both he and Stevens were presented with six others from Bledlow at the Quarter Sessions in Aylesbury for continued non-attendance at the parish church.[52] Costard's house was licensed for Dissenting worship in 1689, and again in 1701, two years before his death.[53] He was the last of the Bledlow Sabbatarians whose name is preserved in any official record. One hundred and seventy families were recorded in the Bledlow parish in 1717 with ten Dissenters of whom seven were 'Anabaptist'. By 1720 the number of families had grown to 200, with six Dissenters given as 'Anabaptist'.[54] There is no mention of any of these Anabaptists being Sabbatarian, but Nathaniel Costard was survived by three sons when he died in 1703, and by a married daughter living in Watlington.[55] It would seem that the Seventh-day church in Bledlow enjoyed a brief but vigorous life for half a century or thereabouts before quietly disappearing at some point early in the eighteenth century.

The Baptist church at nearby Kingston Blount was received into the Abingdon Association in 1655, and at the Association meeting at Tetsworth a year later was represented by two messengers, one of whom was John Belcher.[56] It was at this meeting that the question of Seventh-day observance had been raised, and it seems that Belcher adopted the seventh day at some point between this date and 1660, when he appeared as an itinerant preacher in Gloucestershire advocating the Saturday Sabbath.[57] By 1660 the influence of Seventh-day views was being felt in the Kingston Blount church,

[52] W. Le Hardy (ed.), *Calendar to the Sessions Records (Buckinghamshire)*, i: *1678–1694* (Aylesbury, 1933), 101, 105, 172.

[53] Ibid. 299. Costard was sworn as a petty constable for Bledlow in 1692: ibid. 410; ii (1939), 272.   [54] LAO, Gibson, 2, 10.

[55] Nathaniel, jun., John, and Henry, who in 1676 had been presented for 'stopping up a way to ye parish church lying through the entry of his house to ye hindrance of ye people that repaire thither', BRO, D/A/V, 10, fo. 56. Rebecca Costard married William Devon of Watlington.   [56] White, *Association Records*, iii. 139, 145.

[57] See below, 211.

for in that year the Association records reveal that 'one is gone off to the seventh day Sa[bbath]' from Kingston, 'and two more are inclined to the seventh day'.[58] By 1669 Sabbatarian views had taken deeper root in Kingston Blount, but at this point we have two records, and must attempt to decide which is the more accurate account of the situation which then existed.

One account simply says that by 1669 Kingston Blount had become a Seventh-day church.[59] This is entirely possible, and would have been in keeping with developments in the neighbouring parishes of Bledlow to the east and Watlington to the west. It would also more readily explain the visits to Kingston Blount, reported in the official returns for that year, of John Belcher, now a 'foreigner', who under pretence of receiving the rent travelled to Kingston to preach.[60] Belcher was by then a confirmed and leading Sabbatarian and minister of the Bell Lane church in London, and a continuing interest in the welfare of a congregation with which he had been associated from its beginning would be natural. The 1669 conventicle returns are, however, an isolated account of Dissenting practice in the Oxford diocesan records for the period, and it is quite possible, even likely, that Belcher was preaching at Kingston Blount before or after 1669. Certainly he was not unknown in the district during this period. He provided the preface to Stennett's *The Seventh Day is the Sabbath* in 1664, and one source says that he was converted to the seventh day as a result of Stennett's influence.[61] Belcher was elsewhere reported in Oxfordshire again in 1671.

The other account records that a mixed congregation of between thirty and forty Presbyterians, Independents, Quakers, and Sabbatarians was meeting in Kingston Blount in 1669 in the houses of Richard Chitch, John North, and Mary North, with Chitch and North 'domestic teachers', and a 'Mr Button and one Belcher, foreigners' coming to preach from elsewhere.[62] Thomas Reynolds, vicar of Aston Rowant, the parish in which Kingston Blount was situated, reported in 1682 that most of the conventicles in the parish had been meeting in Chitch's home 'above this twenty years'. This would put the beginnings of this conventicle, regarded by him as the main Dissenting congregation in the parish, if not the only one, in the early 1660s.[63]

---

[58] White, *Association Records*, iii. 195.   [59] *BQ* 26: 20.
[60] *OR* iii. 824.   [61] *SO* 2: 156.
[62] Lambeth MS. 951/1, fo. 112ᵛ; *OR* iii. 824. Button is identified as Ralph Button of Brainford, formerly a canon of Christ Church, Oxford: *CR* 95.
[63] ORO, MS Oxf. Dioc. c.430, fo. 3.

The 1669 return does not mention Anabaptists at all, yet Reynolds describes Chitch in 1682 as an Anabaptist, 'their champion', 'the chief of the Dissenters', adding that 'the several Dissenters and absenters from church' in his parish were 'of the Anabaptist persuasion'.[64] It is not easy to reconcile Reynolds's unusually detailed account with the 1669 records. Although he does not specifically mention Sabbatarians, which the 1669 account does, neither does he mention Presbyterians or Quakers. The predominant classification in 1682 is Anabaptist, and if this is the nearest we can get to Sabbatarianism in Kingston Blount after 1669, it would not be unusual terminology. In view of the fact that both Richard Chitch and John North were named as preachers at Kingston Blount with John Belcher in 1669, a continuing Sabbatarian emphasis there at least until 1682 seems likely.[65] In 1689, Thomas and Martha North were received into fellowship at Pinners' Hall on the recommendation of 'the congregation walking with Mr Ed. Stennett in and about Wallingford'.[66]

Given the notorious unreliability of some episcopal records relating to Dissenters and Dissenting activity, the accuracy of the 1669 return might well be open to question. Even if the information was correct at the time, and a congregation consisting of Presbyterians, Independents, Quakers, and Sabbatarians did meet at that point, the mix is too diverse for lasting stability, and it is not likely to have remained an accurate account of Dissenting practice in Kingston Blount for any length of time. By 1682 Thomas Reynolds's Anabaptists are much more credible, even if they did not appear by name in the 1669 report. What is more to the point, perhaps, is that this conventicle, in whatever form it persisted to 1682, and whatever its composition in 1669, does not appear to have survived the deaths of John North and Richard Chitch, and the activities of the prosecuting authorities. From 1688 Kingston Blount is named as a preaching station of the Ford–Cuddington Baptist church in Buckinghamshire with preachers supplied by Ford and no further hint of a Sabbatarian interest.[67]

---

[64] Ibid., fos. 2–3.

[65] In 1682 a William North and his wife Elizabeth were named as Anabaptists by the incumbent of neighbouring Lewknor who at the same time had reported a Sabbatarian Anabaptist couple as leaving the district to avoid harassment. William and Elizabeth North kept 'their station, continuing stiff in their persuasion and inflexible', ibid., fo. 27.   [66] PHCB 13.

[67] Clapinson (ed.), *Bishop Fell*, 49 n. 22; Whitley, *Church Books of Ford . . . and Amersham*, 3, although it is possible that both First-day and Seventh-day congregations existed simultaneously, as appears also to have been the case at Bledlow by this time.

WATLINGTON, WARBOROUGH, AND BERRICK SALOME

Watlington was the most westerly of four communities lying in almost a straight line along the foot of the Chilterns, in which observance of the seventh day was established at some point during the latter half of the seventeenth century. According to the account in the *Victoria County History*, it could almost be claimed that Watlington was unique among Sabbatarian communities throughout the country, since the Sabbath-keeping Baptists here became the dominant Dissenting sect until the arrival of Methodism.[68] Even after that, a diminished but persistent Seventh-day witness continued into the early years of the nineteenth century before the demise of the last surviving Watlington Sabbatarian.

A Baptist church at Watlington was first represented at the eleventh meeting of the Abingdon Association at Tetsworth in 1655, although it was not until later that any definite evidence came to light of a tendency to Saturday Sabbatarianism.[69] By 1669 a regular congregation of Seventh-day people was worshipping in Watlington, comprised most probably of Baptists who hitherto had kept the first day. White concludes that by that time the Sabbatarians 'appear to have taken over'.[70] Although the Watlington group is often said to have been an offshoot from Wallingford,[71] it seems clear enough that Watlington preceded Wallingford as a separate congregation by as much as ten years. It might be more accurate to suggest a link with Edward Stennett and Abingdon during the early 1660s but, since Bledlow to the east had adopted the seventh day by 1659, an influence from that direction cannot be ruled out. Certainly at a later date, as already noted, a direct link did exist between the two congregations.

Watlington appears to have been an active centre of Dissent in the Oxford diocese in the immediate post-Restoration years, with several large groups of unidentified Dissenters reported to the ecclesiastical authorities from 1660 onwards. Between January 1663 and March 1664 twenty-nine parishioners are recorded as having been excommunicated for refusing to attend services in the parish

---

[68]   *VCH* Oxon., viii. 246.
[69]   White, *Association Records*, iii. 139. The *VCH* reference to Watlington as represented at the first meeting of the Association in 1653 is incorrect, *VCH* Oxon., viii. 245.   [70]   *BQ* 26: 20; White, *Association Records*, iii. 209.
[71]   e.g. Clapinson (ed.), *Bishop Fell*, pp. xxi, 52 n. 52, where the dates given for Stennett's death and his removal to Wallingford should be amended to 1705 and 1671 respectively.

church and related offences.[72] In 1664 Mary East and Gregory West were among those excommunicated 'for not paying the minister's dues', and it was in the houses of these two established Dissenters that Sabbatarian gatherings were reported to Bishop Fell as one of two conventicles meeting in Watlington in 1669. Mary East 'widow' and Gregory West 'weaver' were thus the first named observers of the seventh day in Watlington, and hosts to a regular conventicle of 'Sabbatarians who observe the Saturday'.[73] Unfortunately, the name of the preacher, or teacher, is not included in the return, or there might have been clear evidence of a link with Sabbatarians elsewhere. One account says that they were taught by Stephen Coven, who had been ejected (1660) from Sampford Peverell, near Tiverton, in Devon, and, while this is quite possible, it should be noted that he was licensed in 1672 as an Independent for the house of Thomas Ovey, or Overy, in Watlington.[74]

At about this time a Seventh-day congregation appeared in another village, Warborough, a few miles to the north of Watlington. Warborough had a history of Dissent going back to Jacobean times, for in 1623 several parishioners had been presented for not receiving the sacrament, non-attendance, or failure to pay their church rates.[75] The first hint of a Sabbatarian interest appears in the archdeaconry records for March 1667, when Thomas Gilpin and Margaret Hinton were said to 'keep and hold conventicles at their several houses upon Saturdays and Sundays'.[76] By the time they were reported these meetings had been conducted regularly for at least 'six months past'. The conventicle in Margaret Hinton's house was identified in the 1669 returns as 'Sabbatarian', meeting on Saturdays, with 'Stamp, a brasier, from Abingdon and others, teachers'.[77]

---

[72] ORO, MS Oxf. Dioc. c.99, fos. 239–241ᵛ, cited in Clapinson (ed.), *Bishop Fell*, 65 n. 255.

[73] Clapinson (ed.), *Bishop Fell*, 40, 69 n. 339, n. 340; *OR* iii. 823.

[74] *VCH* Oxon., viii. 245; Clapinson (ed.), *Bishop Fell*, 52 n. 53, 65 n. 255. Coven was noted as 'a wandering Seditious Seminary' licensed for Grub Street, London, as a Presbyterian: *CR* 139. He was the author of *The Militant Christian* (1668).

[75] ORO, MS Archd. Oxon. b.66, fos. 161–4.

[76] Ibid., fo. 169. Gilpin, 'an Olivarian soldier and great seducer' and a Quaker, was summoned to appear before the ecclesiastical courts frequently between 1667 and 1680 for keeping conventicles, Lambeth MS 951/1, fo. 112ᵛ; Clapinson (ed.), *Bishop Fell*, 70 n. 350, where Mercer should read Gilpin.

[77] *OR* iii. 824; Lambeth MS 951/1, fo. 112ᵛ. Hinton was later to be a prominent name in Baptist circles: James Hinton was pastor of the Oxford Baptist church, and John Howard Hinton (1791–1873) minister at Reading. On James's association with the Oxfordshire Sabbatarians, see below, 185.

It was reported to attract between forty and fifty attenders, and was evidently distinct from the First-day Baptists, who were recorded in the same return as meeting monthly, also in Margaret Hinton's house, but under the leadership of John Beesly (or Bisley), Margaret's son, and with different teachers.[78] Margaret Hinton was presented in 1668, and again, together with several other Dissenters not identified by persuasion, in 1671 and 1673, for absence from the parish church.[79]

The fact that there is no record of a meeting-place having been licensed for Sabbatarian worship in Warborough in 1672 does not necessarily indicate that meetings were not taking place. It is probably the reflection of a practice among some Baptists, who refused to apply for a licence on the grounds that to do so would acknowledge the King's prerogative to grant freedom of worship,[80] rather than an indication that the recently thriving Seventh-day cause had abruptly come to an end. There appear to be no extant records which indicate how long the conventicle of forty or fifty reported in 1669 continued to meet, or how many of its members continued to observe the seventh day. A few probably found their way to Berrick Salome or Watlington when the meetings at Warborough finally came to an end.

A similar situation seems to have prevailed in Watlington. Although an active congregation which was to survive the seventeenth century had been well established by 1669,[81] no licence is recorded for Sabbatarian worship in Watlington in 1672. Licences were issued for several Dissenting meeting-houses in the Oxford diocese in places where conventicles had been reported in 1669, but for Watlington licences were granted only for Presbyterian and

[78] Lambeth MS 951/1, fo. 112ᵛ. A John Boosley (or Bisley) and his wife Joan, and Thomas Boosly had been among those presented in 1623.

[79] ORO, MS Archd. Oxon. b.66. fos. 170, 176.

[80] In neighbouring Buckinghamshire and Hertfordshire the General Baptists, led by Thomas Monk, had mostly decided not to apply for the licences available under the Declaration of Indulgence: White, *English Baptists*, 119.

[81] White notes that by 1669 'Sabbatarians appear to have taken over' the Watlington Baptists: *Association Records*, iii. 209. At about this time ' a sort of Sectaries . . . called Anointers' were reported in Oxfordshire, which the *VCH* applies to the Seventh-day Baptists in the Watlington area. If the connection is justifiable, it is more likely to have been related to a literal application of James 5: 14 and prayer for the healing of the sick, than an 'anointing of all persons on admission to membership': Robert Plot, *The Natural History of Oxfordshire* (Oxford, 1677), 204, *VCH* Oxon., viii. 246. Anointing continued into the eighteenth century in some General Baptist congregations: Brown, *English Baptists*, 18.

Independent congregations.[82] It is unlikely that the Watlington Sabbatarians had ceased to meet by 1672, particularly since they are mentioned again in the diocesan records in 1676. Their reluctance to apply for a licence, like that of the Warborough group, should be taken rather as an indication that they shared the sentiments of Seventh-day congregations elsewhere in the country who similarly entertained reservations about the royal authority and freedom of worship.[83] It is possible, of course, even if unlikely, that under the difficulties of the post-Restoration era, and given the good relationship which neighbouring Sabbatarians enjoyed with Presbyterians and other Dissenters, the Watlington Seventh-day people had opted for mixed-communion worship. The other conventicle noted at Watlington in 1669 had been 'mixt of Presbyterians, Anabaptists, etc.', in the house of John Oovey, or Overy,[84] and in 1672 Stephen Coven was licensed to conduct Independent worship in the house of Thomas Ovey, or Overy.[85] A list of thirteen 'Dissenters' in 1685 whose religious affiliations were not noted contains the names of 'Mary, the wife of Gregory West', and 'Thomas Ovey and his wife'.[86]

Meanwhile, Baptist and Sabbatarian interests were developing in Berrick Salome, a village in the parish of Chalgrove, a few miles to the north again of Warborough and Watlington. One of the three main preachers at the Warborough Anabaptist conventicle reported in 1669 under the leadership of John Beesly was William Luggrove, a tobacco cutter from Berrick.[87] This conventicle was said to number up to 100, and, like most of the other village conventicles, would certainly have drawn support from the surrounding communities. Some of those who attended, if not all, would have been aware of the Sabbatarian group which met in the same house on Saturdays, from which it must be concluded that the seventh day was not unknown in Berrick during the late 1660s.

Just when the seeds began to grow has not been recorded, but in 1682, as already noted, Joseph Wise of Berrick and 'of Stannett's church' was reported to Bishop Fell as holding 'the Jewish Sabbath'

---

[82] Clapinson (ed.), *Bishop Fell*, p. xxi.
[83] e.g. cf. Beaminster and Bledlow for 1672.
[84] Lambeth MS 951/1, fo. 112ʳ.
[85] *CR* 139; *OR* ii. 829. Coven was also preaching in Warborough in 1682; ORO, MS Oxf. Dioc. c.430, fo. 7.   [86] ORO, MS Oxf. Dioc. d.708, fo. 124.
[87] Lambeth MS 951/1, fo. 112ᵛ.

and being 'against infant baptism', and three years later Wise and his wife were presented as 'Jews'.[88] Even if the first of the dates is taken as the earliest point at which Wise adopted the seventh day, it still means that he or his family maintained a consistent and effective witness of nearly sixty years for the Saturday Sabbath in Berrick Salome. In 1700 his house in Berrick was licensed as a meeting place, and in 1738 the visitation records of Bishop Secker reported a family of Sabbatarians in Berrick by the name of Wise, with the note that 'There are many of that sect in the neighbouring villages who meet in his house'.[89] Perhaps Berrick Salome, with Watlington at this point meeting only monthly, had superseded both it and Warborough as the locus of Sabbatarian activity in east Berkshire and south Oxfordshire, although the centre of gravity would later shift again to Watlington. Whether or not this was so, it seems clear that the Seventh-day Men were still strong around Berrick in 1738, and on the basis of the Secker visitation records their witness to the seventh day would seem set to continue for a few more years yet.

The 'remnant' which had been reported at Watlington in 1690 under the care of Edward Stennett[90] was destined to last for much longer than either he or they could have foreseen. The persistence of Seventh-day views here was undoubtedly due to the tenacity with which a small group of convinced believers held to an unpopular doctrine, but also to the interest and assistance of Sabbatarians, and others, from London and elsewhere. Indeed, the story of the Watlington Sabbatarians in the eighteenth century, fragmented though it is, owes its existence to support from fellow believers at Mill Yard, Pinners' Hall, and Natton, and from sympathetic Baptist friends from Haddenham[91] and Oxford, all of whom helped to keep the cause alive. It is remarkable that this small congregation remained in existence for more than a century after Stennett's death in 1705, without ever again having the services of a regular elder or teacher.

---

[88] Richard Manning, the incumbent of Chalgrove, to Bishop Fell, June 1682, ORO, MS Oxf. Dioc. c.430, fo. 7; c.708, fo. 117.

[89] W.J. Oldfield (ed.), 'Oxfordshire Quarter Sessions Rolls', viii. 803; H.A. Lloyd Jukes (ed.), *Articles of Enquiry Addressed to the Clergy of the Diocese of Oxford at the Primary Visitation of Dr Thomas Secker, 1738* (Oxford, 1957), 38.

[90] *BQ* 14: 165.

[91] The *VCH* entry for Watlington refers to a Hoare from Haddenham being teacher c.1738: *VCH* Oxon. viii. 246. Edward Hoare became pastor at Haddenham c.1717. Thomas Hoare, his brother, was a member of the same church, *TBHS* 3: 38.

Mill Yard is recorded as the first church that came to the aid of what, even early in the eighteenth century, must have appeared as a struggling cause. In 1717 John Savage, the Mill Yard minister, was authorized to visit the Sabbath-keepers 'in Oxfordshire and Buckinghamshire' to assist them as necessary.[92] The Mill Yard minutes thereafter refer only to 'the church observing the seventh-day Sabbath' in Oxfordshire and/or Buckinghamshire, or 'the Sabbath-keepers of Oxfordshire and Buckinghamshire', without reference to any specific locality. Savage's assistance would have been to preach, to administer the ordinances, and perhaps to engage in some pastoral visitation. In 1724 Mill Yard sent Edmund Townsend to minister to the Oxfordshire and Buckinghamshire believers for two Sabbaths over the Christmas period, and the following February received a letter thanking them for releasing Townsend and expressing the hope that the gesture might be repeated.[93] In the mean time Mill Yard had urged them to 'assemble together often' as best they could for corporate worship 'by praying, reading the Scripture or exposition, or confessing together as the Lord shall assist'.[94]

This new relationship with the Mill Yard General Baptists probably represents a pragmatic understanding to avoid the difficult question of Calvinistic determinism versus Arminian free will in view of the pressing need to uphold the seventh day. Pinners' Hall was similarly in temporary fellowship with Mill Yard at this time, and was not in a position to supply the pastoral help which the Oxfordshire believers needed, and which they might have preferred to seek from a Particular Baptist source, had one readily been available. We are assuming here that Edward Stennett's Particular views, as well as those of the Baptist churches which formed the Abingdon Association, had shaped the developing Berkshire and Oxfordshire Seventh-day Baptists, although the early defection of at least one Watlington Baptist to the 'free-willers' should not be overlooked.[95] That the desire to sustain a witness to the seventh day was of major concern at this time is evident from the case of a former member who was causing some perplexity amongst the Oxfordshire brethren. In December 1722, they had written to Mill Yard for 'advice . . . concerning Mr Mumford', who had previously

---

[92] MYM 228. Mill Yard's interest in the Oxfordshire Sabbatarians extended beyond those in the south-east of the county. In 1722 the church wrote to Bro. Fowler of Duxford reminding him of his 'duty to God and his holy Sabbath', 239.
[93] Ibid. 247–8.   [94] Ibid. 240.   [95] *BQ* 26: 19.

been in fellowship with them 'pretending to keep the Seventh-day Sabbath, and to be a partaker to them [*sic*], but withal pretending to others to keep the first day, and so to bring them to a mixed communion'.[96] Mill Yard's advice was short and to the point, that 'if Mr Mumford be for a mixt communion, not to receive him if he come again'.[97] The maintenance of a distinctive witness was evidently considered more important than any benefit that a mixed fellowship might have brought.

The records of the episcopal visitation of Thomas Secker[98] in 1738 throw further light on Dissenters in the Oxford diocese, probably because the visitation queries had made it plain that Secker would not be satisfied with any mere formality. The third of twelve detailed sets of questions put to the parish incumbents reads as follows:

Are there in your parish any Presbyterians, Independents, or Anabaptists? And how many of each sect, and of what rank? Have they one or more meeting houses in your parish, and are they duly licensed? What are the names of their teachers, and are they qualified according to law? Is their number lessened or increased of late years, and by what means?[99]

The reply from Thomas Toovey, the absentee vicar of Watlington, presumably on the basis of information supplied by his curate and the churchwardens, suggests a declining Sabbatarian cause, which perhaps by now had even capitulated to the exigency of mixed communion:

Very few Protestant Dissenters within this parish, and those few chiefly Sabbatarians and Anabaptists. The principal is one Nathaniel Nash a tanner, of good substance, but very wary and expounds but little to promote their interests. When any meeting is held it is at his house, and this about once a month. They used to have a teacher from Haddenham in Bucks, either a tailor or a shoemaker, I am informed, named Hoare. How and whether their house and teacher is licensed or qualified I can't say, neither did I think it prudent to enquire, for they dwindle by disregard [and] their numbers are decreased.[100]

[96] MYM 240.   [97] Ibid.
[98] Bishop of Oxford 1737–50, Archbishop of Canterbury 1758–68. See *DNB* and *ODCC.*
[99] ORO, MS Oxf. Dioc. d.554, fo. 160ᵛ; Jukes, *Articles of Enquiry*, 4.
[100] ORO, MS Oxf. Dioc. d.554, fo. 160ᵛ. See also Jukes, *Articles of Enquiry,* 163–5 for Toovey's return for Watlington, and *passim* for information on Dissenters in the diocese in general.

Some twenty years later the Sabbatarians were said to be the only remaining Dissenting sect in Watlington, and the Nash family their only representatives, keeping themselves 'pretty much to themselves' and seeming not 'to endeavour to draw others over to their persuasion'.[101]

The end was not yet, however. Although still without a regular minister, something in the mid-eighteenth century brought a measure of new life to the Watlington Sabbatarians, for by 1773 a small Dissenting congregation, 'chiefly Seventh Day Baptists', was reported as meeting occasionally, with 'preaching once in several weeks'.[102] This revived interest was sufficient to attract Thomas Hiller of Natton Seventh-day church and Tewkesbury to preach and administer the ordinances which, despite the distance, he did at regular intervals until his death in 1790. By 1793 two families constituted the Watlington congregation, and a report in 1794 referred to 'the Seventh-day friends at Watlington' having had 'the ordinances administered to them by the late Mr Hiller of Tewksbury . . . now supplied by Mr Hinton of Oxford'.[103] This was James Hinton, minister of the Baptist church at Oxford, who from 1792 preached regularly at Watlington, at one point on Saturday afternoons to a congregation said to number up to forty persons including some from neighbouring villages, but in later years once a month, or as his health permitted, on Friday evenings to the Stringer family.[104] They were the last surviving representatives of a cause that had persisted against all odds for nearly a century and a half. When Mary Stringer, a descendant of the Nash family, died in 1808 the light of the Watlington Sabbatarians was finally extinguished, and with it that of the Berkshire, Oxfordshire, and Buckinghamshire Seventh-day Men as well.

AMERSHAM, CHALFONT ST GILES, AND CHORLEY WOOD

1669 is a convenient date from which to commence a reconstruction of the Seventh-day movement in the south-east corner of Buckinghamshire, even if its beginnings can tentatively be suggested as somewhat earlier. In that year Sabbatarian conventicles were

[101] ORO, MS Oxf. Dioc. d.759, fo. 89; *VCH* Oxon., viii. 246.
[102] Josiah Thompson, 'The State of the Dissenting Interest', DWL, MS 38.5, fo. 30.
[103] *VCH* Oxon., iii. 246–7; John Rippon, *The Baptist Annual Register*, ii (1794), 11.
[104] *VCH* Oxon., viii. 246; J.H. Hinton, *A Biographical Portraiture of the Late Rev. James Hinton. M.A.* (1824), 96, 282, 328.

reported at Amersham[105] and Chorley Wood,[106] and a Fifth Monarchy group at Chalfont St Giles[107] which other evidence indicates was Seventh-day, if not at that point, then soon afterwards. The Amersham congregation was one of four Dissenting conventicles listed for the town in the diocesan records for 1669, the others being Presbyterian, Anabaptist, and Quaker. The Seventh-day people were described as 'Jews, so-called because they observe Saturday Sabbath', usually meeting in Sarah Grimsell's house, with Nicholas Babb, a weaver, their teacher, and 'often their preacher'.[108] Thus by 1669 the Amersham Sabbatarians were distinct from the other Baptists in the town, usually thought to have been General Baptists, who in 1675 divided over the issue of imposition of hands on newly baptized converts.[109] It appears that both the Sabbatarians and General Baptists maintained a reciprocally good relationship before and after 1669, the Sabbatarians here being likely to have leaned towards the free-will and universal redemption doctrines of their First-day brethren.

The more recent view of Baptist historians is that the Amersham General Baptists did not gather much before 1669, even though previous opinion favoured a General Baptist presence in Amersham as early as 1626.[110] This earlier date would have been in keeping with Amersham's history of a deep and lasting interest in Lollard tradition[111] and, even if only a general indication of earlier trends, would suggest an established radical Dissenting background for the existence of the Sabbatarian group prior to 1669. Be that as it may, John Stoning, Thomas Crawley's curate at Amersham, reported somewhat testily in 1669 that 'these Jews have had their meeting ever since I came to this place'.[112] This was in 1660 or very soon thereafter, and it establishes a Sabbatarian presence in Amersham from that time, or even from the late 1650s. In 1667 or early 1668 William Burnet, the Sabbatarian Baptist from Chertsey, represented the Amersham Baptists and others, together with Matthew Caffyn, in a debate against the Quakers held at Amersham,[113] and prompted it seems by the fear of further defections from the Baptist ranks to

[105] LAO, Diss. 8/1, 52.   [106] *BQ* 17: 85.   [107] *OR* i. 78.

[108] LAO, Diss. 8/1, 52. A John 'Grimsdale' was presented at Amersham in 1664 and 1666 for 'standing excommunicate', BRO, D/A/V 8, fo. 3.

[109] White, *English Baptists*, 121.

[110] DWL, Wilson, MS 63, I, 1. fo. 41; White, *English Baptists*, 121.

[111] Cross, *Church and People*, 32–5.   [112] LAO, Diss. 8/1, 52.

[113] Burnet, *The Capital Principles of the . . . Quakers Discovered*, 27.

Quakerism, which neither the Sabbatarians nor the General Baptists could afford. This situation was the main reason behind the publication of Burnet's *The Capital Principles of the . . . Quakers Discovered* (1668), an attempt to avert the Quaker threat to the Baptist churches in Buckinghamshire, Surrey, and Sussex. In the event, both the Seventh-day and First-day Baptists in Amersham survived any danger posed by the Quakers without much difficulty, for which the Sabbatarians must be given their share of credit.

At Chalfont St Giles, a Fifth Monarchy conventicle was one of three established there by 1669, meeting 'now and then' in the home of Henry Cock with teachers 'for the most part strangers'.[114] The key to the ultimate identity of this group is Henry Cock, reported in 1669 as a member 'of quality', and known by 1690 as one of the 'ministering brethren' to the Buckinghamshire Sabbatarians.[115] He had been born in Chalfont St Giles, although he may have descended from a well-known Lincolnshire Baptist family, and had spent some time in Ireland after serving as a soldier at Uxbridge in the Civil War.[116] At what point he or the Chalfont congregation became Seventh-day is not known and it is quite possible that they were already of that mind by 1669. A link with Amersham is established by the fact that his son, daughter, and wife were buried in the Amersham Baptist burial ground in 1689, 1694, and 1695 respectively.[117] He was noted as a General Baptist in 1689, and in 1701 his house was registered for meetings in Chalfont St Giles.[118] Given the 1690 designation, this would indicate that Sabbatarians

---

[114] LAO, Diss. 8/1, 12, where Cock is named Corke. Milton lived there from 1665, but makes no allusion to Sabbatarianism in the *De doctrina Christiana*. Milton's view was that the term Sabbath should be applied only to the seventh day, not to the first, and that those who 'live under the gospel are emancipated from the ordinances of the law', including the Sabbath. Hence 'no one day is appointed for divine worship in preference to another, except such as the church may set apart of its own authority for the voluntary assembling of its members', which may 'conveniently' be the first day: John Milton, *A Treatise of Christian Doctrine* tr. C.R. Sumner (Cambridge, 1825), 600–11.

[115] *OR* i. 28; *BQ* 14: 165. Cock was reported to the bishops in 1669 as a General Baptist, *MGA* i, pp. xlii–xliii.

[116] Edward Cock of Boston, Robert Cock of Westley, and Thomas Cocks of Fenstanton all appeared in the General Baptist *The Faith and Practise of Thirty Congregations Gathered according to the Primitive Pattern* (1651). Joan Cocks was noted in Lollard circles in Buckinghamshire early in the sixteenth century: Cross, *Church and People*, 33. On Henry Cock, see also Le Hardy (ed.), *Session Records (Buckinghamshire)*, i. 400, and *FMM* 246.

[117] Whitley, *Church Books of Ford . . . and Amersham*, 228, 233.

[118] *MGA* i, p. xliii.

were still worshipping at Chalfont early in the eighteenth century, either as a separate group or as part of a wider Buckinghamshire congregation.

The Amersham church was also reported to be in touch with a Sabbatarian group at Chorley Wood in 1669,[119] and had also had connections with Seventh-day believers in the Chesham area since at least 1663. In that year William Russell of Chesham, an erstwhile Sabbatarian himself, published *No Seventh-Day-Sabbath Commanded by Jesus Christ*, in which he apologized for a brief liaison with the Sabbatarians, and defended his renewed allegiance to the first day against Robert Turner, 'Pastor of the Sabbath-People at Bledlo [*sic*] and Charly-Wood [*sic*]'.[120] Russell had been convinced of the Seventh-day position earlier in 1663 when Thomas Tillam had appeared in a public disputation in the Chesham district as a protagonist for the Sabbatarian cause.[121] The Chorley Wood group is referred to again in the Amersham minutes in 1677, in conjunction with Robert Turner's burial in the new Amersham burial ground.[122] Nothing further is heard again specifically of Chalfont St Giles or Chorley Wood, or of Amersham until 1708.

In the 1690 Llanwenarth record of Seventh-day congregations then in existence, William Charsley was named as one of two ministers serving the Seventh-day church in Buckinghamshire, together with Henry Cock.[123] Charsley, and a continuing Seventh-day presence at Amersham, would probably have remained obscure without the attention of John Ball, an Oxford graduate, and later vicar of Chesham, who for some reason held an aversion to Charsley and his congregation.[124] In 1708 Ball launched a somewhat uncharitable attack on Charsley, then an old man, but still ministering to the Amersham Sabbatarians. Ball's intention appears to have been to undermine the validity of Charsley's ministry. In *The Anabaptist Teachers no Ministers of Christ proved in a letter to Mr*

---

[119] *BQ* 17: 85.

[120] William Russel[l], *No Seventh-Day-Sabbath Commanded*, title-page, 37.

[121] Ibid. 1, 12, 34.

[122] Whitley, *Church Books of Ford . . . and Amersham*, 210. The minutes show that Turner represented both Chorley Wood and Bledlow. In 1669 he had been reported as one of the teachers at the Amersham Anabaptist conventicle, Lambeth MS 639, fo. 214^r. Whitley noted that he 'linked the two groups', p. xii. A Captain Turner of Amersham was also reported as the teacher at an unspecified conventicle in Rickmansworth in 1669: *OR* i. 94.   [123] *BQ* 14: 165.

[124] Son of James Ball of Amersham, matriculated St Mary's Hall, Oxford, 1701, vicar of Chesham 1711–50.

Charsley, an Anabaptist Teacher at Agmondesham (1708) he argued the invalidity of Charsley's ministry on the grounds that it lacked the authority of apostolic succession, a proposition not likely to have impressed Baptists at any time. Besides confirming that the Amersham group were still meeting in 1708,[125] Ball's book called up some important links from the past. It referred to John Spittlehouse, the seventeenth-century Fifth Monarchist Sabbatarian, as 'the chief' of Charsley's 'faction', and to other radicals who Ball evidently thought would discredit Charsley and his people, including John James, the London Sabbatarian preacher who had been executed in 1661 for alleged treason.[126] Ball's efforts attracted a reply from Joseph Stennett, whose help the Amersham Sabbatarians had sought in warding off the unwelcome charges against their elder and his right to function as a true minister of Christ.[127] The incident is a substantial link in establishing the continuity of the Amersham Seventh-day people into the eighteenth century.

Even with this evidence the records are scanty and intermittent, and all that can be concluded with any certainty is that a Seventh-day congregation flourished at Amersham during the latter part of the seventeenth century, that it was still in existence early in the eighteenth century, and that it or a Sabbatarian witness of some kind may have lasted longer than that. The Mill Yard records, as has already been noted, refer to the Sabbath-keepers of Buckinghamshire between 1717 and 1724,[128] and inasmuch as Bledlow was extinct by then, it seems logical to conclude that the Buckinghamshire witness to the seventh day centred in the Amersham–Chalfont district. Whether or not it persisted for longer is an open question, but Daniel Noble of Mill Yard was invited to Amersham in 1770 to lay hands on newly baptized members.[129] The question is obvious, but if there was not a Sabbatarian connection, why was Noble invited? One answer could be that it was on account of his General

---

[125] John Ball, *The Anabaptist Teachers no Ministers of Christ, proved in a letter to Mr Charsley, an Anabaptist Teacher at Agmondesham* (1708), 9. Walter Wilson's report that Charsley was elder of the Amersham General Baptists by 1697, DWL, Wilson MS I, 1, fo. 41, can be explained (1) as an error or misunderstanding, (2) if Charsley was serving both First-day and Seventh-day congregations, (3) on the basis that a mixed-communion congregation existed by that date. On balance (2) and (3) are unlikely, although a mixed-communion church is not impossible at a later date.

[126] Ball, *Anabaptist Teachers*, 108.

[127] Joseph Stennett, 'Remarks Upon the letter sent to Mr Charsley', in *Works* iv. 318–35.

[128] MYM 228, 247.   [129] *BQ* 1: 136–7.

Baptist convictions, his standing in the General Baptist community at large, and his attachment to a representative First-day church, but if that was all that was required, others closer at hand might more easily have been found. His presence at Amersham in 1770 remains as a hint, if nothing more, of a lingering Seventh-day interest in Buckinghamshire.[130]

There are two or three further references to the Sabbatarian movement in the Oxfordshire–Chilterns area which should be noted before we leave it. A Baptist church had been established at Watford in Hertfordshire, at the eastern extremity of Chiltern country, *c.*1652, and by 1659 eight members were recorded as having 'gone off to the seventh day'.[131] In an untypically harsh reaction, the church terminated fellowship, and refused further communion with those who had seceded in favour of the Saturday Sabbath. There may have been a link with the Chiltern Sabbatarians to the west, for sixty years or so prior to the founding of the Beechen Grove Baptist church in Watford in 1707, a community of Baptists is said to have existed in West Hertfordshire and adjoining parts of Buckinghamshire with known preaching stations at Watford, Hemel Hempstead, and Chesham. This early Baptist congregation was in fellowship with Baptist churches in London, at Wapping, and Horsleydown, and had as one of its preachers George Eve, later known as a Sabbatarian.[132] Eve may have been one of the eight who seceded in favour of the seventh day in 1658–9. His name was one of the signatories to the *Faithful Testimony Against The Teachers of Circumcision and the Legal Ceremonies*, in 1667, and in 1669 a conventicle of Anabaptists, 'some of considerable estate', was reported at Watford under John Crawley and John (Richard?) Coleman, but without mention of Eve.[133] Nothing further is known of the Watford Sabbatarians. It can only be assumed that they had come to a decision over the seventh day at some point just prior to 1659, and that they continued in Saturday worship for a decade or so at least.

---

[130] Although an unattributed piece in an early *Baptist Quarterly* claims that Noble's visit was to the Amersham General Baptists, *BQ* 1: 136.

[131] White, *Association Records*, iii. 193. Cf. B.R. White, 'Baptist Beginnings in Watford', *BQ* 26: 205 ff.

[132] W. Urwick, *Nonconformity in Herts* (1884), 360–1; J. Stuart, *Beechen Grove Baptist Church, Watford* (1907), 9–11; *BQ* 26: 206. The other preachers were Richard Coleman, John Crawley, and John Reeve.

[133] Urwick, *Nonconformity in Herts*, 361. A meeting-place for Independents was certified by George Eve for Brent Pelham in 1669, ibid. 761.

At the other end of the region surveyed in this chapter, an event of wider significance for the survival of Seventh-day views occurred in Oxford gaol in 1665. Joseph Davis from Chipping Norton, who had become a Baptist at Coventry, was imprisoned at Oxford for ten years between 1662 and 1672, and while there was convinced of the Sabbath, perhaps through the influence of Edward Stennett. Davis shared 'the light' that was thus given 'by the Word and the Spirit' with another prisoner, and they both began to observe the seventh day forthwith.[134] Although it was another seven years before Davis was released from gaol, his attachment to the Saturday Sabbath never wavered, and his subsequent generosity to the Seventh-day cause in life and at death did much to ensure its survival in London and in other strategic locations around the country.[135]

Stennett had referred to 'many scattered disciples' in his correspondence with Newport, Rhode Island, and there were good examples not far away in the Chilterns. In 1682 Richard Parr, rector of Ibstone, wrote a rather sad and revealing letter to his bishop about the state of souls in his parish, complaining at the lack of interest in spiritual matters, 'Christianity being out of fashion', and most of his parishioners convinced that Anglican worship was 'tainted with popery'.[136] This would almost certainly have been the view of Thomas and Hannah Cook, Sabbatarians with whom Parr had apparently discussed the matter of attendance at the parish church and the requirements of government legislation pertaining thereto. He could only report to Bishop Fell 'their final answer', which was 'that if your Lordship can in words shew them an express command of Christ for keeping the Lord's day, they will then keep it, otherwise they must obey God rather than men'.[137]

This was not talk calculated to placate bishops intent on repressing Dissent, and it is not surprising that Thomas Cook and his wife, together with five others from Ibstone and neighbouring Turville, were summoned to the Buckinghamshire Quarter Sessions the following year for continued non-attendance at their parish church.[138] Parr's letter had, in fact, indicated that the Cooks may have been

---

[134] [Davis], *Last Legacy* (1720), 29–30.
[135] On Davis's benefactions to the Sabbatarian cause see above, 87; *Reports from the Commissioners for Charities*, xix, pt. I, 870–3.
[136] ORO, MS Oxf. Dioc. c.430, fo. 24, cited in Clapinson (ed.), *Bishop Fell*, 22–4.
[137] Clapinson (ed.), *Bishop Fell*, 23.
[138] Le Hardy (ed.), *Sessions Records (Buckinghamshire)*, i. 125.

practising Sabbatarians for some years prior to 1682, perhaps since 1665 or 1666, for he had given a similar account on the state of affairs in the parish to Fell's predecessor, Walter Blandford. Parr affirmed that both reports had given 'a true account of the state and condition' of his parish, and ventured to suggest that because nothing had been done to suppress Dissent in the district, matters had grown worse, Dissenters ever since having been 'greater neglectors of the divine service'.[139] It was this spirit, intransigence to the episcopal authorities, devotion to truth to Nonconformists and Dissenters, that also helped to perpetuate observance of the seventh day, in small congregations and in isolated family circles.

[139] Clapinson (ed.), *Bishop Fell*, 23. Blandford was bishop of Oxford 1665–71.

7

The Cotswolds and
the Severn Valley

O f the thirty or so counties in England and Wales in which Seventh-day views are known to have appeared at some point during the seventeenth or eighteenth centuries,[1] it was in Gloucestershire that Sabbatarian groups were most numerous and widely distributed. The Llanwenarth record, which provides such useful information on the state of the Seventh-day movement immediately after the great persecution of the 1680s, notes specifically that two separate congregations existed in Gloucestershire in 1690, each with an elder and 'several ministering brethern'.[2] By congregation, it seems that a church consisting of several scattered groups in a wide geographical area is meant, rather than a specific congregation settled in one location. One such congregation appears to have flourished in the high Cotswold country to the north and east of the county, centring around Bourton-on-the-Water and Stow-on-the-Wold. The other was located in the Severn Valley with its centre in the parish of Ashchurch at the foot of the Cotswolds and just south of the Worcestershire border.

A persistent Seventh-day presence can also be traced in the Horsley–Nailsworth area in the south of the county, although it is not clear whether the Sabbatarians here belonged to one of the other two congregations, or constituted a third and perhaps earlier group which had largely disappeared as an identifiable congregation by 1690. Whatever the status of the Sabbatarians here, they kept alive Seventh-day doctrine well into the eighteenth century, as did the upper Gloucestershire congregation. Those in the Severn

---

[1] See Appendix V for the distribution of the Sabbatarian movement by counties.
[2] *BQ* 14: 165. Perhaps Tyndale's Gloucestershire roots and his zeal for a thoroughly biblical faith, as well as the 'strain of Lollardy' which persisted in the county (Cross, *Church and People*, 75), reflect something in the Gloucestershire mind which made obedience to the literal word of the fourth commandment both easy and necessary. T.M. Parker suggests there may have been a link between Lollardy and the work of Tyndale, *The English Reformation to 1558* (1950), 27–9.

STAFFORDSHIRE

▲ Wolverhampton
Dudley×

WARWICKSHIRE
×
Warwick

WORCESTERSHIRE
★ Alderminster

×Mickleton

Birlingham
Upton-on-Severn ★ ×   Ashton-under-Hill
Bredon's Norton▲ ×Overbury +Pa×ford
Westmancote ×○ ×Kemerton
Tewkesbury● ×Bredon   Stow-on-
Natton ★Oxenton the-Wold
Bishop's Cleeve × Naunton ★ × ★Oddington
Cheltenham ★ Notgrove ★ ×+Bourton-on-the-Water
×Badgeworth
GLOUCESTERSHIRE
×Haresfield Bibury★
×Wheatenhurst   Fairford ▲
★○Kings Stanley

Horsley▲

Hillesley●

Chipping Sodbury▲
★
Stapleton

★ Confirmed Sabbatarian congregation
+ Probable Sabbatarian congregation
● Mixed-communion congregation
× Sabbatarian presence: no known congregation
▲ Possible Sabbatarian interest

MAP 4 Locations in counties in the Severn Valley, the Cotswolds, and Staffordshire associated with seventeenth- and eighteenth-century Sabbatarianism

Valley finally settled on Natton[3] as their centre, and have the distinction of being the most long-lived Sabbatarian congregation in the country outside London.

For a religious movement that only infrequently finds its way into the history books this represents a notable presence. In the period between 1620 and 1770 there are evidences of Saturday Sabbatarianism in at least twenty locations in Gloucestershire, from Mickleton in the far north to Hillesley in the south, and from Oddington on the Oxfordshire border to Tewkesbury on the banks of the Severn. In the seventeenth and eighteenth centuries Sabbatarianism can also be traced in six or seven localities in that part of Worcestershire which bordered Gloucestershire around Tewkesbury and Ashchurch. Not all these locations represent a Sabbatarian group, and when one did exist it was usually small. While Gloucestershire was clearly the focus of Seventh-day observance in this region, Saturday Sabbatarians were also found in neighbouring parts of Oxfordshire and Warwickshire, as well as in Worcestershire. Usually they were isolated adherents to the seventh day and in fellowship with one of the Gloucestershire congregations, but there is evidence that a hitherto unknown group existed at Alderminster in Worcestershire, which may have had some connection with Sabbatarians elsewhere.

In 1664 Robert and Anne Phypps, Frances Phypps, and Alice Robbins and her son William, together with several others from Alderminster whose names have not survived, were presented to the diocesan authorities as 'Sabbatarians' and for refusing to pay their contributions to the church clerk's wages. Anne Phypps, 'a Sabbatarian', was also presented for refusing to make public thanksgiving at the parish church after childbirth, and Alice Robbins and her sons William and Nathaniel were reported for refusing to give an Easter offering to the local Anglican incumbent.[4] It is a classic

---

[3] The Sabbatarian congregation in the Tewkesbury area is usually referred to as the Natton church. Natton is a small hamlet two or three miles to the east of Tewkesbury, and situated in the parish of Ashchurch. The Seventh-day people did not actually settle at Natton until the middle of the eighteenth century. It is therefore anachronistic to speak of the 'Natton church' before that time.

[4] HWRO, 807/2289/1. Only a portion of the relevant document remains. Alderminster was in Worcestershire until 1931 when it was transferred to Warwickshire. In the seventeenth century it was also known as Aldermaston. There may have been some connection with the Alderminster Sabbatarians and Richard Annis, 'a baptised person keeping the Seventh-day Sabbath' and a member of the Baptist Church at Warwick, who was received into fellowship at Pinners' Hall in 1702 on a letter of recommendation from Warwick: PHCB 85–6.

picture of Nonconformist obduracy, for which the reward was, at the least, excommunication from the Anglican fold. Ten years later the records show that Alice Robbins and William Robbins and his wife were again presented as 'Sabbatarians' and 'known sectaries, frequenting conventicles in other parishes'.[5] In 1676 Alice, and William and his wife Eleanor, with William Etheridge, and Thomas and Joan Finder who were already excommunicate since 1666 for their 'Anabaptisticall opinions' and for 'frequenting conventicles in other places', were reported, with others, as 'being Sabbatarians Quakers and Anabaptists'.[6] The last that is heard officially of the Alderminster Sabbatarians is in 1679 when a somewhat under-standably weary churchwarden wrote of 'several reputed heretics or schismatics . . . who have oftentimes been presented by their names, . . . are recorded in the [Bishop's] court at Worcester and are most of them under sentence of excommunication'.[7] A similar fate may have befallen Katherine Nicholls and Jane Smith, who in 1674 had been presented at Birlingham near Pershore, as Sabbatarians.[8] There can be little doubt that the Seventh-day Sabbath was well represented in the south-east corner of Worcestershire for much of the latter half of the seventeenth century.

GLOUCESTERSHIRE BEGINNINGS

The first known evidence of a renewed interest in the seventh day in Gloucestershire appeared at Tewkesbury in 1620. This was earlier than at any other place in the country except London, and possibly those areas in Devon and Cambridgeshire where John Traske had worked prior to going to London in 1615.[9] Indeed, Whitley thought that it was due to Traske's influence that Sabbatarian sentiments surfaced at Tewkesbury,[10] although there seems to be little evidence that Traske or any of his disciples visited Glouces-tershire either before or after he had introduced Seventh-day worship in London. In any attempt to explain why the Saturday Sabbath appeared so early in seventeenth-century Gloucestershire or was widely entertained in that county, it should not be forgotten that in 1448 the Gloucestershire Lollard, William Fuer, had confessed to an interest in the Old Testament Sabbath.[11]

[5] HWRO, 807/2289/1.   [6] Ibid.; DWL, G.L. Turner MS 89/12.
[7] HRWO, 897/2289/1.   [8] HRWO, 802/2884, fo. 170ʳ.   [9] See above, 50–1.
[10] Whitley, 'Men of the Seventh Day', 2/3.   [11] See above, 32.

Whatever the immediate or more distant background, in June 1620 three principal burgesses of Tewkesbury, George Shaw, Roger Plevey, and Edward Hill, were warned that they were in danger of losing their municipal rights, apparently for observing Saturday rather than Sunday as the Sabbath. They were given eight weeks in which to acknowledge that the Christian Sabbath, or Lord's day, was 'God's holy ordinance', and that no man had the right to transfer the Sabbath institution from one day to another. The matter was considered significant enough to refer to the Council for the Welsh Marches, which required the three to appear before the Court of High Commission, should they persist in their views. George Shaw stood his ground for a time, refusing to respond to the Council's ultimatum, but by November all three had been fully exonerated, presumably because they had agreed to an ordinance of the Borough Council which had required their acquiescence concerning the Sabbath.[12] The issue was not whether they would obey the fourth commandment, but which day they should observe in their obedience. The carefully worded action of the Council would, however, with a little thought, have allowed a Sabbatarian to obey the commandment as his conscience dictated.[13] It may have been intentional.

Sabbatarians were reported again in and around Tewkesbury c.1640, and a church with Sabbatarian interests is first supposed to have appeared in the area at about the same time.[14] If a congregation did exist at this date, it may well have been mixed-communion for a number of years. As in other parts of the country, the Seventh-day issue surfaced at Baptist Association gatherings, and in 1657, at a meeting of the Midlands Association at Alcester in Warwickshire, a question from the Tewkesbury church was tabled for discussion. They wanted advice regarding the Sabbath, 'Whether ye last day of ye week commonly called Satterday be to be observed as a Sabbath now under the gospel of Christ.' The consensus was strongly against

---

[12] *VCH* Glos., viii. 149.

[13] They were required to 'acknowledge the Fourth Commandment to be a perpetual moral law of God, and the Christian Sabbath or Lord's Day to be God's holy ordinance, and that it is not in man's power to alter the number of one day in seven for a Sabbath to any other proportion of time', W.B. Willcox, *Gloucestershire: A Study in Local Government 1590–1640* (New Haven, Conn., 1940), 220 n. 50, citing Tewkes. Corp. Rec. 2. Given the argument that the Sabbath was really the Lord's day since He had created it, this was precisely what Sabbatarians stood for.

[14] B.H. Blacker (ed.), *Gloucestershire Notes and Queries*, ii (1884), 354; *SO* 1: 197.

the seventh day, with the exception of one messenger who was not 'fully satisfied'.[15] Presumably he was not the Tewkesbury messenger who had raised the question and who represented a church which itself was undecided about the matter. The question remained open for a time yet at Tewkesbury, for by 1661 some members were still reported as 'owning the Lord's holy Sabbath', in context a clear reference to Saturday, which Whitley interpreted as evidence for 'the growing adoption of Seventh-day tenets by some of the members'. A contemporary list of the Tewkesbury members includes John Cowell, one of the two elders and by then a practising Sabbatarian, John Purser, one of three deacons and already preaching to a Seventh-day group in his home parish of Ashchurch, and Stephen Mumford, soon to plant the seeds of Sabbath doctrine in New England soil.[16]

The 1660s and early 1670s constitute an important era for the Gloucestershire Sabbatarians, particularly those in the Tewkesbury–Ashchurch area, and may be regarded as a time of transition for both them and the Tewkesbury Baptists. It marks the end of what probably was a mixed-communion church at Tewkesbury, and the final establishment of a distinct Sabbatarian congregation in the Ashchurch and Aston-upon-Carrant[17] district with its own organization and ministry, distinct from the continuing Tewkesbury Baptist church. John Cowell and John Purser were the key figures in these events.

Cowell had adopted the seventh day in 1661, and although he abandoned it thirteen years later in 1674, he played an important part in establishing the Seventh-day movement in this area.[18] For most of that time, if not all of it, he was one of the elders of the Tewkesbury Baptist church, with a wider influence in the Sabbatarian movement elsewhere in the country. Initially a strong contender for the Saturday Sabbath, he published *A Beame of Sabbath Light* (1664) and *Divine Oracles* (1664),[19] in which he argued in favour of the seventh day. Already by 1664, however, he had begun to have

---

[15] White, *Association Records*, i. 32. Recorded also in the Leominster church book, 16.

[16] *70th Annual Report of the Seventh Day Baptist Historical Society* (1986), document E, 6; Whitley, 'Men of the Seventh Day', 8/2; GRO, D4944, 2/1, fos. 21ᵛ–23ʳ; D4944 1/2, 1, where Cowell is described as a 'teaching Elder' in 1663.

[17] Or variously Ashton-upon-Carrant, Aston-on-Carron, or Ashton-on-Carrow, or Ashton-upon-Carron.   [18] Cowell, *The Snare Broken*, 1.

[19] Neither Cox, *Literature of the Sabbath Question*, nor Whitley, *Baptist Bibliography*, mention Cowell's *A Beame of Sabbath Light* (1664), of which the only known

some misgivings, largely on account of the 'desperate, dangerous, and pernicious practices' of the Tillam–Pooley faction in East Anglia, who were advocating circumcision, animal sacrifices, and the entire Levitical system, even going to the extent of prohibiting the trimming of beards and wearing garments made of both linen and wool.[20] In 1668, Cowell says, some confusion arose within the Sabbatarian movement over the time at which observance of the Sabbath should begin. Some argued that the Sabbath began at sunset on Friday and should be kept from then until sunset on Saturday, and some said that it should be kept from 'darkness to darkness', i.e. an hour or so after sunset.[21] To Cowell, this contention over what appeared to him a peripheral matter was further evidence of a legalistic element within the ranks of Sabbatarians.

By 1671 he had become convinced that Saturday Sabbatarianism tended inevitably to legalism. 'The practice carries it in its womb,' he said. This growing conviction would not have been modified by one local Sabbath-keeper who, according to Cowell, denied the Messiahship of Christ and disavowed the New Testament, tearing it from her Bible and keeping only the Old Testament. Cowell's association with the Sabbatarian movement at what undoubtedly was its most vulnerable period had led him to the conclusion that 'many Sabbath keepers' had 'turned from the Gospel to the Law, and so from Christ to Moses'.[22] Finally, in 1674, he left the Seventh-day movement, remaining as elder at Tewkesbury, and published his revised convictions in *The Snare Broken* (1677), in which he repudiated his earlier works, confessing that his *Beame of Sabbath Light* had 'since proved a heavy beam' indeed.[23] Cowell seems to have been honest and without malice in his change of heart, although his reversion to Sunday worship does not seem to have had as much effect on the Sabbatarian cause in the Tewkesbury–Ashchurch area as might have been anticipated, except perhaps to precipitate the separation of the local Sabbatarians into a distinct fellowship.

John Purser is recorded as the first known pastor of the Sabbatarian

---

copy is in Edinburgh University Library. Cox does not list *Divine Oracles* either, and, although he quotes liberally from *The Snare Broken*, does not seem to know of Edward Stennett's reply, *The Insnared Taken in the Work of his Hands* (1677), for which Whitley gives an inaccurate title, *BB* i. 108. Stennett rather tartly chides Cowell, 'I thought you had learned better than to judge of the truth by the miscarriage of its professors.'

[20] Cowell, *The Snare Broken*, 4–6, 49.
[21] Ibid. 7–8.   [22] Ibid. 12–15.   [23] Ibid. 6.

congregation in the Ashchurch parish, later the Natton church, a role which he fulfilled for a remarkable sixty years from 1660 until his death in 1720. Purser was descended from a wealthy and influential family, but had been disinherited upon adopting the Seventh-day Sabbath and had turned to farming as a livelihood, settling in Aston-upon-Carrant. He is known to have preached to Sabbath-keepers in his own home from 1660 or thereabouts while he, and at least some of them, were still members of the Tewkesbury Baptist church.[24] There are hints that a group of Sabbatarians had begun to worship in Ashchurch *c.*1650, with Purser as a probationary preacher.[25] Given the earlier history of the area, this is not at all improbable. By the early 1660s, Cowell was the principal preacher to this group, with Purser his assistant, and it seems that while Cowell's interest and influence declined through the 1660s, that of Purser increased until he was recognized as the spiritual head of the Sabbatarian community and his house the principal meeting-place of Sabbatarians in the vicinity. Later there were several preaching stations in other locations as much as twenty-five miles distant. One account states that there were up to a dozen branches of the Aston-upon-Carrant church scattered throughout Gloucestershire and Worcestershire.[26] Some of these small Sabbatarian groups may already have been in existence and served by Purser at the time the work became centred at Aston, or shortly thereafter. Several of them appear intermittently in various records over the next century or so, giving brief but important glimpses into the continuing history of the Seventh-day cause in the Severn Valley.

Meanwhile, at King's Stanley to the south a Seventh-day congregation may have been in existence as early as 1640. King's Stanley was the mother church of the better-known Shortwood, or Horsley, Baptist church (now at Nailsworth), and seems to have originated as a Sabbatarian group. This rather unusual order of events was not unique in Gloucestershire, for at least one other Baptist church arose through the preaching of a Seventh-day Baptist minister before settling as a First-day congregation.[27] The records for King's Stanley

[24] *SR* 2/1: 1; *SDBEA* 1: 45; Tewkesbury church book, GRO, D4944, 2/1, fo. 21ᵛ.
[25] *SO* 1: 197.
[26] *SR* 2/1: 1; *SO* 1: 220–1. Groups at Cheltenham, Oxenton, Ashton-under-Hill, and Upton-on-Severn will be noted, with others, as part of the Aston–Natton church during the eighteenth century. Philip Jones is also said to have preached to Sabbatarians at Paxford.   [27] At Naunton, see below, 213.

are again scarce, since the original church book has not survived, but on the basis of historical fragments from the area, including the Shortwood church book and the Stroud *Free Church News*, a tradition has been preserved which has about it a ring of authenticity:

It is certain that in 1640 there was at King's Stanley a fellowship of baptised believers. Little is known of their doctrines and practices, except that they were Seventh Day Baptists, and that they worshipped from house to house according to the custom of the early church. This may have been a counsel of prudence, for at that time the rectory was in the gift of the king. But during the Commonwealth they doubtless 'lengthened their cords and strengthened their stakes', for when the Restoration let loose the spirit of persecution it met here with a sturdy resistance. Driven from their meetings, the members sought cover in the Penn Wood, where they gathered for worship under a tree, for long years afterwards known and honoured as the 'Gospel Beech', . . . Many of the members suffered fine, persecution and imprisonment; one of them, Samuel Jones (an ancestor of the Rev. Thomas Hillier [Hiller], a Baptist minister of Tewkesbury) was often fined and finally cast into Gloucester gaol, for unswerving devotion to his faith. When the days of toleration came the Church settled in a secluded byway known since as Meeting House Lane.[28]

It is known from other sources that Thomas Hiller, who was born a century later in King's Stanley, came from an established Seventh Day Baptist family. His mother was Mary Jones, sister of Philip Jones, who ministered so effectively to the Natton Sabbatarians during the eighteenth century.[29] Jones and Hiller remained convinced and practising Sabbatarians throughout their lives. Even though the evidence is scarce, it seems well established that a Sabbatarian presence did prevail at King's Stanley for a considerable time, and reasonably clear that, in terms of the Seventh-day movement elsewhere in the country, it began at an early date.

THE SEVERN VALLEY AND THE NATTON CHURCH

Under Purser's diligent care the church at Aston-upon-Carrant was established on a sound doctrinal and spiritual basis, and began to

---

[28] *King's Stanley Baptist Church: 330th Anniversary* (1970), 1, 2. Cf. *BAR* iii. 15, where the Dissenting interest at King's Stanley is said to have been 'the most ancient of any in Gloucestershire'.

[29] DWL, Wilson MS 63, I, V, fo. 10; Rippon, *BAR* i. 155–6.

prosper. Although never numerically large it maintained a consistent membership level over the first hundred years of its life, in spite of harassment during the earlier years of Purser's ministry.[30] Ashchurch at the end of the seventeenth century was only a small parish of some 300 inhabitants, and in Aston-upon-Carrant itself there were only twenty families. The neighbouring hamlet of Natton, which was part of the parish and ultimately the home of the Ashchurch Sabbatarians, was even smaller. It is quite remarkable that the Seventh-day Sabbath struck such deep roots in so small a community. It also helps to explain why the Sabbatarian church here consistently attracted some adherents from neighbouring communities, either as regular or occasional worshippers,[31] or as members who usually worshipped with one of the other groups associated with Natton or even with First-day churches.

Indeed, it might be thought that some of these other Sabbatarian groups would have been of greater significance than Aston itself. Purser also conducted services at Cheltenham, Upton-on-Severn, Paxford, and in the neighbouring parish of Oxenton, most of which had a bigger population than Aston, or even Ashchurch as a whole.[32] By the time Purser died in 1720, there were twenty regular worshippers at Aston, but a further forty at Oxenton.[33] It seems that at this point Oxenton was almost a distinct congregation, although soon after the Aston congregation had transferred to the new meeting-house at Natton the Gloucestershire diocesan records mention Anabaptists only at Oxenton. This is in sharp contrast to the specific listing of Sabbatarians at several other locations in the same returns.[34] It would seem that the Oxenton group was relatively short-lived and that what remained of it from the mid-eighteenth century onward

---

[30] *SR* 2/1: 1; *SO* 1: 212.

[31] Perhaps there is a further indication here of a Gloucestershire tradition. In the records of Laud's archiepiscopal visitation in 1635 there is a note that the people of Gloucestershire were 'much given to straggle from their own parishes to hear strangers', cited in Cross, *Church and People*, 181.

[32] It is not entirely clear whether figures given for Aston or Natton in various records include members from these neighbouring groups or not. No membership or attendance figures for any of these other groups appear until the mid-eighteenth century.

[33] *VCH* Glos., viii. 227; *TBHS* 2: 99. John Evans, 'Dissenting Congregations and Ministers in England and Wales, 1715–1729', DWL, MS 38.4. Evans seems not to have realized that John Persaw (*sic*) 'Seventh Day' of Ashton-upon-Carron, was also the John Purser of Oxenton. Evans gives twenty 'Hearers' for Aston, and forty for Oxenton.   [34] GRO, GDR/397/381A.

merged with the Aston–Natton church. At a distance of nearly four centuries that which seems to have centred the Sabbatarian cause in Ashchurch, as much as anything, was the solid foundation laid by John Purser, and the single-minded dedication of the Purser family to the Seventh-day cause through several generations.[35]

John Purser was succeeded at Aston-upon-Carrant by Edmund Townsend, a member of Aston, whom we have met already as a supply preacher at Mill Yard and pastor of the Pinners' Hall church. These appointments came after his pastorate at Aston, where he began his ministry in 1720, being ordained in 1722 'that he might administer ye ordinances amongst us and preach to other churches in want'.[36] There might be a hint here of an expansion among the Gloucestershire Sabbatarians in the early eighteenth century, or perhaps of a recognition of other Seventh-day groups as congregations in their own right. The Mill Yard minutes refer to a letter received from Gloucestershire in 1717, telling of 'the increase of the Sabbath'.[37] Townsend appears to have travelled about the country in fulfilment of his ordination charge, and one account, with some licence perhaps, even says 'from one end of England to the other' in his quest to extend the Sabbatarian cause.[38] It is known that Townsend lived in London for a time during his Aston pastorate, and that he then supplied the joint Mill Yard–Pinners' Hall pulpit. He was reputed to be an accomplished preacher, and when he finally left the Aston–Natton district for Pinners' Hall, Gloucestershire's loss was clearly London's gain. Mill Yard thought it prudent, in 1726 when Townsend ceased to preach there, to write to Gloucestershire 'to give a narrative of matters, how Mr Townsend and wee came to part from each other'.[39] The letter has not survived, but the minute records that Mill Yard had 'somewhat against' Townsend and suggests that they feared his departure might result in a loss of members. Townsend himself had probably grown increasingly uncomfortable with Mill Yard's Arminianism, and perhaps its incipient Unitarianism. In any case, Cornthwaite was by then available to serve Mill Yard, and Pinners' Hall was accordingly

---

[35] One of the three surviving members of the Natton church in 1901 was John Purser, then living in Tewkesbury, Commissioners for Charities MS 210274/A/7.
[36] *SO* 1: 116; *SR* 2/1: 1.   [37] MYM 228.   [38] *SO* 1: 117.
[39] MYM 253. The same minutes, for 7 Aug. 1726, list ten Mill Yard members already showing an interest in the Cripplegate church, now under Townsend. See also *SO* 1: 117.

pleased to call Townsend. The arrangements suited all concerned except, presumably, those at Aston-upon-Carrant.

When Philip Jones was appointed to follow Townsend in 1727, it is said that 'the golden age of the Natton church'[40] began. Services were still being conducted in the Purser farmhouse at Aston when Jones began his ministry, and the shift to Natton as the focus of Sabbatarian activity in the area was one of the notable developments of this period. Jones, originally from King's Stanley and the son of Samuel Jones, a stalwart of King's Stanley church in its Sabbatarian days, lived at Cheltenham for some years, preaching there and at Aston, Paxford, and 'other towns' in the county.[41] He ministered to these groups for a total of forty-three years, and under his diligent care the Sabbatarian cause at several locations in the Severn Valley reached its greatest prosperity. From a membership of twenty in Ashchurch c.1720,[42] the number grew steadily to twenty-four in 1735,[43] to twenty-six in 1750,[44] and to around thirty by the time Jones died in 1770.[45] The numbers are not large, but given the constituency and comparable figures for the Baptist church at Tewkesbury,[46] neither are they small.

[40] *SO* 1: 212; *SDBEA*, 1: 45. Cf. PHCB 96, where, for 1727, 'ye church at Alston' [Aston or Ashton] is said to be 'under ye care of Mr James' [Jones]. Some accounts refer to a Thomas Boston being considered as a replacement for Townsend, e.g. *SR* 2/1: 1.

[41] *SR* 2/1: 1; Walter Wilson, 'An Account of Various Congregations in England, among the Presbyterians, Independents, and Baptists', DWL, MS 63, I, 3, fo. 339. Jones is said to have preached also at Westmancote and Bredon's Norton in Worcestershire once a month until 1769. Robert Brown, ejected from White Ladies Aston, near Bredon, ministered to a Baptist church in Westmancote in 1679. Baxter described him as a 'fervent, honest Fifth-Monarchy man', *CR* 81. Mary Harvey, previously baptized at Westmancote, was admitted a member at Natton in 1847 on profession of her belief in the Saturday Sabbath. The seventh day appears again at Westmancote and Bredon c.1870 when Sabbatarians from here are listed among the members of the Kinsham church: GRO, D4944 10/1/4; 10/2/1.

[42] John Evans, 'Dissenting Congregations and Ministers in England and Wales', 1715, DWL, MS 38.4, p. 44. The figure of thirty members at Aston-upon-Carrant for 1727, *SO* 1: 220, may include 'hearers', as it may also reflect communicant members from other locations.

[43] GRO, GDR/285B(1), G. Dutton, who transcribed the original diocesan returns for 1735, claimed that the figures returned referred to families rather than individuals, GRO, D1762/4. On this basis, there were twenty-four Sabbatarian families in the Ashchurch parish of 600 inhabitants, which seems unlikely.

[44] GRO, GDR/381A.   [45] DWL, Wilson MS 63, V, fo. 8.

[46] In 1771 there were thirty-seven members at Tewkesbury: Wilson MS, DWL, 63, I, v. fo. 9ᵛ.

The centralization of the Ashchurch work at Natton and the consolidation of the Seventh-day cause in the area as a whole were substantially helped by the provision of a regular meeting-place in 1746, made possible by the generosity of Benjamin Purser. Although modest in size, and little more than the extension of a barn, it served the Sabbatarians of Natton and the adjacent area for a further 150 years and more. When Purser died in 1765 he left the meeting-house and its burial ground to the church.[47] Meanwhile, by the will of Samuel Purser, who died in 1757, half the interest on investments from his estate was eventually to be paid to the ministry of the Natton church 'for ever', and the other half to the poor and needy of the congregation.[48] If events had not taken an unfortunate turn a century later, Samuel's faith in the continuity of the Natton work might have been unexpectedly justified.

In 1731 Philip Jones moved from Cheltenham to Upton-on-Severn and shortly assumed responsibility for the First-day Baptist church there, continuing in that capacity as well as serving as pastor of the Aston–Natton Seventh-day church until his death in 1770.[49] In this instance, the Seventh-day cause seems to have been stronger rather than weaker on account of its minister's First-day interests. He was highly regarded in both First- and Seventh-day circles, serving as moderator at meetings of the Midland Baptist Association on at least five occasions.[50] There are conflicting accounts whether a separate Seventh-day congregation met at Upton under Jones's care and, if so, whether or not it was a branch of the Aston–Natton church, or whether the Sabbatarians there were part of a mixed-communion church with full membership at Natton. The former

---

[47] *VCH* Glos., viii. 187; *SR* 2/1: 1.

[48] GRO, D4944 10/1/1. All income from his invested estate was to be paid to his mother during her life, and thereafter to the Natton minister and congregation.

[49] *SR* 2/1: 1; *BB* i. 221; Benjamin Francis, *An Elegy on the Death of the Reverend Mr. Philip Jones, late Minister of the Gospel at Upton-on-Severn* (1771); H.W. Cox, *A Short History of the Upton Baptist Church: Its Origin, Growth, and Progress 1653–1953* (n.p., 1953). A curious note in the Upton church book may reflect the staunch sentiments of a later Sunday-keeper. Philip Jones, it reads, 'was never really their pastor or member of their church . . . observing the seventh day and having previous to his coming to Upton been ordained pastor over a small Seventh Day Church at Natton'.

[50] In 1738, 1745, 1751, 1754, and 1756: W. Stokes, *The History of the Midland Association of Baptist Churches 1655 to 1855* (1855), 88–9. See *An Elegy, passim*, for an appreciation of 'holy Jones'. G.F. Nuttall describes Jones as a man 'of influence in the Baptist churches', *JEH* 27 (1976), 384.

seems to have been the more likely, at least while there were
sufficient Sabbatarians at Upton to constitute a small congregation.[51]
A Baptist church had existed at Upton since the mid-seventeenth
century, and although its records show a strong contingent of
Pursers[52] for much of the eighteenth century, there are no direct
references to Sabbatarians or the seventh day. 'A Sabbatarian congregation near Upton' is mentioned in one source,[53] although Natton
was near enough to be so described. Elizabeth Purser, 'having settled
in the country', was dismissed from Curriers' Hall to Upton in 1787,[54]
and in 1866 two members were transferred from Upton to Natton.[55]
Once again the evidence is minimal, but sufficient to indicate a
lingering interest in the Seventh-day Sabbath at Upton-on-Severn.

The Gloucestershire diocesan records for the mid-eighteenth
century throw further light on the extent of the Sabbatarian cause
at that period, but do little to clarify its inner structure. A careful
survey of the diocese conducted by Bishop Martin Benson in 1735,
and recorded in his own hand, shows the number of Nonconformists in each parish in the following denominations: Papists, Presbyterians, Anabaptists, Independents, Quakers, Sabbatarians and
Congregationalists, and those whose denomination was not specified. Sabbatarians are thus, in this instance, clearly distinguished
from Anabaptists and Independents.[56] The significance of the classification 'Sabbatarians and Congregationalists' will shortly be noted.

In the parish of Ashchurch there were twenty-four Sabbatarians,[57]
and in the nearby parish of Bishop's Cleeve (sometimes designated
Stoke Orchard) two were reported, with fifteen Anabaptists and a
Quaker meeting with 'Fifth Monarchy Men from other places in a

---

[51] Based on information gathered by John Evans, 'The Baptist Interest under
George I', *TBHS* 2: 106; *Gloucestershire Notes and Queries*, ii. 354. The conclusion
that under Jones 'the Upton church was Calvinistic Seventh-day' is better understood
of a discrete Seventh-day congregation than of the Upton Baptist Church, *TBHS* 5:
235.

[52] The births of eight children to John and Jane Purser between 1745 and 1759,
and of seven to John and Mary Purser between 1768 and 1785, are recorded in the
Upton church book, with many other references to branches of the Purser family.
Philip Jones's daughter Hannah, b. 1737 at Upton, married a William Purser, Upton
church book, *passim.*

[53] Josiah Thompson, 'The Dissenting Interest in England and Wales, 1772–3', DWL,
MS 38.6, fo. 39.

[54] PHCB 130.   [55] GRO, D4944 10/1/2, fo. 5ʳ.

[56] See below, on Oddington, for the significance of the unusual classification
'Sabbatarians and Congregationalists'.   [57] GRO, GDR/285B(1).

poor thatched cottage'.[58] At Badgeworth, between Gloucester and Cheltenham, there were three Sabbatarians in 1735 and again in 1743 and 1750,[59] while at Cheltenham 'seven or eight' Sabbatarians were reported in 1743 and 1750.[60] It is not clear whether the Badgeworth and Cheltenham groups were part of the Ashchurch congregation, which had grown to twenty-six by 1750,[61] or whether they constituted a congregation in their own right. Philip Jones had preached regularly at Cheltenham before moving to Upton in 1731, Townsend's ordination had authorized him to preach to other Sabbatarian churches besides Aston-upon-Carrant, and Purser was said to have preached at Cheltenham in the seventeenth century. The question whether the Cheltenham Sabbatarians were constitutionally part of the Aston church is to some extent academic, the point being that Seventh-day interests appear to have been represented at Cheltenham from the mid-seventeenth century to the mid-eighteenth century. The lone Sabbatarian reported at Haresfield in 1750 and the 'Jew' reported at Wheatenhurst[62] were probably in communion with any remaining Seventh-day interest at nearby King's Stanley. These fragmentary records, valuable though they are, do little more than confirm a small but widespread Sabbatarian presence throughout the lower part of Gloucestershire at the mid-point of the eighteenth century.

The last minister of any standing at Natton was Thomas Hiller, Philip Jones's nephew, who, as previously noted, was also from Sabbatarian stock at King's Stanley. After serving an apprenticeship with a linen manufacturer in Oxenton, he followed his parents to London, where they had been received into fellowship at Curriers' Hall in 1753 'from the church of Christ under the care of Mr Philip Jones in Gloucestershire'.[63] Hiller himself was baptized and received into the Curriers' Hall church in 1759, the congregation 'being satisfied with his faith and experience'.[64] His subsequent association with Goodman's Fields First-day church under Samuel Burford was not a reflection of weakening convictions regarding the seventh

---

[58] Ibid. Stoke Orchard was within the peculiar of Bishop's Cleeve in the eighteenth century. This late reference to the Fifth Monarchy movement could conceivably indicate a Seventh-day presence.   [59] GRO, GDR/285B(1), 397, 381A.

[60] GRO, GDR/397, 381A.   [61] GRO, GDR/381A.

[62] GRO, D1762/7. Known as Whitminster from 1945, although both names were used earlier: I.M. Kirby (ed.), *Diocese of Gloucester: A Catalogue of the Records of the Bishop and Archdeacons* (Gloucester, 1968), 206.

[63] *BAR* i. 156; PHCB 126.   [64] PHCB 127.

day, to which he remained steadfastly committed for life.[65] After attending Bristol Baptist Academy he accepted the pastoral charge at Tewkesbury, in 1769, and in the following year, when Philip Jones died, he succeeded to the Natton pastorate.[66] Although Tewkesbury might have been regarded as his principal charge, he served Natton and its Sabbatarians as faithfully as had Purser and Jones. When later in life he expressed concern at the spread of false doctrine, and the wish that all the 'real friends of Christ would come forward and contend earnestly for the faith once delivered to the saints', they were sentiments presumably acceptable to both congregations.[67] He is said to have preached frequently at farmhouses in neighbouring villages, and even in farmyards when occasion demanded, as well as at Natton each Sabbath consistently for twenty years.[68] Like his uncle, Hiller also played a prominent role in the Midland Baptist Association, preaching at Association meetings and serving as moderator on at least two occasions.[69] The 'Seventh-day Brethren' at Natton, so referred to in the *Baptist Annual Register* for 1790, the year of Hiller's death, still numbered 'about twenty', adequate testimony to the labours of a man 'universally esteemed'.[70]

The traditional view that no minister could be found to accept the Natton pastorate after Hiller does not seem to be correct.[71] In 1792 John Davis succeeded Hiller at Tewkesbury, and supplied Natton regularly until his death in 1803. It may not have been an

---

[65] Wilson noted that Hiller's opinions 'were in favour of the observance of the Seventh day, which he esteemed the true Christian Sabbath, and he persevered in that opinion to his dying day', DWL, MS 63, I, III, fo. 340.

[66] *BAR* i. 156, where it is said that he was briefly pastor at Wantage before returning to Gloucestershire; see also *SO* 1: 213.   [67] *BAR* i. 157.

[68] Ibid. 156–7. Hiller's personal note book reveals a careful record of the texts for all the sermons he preached at Tewkesbury and Natton. Of the 885 sermons at Natton, 578 were from the New Testament, taken from every book except Philemon, and 307 were based on Old Testament texts from all books except Leviticus, Ruth, Ezra, and a few of the Minor Prophets. His first sermon at Natton, on 20 May 1769, may have been planned with care to reflect an eschatological interest in the congregation. It was from Heb. 13: 14, 'For here we have no continuing city, but we seek one to come', GRO, D4944 5/1 fo. 3ʳ and *passim*.

[69] Particularly between 1773 and 1790: *BAR* i. 157.

[70] *BAR* i. 6; Joseph Meen, 'Collections Biographical, Historical and Miscellaneous Relating to the History of Dissenting Churches', New College MS L6/15, 489; Thomas Wilkinson, *Sketch of the History of the Baptist Church, Tewkesbury* (n.d.), 19.

[71] e.g. *SDBEA* 1: 46; *SO* 1: 20. Nineteenth-century historians of the English Sabbatarian movement, mostly American, would not have been aware of relevant material in the archives of the Charity Commissioners.

altogether satisfactory arrangement, for when Davis died Natton decided to have their own minister and not rely further on the Tewkesbury First-day church. John Miller was accordingly appointed and served Natton well for over twenty-five years until 1830 or thereabouts.[72] In 1823 a regular congregation of approximately thirty was reported, with twelve communicant members, but towards the end of Miller's pastorate and shortly thereafter Natton suffered a change in fortunes, largely due to the death of several of its ageing members. Attendance and membership declined and the remaining few were served, not always regularly, by a succession of supply preachers and caretaker pastors. At one point the number of communicant members dropped to two, and the outlook appeared bleak.[73] Yet help was at hand from an unexpected source.

The Natton cause had persisted sufficiently to attract a visit in 1843 from W.H. Black of Mill Yard and G.B. Utter of the Seventh Day Baptist Tract Society in America. This visit resulted in a revival of the work at Natton, and two years later John Francis was appointed as pastor of a church of seven communicant members, which by 1855 had grown to twelve, with a congregation of twenty-five of more.[74] The prospects of a lasting revival looked good until 1867, when disagreements within the congregation caused a split. The majority followed Francis to Kinsham, where a new Sabbatarian church was established on a doctrinal basis which differed in one significant respect from the Natton tradition. Baptism by immersion was no longer required as a condition of membership.[75] Four of five members only remained at Natton, under the care of the Tewkesbury Baptist minister Thomas Wilkinson.[76] The now fragile Sabbatarian cause could not withstand such trauma. Kinsham did not last long, and although Natton was still in existence in name at the turn of the century, its end was also at hand. As the three remaining members died, so did the Natton church, and by 1910 it was defunct. The farm and meeting-house which had served it so well for more than two centuries were replaced by a barn in 1955,[77] leaving only a dilapidated and overgrown burial ground as visible evidence of a

[72] Wilson, DWL, MS 63, I, III, fos. 340–1.
[73] Commissioners for Charities, MS 210274/A/1.
[74] Ibid.; GRO, D4944 10/1/2.
[75] Commissioners for Charities, MS 210274/A/3; Kinsham church book, GRO, D4944 10/1/4 fo. 3[r]; 'But should any person or persons desire to be so baptised, then the Minister or his deputy shall so baptise them.'
[76] GRO, D4944 10/1/4.   [77] *VCH* Glos., viii. 187.

remarkable Sabbatarian church whose history was unique. When the last Natton member died at Tewkesbury there had been a known Sabbatarian interest in the district for almost 300 years.

THE COTSWOLDS

A report in the *Birmingham Weekly Post* in 1901 referred to an eighteenth-century manuscript 'in private hands' which gave details of Seventh-day Sabbatarianism in the Midland counties from 1650. The manuscript, alas, has not survived, or if it has its whereabouts is unknown. The *Post* cited references to a Seventh-day 'society' in Ashchurch, and to Sabbatarians in and 'about Bourton in this last century'.[78] In context this should be understood of the one hundred years or so prior to the account having been written, and thus covers a period from later in the second half of the seventeenth century to a corresponding point in the eighteenth century. This coincides well with information from other sources that the time of greatest known Sabbatarian activity in the Bourton area was from *c.*1660 to *c.*1770. There is evidence of a lingering interest beyond that, but references become increasingly few as the eighteenth century progresses.

Although there are known associations between the Baptist churches at Tewkesbury and Bourton, there does not appear to have been much communication between the Seventh-day church or churches in the Severn Valley and the Sabbatarians in the higher Cotswold country. There are one or two exceptions to this generality, which will be noted in due course, but the two Sabbath-keeping communities largely found their own way, followed their own leaders, bore their own witness, and may have sprung from different roots. Although there is no direct evidence that the free will–predestination debate was ever of great significance among the Gloucestershire Sabbatarians, there are hints of a tendency to Arminianism and General Baptist views among some of the Bourton people, and of a leaning in the opposite direction among those in the valley.[79]

The first local name which comes to light in the north and east of the county, and it is an important one, is that of Thomas Hitchman

---

[78] *Birmingham Weekly Post*, 13 Apr. 1901.
[79] e.g. Thomas Hiller, *The Doctrine of Grace* (1740), a circular letter of the Midland Association, emphasizing election.

of Mickleton, who was presented in 1663 for 'a reputed Anabaptist and keeping Saturday Sabbath'.[80] The Hitchman name is even more central to the Cotswold Sabbatarians than the name of Purser to the Ashchurch–Natton community; we meet it again through several generations and branches over the next 150 years. Hitchman was known and respected in London, for in 1687 the Pinners' Hall Sabbatarians referred to the 'church of Jesus Christ in Gloucestershire walking with our honoured brother Mr Thomas Hitchman'.[81] The Gloucester diocesan records, which are usually fairly accurate, refer to Thomas Hitchman again in 1665, but only as an 'Anabaptist' not attending the parish church.[82] Unfortunately these are the few references known at present to a man who was undoubtedly one of the early leaders of the Sabbatarian movement in north-east Gloucestershire.[83]

The name of John Belcher should also be noted in connection with the first open appearance of Sabbatarianism in upper Gloucestershire. Belcher was regarded as a leading Fifth Monarchist preacher in 1660 and 1661, 'one of the foremost', and at one point was even 'thought likely to rebel'.[84] With other exponents of Fifth Monarchist doctrine he had travelled the country seeking 'to blow up the coals of rebellion', according to one account.[85] The extent of Belcher's radicalism is debatable, but there can be no doubt that he entertained Fifth Monarchy hopes until 1671, or that his eschatological leanings, of whatever hue, were combined with a newly acquired Sabbatarianism. When, in 1660, he appeared as a preacher in the market-place at Stow-on-the-Wold, where 'the Jewish Sabbath' was 'preferred before the Christian Sabbath', and 'at other places' nearby,[86] the question of intention naturally arises. Was this visit to the Bourton locality merely to fan the flames of a recently kindled Sabbatarian fire, or to strengthen a cause which had already existed for some time? For how long had the Jewish Sabbath been preferred above the Christian Sunday in this area? And by how many? Or was Belcher's visit with the intention of proclaiming the Fifth Monarchy manifesto? And if so, did he come to Stow and Bourton

---

[80] GRO, GDR/212.   [81] PHCB 12.   [82] GRO, GDR/214.
[83] The reference to Gloucestershire Seventh Day Baptists in *Gloucestershire Notes and Queries*, ii (1884), 354, makes no mention of Sabbatarian activity in the Cotswolds.   [84] *FMM* 205, 242.
[85] Ibid. 207; Greaves, *Deliver us from Evil*, 81.
[86] *Strange and True Newes from Glocester*, 5; Clark, *The Lying-Wonders*, 5, 16.

precisely because he calculated that an established Seventh-day tradition might reasonably be expected to embrace a biblically based and eminently practical eschatology? The questions are more than rhetorical, and although owing to lack of evidence they cannot be answered with any certainty, they do point to the possibility that a Sabbatarian interest prevailed in this locality well before Thomas Hitchman appeared in 1663.[87]

Bourton and Stow are recognized as having been a centre of Dissent and Nonconformity for some time prior to 1660. Congregationalism seems to have been well established by the early 1650s, and a Baptist church had been gathered by 1655 when it was represented at an Association meeting at Warwick.[88] Its relationship to the Seventh-day movement is not entirely clear, although it does not appear to have been mixed-communion, at least in the seventeenth century. Of greater interest for the purposes of this study is the fact that it drew its membership from surrounding villages, including Oddington, Upper and Lower Slaughter, Naunton, and Notgrove. Benjamin Beddome, the well-known eighteenth-century Baptist minister at Bourton, who was not in general ill disposed towards Sabbatarians, lived at Lower Slaughter.[89] It is the typical picture of an established Dissenting congregation, anchored at a given point in an area, but spread throughout the surrounding community. In this respect it serves as a perfect model for the less obtrusive Seventh-day church in the same locality.

In the light of the Pinners' Hall reference to Thomas Hitchman in 1687, it is virtually certain that he was elder of one of the two Gloucestershire congregations mentioned in the Llanwenarth record for 1690.[90] Nothing further is heard of him, or of Mickleton, or the Sabbatarian church in the Cotswolds, for forty-five years, but the Hitchman family, if no others, persevered in the Sabbatarian faith, for they were at its centre in the Bourton district when records in the eighteenth century reveal glimpses of its life once again. Jonathan Hitchman was baptized and admitted to fellowship at Mill Yard in December 1734, and six months later John Hitchman and his sister

[87] Cf. the *Birmingham Weekly Post* reference to Sabbatarian views existing in Gloucestershire since 1650.

[88] Nuttall, *Visible Saints*, 149, 154; H. Clifford, *History of Bourton-on-the-Water, Gloucestershire* (Stow-on-the-Wold, 1916), 90; White, *Association Records*, i. 20.

[89] Clifford, *History*, 90; AL, MS F.P.C. F1b, *passim*.

[90] 'In Glostersheire ther be two congregations that have each of them an Elder and severall Ministering Brethren', the Llanwenarth church book, cited in *BQ* 14: 165.

Elizabeth were also received into membership at Mill Yard.[91] There are clearly two branches of the Hitchman family represented here, although it is not always easy to distinguish them, especially in the Gloucestershire context. In 1737 Ann Hitchman was admitted to Mill Yard on the strength of a 'satisfactory account from the church to which she belonged'.[92] There is no record of her dismissal from either the Bourton or Gloucestershire Sabbatarians, or, indeed, from any church in the area. There was a tradition at the London churches to accept transient memberships from Sabbath-keepers elsewhere in the country, and the preference for Mill Yard rather than Curriers' Hall shown in these records may say something about the theological leanings of the Bourton Sabbatarians. In 1750 'Dame Alsop', née Hitchman, of Notgrove, was dismissed from Bourton 'for errors in judgement, especially denying the divinity of the Lord Jesus Christ, and his completed satisfaction'.[93]

This may be an appropriate point at which to turn to Notgrove and the neighbouring village of Naunton. They are typical of isolated communities tucked away in the Cotswold valleys which could have harboured Dissent for generations without its being detected, and the registration of an 'Anabaptist' meeting-place in Notgrove in 1705 may only be the first open appearance of those who had long worshipped there.[94] In 1735 eleven Nonconformists were reported at Naunton, six of them Presbyterian, three Anabaptist, and two Sabbatarian.[95] Apparently this was enough for an attempt to establish a congregation, for in 1737 a Seventh-day Baptist, Joseph Hitchman, 'commenced to preach' there, his efforts resulting in the baptism of Robert and Margaret Rowlands in the local river. Another Seventh-day man, a 'Mr Humphries', is known to have preached in a house at Notgrove at about the same period, and this concerted effort resulted in the establishment of a small but lively congregation.[96] The 1743 returns to the Bishop of Gloucester reveal 'at least one' Sabbatarian at Naunton and ten in Notgrove,[97] and in 1750 three at Naunton and ten again in Notgrove,[98] which seems to have remained a centre of Sabbatarianism for some years to come. This

[91] MYM 268.   [92] Ibid. 271.

[93] Bourton-on-the-Water church book, 1719–1802, AL, MS F.P.C. F1b, fo. 66.

[94] GRO, Q/503, in the house of Jane Evans.   [95] *VCH* Glos., vi. 86.

[96] 'Historical Notes of Naunton Baptist Church', in the church secretary's Minute Book, 1849–65, 1.

[97] GRO, GDR/397.   [98] GRO, GDR/381A, 393.

does not mean that all Sabbatarian activity in this area was centred in Notgrove, for we still do not know where Joseph Hitchman or Mr Humphries came from. In 1767 Sarah Alsop, née Hitchman, of Notgrove, was baptized at 'Mr Dadges' by her brother William Hitchman of Hillesley, and later became a member of the Natton church.[99]

Another Notgrove Sabbatarian, Jonathan Hitchman, gained notoriety for his part in an extraordinary incident at Bourton Baptist church in 1764. Benjamin Beddome had preached, by request, on Revelation 1: 10, 'I was in the Spirit on the Lord's day', but had, according to his own account, 'meddled with the change of the Sabbath as little as he could to do justice to his text'.[100] These circumstances in themselves suggest some tension regarding the Sabbath issue, and may also have later led Beddome to present the case for Sunday in preference to Saturday with some detail in his *Scriptural Exposition of the Baptist Catechism* (2nd edition 1776). At the end of the sermon, according to Beddome himself, Hitchman arose 'in the face of the whole congregation, and opposed him'. He made some objections to the content of the sermon, and asked several questions. Beddome attempted by reply, but soon concluded that the matter 'could not easily be brought to an end', telling Hitchman that his conduct was 'indecent and illegal'.[101] Beddome had been taken off guard, and had to decide on the spur of the moment whether to proceed with a public discussion which would possibly have become heated and might have conceded some ground to the Sabbatarians, or to cut it short as he did, thereby risking the impression that he felt unable to deal with the questions raised. It was an unenviable position, and Beddome's pastoral insight led him to opt for discretion.

It appears that the nature of Christ and the way of salvation had been brought up in this exchange, for Beddome recorded that he told Hitchman in the heat of the moment that it was no wonder that he who had so little regard for the Lord Himself as to deny his divinity and set aside His righteousness should have so little regard for his day. Stung by this, Hitchman replied that he knew of no other righteousness but that which led to obedience, to which

[99] Hillesley church book, GRO 2889 2/1, 5.
[100] Bourton-on-the-Water church book, Pastoral Diary 1745–1773, AL, MS F.P.C. F.1c, 26 Feb. 1764.
[101] Ibid. The records of this whole incident are in Beddome's own hand.

Beddome responded that Christian righteousness was not of man's obedience to the gospel, but through Christ's obedience to the law.[102] Evidently the Notgrove Sabbatarians, or some of them, were perceived as being Socinian, whether or not they were so in fact. The Hitchman link with Mill Yard, which at that point was under the influence of Unitarianism, would seem to confirm that such perceptions were not ill founded. It is quite likely, indeed, that divergent views such as these on the divinity of Christ and the Atonement were more problematic to Beddome and the Bourton Baptists than the Seventh-day Sabbath, which many Baptist congregations around the country had accommodated without great difficulty. There is also a suggestion in all this that under normal circumstances Sabbatarians were not excluded from fellowship at Bourton, and there is evidence that Seventh-day people did worship there, at least occasionally. Nancy Alsop, whose membership was 'with the 7th Day people at Natton', sometimes met with the Bourton Baptists, and died shortly after attending one of their services in 1770.[103]

Meanwhile at Oddington to the east and Bibury to the south a development of some interest in the history of the Sabbatarian movement had taken place. An Independent church had existed at Oddington at least since Commonwealth times under William Tray, who with Anthony Palmer of Bourton and others had signed the local returns for the Nominated Parliament in 1653.[104] Tray had been licensed in 1672 to teach in his own house as a Congregationalist. That designation appears again for Oddington some sixty years later, when in the Gloucester diocesan returns for 1735 a group of twenty 'Sabbatarians and Congregationalists' was reported.[105] As noted earlier, this categorization was quite distinct from that of Anabaptists and Independents listed in the same returns, and seems to indicate, in this instance if not in all cases, a Sabbatarian development among paedobaptists. A similar return was made for Oddington in 1750, with Anabaptists being listed separately in 1743 and 1750.[106] In 1735 in the peculiar of Bibury, which included three neighbouring parishes as well as the large parish of Bibury itself, forty Sabbatarians were reported.[107] The 1743 survey of Bibury was even more specific, noting a sect of about forty 'Congregationalists',

[102] Ibid.   [103] Ibid., 6 Aug. 1770.   [104] Nuttall, *Visible Saints*, 149.
[105] GRO, GDR/285B; *VCH* Glos., vi. 97.   [106] GRO, GDR/381A, 397.
[107] GRO, GDR/285B(1).

and went to the unusual extent of including an explanatory note. It described 'a meeting of a sect called Congregationalists. abt. 40. in numb. Jacobs of Oxfdsh. who died about 30 yrs. ago was their Founder. They baptize infants, but refuse to swear upon ye Bible, are rigid Pred.'[108] The entry for 1750 is identical, repeating this note.[109] An Independent congregation had been reported at Bibury c.1715, with forty 'hearers' and a preacher named Humphries.[110] The latter seems to establish a link with the Sabbatarians at Notgrove.

On the strength of this evidence it seems that the Bibury and Oddington Sabbatarian Congregationalists had come into being during the first half of the eighteenth century, possibly at a fairly early point, and in the absence of any other records it may be assumed that a group of their strength would normally have continued for several years beyond the last reported date of existence. The 'unknown denomination' reported at Oddington in 1798[111] may reflect a remnant of that small but historically significant Sabbatarian congregation. Apart from those members of the Hitchman family who were in fellowship with Natton, it is this group which provides the only definable link between the Cotswold Sabbatarians and those who were later established in the Severn Valley. When John Francis formed a Sabbatarian congregation at Kinsham in 1867 from the old Natton church, members were included from Cheltenham, Westmancote, Kemerton, Overbury, Bredon, and other places. Francis claimed that his church had descended from the seventeenth-century witness of Joseph Davis in Oxford gaol and that it was one of only three remaining Sabbatarian congregations in the country. The link which appears to have existed between the Oddington–Bibury Sabbatarians and those at Kinsham was, however, more of a theological nature. The Kinsham people were to be known as Seventh-day Christians, or Sabbatarian Protestant Dissenters, as distinct from the Natton Seventh-day Baptists, and did not require adult baptism by immersion as a condition of membership.[112] It is just possible that Francis followed a precedent set by the Oddington and Bibury Sabbatarian paedobaptists, who were sufficiently extensive in their time to have been known elsewhere in the country, and for whom the 1735 and 1750 returns should certainly not be regarded as a definitive chronological framework.

[108] GRO, GDR/397.   [109] GRO, GDR/393.
[110] Evans, 'Dissenting Congregations and Ministers in England and Wales, 1715–29', DWL, MS 38.4, p. 43.   [111] *VCH* Glos., vi. 97.
[112] Kinsham church book, GRO D4944 10/1/4.

SOUTH GLOUCESTERSHIRE

The Sabbatarian presence in south Gloucestershire during the period covered by this study is shadowy from beginning to end. As noted earlier, it is not clear whether the Sabbatarians here constituted a third Gloucestershire congregation not known to the compiler of the 1690 Llanwenarth list, and distinct from the other two Seventh-day churches in the county, or whether they were part of one of those more clearly identifiable congregations. Whatever the reality, the shadows provide evidence of something more substantial that is rarely seen here as it is in the north and east of the county. In fact, after the early beginnings at King's Stanley *c*.1640, there is no firm evidence of a distinct Seventh-day congregation in this area, which may indicate that the Sabbatarians here were indeed part of the Ashchurch–Natton congregation twenty miles or so to the north. There are indications that this might have been so, as there is also evidence for Sabbatarians worshipping with First-day churches, particularly in the latter half of the eighteenth century. What emerges from this apparent uncertainty is that Saturday Sabbatarianism did prevail in the King's Stanley–Horsley area and neighbouring parishes for several generations, and that some of its staunchest supporters came from Sabbatarian families in this district. It is also clear that one of the last outposts of known Sabbatarian presence in south Gloucestershire was the unlikely village of Hillesley, where the pastor of the Baptist church and his family were of that mind.[113]

It is not known how long the Baptist church in King's Stanley remained wholly or partly Sabbatarian. Philip Jones and Thomas Hiller were both born into Seventh-day Baptist families in King's Stanley, Jones around the turn of the century and Hiller in 1737. Jones's father Samuel suffered persecution and imprisonment during

---

[113] The parishes of Little Sodbury, Wootton-under-Edge, and Coaley were among those in the south of the county where, in the sixteenth century, there had been tangible evidence of 'a long-standing popular tradition of discontent with the unreformed Church'; Cross, *Church and People*, 75–6. It was in this area that Sabbatarianism showed itself in the seventeenth and eighteenth centuries. King's Stanley bordered on Coaley, and Hillesley stood next to Wootton-under-Edge, midway between Coaley and Little Sodbury. It was all Tyndale country, where the seeds of a biblical faith had long been sown and nurtured. Tyndale himself was no Sabbatarian, however: 'We be Lords over the Saboth, and may change it into the Monday, or any other day, as we see need; or make every tenth day holy . . . if we see a cause why,' William Tyndale, *An Answer to Sir Thomas More's Dialogue*, ed. H. Walter (Cambridge, 1850), 97.

the post-Restoration period. Hiller's mother was Samuel Jones's daughter Mary, and thus Philip Jones's sister. Hiller's father came originally from Malmesbury,[114] and, as we have noted previously, Stephen and Mary Hiller moved to London in 1753 and became members of Curriers' Hall. They were received by Edmund Townsend's congregation 'by virtue of a letter of dismission to us from the Church of Christ under ye care of Mr Philip Jones in Gloucestershire'.[115] This is one indication that the King's Stanley Sabbatarians may have been part of the Natton church, at least in a formal sense.

A strong Baptist church is known at King's Stanley throughout the eighteenth century, but with no indication of it being Seventh-day.[116] It would seem that King's Stanley turned away from Seventh-day observance at some point in the late seventeenth century, or else that Sabbatarians there seceded and began to worship by themselves, sustained perhaps by regular visits from John Purser, Philip Jones, and Thomas Hiller.[117] Something, indeed, kept the cause alive well into the eighteenth century after King's Stanley had changed its position, for both the Jones and Hiller families are noted as staunch Seventh-day Baptists,[118] and there is evidence that the seventh day was observed in other local parishes. It has to be remembered that diocesan returns can rarely be regarded as providing a complete record of Nonconformist activity, but the report of a Sabbatarian at Haresfield and a 'Jew' at Wheatenhurst (Whitminster) in 1743 is some indication of continuing interest in the seventh day in this area.[119] It is quite possible, even probable, that there were other Sabbatarians in these and other parishes who were not known or included in the official returns. The three who were reported at Badgeworth in 1735 and 1750 may have been connected with a larger group at Cheltenham,[120] or may have had links with Haresfield, Whitminster, and King's Stanley. In 1750 a 'Mrs. Boulton' was known as a Sabbatarian at Haresfield.[121] It is less likely that she and other Sabbatarians similarly situated would have survived without the support of fellow believers, although, given the tenacity with which Nonconformists usually clung to their beliefs, the possibility cannot be dismissed.

---

[114] *BAR* i. 156.   [115] PHCB 126.

[116] *BAR* i. 6; iii. 15. King's Stanley was represented regularly at meetings of the Western Association from 1733 onwards.   [117] Cf. *SO* 1: 212–13; *BAR* i. 156.

[118] DWL, Wilson MS 63, I, iii, fo. 339, and v, fo. 10.   [119] GRO, D1762/7.

[120] GRO, GDR/285B(1), 397, 381A; D 1762/7.   [121] GRO, GDR/381A.

A comment from Benjamin Francis of Horsley throws a little additional light on the Seventh-day movement at this period. In 1759 Francis wrote to Joshua Thomas that he had no 'scruple to admit a Sabbatarian, or an anti-singer, provided they are peaceable, and leave others to their liberty'.[122] This was in reply to a query from Thomas regarding the 'proper bounds of church communion'. Francis had just moved to Horsley from Chipping Sodbury, where he had been since 1756,[123] when this correspondence took place. Horsley, it will be recalled, had arisen from the earlier Baptist witness at King's Stanley. Evidently Sabbatarians, however few, were known to Francis and were still seeking fellowship with Baptists, probably at Horsley, but perhaps also at Chipping Sodbury in the late 1750s.

A further connection with Natton, and perhaps also with Notgrove, can be traced through William Hitchman, who joined the Hillesley Baptist church in 1762. In that year Hitchman was dismissed from Natton to Hillesley as 'a brother in fellowship with us whose conversation so far as we know has been as becometh the Gospel of Christ'.[124] The notice of dismission makes it clear that Hitchman, while actually a member at Natton, was not well known to Sabbatarians there on account of distance, and implies that he had not worshipped regularly with them.[125] He had been born at Notgrove, in fact, in 1729, the son of William Hitchman and the grandson of John Hitchman.[126] There may also be a link with the upper Gloucestershire Sabbatarians in the fact that his wife came from a parish near to the Oxfordshire border. In 1763 Mary Hitchman

[122] Joshua Thomas, 'Queries and Answers', BBC, MS G98a(5), 31, 34. Cf. G.F. Nuttall, 'Questions and Answers: an Eighteenth-Century Correspondence: Joshua Thomas and Benjamin Francis', *BQ* 27 (1977–8), 2, 85.

[123] John Ryland, *The Presence of Christ the Source of Eternal Bliss* (n.d.), 39.

[124] Cited in K. Chappell, 'Hillesley Baptist Church, 1730–1980', GRO, PA 178/3, 2.

[125] 'To the Church of Christ meeting at Hilsley in the county of Gloucester fondest greetings. Whereas William Hitchman a brother in fellowship with us, (whose conversation so far as we know has been as becometh the Gospel of Christ) hath signified his desire of a Dismission to you. As his distance from us renders him incapable of Answering the Ends of Church Communion with us and as Providence hath at present cast his lot among you; we do therefore dismiss him unto you and commit him to your particular watch and care, desiring you to receive him in the Lord. Our wishes are that he may be useful among you, and that you may be made Mutual Blessings to each other; to which End we commit you and him with you to the Word of His Grace which is able to build you up and to give you an inheritance among them that are sanctified'; Hillesley church book, GRO, D 2889 2/1, 2.

[126] Notgrove Parish register, GRO, P253 IN 1/1. The register indicates that he was baptized on 10 Oct. 1729. Either this branch of the Hitchman family came late to the seventh day, or it had links with the Oddington–Bibury paedobaptist Sabbatarians.

was received as a transient member at Hillesley from Fairford,[127] just south of Bibury and twelve miles or so from Wantage, where Sabbatarian views had been canvassed in the seventeenth century, and where Thomas Hiller had ministered briefly before taking up the Tewkesbury and Natton pastorates.[128]

In 1764 Hitchman was called formally to the Hillesley pastorate, and was ordained in June 'by the general consent of all the members', Hugh Evans[129] and Samuel Stennett officiating. His ministry of thirty-eight years at Hillesley was undoubtedly a success by any account. Ten members were added in his first year, and the membership of twelve in 1762 had grown to sixty-two by 1794, although there is no hint that the church was Sabbatarian at any point in its history. Indeed, the opposite seems to have been the case. One of the conditions under which Hitchman accepted the Hillesley pastorate was that he be allowed three free Sundays each year 'either together or apart, for his own use', and that Hillesley on such occasions provide a supply at their own expense. The church readily agreed. It is equally clear, however, that Hitchman held Sabbatarian views, and that Hillesley called him knowing this to be so. It is also likely that Hillesley accepted Sabbatarians into fellowship, certainly in its earlier years, while holding regular services on Sundays. In 1767 Hitchman baptized his sister Sarah Alsop of Notgrove, although she did not seek admission to Hillesley 'by reason of distance', and subsequently joined Natton. In 1776 he baptized his daughters Sophia and Sarah, who did become members at Hillesley.[130]

The clearest evidence of Hitchman's Sabbatarianism and of Hillesley's acceptance of it comes from another source altogether. From 1766 until 1789 Hitchman received an annuity from the Joseph Davis trust, which was designated only for Seventh-day ministers as long as they and their congregations 'should continue in the faith'.[131] While these conditions may have been modified with the passing of time, a Sabbatarian interest was always necessary as a condition

---

[127] Hillesley church book, 3.

[128] White, *Association Records*, iii. 190; *SO* 1: 213.

[129] On Evans, of Broadmead, Bristol, tutor and principal at Bristol Baptist Academy, and father of Caleb Evans, see *BB* i. 216 and G.F. Nuttall, 'George Whitefield's "Curate": Gloucestershire Dissent and the Revival', *JEH* 27 (1976), 384.

[130] Hillesley church book, *passim*.

[131] *The Case Submitted to the General Body of Protestant Dissenting Ministers of the Three Denominations* (n.d.), appendix, p. 9. See *MYM*, introductory notes by W.H. Black.

of receiving support from this fund. The first payment to Hitchman was recorded in the Hillesley church book with the note, 'A gift from Mill Yard to Sabbatarian ministers', and with the explanation that 'all gifts herein mentioned except the Fund's Bounty are not given to the church, but personally to Mr. Hitchman as a Minister independent of his connection with the church at Hillesley'.[132] From the beginning of his ministry Hitchman had also been supported by contributions from both the General and Particular Baptist funds (the former ceasing in 1788), and from 1766 to 1790 by an additional grant from Dr Stennett's fund.[133] Whether or not the termination of all these grants between 1788 and 1790, with the exception of the support from the Particular Baptists, is a reflection of any change of view on his part regarding the Sabbath, it is difficult to say. It may have been due more to the fact that his wife had died in 1788 and that the church by 1790 was able to support him. His own will, proved in 1802, reveals a comfortable estate.[134]

Evidence of a further and more unusual attachment to the Saturday Sabbath in south Gloucestershire comes from Stapleton, near Bristol, in 1776. The sermon register of John Ryland, jun., reveals that on 20 July of that year he preached at 'Dr Mason's 7 Day', where, in Ryland's words, the company of about thirty were 'almost all mad or asleep'.[135] This is evidently a reference to one of the congregations under the care of Joseph Mason, founder of the Fishponds asylum, and thus would explain Ryland's otherwise uncomplimentary comments. Mason was a member and benefactor of Broadmead Baptist church, Bristol,[136] but appears to have ministered in his own right to this Sabbatarian group and also to a Sunday-keeping congregation in Stapleton, to which Ryland had preached on the preceding Sunday.[137] Mason, who was born in 1711, came originally from the Hillesley area, where his father, also Joseph Mason, had been the first Baptist minister. Dr Joseph Mason of Stapleton was related by marriage to a prominent family with a long Sabbatarian tradition. His third wife Sarah, who predeceased him by four years, was a Stennett, and his will reveals that he left ten guineas 'to my brother-in-law, the Reverend Dr Samuel

---

[132] Hillesley church book, GRO D 2889 2/1, 9–12.   [133] Ibid.
[134] GRO, will of William Hitchman, 17 Aug. 1802.
[135] 'Text Book of John Ryland, D.D., 1766–1825', NoRO, CSBC 2, fo. 41ᵛ. Ryland had preached a month earlier to 'the 7 Day people at Cripplegate', ibid., fo. 40ᵛ.
[136] BrRO, Info. Box IX/48.   [137] NoRO, CSBC 2, fo., 41ᵛ.

Stennett'.[138] Mason died in 1779, and nothing further is heard of his Sabbatarian cause at Stapleton.

With William Hitchman's death in 1802, the shadows of a Sabbatarian presence in south Gloucestershire, which had persisted for so long, finally disappear altogether. So, too, does the name of a family which more than any other in the county had preserved a witness to the seventh day through several generations. Sabbatarianism in the Cotswolds and the Severn Valley had retreated by now to Natton, there to remain for another hundred years or so. The Gloucestershire Sabbatarian tradition, in many ways unique, was certainly as old and as widespread as any in the country. On that account alone it deserves greater recognition than it has received in the records of Dissent and Nonconformity in Gloucestershire, and perhaps in those of the country as a whole.

[138] BrRO, 39801/F17.

8
South Wales and the Borders

THERE is sufficient evidence to conclude that the Saturday Sabbath was well established in the Welsh Marches south of Leominster and in neighbouring parts of Wales from the mid-seventeenth century, if not earlier, and that it persisted in that region well into the eighteenth century. The evidence pertains primarily to the counties of Monmouthshire and Herefordshire, and to the district around Hay-on-Wye, where at that time Herefordshire converged with Radnorshire and Breconshire.[1] While specific Seventh-day congregations can be identified at Leominster and Hay, the first Sabbatarians in south-east Monmouthshire seem to have followed a pattern set in the early days of Welsh Nonconformity, and to have belonged to mixed-communion churches, mainly of the Baptist tradition.

The status of those who persisted into the eighteenth century is not entirely clear, although a lingering interest may have lasted in the Abergavenny area until the 1720s, and a small Seventh-day group appears to have survived at Hay until the 1730s. The Abergavenny–Llanwenarth cause was probably an extension of the Sabbatarian Baptist strand which first appeared in south-east Monmouthshire around Llangwm and Llantrissant in the mid-seventeenth century, and which was fostered there principally by William Milman and in the Usk–Abergavenny area by Nathaniel Morgan.[2] The late interest at Hay-on-Wye and Broadmeadow may represent a gradual retreat of Seventh-day views to their original source in Wales. Certainly the last known foothold of the Seventh-day Men in Wales during the period under consideration was in this district.

---

[1] See Appendix V for current county designations.

[2] Milman is described as 'one of the Seventh-day Baptists' in Monmouthshire, T.M. Bassett, *Bedyddwyr Cymru* (Llandysul, 1977), 17. On Milman, see also T. Richards, *Religious Developments in Wales, 1654–1662* (1923), 188; *A History of the Puritan Movement in Wales . . . 1639–1653* (1920), 208. On Morgan, see Joshua Thomas, 'The History of the Baptist Churches in Wales', BBC, MS G 98 a(1) 120; 'History of Welsh Baptists', NLW, MS 10620E, fos. 190–1. The date at which Milman and Morgan adopted Seventh-day views is unknown.

MAP 5 Locations in South Wales and the border counties associated with
seventeenth- and eighteenth-century Sabbatarianism

The precise origins of Saturday observance in Wales and the
Marches are again shrouded in obscurity, even though there are
some intriguing hints. The Leominster Baptists, for example, referred
to the Seventh-day people there in 1689 as being 'ancient',[3] a term
which clearly held some special significance for the Baptist churches
which had arisen in Leominster since the late 1640s and the appearance of Baptist convictions there under the influence of John

---

[3] Leominster Baptist church book, A, p. vi.

Tombes.[4] According to Joshua Thomas, the historian of early Welsh Nonconformity, the Baptist church at Hay grew out of an earlier antipaedobaptist movement centred at Olchon in the parish of Clodock between Hay and Abergavenny. This area is said to have been the home of the earliest Dissenters in Wales. Thomas describes it, perhaps rather uncritically, as the birthplace of several notable proponents of a free and biblical faith, including the Lollard supporters Walter Brute and Sir John Oldcastle, and William Tyndale and John Penry.[5] John Rhys Howell, one of the two most prominent Seventh-day Men in this region in the latter part of the seventeenth century, came from Olchon and was a member of the Hay Baptist church by 1654.[6]

A close connection is known to have existed between the Particular Baptists of the separated church in Monmouthshire, and the Broadmead church in Bristol.[7] Thomas Richards speaks of an 'intimate' link between the two groups, largely due to the influence of William Thomas, the Baptist leader at Llangwm,[8] on the Broadmead congregation from 1667 onwards. Richards points out that several members at Broadmead during the late 1660s had 'distinctively Welsh surnames' and suggests a direct connection between Broadmead Baptists and those of south-east Monmouthshire. Thomas had administered baptisms at Bristol, and in 1667 advised on the election of elders, resulting in the appointment of Richard White and Edward Terrill.[9] Seventh-day views had been known to Terrill before the Restoration. It is recorded in the Broadmead records that by 1658 he had decided against the Saturday Sabbath, 'the Lord having satisfied him that observation of the seventh day was not necessary'.[10] Presumably there were others in Bristol, as there were

[4] On Tombes, vicar of Leominster and 'perhaps the most learned of all the Baptist's (White, *English Baptists*, 102), see *CR* 487–8; *DNB*. White suggests that the *DNB* entry on Tombes requires revision: *English Baptists*, 142 n. 12.

[5] Thomas, BBC, MS G 98 a(1), 39–46. Of the various Joshua Thomas manuscripts at Bristol Baptist College relating to the early history of Welsh Baptists and Welsh Nonconformity in general, MS G 98 a(1) 'The History of the Baptist Churches in Wales' is cited exclusively in this study.

[6] Ibid. 54; Richards, *The Religious Census of 1676* (1927), 77.

[7] E.B. Underhill (ed.), *Records of a Church of Christ, Meeting in Broadmead, Bristol* (1847), 515–17; Bassett, *Bedyddwyr Cymru*, 36.

[8] To be distinguished from four others of the same name associated with early Puritan and Nonconformist developments in South Wales and the Marches; T. Richards, *Wales under the Penal Code, 1662–1687* (1925), 95.

[9] Ibid.   [10] Underhill (ed.), *Broadmead Records*, 68.

further up the Severn Valley in Gloucestershire and Worcestershire, who were similarly exercised over the matter, but who decided, as Terrill did, in favour of the first day. William Milman, the other most prominent Monmouthshire Sabbatarian, first appears at Magor, just across the Severn from Bristol.[11] It is quite conceivable that the Monmouthshire Sabbatarians learned of the seventh day from the same source as Edward Terrill.

It is also possible that Seventh-day views came to Monmouthshire direct from London. Prior to assuming pastoral leadership of the Llangwm/Llantrissant Baptists, William Thomas had been associated with Walter Cradock at Llanvaches, the mixed-communion 'mother church' of early Welsh Nonconformity. Thomas, and others from Llanvaches, had spent some years in London, as well as in Bristol, during the Civil War, returning to Monmouthshire c.1646.[12] Seventh-day views were circulating in the capital by this time and were adopted shortly thereafter by Henry Jessey, who had been directly involved in the establishment of the first Independent church in Wales at Llanvaches in 1639.[13] It is highly probable that the Llanvaches Separatists re-established contact with him during their London exile. While there is no evidence to suggest that Seventh-day views appeared in the Llanvaches church itself, Jessey's own pattern of Seventh-day observance[14] would have provided a good model for William Thomas's open-communion Baptists at Llangwm, who grew out of the Llanvaches congregation and who evidently included Sabbatarians as communicant members.[15]

While the question of Seventh-day origins in Monmouthshire must in general be left open, it would be imprudent not to recognize any influence which the 'ancient' and established Sabbatarians at Leominster, and those at Tewkesbury and elsewhere in nearby Gloucestershire, might have had on developments in South Wales. At the eighth meeting of the Midlands Particular Baptist Association in September 1657, which proceedings are recorded in the Leominster church book, the messenger from Tewkesbury enquired 'Whether ye last day of ye week commonly called Satterday [*sic*] [was] to be observed as a Sabbath now under the gospel of Christ'.[16] The

[11] Richards, *Puritan Movement in Wales*, 208; *TBHS* 6: 168.
[12] Richards, *Wales under the Penal Code*, 95.
[13] Joshua Thomas, BBC, MS G 98 a(1), 45, 112–13.   [14] See Ch. 4.
[15] Bassett, *Bedyddwyr Cymru*, 17; *TBHS* 6: 169.
[16] White, *Association Records*, i. 32, 41.

assembled representatives of the Baptist churches returned a negative answer to the question, but noted 'one brother declaring himself to be enquiring and not yet fully satisfied'.[17] While Seventh-day congregations were not represented *per se* at the meeting, the episode fairly typifies the relative strength and dispersion of Seventh-day views amongst Baptists in the region during the years immediately preceding the Restoration. Apparently the Sabbath question was significant enough to raise at an Association meeting, but neither of sufficient consequence to impose on all the churches nor to prevent fellowship between otherwise like-minded believers.[18] Thus the 'ancient' Leominster Sabbatarians, and others, would continue to bear witness to the seventh day, and thereby to leaven the thinking of others to the west and to the south who were similarly motivated to 'gospel obedience' by their respect for the authority of Scripture.[19]

MONMOUTHSHIRE: LLANGWM AND LLANTRISSANT

The character of Welsh Sabbatarianism, restricted as it seems to have been to the south-east corner of the principality, can only be understood, as already intimated, in relationship to the broader Baptist movement in this region.[20] The most striking evidence of this proposition is the Llanwenarth Baptist church, whose records, alluded to frequently in earlier chapters, contain a list of Seventh-day churches extant in 1690. This record, which first appeared in the *Baptist Quarterly* in 1951, is of sufficient importance to the

---

[17] Ibid.

[18] Cf. Edward Stennett's assertion in 1677 that 'many Sabbath-keepers', including himself, 'hold communion with such of our brethren that are not Sabbath-keepers', *The Insnared Taken*, 13. Much later, in 1759, Joshua Thomas was advised by Benjamin Francis of Horsley that he had no hesitation in admitting Sabbatarians to church fellowship, since he had not observed that 'any pernicious consequences' followed their sentiments, 'Queries and Answers', BBC, MS G 98 a(5), 31.

[19] Richard Baxter spoke for most in the Puritan-Nonconformist tradition when he said that 'gospel-obedience', or faith and works, was 'the way for those to walk in that are in Christ': *The Saints Everlasting Rest* (1669), 15.

[20] The sometimes confusing development of early Welsh Independent-Baptist history is recorded in the manuscripts of Joshua Thomas, and the works of Thomas Richards, and Thomas Bassett already cited. There are also the following: Joshua Thomas, *Hanes y Bedyddwyr, Ymblith y Cymry* (Caerfyrddin, 1778); *The History of Antipaedobaptists in Wales* (1778); *A History of the Baptist Association in Wales, 1650–1790* (1795), *inter alia*; Thomas Rees, *History of Protestant Nonconformity in Wales* (2nd edn. 1883); and T.M. Bassett, *The Welsh Baptists* (Swansea, 1977). See also W.T. Whitley, 'South Wales till 1753', *TBHS* 6 (1918–19), 163–82.

history of the entire Seventh-day movement to warrant being reproduced again in its more immediate context of Welsh Sabbatarianism, and for the benefit of a wider public. The original spelling
and syntax of this unique document have been retained as far as
possible:

An account of some Sabbathkeepers in England, & the places
of ther aboad.

December 1690

In the citty of london three congregations
1 one to whom Mr John Bellcher & Mr Henry Cooke be
    ministers or Elders
2 another to whom young Mr Stennet is minister
3 the others have Mr Henry Shorsby to ther minister
In the county of Essex
ther is a congregation in the citty of Coltchester
Abraham Chaplin ther minister
and at a seaport called Harwich ther is a Remnant.
In the county of Southffolke
At Woodbridge & Melton there beth A Remnant
In the county of Norffolke
Ther is a congregation at Ingham and Northwalsham
and therabout, Mr John Hagges ther minister
as also A little Remnant at great Yarmouth
In Lincolnsheire
Att A seaport called Boston ther be A small Remnant
In the citty of Nottingham & therabouts be A Remnant
in the county of Bucks or Buckinghamsheire
There be a congregation William Charsley & henry Cock
ministering Brethren
at Wallingford in Barksheire
Ther be a congregation Mr Edward Stennet ther elder
at Watleton in Oxffordsheire
ther be also A Remnant Relating to the sayd Mr Stennet
at Salisbury in Wiltsheire
Ther is a congregation John Laws & John Hall
ministering Brethren, but ther Elder lives at Southampton
whose Name is, Michell Aldridge
in Dorsetsheire ther is also a congregation
som at the citty of Dorsetor & some at Belminster som at
Sherbon

& som at Sturmister all market towns Joseph Newman and
some other Brethren to minister to them
ROBERT   In Glostersheire Ther be two
congregations that have each of them an Elder and
ROBERT WOODS   severall Ministering Brethren
In the county of Surry ther is at A market
town called Cherssey Mr William Burnet ther elder
& Mr Thom Stickland a ministering Brother
December
1690[21]

Dr E.A. Payne commented on the importance of this document, but
did not pursue its significance for the Seventh-day movement in
Wales.[22] Indeed, nobody appears to have raised the most obvious
question arising from the discovery of the Llanwenarth records,
now deposited in the National Library of Wales at Aberystwyth.[23]
Why did the Llanwenarth church, of all the contemporary Baptist
churches in Wales, keep a record of Seventh-day congregations?
The brief introduction to the account refers specifically to
'Sabbathkeepers in England', but does not include the Sabbatarian
groups at Leominster or Hay-on-Wye, which are known from other
sources to have been in existence at the time the list was drawn
up.[24] The compiler of the Llanwenarth list was evidently more
concerned with Seventh-day congregations in England than in Wales,
presumably since the latter were already well known to Welsh
Sabbatarians and other Baptists who might have been interested. It
further appears that both the Leominster and Hay Sabbatarians were
regarded as belonging more to the Welsh community than to fellow believers across the Severn or elsewhere in England.

It might, therefore, reasonably be inferred that there were Sabbatarians at Llanwenarth at the time this list was compiled for whom
confirmation of the survival of Seventh-day congregations, so soon
after the years of persecution, was of importance. The document is
not strong enough in itself to conclude that Sabbatarians amounted
to a majority in the Llanwenarth congregation, but does permit the
conclusion that at least they constituted a significant minority. In
the light of this document, it is also possible to conclude that the

---

[21] *BQ* 14: 165. The significance of Robert Woods for Llanwenarth is not clear. He
is more frequently associated with the Sabbatarian movement in East Anglia. Woods
should also probably be distinguished from the Robert Wood known in Lincolnshire
c.1672.   [22] Ibid. 164.
[23] NLW, Deposit 409 B.   [24] Leominster Baptist church book, A, pp. v, vi.

centre of gravity amongst Monmouthshire Sabbatarians had shifted before the turn of the century from Llangwm–Llantrissant to the Abergavenny–Llanwenarth area. The strength of this possibility will become clearer as we endeavour to piece together the story of the Seventh-day movement in this region from the few historical fragments which remain.

In 1639, as has already been noted, Henry Jessey came down from London to assist William Wroth in the establishment of the first Separatist church in Wales at Llanvaches.[25] Wroth was henceforth known as the father of Welsh Nonconformity, and the Llanvaches congregation as the 'mother church of Nonconformity in Wales'. Earlier, Wroth had been rector of Llanvaches, and had regularly drawn large crowds to his services on account of his powerful and popular preaching. The Separatist congregation which emerged under his influence, and with the help of Henry Jessey in 1639, was initially a mixed-communion church of Independent paedobaptists and Baptists, and remained so until Wroth's death in 1642, when it came under the care of Walter Cradock.[26] It appears that in the early days of the Llanvaches church, Wroth ministered principally to the Independents, while his assistant, William Thomas, cared for Baptist interests. At some point between Wroth's death in 1642 and Cradock's death in 1659, the church more formally divided into two congregations, with the Independents now centred around Magor, and the Baptists concentrated in the Llangwm–Llantrissant area a few miles further north with William Thomas established as their leader.[27]

This open-communion, predominantly Baptist church rapidly established itself throughout the south-east corner of Monmouthshire, first under William Thomas (d. 1671), and then under Thomas Quarrell, who nurtured the Baptist cause in the area until 1709. Joshua Thomas describes Thomas and Quarrell, and Dr Christopher Price, one of their assistants, as 'very substantial ministers'.[28] This

---

[25] Thomas, BBC, MS G 98 a(1), 45, 112–13; [Whiston], *Life of Jessey*, 11. On Wroth, see *DNB*.

[26] Rees, *Nonconformity in Wales*, 49; BBC, MS G 98 a(1), 111–13.

[27] BBC, MS G 98 a(1), 114–15; Rees, *Nonconformity in Wales*, 189.

[28] Bassett describes Price as belonging to a prominent family in Llanffwyst, and a chemist by profession. He is said to have supported John Tombes in a controversy over baptism at Abergavenny in 1653; Bassett, *Bedyddwyr Cymru*, 17. He later represented Llangwm at the General Assembly in London in 1689: Thomas, BBC, MS G 98 a(1), 115. Thomas and Rees refer to him as 'Dr. Price', and Rees states that he

Baptist church is recorded as being 'one of the largest and wealthiest Nonconforming churches in Wales' for many years.[29] It grew to include adherents at Llangibby, Llandegveth, Usk, and Abergavenny, although it appears to have been known principally as the Llangwm church, particularly during the years of Thomas Quarrell's leadership.[30] In addition to the physician Christopher Price, Thomas Quarrell was assisted by two other 'elders', Robert Jones, and William Milman,[31] and it is with the latter that the first clear evidence of Sabbatarianism appears in this broadly based Baptist community.

The accounts of Milman's origins, and his activities both before his association with the Llangwm Baptists and during that time, are incomplete. Thomas Rees, following Joshua Thomas, says that Milman was ejected c.1660 from an unidentified living in Monmouthshire.[32] He is more frequently referred to, however, as a schoolmaster from Magor, c.1650,[33] although the two accounts need not necessarily be incompatible. Whitley thought that he had been appointed as an itinerant preacher by the Commission for Propagating the Gospel in Wales.[34] What is beyond doubt is that at some point Milman espoused Seventh-day views and that thereafter his energies were expended principally in that cause. Richards correctly points out that since Milman's name first appears in conventicle records as a Sabbatarian in 1669, the canons of sure evidence do not allow him to be identified as a preacher prior to that date.[35] However, Joshua Thomas states that Milman was 'a helper in the scattered church' in Monmouthshire throughout the difficult years of restraint and persecution,[36] and it is quite possible that he was active in the Seventh-day cause well before he was first reported to the authorities in 1669. He is elsewhere said to have located in Llangwm by 1660,[37] and in the 1669 conventicle returns appears as

was a physician, *Nonconformity in Wales*, 189. On Thomas, Quarrell and Price, see *DWB*, s.vv.

[29] Rees, *Nonconformity in Wales*, 214.

[30] Bassett, *Bedyddwyr Cymru*, 36–7; *TBHS* 6: 169.

[31] BBC, MS G 98 a(1), 116, where Thomas describes all three as 'elders', and 'perhaps ordained ministers'.

[32] Rees, *Nonconformity in Wales*, 142; BBC, MS G 98 a(1), 117. But not Trelech, which is a misreading of Palmer's revision of Calamy, *The Nonconformist's Memorial* (1802–3), iii. 506; *OR* ii. 1224.

[33] Richards, *Religious Developments in Wales*, 188; Lambeth MS 639. fo. 186; *BQ* 17: 363.   [34] Whitley, 'Men of the Seventh Day', 8/4.

[35] Richards, *Religious Developments in Wales*, 188.

[36] BBC, MS G 98 a(1), 117.   [37] *TBHS* 2: 254.

a 'Sabbatharian Anabaptist' preacher in Llantrissant, and as one of the 'heads and teachers' at mixed conventicles throughout the deanery of Netherwent.[38] He was licensed for the house of William Richards in Llangwm in 1672, and may also have preached in the house of Walter Jones in Magor.[39] He again appears as a teacher in the Caerleon district, together with several others, and is also said to have preached at Usk in association with William Thomas.[40]

The interest in and around Llangwm during these years seems to have been particularly strong. Rees maintains that in the early 1660s, soon after William Thomas had settled at Llantrissant, 'a considerable number of respectable people' came under his pastoral care there, and at Llangwm, Llangibby, and Llandegveth.[41] By 1672, when Milman was licensed for the house of William Richards at Llangwm, five local gentry, 'competent men of breeding', are reported to have opened their homes for his meetings.[42] William Thomas had also preached at Llangibby and Llandegveth, usually to a congregation numbering between thirty and forty, where he was assisted by Milman and sometimes by Walter Prosser of Abergavenny.[43] Bassett believes that it was likely that Llangibby adherents of the closed-communion Abergavenny church attended Prosser's meetings.[44] If so, the ties between Llangwm–Llantrissant–Llangibby Nonconformists and those in the Abergavenny–Llanwenarth area would naturally have been strengthened. Walter Williams was also licensed in 1672 for the house of Edward Waters in Llangibby, a meeting which officially was designated 'Congregational' but which also reflected a Sabbatarian interest.[45] Llandegveth was still listed in 1715 as 'Independent' with about a hundred attenders, including two 'gentlemen' and twelve 'yeomen'.[46] There is little doubt that the openness to mixed-communion congregations which had characterized the early Llanvaches church persisted for several decades and that it

[38] Lambeth Palace Library, Tenison MS 639, fo. 186[v]; *OR* i. 45. Llangwm was situated in the parish of Llantrissant. Conventicles were reported in Netherwent at Caerleon, Magor, St Brides, Llanvaches, Dinham, and Caldecot, with meetings of up to 200 'Independents, Anabaptists, and Quakers'.   [39] *OR* ii. 542; i. 45, 554.

[40] *OR* ii. 1223; *TBHS* 6: 169.   [41] Rees, *Nonconformity in Wales*, 129.

[42] Richards, *Wales under the Penal Code*, 96; *TBHS* 6: 169; *BQ* 4: 284.

[43] Bassett, *Bedyddwyr Cymru*, 36; Richards, *Wales under the Penal Code*, 96.

[44] Bassett, *Bedyddwyr Cymru*, 36. A closed-communion Baptist church at Abergavenny had been founded c.1652: Rees, *Nonconformity in Wales*, 92. Prosser is described by Richards as 'the old strict Baptist', *Wales under the Penal Code*, 97.

[45] *OR* i. 531: *BQ* 4: 284; Richards, *Wales under the Indulgence, 1672–1675* (1928), 199.   [46] Rees, *Nonconformity in Wales*, 260.

permitted Seventh-day observance. For this William Milman, who throughout the period was 'busy in many conventicles in the south-eastern corner of the county',[47] was largely responsible.

Milman is said to have settled eventually at Tintern, where he died shortly after 1690. He is still mentioned at that time as Thomas Quarrell's assistant at Llangwm and Llantrissant,[48] where Seventh-day views are said to have persisted into the eighteenth century.[49] It seems beyond doubt that Milman, once a conformist, but known since 1669 as an itinerating Sabbatarian preacher, was active in many conventicles throughout the deaneries of Netherwent and Usk for at least twenty-five years. It is not clear from the extant records if any of the groups at Llangwm, Llantrissant, Llangibby, or Llandegveth were at any time predominantly Sabbatarian. It seems most likely that they were not.

MONMOUTHSHIRE: USK AND ABERGAVENNY

It is quite clear that from an early date William Thomas's open-communion Llangwm Baptist church included a branch at Usk. The Llangwm–Llantrissant congregations were part of a 'continuous line of conventicles' in the Usk region.[50] Thomas himself preached in Usk Priory, then the home of Mary Jones, before his death in 1671, and was assisted there, as already noted, by William Milman, and by others.[51] Whitley's conclusion that an early Seventh-day congregation was centred at Usk[52] probably derived from the fact that the conventicles originally reported in this area were located in the deanery of Usk, which thereby lent its name readily to Nonconformist groups. By the turn of the century Usk may well have become the centre of Seventh-day activity in the area, particularly since Nathaniel Morgan had by then acquired Usk Castle as his residence and was using it as a meeting-place.[53] Joshua Thomas is sure, however, that

[47] Richards, *Wales under the Penal Code*, 97.
[48] BBC, MS G 98 a(1), 117; Rees, *Nonconformity in Wales*, 142; Palmer (ed.), *Nonconformist's Memorial*, iii. 527.
[49] *TBHS* 6: 169.   [50] Ibid.
[51] Ibid.; Richards, *Wales under the Penal Code*, 95.
[52] Whitley, *British Baptists*, 86. Whitley's view that William Milman obtained his Seventh-day views from Richard Goodgroom of Usk is based on a mistaken identification of Goodgroom with the London Fifth Monarchist/Seventh-day man of the same name: *BQ* 1: 233; *FMM* 250.
[53] *TBHS* 6: 173; Thomas, NLW, MS 10620E, fos. 190–1.

Usk and Abergavenny, when under the care of Christopher Price and Nathaniel Morgan, belonged initially to the William Thomas/ Thomas Quarrell Llangwm Baptist church.[54]

The scattered nature of this church clearly made its pastoral administration difficult, and at some point prior to 1690 the congregation agreed to divide, 'for conveniency'.[55] Thomas Quarrell retained oversight of Llangwm, Llantrissant, Llangibby, and Llandegveth, with William Milman and Walter Williams his assistants. Christopher Price assumed full responsibility for Abergavenny and Usk, with Nathaniel Morgan his occasional assistant.[56] The arrangement suggests that there were Sabbatarians in both branches of the old church. In 1690 the Abergavenny/Usk church was 'in a respectable state, with plenty of good officers', although it appears to have departed from the Llangwm tradition in one respect, in that it was by now a closed-communion Baptist church.[57] Price gave land for a church building at Llanwenarth near Abergavenny, and shortly after his death in 1697 the Abergavenny branch of the original Llangwm church joined with the Llanwenarth Baptists.[58] They, too, were soon to divide, but over the imposition of hands, those who were opposed returning to the open-communion Llangwm–Llantrissant fold, and those who were in favour persevering as a congregation in their own right.[59] The fortunes and dispositions of any Sabbatarians who might have been caught up in these events are not recorded.

It was Nathaniel Morgan, one of the few surviving names of known Sabbatarians in the Marches–Monmouthshire area, and Price's assistant at Usk and Abergavenny, who nurtured the Seventh-day interest in that locality. Joshua Thomas describes Morgan as 'a gentleman of no small repute in the world', and confirms that Morgan was recognized as one of the ministering brethren at Usk and Llangwm.[60] He came originally from St Weonard's in Herefordshire, moving to St Margaret's near Olchon before settling finally in Usk Castle. Thomas notes him as a preacher in each of these localities, frequently holding meetings in his own house, and preaching regularly in Usk Castle from 1689 until his death in 1722.[61] The 1669 conventicle returns had revealed a meeting of 'Anabaptists' at Abergavenny, with Christopher Price, 'apothecarie', William Morgan, 'shoemaker', and John Edward, 'shoemaker', as 'teachers and

[54] BBC, MS G 98 a(1), 115.   [55] Ibid. 116.   [56] Ibid.
[57] Thomas, NLW, MS 10620E, fos. 184–5.   [58] BBC, MS G 98 a(1), 118.
[59] Rees, *Nonconformity in Wales*, 190.   [60] BBC, MS G 98 a(1), 120.
[61] Ibid. 120–1.

seducers',[62] and a congregation of up to 200 at Llangwm, including some 'of competent parts and breeding' in the houses of John Morgan, Nathaniel Morgan, and Thomas Williams, amongst others, with William Thomas and William Milman as teachers.[63] A later record, based on information supplied by Joseph Stennett II in 1717, states that Morgan, *c.*1715, preached to a congregation of fifty at Usk Castle and to 150 at Llangwm.[64]

Joseph Stennett II, previously of Leominster, had been attracted to this area, possibly on two accounts. Dr E.A. Payne recounts that a Stennett began to preach at Abergavenny *c.*1706,[65] but it is improbable this was the young Joseph Stennett II who at the time could have been only 14. If it was his father, Joseph Stennett I, it is likely that the young Joseph II would also have become acquainted with the Abergavenny church. In any event, in 1714 Stennett married one of Nathaniel Morgan's daughters, Mary, who thus was to become the mother of the renowned Dr Samuel Stennett.[66] Another child of Joseph and Mary Stennett died in infancy and was buried

[62] *OR* i. 45.   [63] Ibid. 48.

[64] John Evans, DWL, MS 38.4, 82. According to Stennett, the Usk congregation included three Gentlemen, four Yeomen, seven Tradesmen, five Farmers, and ten Labourers. At Llangwm the number included four Gentlemen, three Yeomen, five Tradesmen, twelve Farmers, and thirty Labourers.

There is some uncertainty regarding the venue of Morgan's meetings at Usk. Stennett reported that they were held at Usk Castle, and Joshua Thomas later added that Morgan had preached in the hall of the castle house from *c.*1689, BBC, MS G 98 a(1), 121; NLW, MS 10620E, fos. 190, 91. However, William Coxe's account of the owners of Usk Castle from Richard III to Lord Clive leaves no room for Nathaniel Morgan; William Coxe, *An Historical Tour in Monmouthshire* (1801), 130–2. Moreover, the great hall is said to have lain in ruins with much of the remainder of the castle since the fifteenth century, although the Gatehouse was extended in the seventeenth century and is currently occupied by the present owners, and could have provided accommodation for a moderately sized congregation. While it seems unlikely that both Stennett and Thomas could have mistaken Usk Castle for Usk Priory, William Thomas and William Milman preached in the Priory to a branch of the Llangwm church. Following its dissolution, the Priory had passed into the hands of Roger Williams of Llangibby, by whose descendants it was later sold to new local owners: Coxe, *Historical Tour*, 133. Richards says that the Priory belonged to the widow of William Jones, a prominent member of the Commission for Propagating the Gospel in Wales, at the time it was used by Thomas and Milman: Richards, *Wales under the Penal Code*, 96.   [65] *BQ* 14: 164.

[66] BBC, MS G 98 a(1), 120; *TBHS* 6: 176. Another of Morgan's daughters married a 'Mr. Roberts' of Abingdon, and another married 'Mr Noble' of Bridgwater: Thomas, *History of the Baptist Association in Wales*, 41. Both Joseph Stennett II and Samuel Stennett were staunch Sabbatarians, even though they ministered principally to congregations which worshipped on Sunday: Joseph at Exeter (1721–37) and Little Wild Street, London (1737–58), and Samuel at Little Wild Street (1758–95), see Ch. 4 n. 103 and Ch. 5 n. 107.

at Llanwenarth in 1717.[67] Dr Payne says that the Stennett association with the Abergavenny–Llanwenarth church would have assured
Welsh Baptists of a knowledge of the Seventh-day tradition.[68] In all
probability, the Stennett connection was more of a late confirmation of knowledge which the Abergavenny–Llanwenarth Baptists
had possessed for some time. Indeed, the Sabbatarians already
established there would account for Stennett's interest in the area
in the first place, since his own Sabbatarian leanings are likely
to have drawn him to Abergavenny as well as to Mary Morgan.
Such a pattern of events would confirm the conclusion that the
Llanwenarth record of Saturday-keeping congregations presupposes
a Sabbatarian interest in that locality *c.*1690. For this, Nathaniel
Morgan, probably William Milman, and perhaps also William
Morgan, were largely responsible.

The brightest years of the Baptist and Seventh-day causes in
south-east Monmouthshire were now over, however. The 'once
flourishing church' of Llangwm and Usk had 'dwindled' to about
200 by 1718.[69] It is difficult to determine whether or not, as Whitley
suggested, the 'peculiar Sabbatarian views' of Milman, Morgan, and
Stennett contributed in any significant manner to the decline and
eventual demise of the Llangwm Baptists.[70] If this was the case, it
rather suggests that Seventh-day views had come to predominate
amongst the Llangwm–Usk Baptists as they had at least for a time,
amongst other mixed-communion Baptist churches elsewhere in
the country, e.g. at Bledlow in Buckinghamshire, and at Ingham in
Norfolk.[71] It is less difficult to see that the departure of its three
leading figures materially contributed to the decline of the Seventh-
day Men throughout this area. Milman had died at Tintern *c.*1691,[72]
faithful and active to the end, and although the Sabbatarian cause
appears to have remained relatively strong for a further twenty or
thirty years, it could not survive the loss of its two remaining
stalwarts. Stennett left to return briefly to Leominster before accepting a call to the South Street Baptist church in Exeter in 1721, and
Nathaniel Morgan died in 1722. Even though Morgan left a bequest
to continue 'the work of the gospel' at Llangwm and Usk,[73] nothing

---

[67] *BQ* 14: 164. Joseph and Mary Stennett returned to Leominster *c.*1718 before
leaving for Exeter in 1721.   [68] Ibid.
[69] *TBHS* 6: 176; DWL, MS 38.4, 82.   [70] *TBHS* 6: 169, 176.
[71] See Ch. 6 on Bledlow, and Ch. 9 on Ingham.
[72] Rees, *Nonconformity in Wales*, 142.   [73] BBC, MS G 98 a(1), 121.

is heard thereafter of the Monmouthshire Sabbatarians. Undoubtedly an interest lingered, perhaps as late as 1737, when a new wave of emigration is said to have taken many Welsh Nonconformists, including some remaining Sabbatarians, to the new world.[74]

HEREFORDSHIRE: LEOMINSTER AND HAY-ON-WYE

Joshua Thomas refers to 'a society of Seventh-day members in Herefordshire' during the seventeenth century and indicates that the group had previously been mentioned in an unidentified letter sent from Hereford to London in 1690.[75] This unnamed congregation appears by then to have been well established, even though it is not included in the Llanwenarth list. The 'ancient' Sabbatarians of Leominster have already been noted, but it is more likely that the Thomas reference is to another Seventh-day congregation, centred around Hay-on-Wye, which almost certainly derived from the early Baptist church at Olchon in the parish of Clodock, on the Herefordshire–Monmouthshire border. The Leominster Baptist church records also allude to a congregation of Seventh-day Men at Hay-on-Wye in 1689, noting that their 'generation' was the last of the Herefordshire Sabbatarians.[76] Certainly the Hay Seventh-day people were the last known Saturday-keeping group to have survived in this region,[77] and, in broad terms, they may also have been the original Herefordshire Sabbatarians and the progenitors of Sabbatarian convictions throughout the entire Herefordshire–Monmouthshire area. The 'good character' of the Hay Seventh-day Men reported in the 1690 letter undoubtedly testifies to their standing in the Baptist community at large,[78] and typifies relationships between Baptists who worshipped on Sunday and those who observed Saturday throughout Herefordshire and Monmouthshire. The bonds of a common origin and an essentially similar theology, and the links forged through hardship and persecution, are sufficient to have ensured mutual respect and toleration.[79]

Once again the Seventh-day Men appear unannounced and without any definite point of origin or departure from the wider

---

[74] *TBHS* 6: 176.   [75] BBC, MS G 98 a(1), 59.

[76] Leominster Baptist church book, A, p. vi.   [77] BBC, MS G 98 a(1), 59.

[78] Ibid.

[79] Thomas records that after 1660 Baptists in the Hay–Olchon area were 'often taken, beaten, abused, fined, and imprisoned', BBC, MS G 98 a(1), 56.

Baptist community. Joshua Thomas maintained that a small Baptist congregation had existed in the remote Olchon region from c.1633,[80] some fifteen or sixteen years before the first known Welsh Baptist congregation, with strict-communion principles, had gathered at Ilston, in 1649. Although Rees dismisses Thomas's assertion as 'groundless',[81] it is not at all impossible, in view of Olchon's predilection for religious dissent, that Baptist convictions did appear there at an early date.[82] Richards notes the uncertainty surrounding Baptist origins in this locality, but concurs with Thomas that Baptists had gathered at Olchon for 'some years' prior to the founding of the Ilston congregation.[83] Thomas himself elsewhere offered the revised date c.1640–1 for Baptist origins at Olchon,[84] although Rees refuses to antedate Baptist beginnings in Wales beyond Ilston and the labours of John Miles in 1649.[85] Whatever the reality might have been at Olchon, it is certain that a Baptist congregation had been formed at nearby Hay by 1649–50,[86] and that the Sabbatarian cause there and at Olchon was advocated and exemplified by John Rhys Howell, a 'Seventh-day man . . . of considerable note and property'.[87] Richards describes Howell as one of the two Seventh-day Baptists recorded in Wales between 1654 and 1662.[88] It seems probable that John Rhys Howell was an early convert to the seventh day in the Olchon–Hay area, even though the origin of his views remains obscure.

Howell was already a member of the Hay Baptist church by 1654,[89] and his name appears in the following year as one of fifteen members of the Hay church who received the laying on of hands from the Baptist church at Llanwenarth.[90] Thomas records that 'the

---

[80] Thomas, *History of the Baptist Association in Wales*, 2.

[81] Rees, *Nonconformity in Wales*, 91.

[82] Richards maintains that the Olchon valley was the cradle of the 'rigid school of Welsh Baptists', and that in the mid-1660s it was still 'a stronghold of the Baptist cause' and 'the home of its strictest gospel and of its most sacred traditions', Richards, *The Religious Census of 1676*, 75–6. This would indicate that the Olchon–Hay Sabbatarians were Particular Baptists with an essentially Calvinistic theology.

[83] Richards, *Puritan Movement in Wales*, 202.   [84] BBC, MS G 98 a(1), 45–6.

[85] Rees, *Nonconformity in Wales*, 91–2. Rees believes that Hay was the second Baptist church to be founded in Wales, c.1649.

[86] Ibid. 92; White, *Association Records*, i. 3.

[87] Thomas, BBC, MS G 98 a(1), 46, 59.

[88] Richards, *Religious Developments in Wales*, 188.

[89] BBC, MS G 98 a(1), 54.

[90] NLW, MS 409 B, fo. 187. Thomas notes that 'several of the first constituents' of the Abergavenny–Llanwenarth church were originally members of the Hay church,

famous Mr John Rhys Howell' was 'very useful' to the church in the Olchon–Hay district, and that as late as 1750 aged people in the locality 'spoke of him with great veneration'.[91] Thomas says that he was an unordained 'occasional assistant in the ministry', an elder of the Baptist church at Olchon and 'the Hay', and confirms that for a considerable period of his life he was 'a Seventh day man'.[92] Thomas does not indicate how many of the early Baptists at Hay or Olchon shared Howell's Sabbatarian convictions, but the Seventh-day group referred to in the Leominster Baptist records in 1689 survived in the Hay–Broadmeadow area until the middle of the eighteenth century. Howell himself died *c.*1692, 'very aged', some time after returning from America where he had emigrated to avoid the persecution of the post-Restoration years.[93] The Sabbatarian cause in south-west Herefordshire probably owed its identity, possibly its survival, and perhaps even its existence, to the long labours of John Rhys Howell both before and after his temporary exile to the new world.

Sabbatarian history in Wales and the border counties suffers much, as it does throughout England, from the fact that in most localities only the barest fragmentary evidence has survived. This might not have been so in the case of the Herefordshire and related Welsh Sabbatarians, or in the case of John Rhys Howell himself, had a chest of papers left by him, relating to early Baptist history, survived. Joshua Thomas had heard of this collection of old documents, and went in search of it *c.*1775,[94] only to find that it had been destroyed. It is a loss that will be lamented by all historians, particularly those with an interest in the Nonconformist, Baptist, and Seventh-day traditions. As it is, the only surviving glimpses of the Sabbatarian movement in this area are of Jacob Francis, a Seventh-day man at Hay, *c.*1706, and the statement by Joshua Thomas that Seventh-day sentiments persisted at Broadmeadow, Clifford, and the Hay 'as late as 1730, or later'.[95] Jacob Francis is noted by Thomas as 'a Baptist, [and] a person of good reputation . . . for piety and gravity', and 'one of those who kept the seventh day as a Sabbath'.[96] Francis married Hannah Davies of Leominster *c.*1714, and she, after his

---

but joined with Abergavenny since 'they lived nearer to Abergavenny' than to Hay, BBC, MS G 98 a(1), 52.

[91] BBC, G 98 a(1), 59, 65.   [92] Ibid. 46, 59.   [93] Ibid. 46.
[94] Ibid.   [95] Ibid. 59.
[96] Thomas, 'History of Leominster Baptist Church', NLW, Minor Deposit 614A, 13.

death, married Benjamin Adams of Leominster.[97] There may be hints here of an established link between the Hay and Leominster Sabbatarians, of a recognizable Sabbatarian group at Hay *c.*1714, and of the survival of the Seventh-day cause at Leominster at least to this date. Although the diocesan records for Herefordshire and Breconshire are strangely silent about Sabbatarianism at any time during the seventeenth and eighteenth centuries, the existence of a Seventh-day group at Hay, and at Leominster, is beyond doubt. What cannot be documented with any certainty is their relationship to each other, and what cannot be documented at all, unfortunately, are the details of their congregational lives.

The cordial relationships between Sabbatarian Baptists and those in the wider Baptist community, evident both in Monmouthshire and in south-west Herefordshire, seem to have been particularly strong in Leominster. The Baptists there spoke warmly of their 'ancient friends who observe the seventh day', and recorded in their church minutes that the Sabbatarians frequently invited them 'to teach in their houses', where they had held 'very considerable meetings'.[98] This refers to events late in the seventeenth and probably also in the early eighteenth century, and by then the Seventh-day people had clearly been established for a relatively long time. One source suggests that the Leominster Sabbatarians were 'flourishing' by 1650,[99] a conclusion which is not impossible in the light of Baptist developments in Leominster and other relevant information recorded in the Leominster church book. Leominster at this period has been described as 'little Amsterdam' on account of the diversity of religious opinion[100] which rapidly developed there during the tolerant years of the Commonwealth. They were favourable circumstances for the rapid growth of Baptist and Sabbatarian views, amongst many other doctrines rediscovered from the Bible.

Baptist origins in Leominster are usually traced to John Tombes, the vicar of Leominster, who adopted Baptist principles *c.*1643, and who thenceforth was known as one of the most articulate and persuasive advocates of believer's baptism. Shortly thereafter, *c.*1647, a predominantly Baptist church emerged at Leominster under Tombes's guidance, although he never took it wholly away from

---

[97] Ibid.   [98] Leominster Baptist church book, A, p. vi.

[99] *SDBEA*, I, 49, based on an article in the *Birmingham Weekly Post*, 13 Apr. 1901.

[100] G.F. Townsend, *The Town and Borough of Leominster* (Leominster, 1863), 134 – 5. Sabbatarianism was reported to be strong at Amsterdam from the 1640s onwards: Edwards, *Gangraena*, 63 (the second so numbered).

the Anglican fold, nor excluded from communion those who continued to hold paedobaptist views.[101] This state of affairs eventually became unacceptable to a segment of Tombes's congregation, and in 1656 several members withdrew on the grounds that he had not sufficiently separated from the Church of England.[102] Those who thus seceded formed a Baptist congregation of their own. A few years later, 'during the times of persecution' to quote Joshua Thomas, another Baptist congregation appeared in Leominster, comprising those who were convinced that the laying on of hands was a New Testament requirement.[103] These congregations account for three of the four Baptist churches in Leominster during the seventeenth century, as recorded in the Etnam Street church book, i.e. those who remained in Tombes's open-communion church, those who seceded in 1656, under 'Mr Price', and those who were gathered in favour of the imposition of hands, under 'Mr. Pardoe'.[104] The fourth group specifically listed in the Etnam Street records is simply designated 'some Seventh-day men'. It is this group which is subsequently described as 'ancient'.[105]

A hint of the obscure origins of the Seventh-day Men in Leominster, traditionally thought to have been General Baptists, may be reflected in the spiritual quest of the Leominster Quaker, John Beevan. In 1660, Beevan addressed his *Loving Salutation To all People who have any desire after the Living God* to those with whom he had formerly been in fellowship, 'especially to the people called Free-Will-Anabaptists'. In recounting his early experiences, Beevan describes how, at the age of 14, before the turmoil of the civil wars, he had worshipped with 'a little flock' in Leominster in an earnest attempt to find the will of God.[106] He recalls the zealous searching of those earlier years. 'Ah, Lord', he sighs, 'Do I not keep all thy commandments?' yet without rest or peace.[107] In 1656, when the Free-Will Baptists had grown strong, 'a multitude of people out

---

[101] Townsend, *Leominster*, 117; White, *English Baptists*, 9, 73.

[102] Leominster Baptist church book, A, p. iii.

[103] Thomas, NLW, Minor Deposit 614A, 6–7.

[104] Leominster Baptist church book, A, p. v. Although he had no known connection with Leominster, the General Baptist William Pardoe was imprisoned at Hereford and Worcester, before settling at Lichfield; *DNB*, and INB, *TBHS* 7: 223. In 1688 Pardoe published *Antient Christianity Revived: Being a Description of the Doctrine, Discipline, and Practice of the Little City of Bethania.*

[105] Leominster Baptist church book, A, pp. v, vi.

[106] John Beevan, *A Loving Salutation To all People who have any desire after the Living God: But especially to the Free-Will-Anabaptists* (1660), 3.

[107] Ibid. 6.

of ye town and country', Beevan found his spiritual home with the
Quakers who emerged at that time largely from among the Baptists
with whom he had formerly been in communion.[108] The identity of
this pre-Civil War Baptist congregation remains unknown, but it is
not impossible that the 'ancient' Leominster Sabbatarians were in
some way linked with Beevan's early 'little flock' of Free-Will Baptists, who clearly antedated William Pardoe's post-Restoration
congregation of General Baptists.

The three Sunday-keeping Baptist congregations under Tombes,
Price, and Pardoe eventually united in 1694 to form the Etnam
Street church,[109] whose records have proved so valuable in iden-
tifying the Leominster Seventh-day Men, thus leaving the Sabbatarian
Baptists as a distinct congregation at the end of the seventeenth
century. The 'very considerable meetings' which the Leominster
Baptists held in the homes of Sabbatarians at this period, and early
in the eighteenth century, suggest that at least some of the Seventh-
day people were comfortably placed members of the community
with houses commodious enough to accommodate relatively large
groups. In context, it could reasonably be deduced that the
Leominster Sabbatarians were at least as old as the original Baptists
who had worshipped with John Tombes in the late 1640s, and that
probably they were even older than that.

John Tombes's own stance on the Sabbath question is not known,
although it has been suggested that his original mixed-communion
congregation included Sabbatarians c.1647.[110] While this is largely
conjecture, given the nature of that congregation and Tombes's
own early tolerant attitude to Dissenting views, it is not impossible.
It is less likely that Tombes himself privately held Sabbatarian
convictions,[111] as did Henry Jessey, his contemporary and fellow
labourer in the open Baptist cause. It is also unlikely that he was
directly responsible for gathering the Sabbatarian church at

---

[108] N. Penney (ed.), *The First Publishers of Truth* (1907), 117. The Quakers were
opposed by John Tombes, *inter alios*.

[109] Leominster Baptist church book, A, p. iii; NLW, Minor Deposit 614A, 9–10.

[110] *SO* 3: 5.

[111] Although Tombes had been wary of 'Judaisme' and the 'burthen of Jewish
rites' since 1645 (*Two Treatises . . . concerning Infant Baptism* (1645), 6, 7), he did
concur with the Sabbatarians at least to the extent of recognizing the identity of the
biblical Sabbath: 'I find not where the term [Sabbath day] is meant or applied to any
other than the seventh day of the week. . . . No where that I yet find is any day
besides the last day of the week termed the Sabbath day . . . that day was the seventh in order after the six days in which [God] created his work'; John Tombes, *Anti-
Paedobaptism, or the Third Part . . .* (1657), 674–5.

Leominster. Nor is there any evidence that he preached for the Salisbury Sabbatarians when in later life he moved from Leominster to Salisbury.[112] The evidence supports the view that his personal sympathies remained with the established Church until the end, for in his last years he appears as a communicant at St Edmund's, Salisbury, hearing the Book of Common Prayer, receiving the sacrament, and confessing that he dared not separate from essential communion with the Church of England.[113] For all that, it remains true that his early ministry at Leominster and his vigorous advocacy of believer's baptism created a climate in which the seeds of Sabbatarianism would spring up and take deep root. There may, or may not, be significance in the fact that Tombes, the pamphleteer and controversialist who wrote against paedobaptists, Quakers, Socinians, Papists, and Fifth Monarchy Men,[114] did not at the same time enter the Sabbatarian debate when it was attracting wide attention from the early 1650s to the late 1670s.[115]

The fortunes of the Leominster Sabbatarians from the end of the seventeenth century and in the eighteenth century can only be surmised. There are no direct references to them beyond 1690 in the Leominster church book or in other sources. It is quite possible that they continued for several years as a separate community without attracting further attention, as did other Seventh-day congregations elsewhere in the country. It is also possible, perhaps probable, that a diminishing remnant were ultimately accorded fellowship with Etnam Street Baptists at some point early in the eighteenth century. This would help to explain the young Joseph Stennett II's interest in Leominster between 1714 and 1721, and the fact that he served as assistant to Thomas Holder at Etnam Street prior to moving to Exeter.[116] It might also help to explain the

---

[112] *SO* 3: 5.   [113] *CR* 488.

[114] e.g., *Saints no Smiters: or Smiting Civil Powers not the Work of Saints, Being a Treatise Shewing the Doctrine and Attempts of Quinto-Monarchians, or Fifth-Monarchy-Men, about Smiting Powers, to be damnable and Antichristian* (1664). The eschatological theme was still strong in Welsh Baptist theology in the eighteenth century, when Rees says that c.1720–30 most Baptists were also millenarians; Rees, *Nonconformity in Wales*, 280.

[115] See Appendix IV for the extent of the Sabbatarian debate, from the anonymous *Moralitie of the Fourth Commandement* (1652) and William Saller's *Sundry Queries* (1653), to Edward Stennett's *The Insnared Taken in the Work of his Hands* (1677) and Francis Bampfield's *A Name, an After One* (1681).

[116] NLW, MS 11095 E. Holder had been a member of Baptist churches at Lichfield and Worcester before moving to Leominster, where he became a 'leader in the Severn Valley'. It was under his guidance that the three Baptist congregations at Leominster united in 1694: INB, *TBHS* 7: 208.

references to Sabbatarians in the Etnam Street records. Holder, who probably wrote up these early records, and Stennett, are likely to have been the principal teachers at the 'very considerable meetings' held in the homes of the Leominster Seventh-day people early in the eighteenth century. The marriage of Jacob Francis's widow, Hannah, to Benjamin Adams of Leominster may also indicate a Seventh-day presence at approximately the same time. The interest at Hay continued, as already noted, at least until the 1730s,[117] and although definitive evidence is lacking, these otherwise unrelated events may suggest that a corresponding interest survived at Leominster. By then, however, it would have been weak, and without the presence of a Tombes or a Stennett, or the catalytic atmosphere of earlier more religious and spirited times, incapable of further survival.

[117] BBC, MS G 98 a(1), 59.

9

East Anglia

THE first definitive work in favour of the Seventh-day Sabbath, as noted in an earlier chapter, came from Theophilus Brabourne of Norwich, in 1628. Brabourne could hardly have anticipated the extent to which literal obedience to the fourth commandment would appeal to his fellow countrymen in East Anglia and further afield. Nor could he have foreseen that his own publications advocating observance of the seventh day would help to persuade more Independents and Baptists than Anglicans of their obligations to keep Saturday instead of Sunday.[1] Brabourne's influence on the development of Sabbatarianism in non-Anglican congregations in Norfolk and throughout East Anglia was arguably greater than his own reluctance to leave the established Church might suggest. That his sympathies lay with those who corporately observed the seventh day is clear from his bequest to provide for the poor of a Sabbatarian congregation in Norwich. By then, in 1662, or soon afterwards, other Sabbatarian congregations had been established at various places in Norfolk, Suffolk, Essex, and Cambridgeshire, several of which were to become recognized strongholds of Saturday observance, some for a century or more.

It would be misleading, however, to exaggerate Brabourne's influence on Sabbatarian developments in East Anglia. It has already been said that the English Seventh-day movement arose in the context of a wider Puritan Sabbatarianism, initially an East Anglian phenomenon itself, born in Suffolk and nurtured at Cambridge.[2] Nicholas Bound's fundamental argument regarding the continuity of the Sabbath commandment was suited perfectly for the proposition which the Saturday Sabbatarians would later seek to draw from it. It was, moreover, an argument that had been well tested by the time it was needed by the Seventh-day Men. It would also be imprudent to overlook the impact which Continental Sabbatarianism may have had on developments in East Anglian counties. Patrick

---

[1] On Brabourne and his works, see above, Ch. 2.   [2] See above, 41–2.

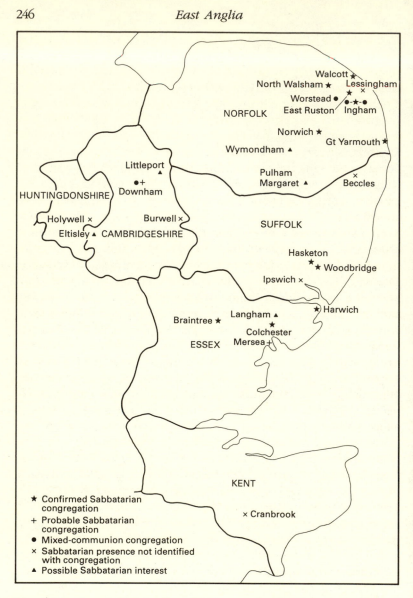

MAP 6 Locations in East Anglia and Kent associated with seventeenth- and eighteenth-century Sabbatarianism

Collinson has argued for the influence of Calvinistic and Zwinglian theology on English Puritan Sabbatarianism, and specifically reminds us that 'English Sabbatarianism was elaborated in full awareness of the progress of the question in learned circles overseas.'[3] Collinson himself points out that before the turn of the century a Sabbatarian movement had appeared in The Netherlands with interests somewhat parallel to those which marked its counterpart in England.[4]

East Anglia had by then already long been open to Continental influences. Dutch and Flemish Anabaptists had settled in large numbers in England early in the sixteenth century, finding an affinity with the remnants of English Lollardy to such an extent that, as G.H. Williams remarks, 'new Anabaptist was but old Lollard writ Dutch'.[5] Many Dutch Anabaptists suffered martyrdom in the eastern counties of England during the sixteenth century, and in London as late as 1575. By 1571, French and Dutch immigrants already constituted a significant proportion of the people living in Norwich, and only sixteen years later Continental immigrants accounted for a majority of that city's population.[6] Following a well-established Separatist tradition, English refugees from Norwich and Yarmouth settled temporarily in Holland in 1635 'to enjoy ye libertie of their conscience in God's worship, and to free themselves from humane Inventions'.[7] Sabbatarianism had been established at Amsterdam in the sixteenth century, and Anabaptists there and at Rotterdam and other Dutch centres would almost certainly have known of the contemporary Sabbatarian movements in Silesia, Moravia, and Transylvania.[8] It is of note that the earliest identifiable reference to Seventh-day observance in East Anglia, in 1645, comes from a Dutch source.[9] It is not at all improbable that sixteenth-century Dutch immigrants and English exiles returning to Norwich and Yarmouth brought with them a knowledge of the Saturday Sabbath, if indeed some of them did not already observe it themselves.

---

[3] Collinson, in *Studies in Church History*, i. 215.   [4] Ibid. 210, 213.

[5] Williams, *The Radical Reformation*, 401.

[6] Ibid. 784.   [7] *BQ* 23: 171.

[8] On the wider Continental Sabbatarian movements, see above, Ch. 1; Williams, *The Radical Reformation, passim*, s.vv. Judaizers and Sabbatarians; and E.M. Wilbur, *Our Unitarian Heritage* (Boston, Mass., 1926) 251–5, and *A History of Unitarianism*, 106–18.

[9] Georgius Hornius, *De statu Ecclesiae Britannicae hodierno* (Danzig, 1647), 102–3.

It was in the more immediate context of the Baptist/Fifth Monarchy developments during the late 1640s and 1650s that seventeenth-century Sabbatarianism first appeared openly in Norfolk. An Independent church had been established at Norwich in 1644, when it was agreed that the Norwich members of a Congregational church at Great Yarmouth, under William Bridge, should organize themselves as a separate group.[10] Within a year or so the membership of this congregation had grown to more than a hundred, and eventually several members became convinced of the invalidity of infant baptism, ultimately seceding to establish a separate Baptist church.[11] At about the same time an Independent church established at Pulham, *c*.1643–4, had become Baptist,[12] while at Wymondham the baptismal debate eventually resulted in the establishment there of a paedobaptist congregation.[13] The establishment of an Independent church at North Walsham in 1652 was attended by messengers from Norwich, and representatives of both Norwich and Yarmouth attended the organization of the Stalham–Ingham church in 1653.[14] Both North Walsham and Ingham soon adopted Baptist principles. An Independent church had also been established at Beccles, on the Norfolk–Suffolk border, with assistance from Norwich and Yarmouth.[15] The interrelationship of these early Independent-Baptist congregations is an important factor in the development of Norfolk Sabbatarianism.

During the 1650s Fifth Monarchist doctrines became popular at Norwich, North Walsham, Yarmouth, and Wymondham, and possibly also at Pulham, which remained in contact with Yarmouth and 'the dominating influence' of Yarmouth's millenarian minister William Bridge.[16] Pulham also established contact with Beccles.[17] Despite Capp's view that nearly all the Fifth Monarchist ministers in

---

[10] *BQ* 23: 173. Bridge, previously rector of St Peter Hungate, and St George Tombland, Norwich, had fled to Holland in 1636 after having been ejected and excommunicated by Matthew Wren, Bishop of Norwich, *CR* 74; *BQ* 23: 171.

[11] M.F. Hewett, 'Historical Record of the Baptists of Norfolk and their Churches', 1942–7, NRO, MS 4260, s.v. Norwich St Mary's.

[12] J. Browne, *History of Congregationalism, and Memorials of the Churches in Norfolk and Suffolk* (1877), 285, 547–8.   [13] *BQ* 23: 174.

[14] Ibid. 173; C.B. Jewson, *Stalham Baptist Church, 1653–1953* (n.d.), 1.

[15] T.J. Hosken, *History of Congregationalism and Memorials of the Churches . . . in Suffolk* (Ipswich, 1920), 199.   [16] *FMM* 77–9.

[17] Browne, *History of Congregationalism*, 549.

East Anglia began their careers under Bridge and continued to come under his influence after becoming Fifth Monarchists,[18] it remains true that the figure who appears most frequently in these early Baptist/Fifth Monarchist developments in south-east Norfolk and east Suffolk is the Cambridge graduate and former captain in the Parliamentary army Christopher Pooley, subsequently known as 'the grand dipper in Norfolk'.[19] It may safely be assumed that under Pooley's later guidance—between 1656 and 1668 he is said to have 'haunted the district'[20]—many Baptists and Fifth Monarchists in these churches also turned to the Seventh-day Sabbath.

Pooley first appears, without Sabbatarian convictions, as curate of Thwaite in Suffolk in 1643, and after the Civil War as leader of an Independent congregation at Wymondham in 1653.[21] The decision of this church to remain paedobaptist may have led Pooley to leave for a more congenial atmosphere, for by 1656 he had adopted Baptist beliefs and was prominent in the Baptist/Fifth Monarchist church at North Walsham.[22] The year 1656 was, in fact, of some significance for the Fifth Monarchy movement in East Anglia. In March messengers from the churches met in Norwich to discuss 'the visible reigne of Christ and the duty of the Saints towards the Governments of the world'.[23] While they concluded that in the latter days there would be 'a Glorious and visible Kingdom of Christ, wherein the Saints should rule', it was also agreed that it was the duty of saints 'to give subjection', and that to do otherwise would be 'a matter of griefe and great offence'.[24] Such laudable sentiments were not to prevail for long. In July Secretary of State Thurloe was advised that many Norwich Fifth Monarchy Men had 'turned anabaptists', and, more alarmingly, that the North Walsham Fifth Monarchists, 'lately dipped', had grown 'exceeding high in their expressions, and that tending to blood'. Pooley was named as one of the 'chieftaines' of the North Walsham group, together with two other known militants, Thomas Buttevant and Thomas Rudduck.[25]

Pooley was also busy at this time in at least two other centres, Norwich and Beccles. Many of the details of his widespread activities

---

[18] *FMM* 79.

[19] *TBHS* 2: 249. On Pooley, who should be distinguished from Christopher Pooley, rector of Great Massingham, Norfolk, 1619–53, see Capp, *FMM* 258; *BDBR* iii. 49–50.   [20] *TBHS* 2: 249.

[21] *FMM* 258. Cf. Browne, *History of Congregationalism*, 291.

[22] *BQ* 23: 174.   [23] Ibid.   [24] Ibid.   [25] Ibid.

have not survived, but it is recorded that in August 1656 he baptized Mary Gill of Norwich and a Mrs Boote of Beccles, both of
whom at the time were members of the Beccles Independent church.
The church took exception to these events, and called a meeting to
consider 'the disorderly breaking off of two of the sisters who had
joined themselves to another society without the church's consent'.[26]
It would seem that Pooley was by now leading a congregation
elsewhere, probably centred in Norwich, which was soon to become
Seventh-day, if indeed it was not already so inclined. One source
suggests that in 1656 a group of militant Fifth Monarchists under
Pooley had seceded from an Independent-Baptist church which
met in St George's Tombland in Norwich, to form a Seventh-day
congregation.[27] Given the fluidity of religious thought in Norwich
at the time, this is not impossible. In 1658 Pooley appeared in a
Norwich court and openly declared that Sunday was not to be kept
holy, that Saturday was the Sabbath, and that the rulers of the
nation were antichristian, 'and the magistrates of the city, limbs of
the beast'.[28] In July of that same year Thomas Tillam of Colchester,
by now a convinced Sabbatarian, preached in St Giles, Norwich, in
favour of the Saturday Sabbath, saying that 'All Christians are bound
to keep the sabbath on the seventh day of the week.'[29] The combined efforts of Pooley and Tillam would unquestionably have
strengthened the Sabbatarian cause in Norwich, and it is clear that
by 1658 a Seventh-day congregation was firmly established.[30]

What is not clear is whether Pooley's Sabbatarian congregation
was in any way related to the Baptist church, since known as St
Mary's, which was organized in Norwich in 1669. Baptists were
certainly present and worshipping corporately in Norwich before
this as part of a broader Independent congregation, but apparently
did not coalesce as a separate Baptist community until the early
1660s.[31] Although Sabbatarian and Fifth Monarchy views were
'widely held' by Norfolk Baptists in the late 1650s and 1660s, and
the early Norwich Baptists 'cannot have been uninfluenced by

---

[26] Browne, *History of Congregationalism*, 572.

[27] Hewett, NRO, MS 4260, s.v. Norwich St Mary's.

[28] Francis Blomefield, *An Essay towards a Topographical History of the County of
Norfolk . . .*, iii (1806), 401.

[29] Bodl., MS Tanner 311, fo. 39ʳ, cited in Katz, *Sabbath and Sectarianism*, 37. See
also Thomas Tillam, *The Temple of Lively Stones. Or the Promised glory of the last
days* (1660), 32.   [30] *BQ* 23: 175.

[31] *BQ* 4: 118.

them',[32] it none the less seems more likely that Pooley's congregation was not an embryonic form of St Mary's. Pooley's 1656 secession probably represents an earlier breakaway from the nascent Independent-Baptist community in Norwich.

The Norwich group appears, moreover, to have been one of the more short-lived Seventh-day congregations in the country. The last extant specific reference to the Norwich Sabbatarians is dated 1662, when by the will of Theophilus Brabourne £10 was bequeathed to needy Sabbath-keepers in Norwich, to be distributed by 'Mr Pooley and his elders'.[33] The wording suggests that Brabourne knew of a thriving congregation in these early post-Restoration years, and its somewhat surprising disappearance is probably due to Pooley's association with Thomas Tillam of Colchester, and their joint venture in the 1660s to settle a community of Sabbatarian immigrant families in the Palatinate. This ambitious and eschatologically motivated scheme, which is discussed in more detail elsewhere,[34] must inevitably have taken its toll of Pooley's own congregation. Pooley himself continued to work in the district until 1666, or thereabouts, and without doubt his congregation survived until then, and in a decimated condition perhaps for even longer. But it does not appear, even as a 'remnant', in the 1690 Llanwenarth list, as do other small, surviving Seventh-day groups, such as those at Harwich and Boston.[35] The damage inflicted on the otherwise theologically respectable Baptist Sabbatarians by the militant millenarianism of Pooley and Tillam was considerable, and Norwich was only one of several Seventh-day congregations to have suffered irretrievably from their radical eschatology.

Whether or not an interest in the seventh day reappeared in Norwich in the eighteenth century, is a matter of some conjecture. An Edward Mumford, whom Whitley identifies as one of the Mumford family which 'leaned to the observance of the seventh day', and who had been a member at Horsleydown, 'where Keach had needed to combat the principle of observing the seventh day', ministered at Norwich St Mary's between 1727 and 1737.[36] After his death the church was supplied on occasion by Benjamin Stennett of Ingham, 'which church had always been flavoured with seventh-day principles'. Edward Trivett of Worstead and John Miller of

---

[32] Hewett, NRO, MS 4260, s.v. Norwich St Mary's.
[33] NRO, NCC Wills 1662, OW80.   [34] See Ch. 10.
[35] Cf. above, 228.   [36] *BQ* 10: 235, 288.

Pulham, both from churches with Seventh-day connections, were also associated with Norwich during the eighteenth century.[37] It would be easy enough to conclude that, at the very least, Sabbatarian sympathies circulated there during these years.

A hint of Sabbatarianism in the Norwich–Yarmouth area towards the end of the seventeenth century comes with the appearance of General Baptists in Norfolk. Up to this time Baptists in the county, including Sabbatarians, had been of the Calvinistic Particular school. In 1685 and 1686 Thomas Grantham established General Baptist congregations in Norwich and Yarmouth respectively, in the hope that Baptists of all opinions, Sabbatarians included, might be brought together in unified communities.[38] It was a worthy, if somewhat forlorn hope, and there is nothing to indicate that the General Baptist churches thus founded included Sabbatarians. Grantham had probably recognized that a measure of Sabbatarianism did remain among Baptists in Norwich and Yarmouth, as he would also perhaps have recognized the need for a more open attitude than his *Seventh-Day Sabbath Ceased* (1667) had earlier suggested.

There are few further references of any substance to Sabbatarian developments in these localities which had been associated with the early Baptist/Fifth Monarchist movement in south-east Norfolk. A Seventh-day group at Yarmouth appears as 'a little remnant' in the Llanwenarth list in 1690, but nothing has come to light concerning its origin. Yarmouth was early disposed to radical Nonconformist doctrine, and the presence of a Sabbatarian group there is not surprising. In 1678 Henry Fryoring was presented to the ecclesiastical authorities at Yarmouth 'for being a Sabbatarian' and for non-attendance at his parish church.[39] No other names have survived. Yarmouth, it appears, was a good example of those Sabbatarian congregations which Henri Misson came across in his travels and later described as making 'little noise'. Something similar might perhaps be said of Wymondham, for the only suggestion of seventeenth-century Sabbatarianism there comes from a later date.[40]

---

[37] Ibid. 285, 289.

[38] White, *English Baptists*, 116; C.B. Jewson, *The Baptists in Norfolk* (1957), 30. On Grantham, see *DNB*. Whitley says that Grantham was 'one of the great unifying forces' in the late seventeenth-century Baptist churches, and points out that the Lincolnshire Baptist community, from which Grantham had come to Norfolk, upheld 'the old customs such as feet-washing (and) abstinence from blood'; *British Baptists*, 168.   [39] NRO, VIS7/3, s.vv. Flegge and Yarmouth.

[40] *SO* 2: 109.

Whitley cautiously states that Pulham Baptists were 'aware' of Seventh-day views,[41] and it is of interest that when Pulham ceased to exist, *c.*1714, St Mary's, Norwich, agreed to receive remaining Pulham members on the condition 'that they agree with us in doctrine, worship, and discipline'.[42] There may have been some point to the conditions imposed by St Mary's. Shortly before Pulham's congregational demise, John Rutland of Woodbridge, a lifelong Sabbatarian, had been invited to preach on several occasions in the Baptist meeting-place at Pulham Margaret. Rutland's sermons were posthumously published in 1720, and he was quoted as emphasizing, in the context of rejecting 'Popish doctrines and discipline', that there were those who still rested 'on the Sabbath day according to the commandment'.[43] It was also noted that Rutland, in later life, 'did more earnestly preach and contend' for the seventh day.[44] Rutland had died in 1718, and the clear inference is that his invitation to Pulham was based on Sabbatarian preferences. The least that can be said is that an awareness of the Seventh-day Sabbath survived at Pulham into the eighteenth century.

While it is evident that the Seventh-day Sabbath attracted many adherents at Norwich, Yarmouth, Beccles, and probably also at Pulham, and that its most prominent and zealous champions were Brabourne, Pooley, and Tillam, the real strength of Norfolk Sabbatarianism lay further to the north and with advocates who were somewhat less controversial. North Walsham, Walcott, Worstead, and particularly Ingham, and neighbouring villages, represent the heart of the Seventh-day movement in Norfolk, and an important Sabbatarian stronghold in the country as a whole. Here the Seventh-day cause persisted for several generations, long after it had been eclipsed at Norwich and other places further south.

NORTH WALSHAM, EAST RUSTON, WALCOTT, AND INGHAM

The Sabbatarians at North Walsham could be counted among the relatively few Seventh-day congregations in the country to support

[41] *BQ* 10: 289.   [42] Browne, *History of Congregationalism*, 549.

[43] John Rutland, *A Vindication of the Divine Decrees of Election and Reprobation* (1720), preface, p. x, sig. C^r. According to Joseph Willett, *Some Observations on a Pretended Dialogue Between a Baptist and a Quaker* (1720), 7, 81, Rutland had been one of four Particular Baptists engaged in a dispute with Quakers at Pulham Margaret, now Pulham Market, which had resulted in his preaching there.

[44] Rutland, *Divine Decrees*, sig. C2^r.

Whitley's thesis that the Seventh-day movement evolved from the earlier and strongly eschatologically oriented Fifth Monarchy Men.[45] By the time the radical millenarian excitement of the early to mid-1650s began to subside in Norfolk, a Sabbatarian group had come into the light at North Walsham. Gathered initially, it is believed, under the influence of Christopher Pooley and therefore heavily tinged with Fifth Monarchist doctrine,[46] it soon stabilized as a more respectable Nonconformist congregation under the pastoral attention of John Woolstone, John Aggas, and Robert Woods. Woolstone and Aggas also ministered successively to the less radical Sabbatarian congregation at nearby Stalham and Ingham, and Woods, in 1667, signed the *Faithful Testimony* against the extremism of Pooley and Tillam. Although a precise date for Sabbatarian beginnings at North Walsham is lacking, it is most likely to have been in 1656 or early 1657 that most of the Fifth Monarchist/Baptists there adopted the seventh day. By 1657 the Fifth Monarchist cause in North Walsham had already begun to wane, just when internal controversy over the Seventh-day Sabbath was troubling Fifth Monarchy congregations elsewhere in the country.[47] In 1669 a clear reference to established North Walsham Sabbatarians appears in the official records, when one of three conventicles reported in the town was said to be composed of 'Saturday observers'.[48] There can be little doubt that this group represented a settled interest in the seventh day generated by Pooley in conjunction with his Fifth Monarchy interests at North Walsham and at Norwich in the mid-1650s.

John Woolstone is principally remembered as the first minister of the Stalham–Ingham Sabbatarian Baptist church, a responsibility he carried for at least twenty years, from the time of his ordination in 1657 until his death in 1677.[49] Woolstone had been a member of the Yarmouth Baptist church prior to his association with Ingham, which probably began when the church was formally organized in

---

[45] *BQ* 12: 253; *British Baptists*, 86. Capp notes that a relatively small proportion of Fifth Monarchy Men were disposed to Sabbatarian principles, and comments that Pooley, and others, 'seem to have adopted the Seventh Day Sabbath as an addition to their Fifth Monarchist beliefs, not as a replacement', *FMM* 224. This would certainly seem to have been true of Pooley, even if his eschatology did take a different direction after 1660.

[46] *FMM* 112; Klaiber, *Suffolk Baptists*, 26–7; Hewett, NRO, MS 4260, s.v. North Walsham.   [47] *FMM* 113.

[48] *OR* i. 100. The other two congregations were of Quakers and Independents.

[49] Browne, *History of Congregationalism*, 554.

1653, or shortly afterwards.[50] Woolstone was succeeded at Ingham by John Aggas (or Haggas), who was designated in the Llanwenarth list in 1690 as minister of the Sabbatarian congregation 'at Ingham and Northwalsham, and therabout'.[51] A 'little remnant' remained at Great Yarmouth at the same time, and, whether or not there was any link between the Yarmouth and Ingham Sabbatarians, the Llanwenarth record is an important clue to the scattered nature of this essentially rural Sabbatarian community in north-east Norfolk. During the latter half of the seventeenth century Seventh-day ob-servance appears in several locations, and it is not always clear whether North Walsham and Ingham were separate centres of Sabbatarian influence, or whether they were essentially branches of a single congregation, as the Llanwenarth record suggests they were by 1690. In 1669 John Woolstone had been reported as a preacher in his own house at Walcott, and also at a conventicle in East Ruston,[52] and in 1672 he was licensed as an 'Anabaptist' for Samuel Durrant's house at Ingham.[53] Henry Symonds was licensed for the house of John Aggas (Hagges) at North Walsham in 1672.[54] At Walcott, in 1669, Woolstone also preached in the house of Anne Thompson, as did Robert Woods,[55] who two years earlier had signed the *Faithful Testimony*.

It is, in fact, Woods who emerges as one of the principal figures in this Sabbatarian community during its formative years. His sig-nature to the *Faithful Testimony*, together with other prominent Sabbatarians elsewhere in the country, including Arthur Squibb, John Belcher, George Eve, and Edward Stennett,[56] suggests that he was already by this time established as a leader amongst the Norfolk Sabbatarians. Indeed, his opposition to the legalistic and divisive work of Pooley and Tillam may have been crucial to the survival of Sabbatarianism in Norfolk, where during the late 1660s Tillam's agents, Pooley amongst them, had successfully recruited several

---

[50] AL, MS 30. a. 8(p), 15; Wilson, 'An Account of Various Congregations in Eng-land Among the Presbyterians, Independents, and Baptists', DWL, MS 63, I, 3, s.v. Ingham, fo. 15.

[51] *BQ* 14: 165. The complete list of Ingham ministers is recorded in several places, e.g. Browne, *History of Congregationalism*, 544; Josiah Thompson, 'History of Protestant Dissenting Congregations', DWL, MS 38.10, fo. 24.

[52] *OR* i. 100.   [53] Ibid. 534.

[54] *BQ* 18: 308; *OR* i. 535; cf. ii. 900, where Aggas is incorrectly called Henry. Symonds is not to be confused with Henry Symons, ejected rector of Southfleet, Kent, and author of *The Lord Jesus His Commission* (1657), on whom see *CR* 442.

[55] *OR* i. 100.   [56] See *BB* i. 14–667.

Sabbatarian families for the misguided emigration scheme to the Palatinate.[57] In 1669 Woods, 'a shoemaker', had been reported as the teacher at a conventicle in widow Kibbald's house at Lessingham and at John Woolstone's house at Walcott, while a congregation of a hundred or so was reported as meeting in his own house at East Ruston, under John Woolstone and 'one Tracey'.[58] In 1672 Woods was licensed as an Anabaptist for Elizabeth Becker's house in East Ruston.[59]

The fact that Woods's name does not appear at any time in the known list of Ingham ministers may indicate that there were two distinct Sabbatarian congregations in north-east Norfolk, one centred at North Walsham, and including adherents at Walcott, Lessingham, and East Ruston, and the other centred at Stalham and Ingham. The chief objection to this possibility is that East Ruston and Lessingham were so near to Ingham that normally believers at either place would have been included with a congregation at Ingham. It is unlikely that theological differences would have separated Sabbatarians at this time as they might have done later, so perhaps Robert Woods's name is missing from Ingham and North Walsham lists because he was regarded as messenger for the Norfolk Sabbatarians as a whole. Certainly the emphasized inclusion of his name in the Llanwenarth list without relationship to any specific congregation indicates that he was widely known in Sabbatarian circles across the country in 1690.[60] Whatever the precise relationship Woods may have had with North Walsham or with Ingham, and whatever the relationship North Walsham and Ingham might have had with each other, it cannot be doubted that Sabbatarianism flourished at several points roughly on a line between Yarmouth and North Walsham during the second part of the seventeenth century. North Walsham is heard of again in 1706, as one of the Sabbatarian congregations to benefit from the will of Joseph Davis, sen., of Mill Yard[61] (although Ingham was not included in the Davis will), and once more in 1719, when correspondence is recorded between Mill Yard and Ingham 'near North Walsom'.[62] By this time North Walsham may well have conceded its identity to Ingham,

[57] *FMM* 201.
[58] *OR* i. 100. There may be a link here with Yarmouth, where in 1673 Thomas Tracey was licensed as a Baptist, 585.   [59] Ibid. 534.
[60] Whitley describes him simply as 'Seventh-day, of East Ruston', *BB* i. 231.
[61] See Black (ed.), *Last Legacy*, 77–8.   [62] MYM 231.

although, as we shall see, a Sabbatarian interest appeared again in the vicinity of North Walsham with the settling of a Baptist congregation at Worstead early in the eighteenth century.

It is Ingham, however, that finally emerges as the centre of a strong Sabbatarian cause in Norfolk, and where under a succession of able ministers, the seventh day was observed for more than a century. Some records suggest that Baptists had been meeting at Ingham since 1637,[63] sixteen years before the church was formally constituted, and twenty years before John Woolstone was officially ordained as its first minister. It is not known when either Woolstone or Ingham adopted the seventh day, but it is certain to have been prior to 1660. One source states, somewhat cautiously, that Ingham was 'always flavoured with Seventh day principles',[64] and another suggests that most of the Ingham members 'were of the seventh-day persuasion' at 'an early stage' in the church's history.[65] Given the development of Sabbatarian congregations at Norwich and North Walsham, it is most likely to have been during the mid-1650s that Baptists began to observe the seventh day at Ingham. In the troubled years immediately after the Restoration, the church met on Saturday evenings in a roadside cottage in the parish of Ingham, but near to the neighbouring village of Stalham. John Woolstone, who at the time lived four or five miles away at Walcott, would frequently arrive to conduct worship disguised as a drover and carrying a whip to allay suspicion. The large, lower room of the cottage would be laid out as a dining-room, and Woolstone would preach from a seat at the table, to a congregation assembled in the upper rooms.[66] On other occasions, meetings were held in a barn at the rear of the cottage, and look-outs were posted at strategic points to warn of the approach of informers. Many of the worshippers lived at a distance from the meeting-place, and would travel home by various routes to avoid detection. It was a situation typical of many Nonconformist gatherings throughout the country at the time.

John Aggas succeeded to the Ingham–Stalham pastorate when Woolstone died in 1677, and remained in charge until 1693, when 'a flourishing congregation of between two and three hundred' was

[63] e.g. Josiah Thompson, DWL, MS 38.10, fo. 24.   [64] *BQ* 10: 289.
[65] Wilson, DWL, MS 63, I, 3, fo. 14ᵛ.
[66] 'An Outline of the History of the Baptist Church at Ingham', AL, MS 30. a. 8(p), 15; Hewett, NRO, MS 4261, s.v. Stalham; Jewson, *Stalham Baptist Church*, 1, 2.

reported.[67] The rather surprising strength of this somewhat isolated congregation throughout these years testifies to the diligent pastoral care of Woolstone and Aggas as much as to any predisposition to Nonconformity which might have characterized the rural Norfolk mind. Ingham's vitality may also have been due in part to the frequent preaching of William Belcher, noted in one source as an assistant to Woolstone, and in another simply as a preacher during the ministries of both Woolstone and Aggas.[68] Belcher, father of the better-known Fifth Monarchist Sabbatarian John Belcher, had been ejected from Ulcombe, Kent, in 1662, and appears have settled in Norfolk, preaching regularly at Ingham both before and after the Declaration of Indulgence in 1672.[69]

When John Aggas died in 1693, he was succeeded at Ingham by Samuel Durrant, in whose home meetings had been held since 1672. Durrant ministered to the Ingham Sabbatarians for twenty-one years. It was a time of continuing growth, and C.B. Jewson comments that, 'despite the practical disadvantages of Saturday worship', the Ingham church 'flourished so greatly that at the beginning of the eighteenth century an assistant minister was employed'.[70] This was James Brewster, who was in turn appointed to the pastorate on Durrant's demise in 1714 and who served the congregation for the next ten years. Again, Ingham is said to have 'flourished' under the ministries of both Durrant and Brewster.[71] By the time Brewster passed from the scene in 1724 the church was more than 70 years old, and for almost the whole of this time, through years of persecution, formalism and general indifference, had borne its single-minded testimony to the Seventh-day Sabbath. But Ingham's years of plenty were now coming to an end. Soon after John Ridley took over the pastoral office in 1724 clouds began to appear on the horizon and when his ministry at Ingham terminated in 1734 a storm was imminent.[72] The long and harmonious witness of one of the staunchest Seventh-day congregations in the country

---

[67] Browne, *History of Congregationalism*, 554; Wilson, DWL, MS 63, I, 3, fo. 15ʳ.

[68] *SO* 2: 137; Thompson, DWL, MS 38.10, fo. 24ʳ.

[69] Browne, *History of Congregationalism*, 554; Wilson, DWL, MS 63, I, 3, fo. 15ʳ.

[70] Browne, *History of Congregationalism*, 554; Jewson, *Stalham Baptist Church*, 2.

[71] DWL, MS 63, I, 3, fo. 16ʳ. Correspondence between Ingham and Mill Yard suggests that there may have been some question in 1720 regarding Brewster's continuing eldership: MYM 231.

[72] Little is known of Ridley, but it appears that he should not be identified with John Ridley of Woodbridge.

was almost over, even though there would be Sabbatarians at Ingham for many years yet.

The slow decline in the fortunes of the Ingham Sabbatarians which had set in during Ridley's years as elder gathered pace when, in 1734, no one could be found to succeed him. For the next two years Ingham was supplied by James Rudd (or Rhudd) of Wapping, a Baptist who was shortly dismissed by Wapping for Unitarianism and who soon after that conformed to the Church of England.[73] Rudd's tentative ministry to a congregation in which the seeds of doubt had already germinated was not destined to be very effective, and it is not surprising that during this period of instability controversy arose at Ingham regarding the seventh day.[74] The 1720s and 1730s were a time of renewed debate over the Sabbath issue throughout the country, and it is unlikely that Ingham remained untouched by the arguments for and against the seventh day which were exchanged in pulpit and in print during these years. George Carlow of Woodbridge, and John Maulden and Robert Cornthwaite of Mill Yard, had all published in favour of the seventh day by 1731,[75] and Dr Samuel Wright, Robert Hill, rector of Stanhoe in Norfolk, and Caleb Fleming, a London minister with Socinian leanings, may be noted amongst those who, by 1736, had responded in defence of the first day.[76] The tension at Ingham appears to have been short-lived, but the Seventh-day Sabbath had lost ground, and

[73] Wilson, DWL, MS 63, I, 3, fo. 17ʳ.   [74] *SO* 2: 140.

[75] George Carlow, *Truth Defended; or, Observations on Mr Ward's Expository Discourses from the 8th, 9th, 10th, and 11th verses of the 20th chapter of Exodus, concerning the Sabbath* (1724); John Maulden, *The Ancient and Honourable Way and Truth of God's Sacred Rest of the Seventh-Day Sabbath* (1724); Robert Cornthwaite, *Reflections on Dr Wright's Treatise on the Religious Observation of the Lord's Day, According to the express Words of the Fourth Commandment. Shewing the Inconclusiveness of the Doctor's Reasoning on that Subject, and the Impossibility of grounding the First-Day Sabbath on the Fourth Commandment, or any other Text of Scripture, produced by him for that Purpose* (1731).

[76] [Samuel Wright], *A Treatise on the Religious Observation of the Lord's Day, according to the express Words of the Fourth Commandment* (1724); Robert Hill, *A Discourse upon the Fourth Commandment* (1728); Caleb Fleming, *The Fourth Commandment Abrogated by the Gospel: Or, the Fourth Commandment's enjoining the Observance of the Seventh Day of the Week as a Religious Rest, was only obligatory and binding within the Jewish State. But the Law of the Sabbath being destroy'd, the Christian Institution authoriseth the Christian's Observance of the First Day of the Week, as an Holy Festival* (1736), and *A Plain and Rational Account of the Law of the Sabbath; Being a Defence of a late Pamphlet, intitled, 'The Fourth Commandment abrogated by the Gospel'; or An Answer to Mr Robert Cornthwaite's farther Defence of the Seventh-Day Sabbath; in which Gen. ii, 2, 3*

the congregation was thereafter always mixed-communion, until the last Sabbatarian died more than fifty years later.[77] Referring to these events, Josiah Thompson subsequently noted that originally the Seventh-day view 'was the sentiment that generally if not universally' had prevailed at Ingham.[78]

In 1736 the church called as its minister Benjamin Stennett, Joseph Stennett I's younger son, presumably because the Stennett family had established a reputation for ministering successfully to Baptist congregations with both Sabbatarian and First-day interests. Stennett stayed for twelve years, and under his care Ingham revived for a time. The church was stabilized, a tolerant spirit was cultivated, and when in 1745 a meeting-house was built on land donated by a member, it seemed that a new and prosperous era had begun.[79] By this time, however, a growing proportion of the congregation had adopted Sunday as their day of worship, and in 1747, a year before Stennett left, the meeting-house and adjoining land were conveyed by him to the 'first-day Baptists . . . to the end of time'.[80] The reasons for Stennett's action in this matter have not been preserved, but it must have seemed a strange turn of events, if not an outright act of perfidy, to many of the Sabbatarians who still remained. They would hardly have been appeased when, a year later, Stennett married into a Sabbatarian family, taking as his wife the daughter of John Ridley of Woodbridge.[81] The trend away from the Saturday Sabbath was now irreversible, and by the middle of the eighteenth century, as Jewson notes, 'interest in the seventh-day doctrine had waned'.[82] Jonathan Brown, who followed Stennett, did little to revive it, and when he died in 1764 he left 'a cause almost dwindled away'.[83] By 1773–4, out of a membership of thirty-four and a congregation of 200, there were only five or six 'of ye 7th day persuasion' left at Ingham.[84] If this remnant survived for a further decade

---

(called by him the Original Institution) is more particularly considered, and his most material Objections and Criticisms refuted (1736). Cornthwaite had quickly replied to Fleming's earlier publication with The Seventh-Day Sabbath Farther Vindicated . . . (1736). On Wright, see DNB; on Hill, see Cox, Literature of the Sabbath Question, ii. 172; on Fleming, see DNB and Cox, Literature of the Sabbath Question, ii. 186.

[77] SO 2: 140.   [78] DWL, MS 38.6, fo. 56ᵛ.
[79] DWL, MS 38.10, fo. 24ᵛ; Jewson, Stalham Baptist Church, 2.
[80] SO 2: 140.   [81] Klaiber, Suffolk Baptists, 34.
[82] Jewson, Stalham Baptist Church, 2.   [83] DWL, MS 38.10, fo. 24ᵛ.
[84] DWL, MS 63, I, 3, fo. 18ʳ; Thompson, DWL, MS 38.6, fo. 56ᵛ.

or so, which is not an unreasonable supposition, there would have been an unbroken line of Sabbatarians at Ingham for at least 130 years.

Notwithstanding Ingham's long witness to the seventh day, it is not there but at Worstead, a few miles to the east, and only two or three miles from North Walsham, that the last traces of Sabbatarianism in Norfolk are found. A Baptist church had been formed at Worstead in 1717, by an amicable secession from Ingham, then thriving under the care of James Brewster.[85] Any secession from Ingham in its heyday, particularly if on grounds of convenience or the geographical distribution of members, is most likely to have been tinged with a degree of Sabbatarianism, however mild. It is true that currently there is no known reference to Seventh-day observance at Worstead in its early days, but this is not surprising if Worstead seceded from Ingham in an agreed and orderly manner as seems to have been the case, and if Worstead was established as a mixed-communion fellowship, or at least with a tolerance for those who observed the seventh day. Later references to Sabbatarianism at Worstead suggest that the Saturday Sabbath had been acceptable in principle to the Worstead fellowship for a long time.

For the first twenty-five years or so little of note marked the life of the Worstead church, and there are few hints of the presence, or absence, of Sabbatarian practice. In 1733, one Thomas Wright was dismissed for 'neglect of his keeping fellowship', and for 'breach of the Sabbath day, and riding about his worldly employment on that Day . . . when he ought to have been looking after the good of his soul'.[86] Given the circumstances, this could reasonably be understood of a Sabbatarianism Worstead might have inherited from Ingham. But it more probably referred to the offender's failure to observe Sunday as the majority of the church thought fit, and cannot

[85] AL, MS 30. a. 8(p), 28. Some sources suggest that Worstead originated from a Baptist cause already established at nearby Smallburgh (NRO, MS 4261, s.v. Worstead; Browne, *History of Congregationalism*, 564), but the connection is doubtful. Smallburgh had been founded by the General Baptist Thomas Grantham. Worstead was established on Particular, Calvinistic principles in the Ingham tradition.

[86] NRO, MS FC 42/1, fo. 8.

therefore arbitrarily be construed as proof of Saturday observance.[87] Such evidence would come later.

It was with the appointment of Edward Trivett as minister in 1742 that Worstead became an active centre of Baptist witness, and Trivett himself a recognized leader among the Norfolk Baptists.[88] Indeed, the decline in Ingham's fortunes which had set in shortly before this, and which continued with increasing pace after the Benjamin Stennett era, may also be linked to the strong leadership given by Trivett for half a century at nearby Worstead. For several generations many of the Ingham members had lived at a distance from their meeting-place near Stalham, and it would have been as easy for them to travel to Worstead as to Ingham for worship. Trivett's growing reputation would have made this an attractive option for many. Trivett would certainly have been aware of the Sabbath issue and, in view of the fact that at least one of his sons observed the seventh day,[89] may himself have leaned in that direction without publicly advocating its observance. Such a stance would have been in keeping with the position adopted by other Baptist ministers in the eighteenth century who were tolerant of the Seventh-day position.[90] In any event, under Trivett's diligent care, the centre of Baptist influence in this part of Norfolk moved from Ingham to Worstead, and with it a tacit acceptance of those who might have wished to observe the seventh day.

Trivett's fifty-year pastorate at Worstead is one of the more notable rural Baptist ministries of the eighteenth century. By the time he died in 1792, at the age of 80, 391 new members had been added to the Worstead fellowship by baptism or profession of faith. It was a remarkable achievement, by any standard. Between 1751

[87] Although by this time it was more usual to refer to Sunday as the Lord's day.

[88] NRO, MS FC 42/1, fo. 35; *BQ* 11: 168; INB, *TBHS* 7: 235.

[89] NRO, MS 4261, s.v. Worstead.

[90] e.g. Joseph Stennett II and Samuel Stennett, Ch. 8 n. 66; Benjamin Beddome, above, 212, and Benjamin Francis, above, 219. Cf. Isaac Watts, who in advocating observance of the Lord's day noted, 'I can never pronounce anything hard or severe upon any fellow-Christian who maintains real piety in heart and life, though his opinion may be different from mine on this subject. Nor does any man, who is humbly and sincerely studious of truth and duty . . . deserve any reproach or censure upon the account of different opinions about meats and days; unless he assume such haughty airs of assurance as arise far beyond all his evidence and proof, or indulge a persecuting spirit, and reproach his brethren who differ from him'; Isaac Watts, *The Holiness of Times, Places, and People under the Jewish and Christian Dispensations Considered and Compared, in several Discourses, viz.: 1. On the Perpetuity of a Sabbath, and the Observation of the Lord's-Day . . .* (1738), 69–70.

and 1789 Trivett is also said to have trained eleven young men for the ministry, including Zenas, his youngest son.[91] Two years after being sent out to begin his pastoral work in 1776, Zenas Trivett was called to the Baptist church at Langham, in Essex, where he remained for the rest of his active life, until retiring in 1819.[92] Langham is not known for Sabbatarianism, although it is near enough to Colchester to be of interest, and in view of Zenas Trivett's own convictions, the possibility cannot be dismissed. Upon retirement, Zenas returned to Worstead, continuing to preach until his death in 1831.[93] A note in the burial register says of Zenas Trivett: 'The last of the family of Edward Trivett. For many years a faithful preacher of the gospel. The last of the Sabbatarians at Worstead.'[94] It is not clear whether Trivett upheld Sabbatarian principles throughout his life, or whether he adopted them, or returned to them, upon his retirement to Worstead.

Hewett states that the burial register entry quoted above is 'the only known reference to any sympathy with Seventh Day Baptist ideas either on the part of the Worstead church, or of the Trivett family'.[95] This may be true in a strictly literal sense, but it overlooks the obvious inference that if Zenas Trivett was the last of the Worstead Sabbatarians, there had been others before him. In this context, it should not be overlooked that Edward Trivett had been followed as minister at Worstead in 1794 by James Beard, who came from the Sabbatarian church at Woodbridge, and who had been introduced at his ordination by a 'Bro. Ridley, of Ipswich'.[96] Under Beard's ministry Worstead continued to prosper, and a further 127 were baptized in total.[97] Beard, who died in 1811, would almost certainly also have been sympathetic to Sabbatarianism, and it thus seems clear that Worstead would have willingly entertained Seventh-day observance at least until the early part of the nineteenth century. In 1800 Benjamin Simpson, a member at Worstead, moved to London and sought membership with the Sabbatarian church at Curriers' Hall, then under Robert Burnside.[98] Simpson was received into fellowship later that year on a letter of recommendation from

---

[91] NRO, MS FC 42/1, fo. 34; *BQ* 11: 168; Browne, *History of Congregationalism*, 564.   [92] NRO, MS 4261, s.v. Worstead.
[93] Ibid.   [94] Ibid.   [95] Ibid.
[96] Ibid.; NRO, MS FC 42/1, fo. 12; *BQ* 11: 170.
[97] NRO, MS 4261, s.v. Worstead; *BQ* 11: 171.
[98] PHCB 131. The Worstead church book merely notes of Simpson, 'dismissed to London', NRO, FC 42/1, fo. 49.

Worstead, even though corporate worship was regularly conducted at Worstead on Sunday.[99]

At some point, possibly in the eighteenth century, Worstead established, or re-established, a connection with North Walsham, where, since the formation of independent congregations in the 1650s, Dissenting interests had tended to look for support from like-minded communities locally and further afield. The North Walsham Fifth Monarchists of the 1650s were in touch with ideologically compatible groups in Norfolk and elsewhere in the county, and similar relationships were established between Independents.[100] The link between Sabbatarians at North Walsham and those at Ingham and other villages later in the seventeenth century has already been noted. As late as the 1830s, Worstead Baptists are recorded as holding regular services for fellow believers at North Walsham.[101] A Sabbatarian interest was kept alive at North Walsham well into the eighteenth century, as we have seen, and whether or not this late connection with Worstead represents a continuation of that interest is open to conjecture. It seems that the difficulty in tracing Sabbatarianism at Worstead is not in demonstrating that it existed, but in determining when it began, and how widely it extended. What is not in doubt is that Worstead has the distinction of being the last retreat of the Seventh-day Men who had once dominated the Baptist churches in this part of Norfolk. By the time they died out with Zenas Trivett in 1831, they had been accepted in the district for the greater part of two centuries.

BRAINTREE AND COLCHESTER

The Dutch theologian Georgius Hornius, in describing the contemporary church in Britain in 1645, reported that the Jewish Sabbath was being advocated in Colchester and that converts to Saturday observance were being made.[102] It is one of the earliest references

---

[99] In 1815 the Norfolk and Suffolk Association met at Worstead, an indication perhaps of a Calvinistic, closed-communion theology, as well as observance of the Lord's day, *BB* ii 92; Browne, *English Baptists*, 129.

[100] *FMM* 111; see also DWL, 'An historical outline of Bradfield and North Walsham Congregational Church, Norfolk' (1957), and the 'Copy of The Church Book of the United Churches of Tunstead, Bradfield and North Walsham', a copy of which, transcribed by Joseph Davey, is also in DWL, MS 76.13.

[101] NRO, MS 4260, s.v. North Walsham.

[102] 'Alicubi Judaicum Sabbatum in usum revocarunt fenestris clausis. Colcestriae ipsum Judaismum propagunt, et proselytos facjunt,' Hornius, *De statu Ecclesiae*, 102–3.

to established Sabbatarian practice in England outside London, and suggests a measure of concerted effort to disseminate Seventh-day views and perhaps also an attempt at congregational consolidation. There is no indication that at this point these Essex Sabbatarians existed beyond Colchester, although there is the hint of a connection with Kent. Later sources explicitly state that Colchester had become the centre of a Sabbath-observing community which included adherents in neighbouring country areas. In 1659 Edmund Warren, vicar of St Peter's, Colchester, deplored 'the spreading of this Jewish leaven', and dedicated *The Jews Sabbath Antiquated* to his 'Christian friends and hearers, in and about the town of Colchester'.[103] And in 1695 Anthony Elton was recommended from Pinners' Hall to 'the Sabbath-keeping church in and about Colchester'.[104] The 1690 Llanwenarth list included a Sabbatarian congregation at Colchester but not at Braintree, while in 1706 a deed executed by Joseph Davis, sen., mentioned Braintree but not Colchester, which, from other sources, is known to have been in a strong condition at this date. Perhaps at some point the Braintree Sabbatarians were included in the Colchester community, although Braintree was far enough from Colchester, and sufficiently inclined to radical religious practice, to sustain a group of its own.

By the seventeenth century both Braintree and Colchester could boast a long-established tradition of Nonconformity and Dissent which would have encouraged the early emergence of Sabbatarianism and helped to conceal its presence. In 1631, Samuel Collins, vicar of Braintree, wrote of the 'unconformitie' in his parish, and complained to Sir Arthur Duck, Laud's chancellor in the diocese of London, that it was no easy matter 'to reduce a numerous congregation into order, that hath been disorderly these fifty years'.[105] The cure of Braintree had been with Collins since 1610, but even so his estimate of fifty years since Nonconformity had appeared in the parish was probably conservative. In 1550 Separatist 'sectaries' had been reported in Essex and Kent who rejected infant baptism and taught, *inter alia*, that election 'was meeter for devils, than for Christian men', and that no man was 'so reprobate, but that he

---

[103] Warren, *The Jews Sabbath Antiquated*, Ep. Ded., sig. A3ʳ. Calamy gives Warren's name as Edward, *CR* 511, and Whitley calls him both Edmund and Edward, *BB* i. 71, 230. [104] PHCB 45.
[105] Cited in T.W. Davids, *Annals of Evangelical Nonconformity in the County of Essex from the time of Wycliffe to the Restoration* (1863), 168.

might keep God's commandments, and be saved'.[106] Man's free will
gave him the choice between obedience or disobedience. 'Christ
saith, "He that loveth me, keepeth my commandments" . . . And
will we say we are not able to keep it? . . . Saint James saith,
"Whosoever shall keep the whole law, and yet fail in one point, he
is guilty of all" . . . Here is nothing required of us, but that is reasonable, and lieth in our power.'[107] These are the very arguments that,
a hundred years later, Sabbatarian apologists would use to argue
the binding claims of the entire Decalogue.

In January of the following year, 1551, several residents at Bocking
were apprehended for attending conventicles, discussing the
teachings of Scripture, and refusing communion at the parish
church.[108] Before that, a 'vigorous Lollard community' flourished in
Essex, 'centred upon Colchester' and around John Pykas, who taught
others the Lord's Prayer and the Ten Commandments in English, as
well as the epistles of James and John.[109] Marion Matthew of Colchester possessed manuscripts of the Gospel of Matthew and the
Book of Revelation, and her house was a meeting-place for a group
of twenty or so like-minded souls. Soon after copies of Tyndale's
New Testament had reached Colchester in 1526, fifty-five people
were arrested there and in Braintree and neighbouring villages.[110]
In 1532 a further eighty-one were apprehended and brought before
the authorities, and Strype records the sufferings of others shortly
thereafter in the Colchester–Braintree area for attending 'secret
meetings wherein they instructed one another out of God's Word',
'for talke of Scripture', and for advocating compliance with 'the
commandment(s) of God'.[111] The claim that Sabbath-keepers had
been known at Braintree since 1527, while unsubstantiated, may
not be entirely without foundation.[112]

The Braintree Sabbatarians who emerge clearly from the shadows only in the eighteenth century were Seventh-day Baptists. It is
not surprising that so little is known of them prior to 1706 when

---

[106] Cited in G.D. Witard, *The History of Braintree Baptist Church, Essex* (1955),
13. On the connection of this group with Kent and Essex, see Cross, *Church and
People,* 98.

[107] Cited in J. Strype, *Historical Memorials, Ecclesiastical and Civil* (1721), iii.
appendix, 114–15.

[108] Davids, *Evangelical Nonconformity in . . . Essex,* 22; J.R. Dasent (ed.), *Acts of
the Privy Council of England,* iii (1891), 198–9.

[109] Cross, *Church and People,* 37–8.

[110] Davids, *Evangelical Nonconformity in . . . Essex,* 6–8.

[111] Ibid. 6–18.   [112] *SO* 2: 68.

they were recognized by Joseph Davis, sen., since there is a dearth of information relating to all Baptists in Braintree throughout the seventeenth century. A General Baptist church is known to have existed since the early 1660s, although it too traces its origin to the 'sectaries' and 'unlawful conventicles' of 1550 and 1551.[113] A small group of six 'Anabaptists' was reported at Braintree during the episcopal visitation of 1664, for refusing to have their children baptized.[114] Twenty years later, Samuel Bentoft was presented for not attending the parish church at Easter and for keeping a conventicle, and thirty-three others were presented for absenteeism and for not receiving the sacrament.[115] An intriguing entry occurs in the churchwardens' presentments for 1677, when the name of John Rootsey appears, without comment, at the bottom of a page where the report is otherwise *omnia bene.*[116] Rootsey's name is not found in either the 1664 or 1684 lists, but he was later installed as minister at Eld Lane Baptist church, Colchester, when one of the officiating ministers was John Rutland, the Seventh-day Baptist from Woodbridge.[117]

The inclusion of Braintree in the provisions made by Joseph Davis, sen., in 1706, as one of the deserving Sabbatarian congregations, suggests that by then it had been established for some time. No minister's name is known until Daniel Wright appears in 1702, in conjunction with Colchester, and with Abraham Chaplin, and John Rutland, both known later as Sabbatarians.[118] From the surviving references, Wright seems to have played a leading role amongst Essex Sabbatarians throughout the first quarter of the eighteenth century. In 1711 an application was made for a licence to use the houses of Daniel Wright and John Worden of Bocking 'for Protestant Dissenters called Anabaptists'.[119] In 1727 'Mr Wright of Braintree' is mentioned in the Mill Yard records, with more than a hint of respect among the wider Sabbatarian community. He had been invited to participate in the ordination of Robert Cornthwaite, but had declined, apparently on the grounds that Cornthwaite was suspected of antinomianism.[120] The charge is surprising, since

[113] Witard, *Braintree Baptist Church*, 19; *The Baptist Union Directory* (1985–6), 71.
[114] GL, MS 9583/2, pt. 2.   [115] ERO, D/ABV 2, fos. 140, 41.
[116] GL, MS 9583/2, pt. 2.
[117] [E. Spurrier], *Memorials of the Baptist Church Worshipping in Eld Lane Chapel, Colchester* (Colchester, 1889), 17–18.
[118] Ibid. 13; ERO, D/NB 4/1. A 'Mr Hinchman', of Braintree, is also mentioned.
[119] ERO, Q/SBb 52 (20).   [120] MYM 255; *SO* 2: 69.

presumably a strict interpretation of the fourth commandment would have been one of the first encumbrances to be discarded by any earnest antinomian. It is more likely that Wright was apprehensive of Cornthwaite's alleged Socinianism than of antinomianism. Daniel Wright, 'of Colchester', prominent in that Sabbatarian community for more than three decades, was mentioned again in the will of Joseph Davis, jun., in 1731.[121] In 1767 a 'Mr Wright' was recorded as preaching for Braintree Seventh-day Baptists, although this is likely to have been William Wright, then one of the elders of the First-day Braintree Particular Baptists.[122] Once again, the evidence is scant, and does little more than confirm the existence of a Sabbatarian congregation at Braintree during the seventeenth and eighteenth centuries.

The information for Colchester is fortunately more adequate. From the testimony of Georgius Hornius, previously referred to, Seventh-day observance had taken root in Colchester well before the arrival of Thomas Tillam late in 1655 or early 1656. Indeed, its existence may have been one of the reasons for Tillam's decision to leave Hexham in preference for Colchester, possibly at the suggestion of Peter Chamberlen or Henry Jessey, and after he had been persuaded of the Saturday Sabbath by Chamberlen *c*.1654–5.[123] Again, there can be little doubt that Lollardy, at the very least, set the scene for the later appearance of the Seventh-day Sabbath in Colchester. William and Alice Mount and Rose Allin, burnt at the stake in Colchester in 1557, represented that 'detestable sort of schismaticks . . . obstinate heretics, anabaptists' who absented themselves from church and met in conventicles.[124] It is to some extent immaterial whether or not these early Nonconformists practised rebaptism, although some of them probably did. Besides John Pykas, who had taught Essex Lollards the Ten Commandments and other parts of Scripture, Colchester had been leavened by the itinerant preaching of Thomas Man and John Hacker, and later by the ministry of John Tyball. Man preached to Lollard congregations in Colchester and Amersham, and at other places in Norfolk and Suffolk, and Hacker, in addition

[121] Black (ed.), *Last Legacy*, 72–3.

[122] Witard, *Braintree Baptist Church*, 23. W.F. Quin, *A History of Braintree and Bocking* (Lavenham, 1981), 111.

[123] E.A. Payne, 'Thomas Tillam', *BQ* 17 (1957–8), 62–3; Whitley, 'Men of the Seventh Day', 4/3, 4.

[124] G.D. Witard, *Bibles in Barrels: A History of Essex Baptists* (1962), 8–9; Cross, *Church and People*, 117.

to preaching, read from Scripture and Lollard literature, including the Ten Commandments and *The Prick of Conscience*. In the early sixteenth century Tyball's 'mixture of religious idealism, scriptural fundamentalism and anti-clericalism', derived in part from his contact with Colchester Lollards, was in turn communicated to others in north-east Essex. So, in Colchester and other parts of East Anglia, as well as in many other areas of England, Lollardy, as Claire Cross notes, 'survived as a living movement, with fairly coherent doctrines, and with books, until the Protestant Reformation'.[125] Without further definitive evidence, however, one is reluctant to endorse the conclusion that the fifteenth-century Lollard Walter White, and the early sixteenth-century martyr William Sweeting, were Sabbatarians, or that a 'large and flourishing' Seventh-day congregation was known in Colchester *c*.1600.[126] The most that can be said with certainty is that here, as elsewhere, Lollard preference for a biblical faith, and its emphasis on obedience to the Ten Commandments, paved the way for a later Sabbatarian movement which may have been preceded by earlier observers of the seventh day.

The name most often associated with Essex Sabbatarianism during the seventeenth century is Thomas Tillam, who by 1656 was firmly established as the leader of the Colchester congregation. Tillam's earlier career has been traced in detail elsewhere,[127] and here and in the following chapter reference will be made only to the last twenty or so years of his life, after he had adopted Seventh-day principles. Perhaps it should be said that prior to that, and even during the early years of his Sabbatarianism, Tillam had been held in high esteem in Baptist and Independent circles elsewhere in the country.[128] Even Cromwell had reported 'good satisfaction' at the 'piety and ability of Mr Tillam'.[129] Tillam arrived in Colchester late in 1655,[130] and was soon engaged in public disputation with the Quaker James Parnell and the town lecturer William Archer.[131] Whether or not it was due to Colchester's strong predilection for Nonconformity, Tillam found the work much easier than it had been at Hexham, and by May 1656 it was reported that he had

---

[125] Cross, *Church and People*, 37–41.   [126] *SO* 2: 20.
[127] Payne, *BQ* 17: 61–6; Katz, *Sabbath and Sectarianism, passim*, particularly 21–47. See also *FMM* 266, and *BDBR* iii. 240–1.   [128] *BQ* 17: 62.
[129] *CSPD* 1655–6, 342.
[130] Possibly by June 1655, Penney, *The First Publishers of Truth*, 96.
[131] *TBHS* 6: 230.

baptized a hundred or more new converts.[132] These fruitful, early labours were shortly consolidated when, on Cromwell's recommendation, the Council of State approved a request from the mayor and aldermen of Colchester that Tillam and his followers be provided with 'a convenient place of worship'.[133] By January of the following year Ralph Josselin, an Essex clergyman, noted that Tillam had 'set up the practice of the Saturday Sabbath'.[134] It is almost certain that Josselin's report referred to events which had occurred during 1656, when, according to another source, Tillam had closed the parish church on Sundays and opened it for worship on Saturdays, encouraging his people to ply their trades as normal on the first day of the week.[135] The exact sequence of Tillam's progression to open Sabbatarianism is not recorded, but even if observance of the seventh day was not formally part of his public credo in the early months of 1656, it soon became so.

By 1657 events had taken an unexpected turn, and Tillam was in prison, presumably for overstepping the mark in the eyes of the authorities. While in gaol, Tillam published *The Seventh-Day Sabbath Sought out and celebrated*, for 'the church of Christ which is at Colchester, gathered by God's grace with the Author's ministry into the beautiful order of the Gospel'.[136] In terms of the times, Tillam's book was moderate enough. The argument that the Sabbath had been changed, and Sunday substituted for Saturday, by the Little Horn of Daniel 7 would have been well understood by the majority of his readers, as would the proposition that universal adoption of the seventh day throughout Christendom would assist in the conversion of the Jews. In urging that it was 'high time wholly to depart from Popish pollutions', Tillam also admonished, 'Let not the unscriptural odium of a Jewish Sabbath startle us any more than a Jewish Saviour.'[137] Moreover, if the Sabbath was to be rejected by Christians because it was 'Jewish', then so too for the

---

[132] Ralph Josselin, *The Diary of Ralph Josselin 1616–1683*, ed. A MacFarlane (1976), 368. [133] *CSPD* 1655–6, 340, 342.

[134] Josselin, *Diary*, 388. [135] *BQ* 17: 63.

[136] Tillam, *Seventh-Day Sabbath*, Ep. Ded. Katz seems unaware that a copy of this rare work is in the Angus Library at Regent's Park College, Oxford, *Sabbath and Sectarianism*, 36 n. 49.

[137] Tillam, *Seventh-Day Sabbath*, 4, 5, 52. Tillam argued that Sunday worship was a great stumbling block to the Jews, and reported that some Jews in London had been influenced by the observance of the seventh day and frequently attended Sabbatarian meetings, 50–1.

same reason should the rest of the Decalogue and the Bible in its entirety.[138] Tillam's case for the seventh day was presented with balance throughout, and if his argument that Sabbatarians could 'as freely preach and hear on the first day as on any other week day'[139] was representative of Seventh-day thought in general, it helps to explain why so many of them were not uncomfortable in association with Sunday-keeping congregations.

By the time his next book appeared in 1658, Tillam claimed to be in 'sweet communion' with 'more than two hundred baptized disciples, celebrating Jehovah's Sabbath'.[140] *The Lasher Proved Lyer* [1658] was a rather scathing reply to William Jennison's attack on Tillam published earlier that year under the title *A Lash for a Lyar*. Obviously smarting under Jennison's criticisms *ad hominem*, Tillam replied in the same vein, describing Jennison as his 'sordid adversary', an 'abusive beadle, much fitter to converse with those savages or wild heathens in America (from whence he came) than with any civil man'.[141] It was the first real sign of immoderation on Tillam's part, and even so fell barely outside the acceptable limits of contemporary polemic. On the subject, Tillam argued that the seventh day had been 'firmly established by the Father's institution, the Son's confirmation, the Spirit's approbation, and the Saints' observation'.[142] Not surprisingly, *The Lasher Proved Lyer* was rather less convincing than *The Seventh-Day Sabbath Sought out and celebrated*, which, despite Tillam's later excesses, proves on examination to have been a persuasive defence of the seventh day, comparable to the works of other contemporary Sabbatarian apologists. Its evangelical tone might have been expected to convince even the most obdurate anti-Sabbatarian of the author's essential orthodoxy, at least at the time of writing. Tillam speaks of 'gospel grace', 'evangelical light, forming Christ in the soul', and urges his readers to 'delight in Christ's shadow, and sit with soul-satisfaction under the spread wings of the eternal Saviour'.[143] The lordship of Christ over the Sabbath, demonstrated by 'His words and His works', is one of the fundamental reasons for its observance by Christians.[144]

Tillam has been described, rather imprecisely, as a Fifth

---

[138] Ibid. 49.   [139] Ibid. 61.
[140] Thomas Tillam, *The Lasher Proved Lyer* [1658], 9.   [141] Ibid. 1.
[142] Ibid. 12.   [143] Tillam, *Seventh-Day Sabbath*, Ep. Ded.
[144] Ibid. 72–80.

Monarchist.[145] It would be more accurate to locate him, as does Capp, 'on the fringe of the Fifth Monarchy Movement',[146] an apolitical advocate of the coming kingdom, whose millenarianism should not be interpreted in terms of the contemporary eschatological radicalism which hoped to transform the present kingdoms of the world into the kingdom of God. From the publication of *The Two Witnesses* in 1651, an exposition of Revelation 11, Tillam had consistently demonstrated an eschatological consciousness which always fell short of outright Fifth Monarchism. His Sabbatarianism, however, was from the beginning eschatologically motivated, and, when linked with the evangelical emphasis already apparent in *The Seventh-Day Sabbath Sought out and celebrated*, it proved a powerful attraction to those who came under his influence. To Tillam, the Sabbath had become the central issue in the last conflict between good and evil. The saints who sought out the Seventh-day Sabbath and celebrated it by so doing were 'obtaining the victory over the mark of the Beast'. 'In these very last days', Tillam declared, contention over the Sabbath was 'the last great controversy between the saints and the man of sin'. The signs of Christ's second coming, 'so fairly visible', were an incentive to slumbering saints to be ready for the final events. 'Although the day and hour be not known, yet doubtless this generation shall not pass till the new Jerusalem's glory shall crown obedient saints with everlasting rest.'[147] Naturally, observance of the seventh day was implicit in Tillam's understanding of obedience.

Two years later, again from prison, Tillam's eschatological Sabbatarianism had taken on the added dimension of a distinctly remnant theology. Total obedience to the will of God in all things was the next and penultimate step in the process of withdrawal from this present evil world in preparation for the establishment of a Sabbath-keeping community in 'the wilderness' of the Palatinate. Drawing on the rapid fulfilment of end-time prophecies from the book of Revelation, Tillam set out his last published theological statement in a work with the title *The Temple of Lively Stones* (1660): 'The voice of the seventh angel (now sounding) hath produced a small remnant of the woman's seed in these Islands, waiting for the advance of the Law of God, who by their entire separation are become victors over the Beast, his image, his mark, and the number

---

[145] Greaves, *Deliver us from Evil*, 92; *BDBR* iii. 240.
[146] *FMM* 266, even though Capp frequently alludes to Tillam as though he were a Fifth Monarchist.   [147] Tillam, *Seventh-Day Sabbath*, 1–2.

of his name.'[148] This latter-day prophetic remnant 'are visible, in view of and therefore persecuted by the world . . . have wholly abandoned Babylon's customs and traditions [and] keep the commandments of God, and have the testimony of Jesus Christ . . . recovering the sanctified Sabbath from that foot of pride which hath so long trampled upon it'.[149] In *The Temple of Lively Stones* Tillam advocated a complete return to New Testament practice including, in addition to observance of the seventh day, the blessing of children, believer's baptism, foot-washing, laying on of hands, marriage only with believers, and anointing the sick with oil.[150] Although the book itself gave little evidence of any overt tendency to Judaism, it is a fact that shortly after its publication Tillam and Pooley launched the Palatinate scheme with which their Judaizing practices have since been associated, and which had such disastrous consequences for the Sabbatarian movement throughout East Anglia and elsewhere in the country. John Traske and his followers had previously shown that to some minds in the seventeenth century there was essentially no distinction between unquestioning obedience to the requirements of the New Testament and unquestioning obedience to those of the Old, and that only a short step existed between the two. Events soon demonstrated that it was a step Tillam was prepared to take.

Christopher Pooley, whose earlier Fifth Monarchist activism had been moderated by subsequent events, had provided the introduction to Tillam's *Temple of Lively Stones*. Thereafter he and Tillam were inseparably linked as the chief architects of the Palatinate scheme, and by 1661 were already known to the nervous authorities as 'dangerous men' and 'seducers of the people'.[151] On 31 July Tillam, under the pseudonym Mallit, 'formerly a proselyter to Judaism', Pooley, 'known to have been a grand dipper in Norfolk and Suffolk', and a Dr Love, 'a [pretended] doctor of physic at Rotterdam', were reported to have landed at Lowestoft *en route* from Holland and the Palatinate.[152] For the next six or seven years

---

[148] Tillam, *The Temple of Lively Stones*, 2.   [149] Ibid. 3–5.

[150] Ibid., *passim*. Even at this point, Tillam appears to have been willing to recognize that observance of the seventh day should not be regarded as a test of church fellowship: ibid. 345.   [151] PRO, SPD 29/41/1.

[152] Ibid. Katz believes that 'Dr Love' was Paul Hobson, formerly of Newcastle, whom Tillam had known while at Hexham, *Sabbath and Sectarianism*, 40. There is no other evidence that Hobson was a Sabbatarian, and no reason to conclude that in this instance he was travelling together with Tillam and Pooley in Sabbatarian interests.

Tillam and/or his associates would frequently cross the North Sea, usually embarking and disembarking at Lowestoft or Harwich, and always in pursuit of the same ultimate objective, a Sabbatarian community totally bound to the most literal interpretation of Scripture, and totally free from the restrictions of post-Restoration legislation in England. There are no records to indicate just how productive their labours were, or precisely how many Sabbatarian families they succeeded in settling in Germany. In 1664 the activities of Tillam and his followers on the Continent were said to have brought reproach on English settlers in Rotterdam, and Tillam was reported to be 'afraid to show himself' in England and to have sent Pooley to spread the word 'of plenty and comfort in Germany'.[153] In 1668 a boat carrying eight or nine passengers bound for 'a monastery granted by the Duke of Brandenburg to one Tillam' was held up by bad weather at Harwich for several days. It was noted that Tillam by then had 'plenty' of disciples, 'both male and female', and that he preached 'circumcision, the Seventh-day Sabbath, Jewish rites, community of goods (and they say, of wives) and as many concubines as they please'.[154] There may have been some distortion, even malice, in this report, but the word reaching England had been sufficiently worrying to prompt other leading Sabbatarians to dissociate themselves and their cause from the Pooley/Tillam faction.[155] Pooley is said ultimately to have repented of his excesses and returned to the moderate Sabbatarian fold. Tillam is reported to have died in Germany in 1674, unrepentant and 'a great blemish to the truth'.[156] By then it seems reasonably clear that many English Sabbatarian families had indeed made the journey to Germany, to the lasting detriment of several Seventh-day churches in Essex, Norfolk, Suffolk, and counties further north.[157]

[153] *CSPD* 1664–5, pt. 1, 101, 2.

[154] PRO, SP 29/236/14. An earlier report had informed Pooley's wife that he had taken another wife in Germany: PRO, SP 29/106/11.

[155] Cf. *A Faithful Testimony Against The Teachers of Circumcision and the Legal Ceremonies; who are lately gone into Germany*, published in 1667 and signed by seven leading Sabbatarians; see Appendix IV for details.

[156] Stennett, *The Insnared Taken*, 7; Joseph Davis to Newport, Rhode Island, 5 Aug. 1674, SDBHS, MS 194x.6, 76.

[157] Hewett rightly says that some Sabbatarians remained in most places where Tillam and Pooley had been active, including Colchester, Mersea, and Stalham/ Ingham, NRO, MS 4261, s.v. Stalham. A 'remnant' was reported at Harwich in 1690, which presumably had some connection with the earlier labours of Pooley and Tillam. There are no other known references to Sabbatarianism at Mersea or Harwich. On the influence of Tillam and Pooley in the North, see below, Ch. 10, *passim*.

The strength of the Seventh-day movement in Colchester is attested to by its survival for more than a hundred years after the efforts of Tillam and Pooley in the 1660s had drawn off a number of its adherents. Whitley suggests that John Smith, a later rector of St Mary's, Colchester, published *The Doctrine of the Church of England concerning the Lords Day, or Sunday-Sabbath* in 1683 as an antidote to Tillam's posthumous influence.[158] Both General and Particular Seventh-day Baptists are said to have existed simultaneously at Colchester during the seventeenth century, although it is not clear whether independently, or in communion with each other.[159] In 1693 a letter was sent to Pinners' Hall from 'the Sabbath-keeping church at Colchester' regarding the transfer of a member. The letter was signed by six Colchester members, including John Rutland, Abraham Chaplin, and Abraham King.[160] Rutland was later known as the minister of the Woodbridge Sabbatarians, and Chaplin and King were both signatories to an application to register a meeting-house in Colchester 'for ye worship of God after ye way of ye people called Seventh day People'. This was in 1706, and the house, situated in St Leonard's parish and formerly belonging to 'Mr. Lucas', had 'antiently' been in use as a place of worship for the Colchester Sabbatarians.[161] Two dismissals to the Sabbatarians from the Eld Lane First-day church, of Mary Munnings in 1707 and of a Mr Mumford in 1709, suggest that the seventh day was a live issue there at this period.[162] In 1712 a letter from Colchester is referred to in the Mill Yard minutes,[163] and in 1721 Daniel Wright, by then firmly established as leader of the Colchester Sabbatarians, administered the Lord's Supper at a joint service for the two London Sabbatarian churches at Mill Yard, meeting together 'though as two congregations'.[164] This is all substantial evidence of a thriving congregation during the latter part of the seventeenth century and the first quarter of the eighteenth century.

John Rutland, whom we met earlier as occasional preacher at Pulham Margaret in Norfolk, had moved to Woodbridge in 1705, assuming the pastoral office there in 1711.[165] As we have also seen,

---

[158] Whitley, 'Men of the Seventh Day', 4/19.
[159] Coomer, *English Dissent under the Early Hanoverians*, 26.
[160] PHCB 31.
[161] ERO, Colchester: Colchester Borough Quarter Sessions Roll, Epiphany 1705/6.
[162] ERO, D/NB 4/24; *BQ* 10: 288.   [163] MYM 206.   [164] Ibid. 235.
[165] Klaiber, *Suffolk Baptists*, 31.

in that same year he officiated at the ordination of John Rootsey at Eld Lane, Colchester. Rutland also preached at Eld Lane until his untimely death in 1718. Daniel Wright had been known as a Sabbatarian preacher in Colchester since 1702, and was still prominent there thirty years later when, under the provisions of the will of Joseph Davis, jun., of Mill Yard, he received a life interest in 'the meeting-house, burying grounds, and all the houses on the premises at the Hithe in Colchester'.[166] Rutland was a confirmed Calvinist, and Davis, and perhaps by inference Wright, were confirmed Arminians. Possibly there were both General and Particular Sabbatarians at Colchester well into the eighteenth century.

John Ridley, who was ministering at Woodbridge by 1731, is also recorded as minister at Colchester between 1731 and 1739. This is a further indication of the link between the two congregations. Ridley is the last known minister of the Colchester Sabbatarians, and it is said that during his pastorate several members from Eld Lane joined the Seventh-day people, and that after his death in 1739 the Seventh-day cause remained alive for many years.[167] As the eighteenth century progressed, however, Eld Lane, whose chequered early years had been consolidated by 1739, gradually assumed dominance as the major Baptist witness in the town, and from 1774 onwards, during the ministry of Thomas Stevens, it slowly absorbed the remaining Sabbatarians. Joshua Thomas records that Eld Lane 'gradually swallowed' the General Baptists and the Seventh-day Baptists, and that in 1784 the last Colchester Sabbatarian died in communion with Eld Lane.[168] The assertion that during the eighteenth century, the Seventh-day Baptist church at Colchester consisted of nearly 200 members is probably over-optimistic.[169]

WOODBRIDGE, HASKETON, AND MELTON

A.J. Klaiber, the historian of the early Suffolk Baptist movement, quaintly noted that the third quarter of the seventeenth century was remarkable 'for certain activities in the interests of a Seventh-day Sunday'.[170] In fact, the activity centred chiefly around the Woodbridge

---

[166] Black (ed.), *Last Legacy*, 73; Whitley, 'Men of the Seventh Day', 4/19.
[167] [Spurrier], *Memorials of . . . Eld Lane*, 23. e.g. Nicholas and Sarah Pain and Sarah Pryer who in 1739 'sat down in communion with Mr Ridley and the other Sabbatarians', ERO, D/NB 4/26.   [168] Spurrier, *Memorials of . . . Eld Lane*, 27.
[169] *SR* 51/25: 396.   [170] *BQ* 4: 118.

district, where Saturday Sabbatarianism may have taken root even before the end of the Commonwealth era.[171] Beyond that, there are few traces in the county, even though Christopher Pooley's evangelistic zeal throughout Norfolk and Suffolk in the 1650s may have stirred an interest in other areas for which no records have survived. One contemporary account records that the people of Woodbridge were 'miserably divided' in their religious convictions, with half the population being orthodox in their allegiance to the Church of England, 'the rest heterodox, with Sectaries of almost all denominations, as Presbyterians, Independents, Anabaptists, Sabbatarians, Jews, and what are worse, Quakers in great plenty'.[172] The covenant of the early Independent church alluded to the fraternal responsibilities of its members, 'that we may give no offence to Jew nor Gentile', a reference which Klaiber interpreted as evidence of a Sabbatarian presence in 1652.[173] Edmund Warren's reply to Tillam's *Seventh-Day Sabbath Sought out and celebrated* was published at Ipswich for a citizen of that town, and may indicate that Sabbatarian ideas were being entertained there by the late 1650s.

The covenant of the Woodbridge Independents, drawn up under Frederick Woodall, urged deeper knowledge of the Scriptures, 'which only are able to make us wise unto salvation', and committed those who subscribed to it to 'walk in all the ways laid out for us therein'. It was without doubt a sound basis for the emergence of Seventh-day observance. Woodall is described as 'a man of learning, ability, and piety, and . . . zealous for the Fifth Monarchy'.[174] Tillam and Pooley had both been active in the district, and by the late 1650s Woodbridge was known as a relatively strong Fifth Monarchist centre.[175] The Woodbridge Sabbatarians, moreover, are reported to have had an early and lasting connection with Colchester—Tillam's centre of operation until his defection to the Continent in the 1660s. It thus seems likely that the beginnings of Woodbridge Sabbatarianism in the 1650s were similar to those of the Seventh-day Men elsewhere in Norfolk and Suffolk who had come under the influence of Pooley and Tillam, and whose fundamental stance

[171] Klaiber, *Suffolk Baptists*. 29.

[172] SRO, Hundred Collects, Loes Hundred, GZ Woodbridge, fo. 63ʳ. See also V.B. Redstone, *Bygone Woodbridge* (Woodbridge, 1893), 49.

[173] Hosken, *History of Congregationalism*, 191; Klaiber, *Suffolk Baptists*, 29.

[174] Hosken, *History of Congregationalism*, 190–2. On Woodall, lecturer at Woodbridge and minister of the Independent church, see *CR* 542 and Capp, *FMM* 269.

[175] *FMM* 81–2.

in those early days was obedience to 'all the precepts' of the Word and all the promptings of the Spirit.[176] There is no evidence at present to suggest that the earlier Sabbatarianism at Colchester had any wider impact. The 'remnant' which survived at Woodbridge and Melton in 1690 to become a 'stronghold' of Sabbatarianism in the eighteenth century[177] suggests that these early Suffolk Sabbatarians withstood the later blandishments of Tillam and Pooley rather better than some. Certainly the Woodbridge congregation was still sufficiently active in 1706 to sustain a 'teacher', and to warrant inclusion in the will of Joseph Davis, sen., as one of the existing congregations whose ministers were worthy of support.[178]

For a congregation which almost certainly worshipped corporately for more than a hundred years, few names have survived. John Rutland (or Rudland) appears *c*.1705 as the first of two recorded ministers at Woodbridge.[179] He had also been known at Colchester at least since 1693, and in view of the link between the two congregations it is quite possible that he had ministered to both groups since the late seventeenth century. A meeting-place for Anabaptists was also certified by Rutland in Bishop's Stortford in 1702.[180] His activities at Pulham Margaret shortly before his death in 1718, and his participation in the ordination of John Rootsey at Colchester, Eld Lane, in 1711 indicate a broad respect for the man and tolerance of his divergent views. In 1719, Mill Yard wrote to Woodbridge concerning a Joseph Boatham, and in 1738, John Spurling was dismissed from Eld Lane to the Woodbridge Sabbatarians.[181] Once again, these fleeting glimpses into the life of an elusive congregation do little more than confirm its existence.

Apart from John Ridley, the second of Woodbridge's two known ministers, George Carlow, is the only other surviving name of any significance. His admittance to the Mill Yard fellowship in 1706 does not appear to have lessened his support of the Woodbridge cause, or his concern for the town's local needy. When he died in 1738, he had made provision in his will for the distribution to the poor of twenty shillings worth of 'good wheaten bread' every Candlemas day except, strangely enough, when that day fell on Saturday.[182] In

---

[176] Hosken, *History of Congregationalism*, 190. [177] *BQ* 14: 165; 10: 289.
[178] Cox, *Literature of the Sabbath Question*, ii. 81.
[179] Klaiber, *Suffolk Baptists*, 31; *SO* 2: 149.
[180] Urwick, *Nonconformity in Herts*, 704. [181] MYM 231; ERO, D/NB 4/24.
[182] MYM 169; Redstone, *Bygone Woodbridge*, 97.

1724 Carlow published *Truth Defended: or, Observations on Mr Ward's Expository Discourses . . . concerning the Sabbath*, one of the first substantial works to advocate Seventh-day observance to appear in print in the revived Sabbatarian debate of the 1720s and 1730s.[183] Carlow's book may also have been intended to counter the effect of an anonymous anti-Sabbatarian tract which appeared that same year, *The Seventh-Day-Man in his Vanity of his Jewish Sabbath, and Presumptuous Contempt of Gospel Rest, together with the Sabbath Day Error*.[184] Carlow and his contemporaries, whoever they were, would not have appreciated such thinly veiled innuendo, and in the ensuing five or six years Edward Elwall, John Maulden, and Robert Cornthwaite all came to the defence of the Saturday Sabbath, although it must be said that Elwall frequently appears to have been speaking to a revised agenda.[185] Carlow's book was deemed worthy of reprinting in the nineteenth century, as an effective apology for Seventh-day observance.

These early decades of the eighteenth century, when John Ridley was minister, were among the most prosperous for the Woodbridge Sabbatarians. Ridley's perceived eccentricities and his local image as a 'Jew' do not appear to have detracted immediately from the general welfare of his congregation.[186] The majority of Baptists in the district are said to have been Seventh-day during these years. Browne records that they were 'numerous', and Klaiber adds that at this period Seventh-day Baptist life in the area centred around Hasketon, two miles or so from Woodbridge itself.[187] In 1724 representatives of the Woodbridge–Hasketon Sabbatarians met with the Baptist Board to request assistance with the erection of a meeting-house. Negotiations did not proceed smoothly, and the Suffolk

---

[183] Carlow's book was written in reply to Henry Ward, the Independent minister at Woodbridge 1707–34, who had attacked the Sabbatarian position in a series of sermons.

[184] Which Whitley suggests was based on Bodl. MS Rawl. D. 1350, fos. 296–9 (*BB* i. 4–724), although the title of this six-page piece reads 'The seventh day man, or restless Christian, in the vanity of his jewish Sabbath, and presumptuous contempt of Gospel-rest . . . and the Lord's Day justified as the true Christian Sabbath'.

[185] On Elwall, Maulden, and Cornthwaite, see above, Ch. 3. Elwall's desire to defend Unitarianism as much as Sabbatarianism appears in some of his titles, e.g. *A True Testimony for God and for His Sacred Law. Being a Plain, Honest, Defence of the First Commandment of God Against all the Trinitarians under Heaven* (1724), and *The Supernatural Incarnation of Jesus Christ proved to be false . . .* (1743).

[186] *SO* ii. 149; Brown, *History of Congregationalism*, 572.

[187] *TBHS* 5: 109; Browne, *History of Congregationalism*, 572; Klaiber, *Suffolk Baptists*, 29.

Sabbatarians were 'advised to be more modest in their demands'.[188] Although the meeting-house never materialized, the congregation continued to meet for many years to come. In 1738 and 1739 members were still being 'dismissed' to the Woodbridge Sabbatarian church from Colchester and other local Baptist and Sabbatarian congregations, 'Mr. Ridley being elder [and] Benjamin Pite coming as messenger for him'.[189] This is the last dated reference to Ridley at Woodbridge, and it is recorded that after his death the cause there lapsed. Carlow had died in 1738, both Rutland's and Ridley's sons forsook the faith of their fathers and joined the Independents, and the surviving Sabbatarians eventually sought fellowship with Colchester, Eld Lane, as the remaining Colchester Sabbatarians had done. Woodbridge continued to decline, owing to the 'death of aged members, and the defection of others', until its witness finally came to an end when the last member died in 1784, again in fellowship with Colchester.[190]

DOWNHAM

Conventicles of 'Quakers, Anabaptists, and Sabbatarians' were reported in the episcopal returns for Downham in 1669. Meetings were held in the houses of Thomas Crab, 'husbandman', and John Rattum, 'excommunicate', with Samuel Cater (or Cator) designated as teacher.[191] Although Cater, of Downham, is described by Whitley as a General Baptist *c*.1661,[192] it is more likely that by then his sympathies lay with the Quakers.[193] He appears to have been dismissed from the Littleport Baptist church with his brother in 1655. To the notice of dismissal delivered by the Baptist elder, the Caters are recorded to have observed, 'You made us elders in your church, who call yourselves Jews, and are not, but the synagogue of Satan, out of which you have cast us.'[194] Unfortunately, the Littleport

---

[188] *TBHS* 5: 100.   [189] Ibid. 109; ERO, D/NB 4/24.

[190] Klaiber, *Suffolk Baptists*, 34; *TBHS* 5: 110.

[191] *OR* i. 35; UCL, MS Palmer B25, 1.   [192] *MGA* i, p. xliii.

[193] For Cater, the 'ex-Baptist' who later espoused Quaker views, see H. Barbour and A. Roberts (eds.), *Early Quaker Writings 1650–1700* (1973), 587; N. Penney (ed.), *Extracts from State Papers Relating to Friends, 1654–1672* (1913), 6, 110.

[194] J.J. Green, 'A Biographical Account of Samuel Cater, of Littleport in the Isle of Ely, Baptist Elder and Quaker Preacher, 1627–1711', Friends House Library, MSS, vol. v, 178/1, 3–11.

Jewish connection is nowhere further defined, and may or may not be an obscure hint of Sabbatarianism. In the 1669 returns Cater is again listed as the preacher at other neighbouring conventicles in the Ely diocese, including one at Littleport of about a hundred 'Quakers', and one at Haddenham of sixty or seventy, again of 'Quakers'. Cater is also reported to have preached in the house of John Harvey at Linton, and at Littleport.[195]

In attempting to interpret the significance of this meagre and somewhat confusing evidence, it may be helpful to consider three factors. In the first place, the possibility of a mixed-communion congregation cannot be dismissed. Sabbatarians elsewhere in the country at this period were not always clearly distinguished from other Nonconformist groups, sometimes meeting in company with them. Secondly, the reports of informers were frequently inaccurate. Katz correctly comments with reference to the information provided in the 1669 returns that denominational designations 'are often suspect'.[196] And thirdly, and perhaps in this instance of most significance, the fluidity of individual convictions and allegiances must be given due consideration. In the traumatic days of the Commonwealth and the Protectorate, a man could quite easily be an Independent, then a Baptist, then a Quaker, or a Sabbatarian, all within the space of a year. B.R. White notes that 'convictions grew from seedling to harvest at breakneck speed' during this period.[197] The ebb and flow of developing and changing opinions seems to have been particularly strong in this district, and the fact that Samuel Cater had links with Quakers and Sabbatarians need not necessarily confuse us, much less the fact that Quakers, Anabaptists, and Sabbatarians are reported to have met together in conventicles. The information can, indeed, be interpreted to indicate that one group met in the house of Thomas Crab and that another met in John Rattum's house, and that one group was Quaker, and the other Anabaptist and Sabbatarian. What is beyond doubt is that Sabbatarianism had been identified at Downham in 1669. It may also have been present in other parishes in the diocese, and for even somewhat longer.

In 1614, as noted in Chapter 3, John Traske had appeared in the district, and several people from at least five local parishes had

---

[195] *OR* i. 34, 40–1; UCL, MS Palmer B25, 1, 6.
[196] Katz, *Sabbath and Sectarianism*, 105.   [197] White, *English Baptists*, 31.

been presented in December of that year for attending his meetings. It is recorded that he preached on at least two occasions, once in a house 'upon a Saboth day at night' and once in the Littleport church 'on ye week day'. Those who attended at Littleport included parishioners from Chettisham, Downham, Ely St Mary's, Ely Holy Trinity, and Sutton.[198] The records pertaining to Littleport have comparatively few entries for 1614, and make no mention of Traske's meeting. It is inconceivable that no Littleport residents were present, however, and the paucity of information may indicate a laxness in the parish which gave Traske opportunity to fill an empty pulpit. Richard Aspland, one of those from Downham present at the Littleport meeting, reported that he had heard that Traske was 'an excellent preacher, and a good man'.[199] Traske also conducted a meeting in the church at Chettisham, when it was noted that he had said prayers 'not by the booke'.[200] Unfortunately, there are no extant records for any of these parishes for the years immediately following which might indicate any continuing activity in the wake of Traske's visit or, indeed, any sign of further visits. Nor is there any explanation of Traske's presence in the Ely diocese in the first place. Presumably there had been some prior contact between him and the parish, and somebody must have been responsible for making whatever arrangements were necessary. It is true, of course, that Traske's recorded activities in this district occurred before he is traditionally thought to have adopted the Seventh-day Sabbath, c.1616–17.[201] Even so, the presence of the first known English Sabbatarian of the seventeenth century in this corner of Cambridgeshire where Seventh-day observance later came into the open is, at the very least, a matter of some interest.

There are hints of a Sabbatarian interest at other parts in the county not far distant. Henry Denne, formerly a minister in the Church of England, had founded General Baptist congregations at Fenstanton and Warboys c.1644–5, and had also obtained the living at nearby Eltisley at about the same time.[202] By 1645, Denne had published on the discovery of the man of sin and the unmasking of the Antichrist, whom he saw at work 'in the pulpits of England',

---

[198] UCL, EDR B/2/35, fos. 3ʳ, 62ʳ, 76ᵛ–77ᵛ, 78ʳ, 113ᵛ, 114ʳ, 190ʳ·ᵛ.

[199] Ibid., fo. 62ʳ.   [200] Ibid., fo. 3ʳ.

[201] On the possibility that Traske might have adopted Sabbatarianism earlier than this, see above, 50–3.

[202] White, *English Baptists*, 39–41. On Denne, see also *DNB*.

and for which view he had been imprisoned.[203] Denne's eschatological interests are unmistakable. According to Thomas Edwards,
Philip Tandy, 'a great sectary' from the North with second advent
expectations based on the prophecies of the Book of Revelation,
and a confirmed Sabbatarian, appeared as occasional preacher to
Denne's congregation at Eltisley, c.1646.[204] While their shared
convictions did not extend to observance of the seventh day, Tandy's
Sabbatarianism would have been known to Denne and presumably
to at least some in his congregation.[205] As late as 1717 a letter was
received by Mill Yard from nearby Hopewell (Holywell?), 'in the
county of Hutterdon' (*sic*).[206]

Joseph Davis recounts a story, first related by John Rutland, of a
blind widow living at Burwell on the Cambridgeshire–Suffolk border, who had been greatly troubled in conscience over the Sabbath
issue. She was said to have miraculously received her sight in answer
to a prayer that if the seventh day was indeed the true Sabbath,
God would heal her so that she might read his word and keep His
holy day. Davis records that subsequently she was 'fully convinced
of the truth of the Sabbath', and kept it 'according to the Commandment upwards of forty years' thereafter.[207] It is the only recorded
instance of Sabbatarianism at Burwell, and whether or not the story
had gathered accretions in the telling, the fact remains that only by
discussion with others, or personal instruction, could a blind woman
have learned of the Seventh-day doctrine. Perhaps the Downham
influence was wider than the official records suggest.

Meanwhile at Downham itself observance of the seventh day
seems to have continued, apparently with a Unitarian flavour, for
some years after it had first been reported in 1669. In 1682 George
Washington was presented at the episcopal visitation for 'denying
ye Godhead of our Lord Jesus Christ, and professing himself a
Jew'.[208] Two years later he was again cited, this time 'for refusing

---

[203] Henry Denne, *Antichrist Unmasked in two Treatises . . . The second, The man
of Sinne discovered in Doctrine; the root and foundation of Antichrist laid open.*
(1645).

[204] Edwards, *Gangraena*, pt. i, 23 (the second so numbered), *The third Part of
Gangraena* (1646), 54. On Tandy's work in the North, see Ch. 10.

[205] Denne later appears to have opposed the seventh day. In 1658 he attended the
Stone Chapel debate in London, apparently in support of Jeremiah Ives who contended against Thomas Tillam and the Saturday Sabbath, E.B. Underhill (ed.), *Records
of the Churches of Christ, Gathered at Fenstanton, Warboys, and Hexham 1644–
1720* (1854), p. xxvi.   [206] MYM 227.

[207] Davis, *Last Legacy*, 34–6.   [208] EDR, B/2/68, fo. 7ʳ.

to have his children baptized'.[209] Unitarian ideas had been canvassed at various places in the country well before this, and it is not
impossible that a Sabbatarianism similar to the kind that later flourished at Mill Yard was reflected in George Washington's beliefs.
Certainly any Baptists in this area at this period are likely to have
been General Baptists, and the Quaker influence already present at
Downham in 1669 in conjunction with Anabaptists and Sabbatarians
is sufficient to demonstrate an openness to diversity. It need not
be argued that, when Washington was reported to have professed
himself a 'Jew', it was a tacit admission of Seventh-day observance.

[209] Ibid., fo. 46ʳ.

10

The Northern Counties

THE preceding chapters in this study have demonstrated that the heaviest concentration of Sabbatarians in England and Wales between 1650 and 1750 resided in the southern half of the country, in broad terms south and south-east of a line drawn between Norwich and Worcester and extending through Hereford to Swansea. It has been suggested, however, that during the second half of the seventeenth century 'comparatively large and flourishing congregations' of Seventh-day Christians existed throughout the land, and even more specifically that 'many persons in the North', isolated individuals as well as gathered congregations, had observed Saturday as the Sabbath.[1] Precisely which parts of the country were in this instance designated by 'the North' is unclear, but the evidence which has survived indicates that Saturday observers north of the Norwich–Worcester line were located mainly in the region to the north of the Wash and to the east of the Pennines, and that several congregations were established, probably in the 1650s and 1660s, in Lincolnshire, Nottinghamshire, Yorkshire, Durham, and Northumberland.[2] As has been observed with reference to Sabbatarianism in other areas, traces of the practice also lingered in some of these counties into the eighteenth century.

Again, as with the Sabbatarian movement elsewhere, county boundaries prove to be convenient but arbitrary lines of demarcation, which do not adequately represent the flow of contemporary religious belief or the strength of personal conviction. Thus, when Thomas Tillam's emissaries, Christopher Pooley and John Foxey, preached at Raby Castle in Durham, it is certain that their hearers included residents of Northumberland and highly probable that followers from Yorkshire were also present.[3] And, given the

---

[1] Mellone, *JQR*, 10: 405–6; cf. *TBHS* 2: 114.

[2] A Sabbatarian congregation is said to have existed at Manchester from *c.*1730 (*SDBEA* 1: 56, *SR* 83/16: 499), but no substantiating evidence has to date come to light. See Appendix II, 'Notes on Supposed Sabbatarian Congregations, 1650–1750'.

[3] PRO, SP 29/232/10.

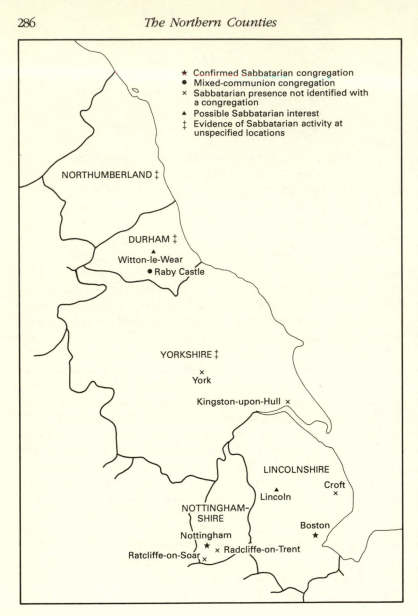

★ Confirmed Sabbatarian congregation
● Mixed-communion congregation
× Sabbatarian presence not identified with
   a congregation
▲ Possible Sabbatarian interest
‡ Evidence of Sabbatarian activity at
   unspecified locations

NORTHUMBERLAND ‡

DURHAM ‡
▲
Witton-le-Wear
● Raby Castle

YORKSHIRE ‡

×
York

Kingston-upon-Hull ×

LINCOLNSHIRE

▲   Croft
Lincoln   ×

NOTTINGHAM-
  SHIRE
                            Boston
Nottingham   ★
          ★ × Radcliffe-on-Trent
Ratcliffe-on-Soar ×

MAP 7 Locations in northern counties associated with seventeenth- and
       eighteenth-century Sabbatarianism

predisposition of Sabbatarians to travel long distances to meet with others of like faith, the 'remnant' that survived at Nottingham in 1690[4] may well have represented kindred spirits who, in more congenial times, had come from neighbouring Derbyshire. Nor is it impossible that the seventeenth-century interest at Kingston upon Hull[5] and the eighteenth-century interest in Northamptonshire[6] were, in some way, however tenuous, derived from a long-standing conviction about the distinctiveness of the seventh day which had been evident in Lincolnshire from at least the fourteenth century, if not earlier.[7] Be all this as it may, the picture emerges of a Sabbatarianism in the north-eastern counties which was intrinsically a part of that wider and more easily defined movement which contemporaneously spread through so many counties to the south.

LINCOLNSHIRE AND NOTTINGHAMSHIRE

In view of certain religious trends in Lincolnshire during the preceding three centuries, as well as that county's geographical proximity to Norfolk, Nottinghamshire, and Yorkshire, in all of which Seventh-day congregations had been established by the mid-seventeenth century, it is somewhat surprising that only one Lincolnshire Sabbatarian group is now identifiable. The 'small remnant' which survived at Boston in 1690, according to the Llanwenarth record,[8] is notable also on account of the fact that its existence can currently be verified only by this one document. This frustrating lack of definitive evidence can to some extent be mitigated by attempting to see Boston Sabbatarianism in the context of other

---

[4] *BQ* 14: 165.

[5] Mary Houlton, a member of an Independent church at Kingston-upon-Hull who observed the seventh day, was admitted to membership at Pinners' Hall in 1696, PHCB 47.

[6] In 1740 William Beck, a member of Philip Doddridge's church in Northampton, was proposed for membership at Pinners' Hall, and was admitted following receipt of a letter of recommendation from Doddridge, PHCB 110–11. A letter from the messengers of the Northamptonshire Baptist Association in 1786 recognized 'a difference in opinion between us and some of our Christian friends' concerning the day on which the Sabbath ought to be observed. It was, however, 'a matter of small importance' compared to the 'obligation to observe a Sabbath at all', and they concluded 'we can readily embrace such as differ from us in this particular, in the armes of Christian affection', *The Authority and Sanctification of the Lord's Day Explained and Enforced* (1786), 5.

[7] Dorothy M. Owen, *Church and Society in Medieval Lincolnshire* (Lincoln, 1971), 110.   [8] *BQ* 14: 165.

earlier and contemporary ideas which are known to have been present in the religious thought of Lincolnshire people since the fourteenth century. Considered together, these related beliefs and practices substantiate the conclusion that Saturday Sabbatarianism was seldom generated in a vacuum.

Although Lollardy as such was not openly as strong in Lincolnshire as in some neighbouring counties,[9] there is none the less unmistakable evidence there of a preference for that kind of biblical faith which would later be the hallmark of thoroughgoing Protestantism. As the English Reformation began to gather momentum, the people of Lincolnshire, as well as the more godly amongst the clergy, readily warmed to 'conferences, disputations, reasonings, prayers, singing of psalmes, preachings, readings, prophesyings . . . and such like holy exercises'[10] which elevated the word of God, exposed the formulations of men, and edified and confirmed the faithful. This attitude of mind, as we have seen elsewhere, readily contributed to the adoption of beliefs and practices which could easily be validated by reference to the biblical text, the observance of the Seventh-day Sabbath amongst them. Moreover, in Lincolnshire it was not new. In this vein, according to the careful research of Dorothy Owen, a form of Saturday observance had been known in the county from medieval times. In the mid-fourteenth century 'the old Lincolnshire heresy of observing Saturday as a feast day' had been revived as 'a new evil', to the extent that in 1360 Bishop Gynwell found it necessary formally to forbid the custom.[11] While this particular version of Seventh-day observance may well have been practised in conjunction with Sunday-keeping, it none the less reflects a regard for the special nature of Saturday reminiscent of the Celtic tradition traced in Chapter 1. Bishop Reginald Pecock's complaint that Lollards would 'fetch and learn their faith at the Bible of Holy Scripture' rather than at the hands of duly appointed teachers of the church[12] was equally true of many not specifically

---

[9] Claire Cross notes the strength of Lollardy in Leicestershire and Northamptonshire, *Church and People*, 20–1.

[10] 'Wiggenton's Visitation', *TCHS* 3 (1907), 31. On Giles Wiggenton, or Wigginton, non-conforming vicar of Sedbeurgh, fl. 1579, see *DNB*.

[11] Owen, *Church and Society*, 32, 110. On John Gynwell, or Gynewell, Bishop of Lincoln 1347–62, see *Fasti Ecclesiae Anglicanae 1300–1541, i: Lincoln Diocese* (1962), 1.

[12] Green, *Bishop Reginald Pecock*, 141. Even Pecock allowed that Saturday was the biblical Sabbath, but argued that it was in no way related to the Christian Sunday, ibid. 181–2.

to be categorized as Lollards, in Lincolnshire as elsewhere. It was a tendency which undoubtedly contributed to the respect shown for the Seventh-day Sabbath of the fourth commandment.

In Lincolnshire this preference for a more thoroughly reformed faith became more apparent during the sixteenth and seventeenth centuries. The indictment of Anne Askew, daughter of Sir William Askew of Stallingborough, ostensibly for rejecting the doctrine of transubstantiation, but more accurately for her knowledge and promulgation of the broader teachings of the Bible;[13] the 'quiet' Lincolnshire support for the 'protestant underground' during the Marian ascendancy;[14] the 'prophesyings' and 'exercises' in several market towns of Lincolnshire during Elizabeth's reign,[15] regular gatherings at which the Scriptures were publicly expounded—all are indications of a shift to a more biblically based religion which would ultimately manifest itself in separation from the Church of England, the early emergence of Baptist congregations, and the adoption of controverted rites and practices, including observance of the Saturday Sabbath. The establishment of a Separatist church at Gainsborough in 1606, under John Smyth and Thomas Helwys,[16] both soon to adopt believers' baptism, the formation of a General Baptist congregation at Lincoln c.1626,[17] one of the earliest Baptist churches in the country, and John Cotton's departure from Boston for Massachusetts in 1633, 'with a considerable number of his Lincolnshire congregation',[18] are all further signs of a developing preference for biblical norms in pre-Commonwealth Lincolnshire. Given a similar pattern of events in other counties where Sabbatarianism established a foothold, it might even be said that Seventh-day observance was an inevitable corollary to the Lincolnshire quest.

At what point the Boston Sabbatarians first appeared as a separate congregation is not known. Several Baptist churches had been formed in Lincolnshire well before 1650. The absence of any

---

[13] Cf. Cross, *Church and People*, 78.

[14] Cf. Dickens, *The English Reformation*, 272–3.

[15] P. Collinson, *The Elizabethan Puritan Movement* (1967), 174. Collinson provides a helpful synopsis of the development of 'prophesyings' in the Continental Reformed tradition, explaining that 'At the one extreme, the prophesying was a learned expository labour, conducted in Latin among scholars and students; at the other, it could be a lively occasion for exercising the liberty of the children of God', and noting that 'it was subsequently a regular part of the worship of some English separatists', 169–70.   [16] Cf. Cross, *Church and People*, 167.

[17] White, *English Baptists*, 29.   [18] Cross, *Church and People*, 194.

reference to Sabbatarians or Sabbatarianism in the relevant diocesan records for the period 1660–90 cannot be taken as evidence
that they did not then exist. The same records make only occasional
mention of Anabaptists, yet Baptist churches had been formed at
Boston itself in 1635, at Bourne in 1645 and at Spalding in 1646.[19]
Thomas Grantham, who in 1667 wrote against the Seventh-day
Sabbath, had been elder at Bourne by the time he was 22.[20] At
Bourne, and also at nearby Hacconby, foot-washing and abstinence
from blood and things strangled were advocated as gospel requirements.[21] They were practices not infrequently associated with
Seventh-day observance. Mill Yard had entertained foot-washing at
one point,[22] and Henri Misson had specifically noted abstinence
from blood as one of the distinguishing characteristics of English
Sabbatarianism *c.*1690.[23] Edward Stennett, who was so influential in
consolidating the Seventh-day movement in London, Berkshire, and
Oxfordshire, and who had publicly adopted the seventh day by
1658, was descended from a Lincolnshire family.[24] Robert Shalder,
a Sabbatarian from Croft, only fifteen miles from Boston, whom
Benedict and Neal both refer to, suffered much for his faith during
the 1660s and died shortly after being released from prison in 1666.[25]
Early in 1667, a Mr Cocks,[26] who lived at Raby Castle in Durham,
as steward to Frances, Lady Vane, and who was associated there

---

[19] W. Elliott, 'Notes on the Baptists' in *Local Historian*, 34, 35 (July 1942), The
Lindsey Local History Society, p. 8, LAO, 2, Brace 4. During the 1630s fourteen
Anabaptists and Brownists had been reported at Gainsborough, and in 1641 a simi-
lar number of Anabaptists were listed at Lincoln. Baptists, Quakers, Levellers,
Manifestarians, *et al.* are recorded as having appeared in Lincolnshire during the
1640s. By 1664, Quakers, Anabaptists 'and other sectaries' were concentrated in the
Isle of Axholme and 'the Marish', C. Holmes, *Seventeenth-Century Lincolnshire*
(Lincoln, 1980), 41, 198–9, 45.

[20] Elliott, 'Notes on the Baptists', 8; Grantham, *The Seventh-Day Sabbath Ceased
as Ceremonial.* In *Christianismus Primitivus* (1678), Grantham again set forth 'the
reasons why the Christian Church is not bound to the observation of the Seventh-
days [sic] Sabbath', 156.   [21] Elliott, 'Notes on the Baptists', 8.

[22] Above, 89.   [23] Ozell (tr.), *Misson's Memoirs*, 235.

[24] Payne, *The Baptists of Berkshire*, 47.

[25] *SDBEA* 1: 91; David Benedict, *A General History of the Baptist Denomination*
(Boston, Mass., 1813), ii. 417; D. Neal, *The History of the Puritans* (1822), v. 171.

[26] John Cocks, according to Margaret S. Child, 'Prelude to Revolution: The Structure of Politics in County Durham, 1678–88' (unpublished Ph.D. thesis, University
of Maryland, 1972), 298. Child believes that Cocks may have had Quaker sympathies, since several of those meeting at Raby in the late 1660s were Quakers. However, correspondence between William Haggett and Sir Philip Musgrave refers to a
letter from Cocks and 'two other chiefs of the Anabaptists', PRO, SP 263/54/1.

with Pooley and Foxey in their efforts to obtain further recruits for the Palatinate settlement, was reported to be in Lincolnshire en route south to visit Lady Vane at her residence in Kent.[27] The Vanes also owned a residence at Belleau in Lincolnshire, which, according to one source, Sir Henry, in his later years, 'continued to prefer'.[28] It may, or may not, be significant that Robert Cornthwaite spent a year at Boston in charge of a Baptist congregation just before being called to Mill Yard in 1725.[29] The evidence, admittedly, is circumstantial, but suggests none the less that a Seventh-day Baptist presence could well have appeared relatively early at Boston, deriving in part from an awareness of Sabbatarian principles which had been present in local religious consciousness for several generations. The last that is heard formally of Sabbatarianism in the county was in 1722, when John Dent 'of Lincolnshire' was recommended for baptism at Mill Yard.[30]

A somewhat similar picture emerges for Nottinghamshire, where clear evidence for a Sabbatarian presence is only marginally stronger than it is for Lincolnshire. Apart from the significant move to separation at Scrooby and other locations in the county *c.*1606–7 under William Brewster and John Robinson, Nottinghamshire in general seems to have offered moderate support for Puritan initiatives for reform. During the years of suppression following the post-Restoration legislation against Dissent, several sizeable conventicles were reported in and around Nottingham itself,[31] but there appears to be only one instance in which reference is made to Sabbatarianism. In 1669, one of seven conventicles delated to the authorities in the city was said to consist of 'Jewes . . . but few', whose teacher had been 'silenced for Nonconformity'.[32] No names were recorded. Two years earlier, in February 1667, it had been reported

---

[27] PRO, SP 29/190/104. On Lady Vane's husband, Sir Henry Vane the younger, who had received Raby Castle from his father Sir Henry Vane the elder in 1640, and who was executed in 1662, see John Willcock, *The Life of Sir Henry Vane the Younger* (1913); F.J.C. Hearnshaw, *The Life of Sir Henry Vane the Younger, Puritan Idealist*, ([1910]); V.A. Rowe, *Sir Henry Vane the Younger* (1970) and *BDBR* iii. 262–5. Lady Vane subsequently lived near Shipbourne in Kent, where both she and her husband were buried.

[28] Hearnshaw, *Life of Sir Henry Vane the Younger* 54. It was reported in 1656 that efforts had been made to secure Vane's nomination for Parliament, first for Boston, and then for the county of Lincolnshire: ibid. 60.

[29] *PDM* 6: 2.   [30] MYM 241.

[31] e.g. YDR, Nottingham Archdeaconry, V1662–3, CB1; V1674, CB 166; Misc. 258.

[32] *OR* i. 164.

that the 'two seducing spirits', Christopher Pooley and John Foxey, were in Nottingham at the homes of Joseph Banfeather, near the Bridge, and Mr Alsoph, at Gravell Lane, in Ratcliffe,[33] 'pretending to know if any of their judgement (i.e. Sabbatarians) would go into the Palatinate'.[34] It is likely, though unconfirmed, that this was not the only visit to Nottingham either by Tillam or his representatives. Banfeather and Alsoph presumably were members of the decimated congregation of 'Jewes' reported in 1669, which in turn was presumably the antecedent of the Sabbatarian 'remnant' said to have been in existence at Nottingham in 1690.[35]

The presence of Tillam's agents in the northern counties between 1666 and 1668 gives some indication of the relative strength of the Seventh-day movement, and as such should not be underestimated. One report has suggested that as many as 200 Sabbath-keeping families may have emigrated to the Palatinate under the influence of Tillam and his associates.[36] While it is not known just how many of Tillam's disciples actually followed him to the Continent, or how many of these came from the North, it may be assumed that these protracted recruiting itineraries, which extended from Suffolk to Durham via Lincolnshire, Nottinghamshire, and Yorkshire, would not have been undertaken by Pooley and Foxey had there not been at least a moderate chance of success. The Nottingham congregation was in all probability weakened on account of these overtures, particularly since it was stated that the Palsgrave had assigned to would-be immigrants to the Palatinate 'a pleasant part of the country to live in', as well as other 'great favours', and that it was the duty of true saints to leave England as quickly as possible on account of the 'great' sins of that kingdom, and the impending judgements of God.[37] Even so, the 1690 remnant 'in the city of Nottingham and thereabouts'[38] indicates that in its heyday the Nottingham congregation probably included adherents from adjacent country areas, as well as from within the city itself. In this respect, it may be noted that Mr Alsoph's residence in Ratcliffe was less than a mile from Nottinghamshire's borders with Derbyshire and Leicestershire.[39]

For whatever reasons, the Lincolnshire and Nottinghamshire

---

[33] Ratcliffe on Soar, or, possibly, Radcliffe on Trent.
[34] PRO, SP 29/190/104.   [35] *BQ* 14: 165.   [36] PRO, SP 29/41/1, 2.
[37] PRO, SP 29/181/116.   [38] *BQ* 14: 165.
[39] If the reference to 'Ratcliffe' was, in fact, to Ratcliffe on Soar.

Sabbatarians, whose existence cannot for a moment be doubted, did not find their way into the contemporary records. They remain among the least documented groups in the country, with few names and little tangible history for posterity to consider. They are, in fact, classic examples of that quietistic passivity which Henri Misson had observed in his contacts with English Sabbatarianism c.1690; they made 'but little noise'[40] and therefore little impact. Indeed, it might even be argued that the survival of the Seventh-day Men in both counties had been impeded, if not rendered impossible, by their failure to create a recognizable identity in the minds of either the authorities or the common people. Certainly, in other places the attention of the authorities, however unwelcome, usually indicated a vigorous Sabbatarian community.

YORKSHIRE

Two identifiable names have survived from the city of York, which point to a Sabbatarian presence having prevailed there and in adjoining localities for much of the seventeenth century. Philip Tandy (or Tanny), 'a great sectary . . . in the North parts and at York',[41] was known there during the 1640s and 1650s, before moving to Northern Ireland. And John Cox, the erstwhile Quaker, who in 1702 was accused by the General Baptists of Lincolnshire[42] of preaching 'Judaism' at York, represented Yorkshire General Baptists at the General Assembly in 1692 and was a subject of discussion at the Assembly in 1697.[43] Tandy had also been aware of the charge of Judaizing, and had himself written to an adversary in York in 1646 regarding his convictions, 'after the way you call Judaism, worship I the God of my fathers'.[44] Both Tandy and Cox, although for different reasons, appear to have been more on the fringes of the Sabbatarian movement than at its heart. There is some evidence to indicate that in later years Tandy may have abandoned the seventh day in favour of the more orthodox observance of Sunday,[45]

---

[40] Ozell (tr.), *Misson's Memoirs*, 235.
[41] Edwards, *The third Part of Gangraena*, 54.   [42] *MGA* i. 74.
[43] Ibid. 36, 52.   [44] Edwards, *The third Part of Gangraena*, 58.
[45] In 1658 he appears as the incumbent (Presbyterian) at Lisburn, Co. Antrim, St J.D. Seymour, *The Puritans in Ireland, 1647–1661* (Oxford, 1921), 171. A Francis Tandy, 'son of Philip, clerk, deceased, of Lisburn, Ulster', was admitted to Magdalene College, Cambridge, in 1670: *Alumni Cantabrigienses*, i. 4, 199. On the Sabbatarian movement in Northern Ireland, see Appendix I.

and Cox and his followers at York may have provided some of the evidence for the later assertions that Traskites had persisted as a distinct sect until well into the eighteenth century.[46]

Tandy is said to have been a clergyman in the established Church before becoming a Baptist and then a Sabbatarian.[47] He had proceeded BA from Gloucester Hall, Oxford, in 1632,[48] a fact which is somewhat difficult to reconcile with the view that he had begun to promulgate Sabbatarian doctrine in York *c.*1628.[49] It is unclear whether Tandy was in fellowship with the Anabaptist congregation known to have been in existence at York *c.*1646,[50] although he is mentioned elsewhere as one of the early Yorkshire Baptists.[51] Certainly by that date he had been engaged in disputations in the city over baptism and observance of the seventh day. Brook says that he was a man of 'great abilities and piety . . . remarkably zealous to promote his own views of divine truth'.[52] In the same year he had been reported to the polemicist, Thomas Edwards, as labouring in York as a Sabbatarian Baptist.[53] Edwards quotes at some length from correspondence between Tandy and an unknown York clergyman, in which Tandy argued that believers' baptism and the Seventh-day Sabbath were two apostolic truths.[54] The eschatological dimension so evident in the early Sabbatarian movement is clearly visible in Tandy, who on the basis of fulfilled prophecies in the book of Revelation, strongly believed in Christ's imminent second advent.[55] It was, indeed, just such a conviction of impending judgement that spurred him on to pursue a life of obedience. 'I am

---

[46] See Whiting, *Studies in English Puritanism*, 316, and above, Ch. 2.

[47] *SR* 1/2: 5; Brook, *Lives of the Puritans*, iii. 30. Tandy is first heard of in Yorkshire at Otley in 1642, where he is recorded as having preached on Easter Sunday: W.J. Sheils letter to author, 1 June 1984. Dr Sheils states that this information comes from a volume of notes on sermons preached in and around Otley in the spring and summer of 1642 'by clergy who were, for the most part, of known Puritan persuasion'.

[48] *Alumni Oxonienses*, iv (1892), 1455.   [49] *SR* 32/19: 2.

[50] *VCH* Yorks., The City of York, 407.

[51] C.E. Shipley (ed.), *The Baptists of Yorkshire* (1912), p. xvii.

[52] Brook, *Lives of the Puritans*, iii. 30.

[53] Edwards, *The third Part of Gangraena*, 54–9. Sarah Pierce and Dorothy Pierce from 'Yorkshire' were listed as transient members of the More–Chamberlen church which met in Lothbury Square, London, in the early 1650s: Bodl. MS Rawl. D. 828. If, as is suggested elsewhere (Appendix III), this congregation was by then Seventh-day, the acceptance of members from Yorkshire might indicate that Tandy's followers in the York area in the late 1640s and early 1650s were insufficient to form a congregation of their own.   [54] Edwards, *The third Part of Gangraena*, 56.

[55] Ibid. 55.

confident', he wrote in 1646, 'that within these very few years I shall see Him whom my soul loveth, and much will it go to my heart, if I oppose a truth or maintain an error.'[56] The mystery of Antichrist 'sitting in the Temple of God as God' was proof of the approaching end, and sufficient reason to 'lay aside tradition, custom, and the reputation of learning' in the effort to render an acceptable 'account' at the coming day of the Lord.[57]

Tandy is not heard of again until 1655, when he published his only known work, *Christ Knocking at the Door*, the text of a sermon 'intended to be preached at Paul's Cross' in April of the preceding year. The title-page of this piece explains that the sermon had not been delivered by Tandy at the time appointed, 'by reason of a sudden obstruction of that liberty which was promised him'.[58] There are obvious inferences here regarding Tandy's orthodoxy and acceptability, even in the generous atmosphere of Commonwealth times. Perhaps the authorities were apprehensive of what Tandy might say in the light of developing eschatological hopes and growing convictions regarding the seventh day currently being disseminated in the capital. Tandy dedicated the sermon, albeit in vain, to Cromwell, with the plea that he was 'no sower of sedition', and lamenting that he had not appeared in a pulpit for nine years.[59] The implications of this latter statement are somewhat obscure, unless it was a tacit complaint that he had been excluded from any kind of preferment or recognition on account of his perceived heterodoxy.

The sermon itself rather belies any fears which the authorities may have held with regard to Tandy's intentions, as it does the charge of Judaizing laid against him. It was an evangelical message in the true Puritan tradition, was based on Revelation 3: 20,[60] made no reference to the Sabbath or any other controverted point of doctrine, and confirms the conclusion that the Sabbatarian Baptists were essentially in the mainstream of Protestant soteriological orthodoxy. Given the tensions of the early to mid-1650s, and the hopes and fears of the nascent Sabbatarian movement, it may well have been published precisely to substantiate this very point.

---

[56] Ibid.   [57] Ibid. 55–6.

[58] Philip Tandy, *Christ Knocking at the Door* (1655), title-page.

[59] Ibid. sig. A3^v.

[60] 'Behold, I stand at the door, and knock: if any man hear my voice, and open the door, I will come in to him, and will sup with him, and he with me,' Rev. 3: 20, AV.

By 1658 Tandy had moved back to Northern Ireland, leaving the Seventh-day cause in Yorkshire without known leadership for thirty years or more. It is more likely to have survived during this period than to have reappeared as a new strand of Baptist belief under the ministrations of John Cox in the 1690s. Indeed, there are clear indications of such a survival. In 1661, John Belcher, by then a leading Sabbatarian spokesman, itinerated in Yorkshire and Durham, amongst other northern counties, ostensibly to keep alive the Fifth Monarchy interest.[61] It is highly probable that he visited York, and any other Sabbatarian cells in the county, and highly probable that his contacts there and elsewhere in the North included fellow Sabbatarians who, as has been noted in several instances, were predisposed to millenarianism and kindred eschatological hopes. Richard Goodgroom, who in 1671 was arrested in London as 'a dangerous person', in company with several other Sabbatarian Fifth Monarchy Men, had been imprisoned at Hull between 1660 and 1667.[62] John Foxey and Christopher Pooley also visited Yorkshire in 1666–7 in the interests of the Palatinate scheme of Thomas Tillam,[63] who himself had fled 'to the North parts' in 1660 soon after the Restoration.[64] Clearly, Tillam and his associates had friends in Yorkshire and elsewhere in the North throughout the 1660s, who shared both their eschatology and their Sabbatarianism.

While the Tillam/Pooley/Foxey visits of the 1660s are likely to have drawn off some followers from the Nottinghamshire, Yorkshire, and Durham Sabbatarian congregations, it is also likely that some resisted the invitation to emigrate, not sufficiently convinced to leave all for an uncertain future in a foreign land. Whether or not this was the case is now largely a matter for conjecture. The records for York for the 1670s and much of the 1680s, and for the county in general, are silent in respect of Sabbatarian activity. It is not until 1689 that hints of Sabbatarianism are found again, now in the writings of John Cox, then a Quaker, but soon to become a Baptist.

Cox, formerly 'a minister' from Holderness, first appears at York in 1682, where at a Quaker quarterly meeting he read a paper on

---

[61] See *FMM* 207. The Fifth Monarchy Men were reported to be 'strongly at work in Yorkshire and Durham' in 1661: *CSPD* 1661–2, 161.

[62] PRO, SP 29/236/207; *FMM* 250; Whitley, 'Men of the Seventh Day', 8/5.

[63] PRO, SP 29/181/116; 29/190/104.   [64] PRO, SP 29/4/18.

remarriage 'in a boisterous kind of an uncomely manner'.[65] It was, perhaps, this lack of decorum as well as doubts over his doctrinal stance, which later made the Baptists wary of him.[66] In 1684 Cox led a group away from the main Quaker meeting at York on the grounds that some practices, at least in the York meeting, were 'contrary to their [Quaker] primitive practices and the Holy Scriptures', and that the York Quakers had 'gone into Apostasy and the like'.[67] The direction in which Cox appeared to be going by this secession was confirmed in 1689 with the publication of his *Articles of Christian Faith*. It becomes clear that during the intervening five years Cox had materially retreated from standard Quaker belief, and now argued that all points of faith and life were to be tried 'by the Holy Scriptures' to determine whether they were 'conformable to the doctrine and precepts of our Lord Jesus Christ, the Prophets, the Apostles and evangelists of the true church of God'.[68] The fourth article of Cox's confession, 'Of the Sacred Scriptures', postulated the totality of the biblical revelation as the norm for Christian belief and practice, with particular emphasis on the known commandments of God:

I believe the Holy Scriptures of the Old and New Testaments, called the Bible, were written by inspiration for our learning by the Holy Ghost, and answers to His own testimony in all mens hearts, and are a Rule to walk by, especially the Commandments and Doctrines and all that which they teach for Salvation I do believe.[69]

While there is no specific mention of the Sabbath here, or in the Articles as a whole, Cox goes on to argue that all tradition 'not according to Scriptures' is unacceptable and constitutes 'the mark

---

[65] W.C. Braithwaite, *The Second Period of Quakerism* (1919), 476.

[66] Ibid. 478. Steven Crisp had 'never taken him for a religious man' and had counselled him 'thirty years before, to sell his horse and boots and follow his employ', ibid.

[67] *Truth Exalted and the Peaceable Fellowship and Exercise thereof Vindicated Against the Abusive Clamours of a Dividing False Spirit* (1685), 12. Edward Nightingale, Thomas Dennison, and John Winnard were among those who seceded with Cox: George Myers, *A Serious Examination of a Pretended Answer to a Paper of Judgement past at Yorke, with a Reply thereto* (1686), 3. Cox also objected to two meetings on the Lord's day: Braithwaite, *Second Period of Quakerism*, 476.

[68] John Cox, *Articles of Christian Faith Believed and Written by me, John Cox, of York* (1689), sig. A2ʳ. Other works by Cox included *A General Epistle to the Christian Churches* (1683); *An Epistle to all the Lord's People* ([1685]); *To All that Believe in God* ([1687]).　　　　[69] Cox, *Articles of Christian Faith*, 7.

of the Beast'.[70] It was language that would have been readily understood and endorsed by most Sabbatarians of the time.[71]

Cox formally became a Baptist in London in 1691,[72] but from the
beginning seems to have run into difficulty with his newly espoused
brethren. Braithwaite says that the London Baptists were shy of him
and advised him to gather a church in his home locality, where he
was known.[73] Cox appears to have taken this advice, for in 1692 he
represented Yorkshire General Baptists at the General Assembly in
Goodman's Fields. Even so, his credentials were not wholly to the
liking of the assembled brethren, for they commissioned William
Reeve and William Pardoe to evangelize Yorkshire, 'and to set those
in order that are there', only asking Cox to assist them.[74] Five years
later, he requested the General Assembly to reconsider the continuing evangelization of Yorkshire, apparently on the grounds that his
authority in the churches should now be recognized. The brethren,
however, were not disposed to change their minds regarding his
suitability, and concluded that they could not at present 'orderly
depute him' to be one of their 'public ministers'.[75] Again, in 1700,
the General Assembly decided that Cox could not be considered as
a Messenger among the churches until he was recommended by
letter from a recognized Association.[76] Such recognition was never
forthcoming.

There is no explicit reason in the General Assembly records, until
1702, for this persistent reluctance to accredit John Cox as a General Baptist spokesman. In that year, Joseph Hook, messenger of
the Lincolnshire Association, reported to the Assembly in London
regarding the 'corrupt principles and insinuating practices of John
Cox of York', specifically charging that he was 'endeavouring to
leaven the churches with Judaism'.[77] The churches involved were
not named, but it seems clear enough that Cox's influence by now

[70] Ibid. 16.

[71] Cf. Tillam, *Seventh-Day Sabbath*, 1. Even in 1741 Edward Elwall confessed that
it was his intention to 'lead men out of Babylon, and bring them back to Christianity
in its native purity, knowing full well how far the generality of professors have
deviated from it, and do now shamefully wear the marks of the Beast, the skirts and
rags of the scarlet whore, and even the most evident badges of Antichrist', *A
Declaration Against all the Kings and Temporal Powers under Heaven* (4th edn.
1741), 91. (The 1st edition of 1732 bore the title *A Declaration Against George, King
of Great Britain and Ireland ... and against Lewis, King of France, and Philip,
King of Spain*.)   [72] Braithwaite, *Second Period of Quakerism*, 478.

[73] Ibid.   [74] *MGA* i. 36.   [75] Ibid. 52.

[76] Ibid. 66.   [77] Ibid. 74.

extended beyond York itself. As a result of this forthright denunciation, all the churches represented at the Assembly were admonished not to 'receive the said John Cox into their assemblies, nor entertain him as a Christian until that time as he shall purge himself from such errors'.[78] It was strong advice, which the Assembly is not recorded as having taken in respect of other General Baptist Sabbatarians. While Whitley concludes that Cox was 'perhaps a Seventh Day Baptist',[79] it is also possible that his 'Judaism' extended beyond observance of the seventh day, and that it included Old Testament rites and practices in the tradition of the earlier Traskites. If that was the case it would help to substantiate the claim that Traskites were known in some parts of the country until the eighteenth century. Whether or not this was so, it seems reasonably certain that advocates of the Saturday Sabbath practised their religion at York and other points in the county throughout the latter half of the seventeenth century and in the early 1700s.

DURHAM AND NORTHUMBERLAND

Sabbatarianism in Durham and Northumberland can only be documented with certainty between 1666 and 1668, in connection with the activities of John Foxey and Christopher Pooley. It is, however, likely to have been present undetected in the region at least since the late 1650s, and to have survived the sustained and zealous recruiting missions of Foxey and Pooley, the last of which is recorded as having occurred in the latter part of 1667 and early in 1668.[80] Thomas Tillam went north briefly, as has already been noted, immediately following the Restoration, presumably to avoid the authorities, who nevertheless caught up with him on his return to London in June, 1660.[81] This was three years after the publication of his *Seventh-Day Sabbath Sought out and celebrated*, four years after he had assumed pastoral responsibility for the Sabbatarian church at Colchester, and nearly five years since his conversion to Seventh-day doctrine. It is inconceivable that his journey north in the early summer of 1660 would not have been to seek the support and encouragement of fellow Sabbatarians. Indeed, it is likely that the scheme to establish a Sabbatarian community on the Continent was by this time forming in Tillam's mind, and his contacts with

[78] Ibid.   [79] Ibid.   [80] PRO, SP 29/232/10.   [81] PRO, SP 29/4/18.

Sabbatarians in 'the North parts' would have been of material assistance in determining the feasibility of the project. Within months of returning to London, and while still in gaol, Tillam, 'a prisoner of hope', produced his *Temple of Lively Stones*, the most thorough exposition of Sabbatarian theology worked out to its logical conclusion, in which the harassed saints eventually triumph as the eschatological remnant worthy to inherit the kingdom.[82] Without doubt, the *Temple of Lively Stones* set forth the theological basis of the Palatinate scheme, a plan which by then Tillam was convinced would attract support from the north, as well as from Sabbatarian communities in East Anglia. It is equally inconceivable that all observance of the seventh day in these north-eastern counties came to an abrupt end in 1668, following the last known visit of Foxey and Pooley, even though there is no extant trace of later Sabbatarianism in either Durham or Northumberland, as there is for Lincolnshire, Nottinghamshire, and Yorkshire.

The surviving records of early Nonconformity in the region, both before 1666 and after 1668, scant though they are, confirm the impression that the climate was congenial for the emergence and growth of Seventh-day doctrine. The relevant Durham diocesan visitation records which have survived, while not mentioning Sabbatarians *per se*, make frequent reference to Anabaptists, Quakers, Nonconformists, and 'Schismaticks'.[83] Despite the confusion over identity which undoubtedly existed in these formative years, with Presbyterians often being taken for Independents, and Independents for Baptists, the emergence of a vigorous Baptist community in the north-east during the Commonwealth, with centres at Newcastle, Hexham, and Muggleswick, is well established. The appeal of the Quaker gospel in the north of England, described by one authority as 'the crucial region of early Quakerism',[84] was particularly evident in the south and east of county Durham, and in neighbouring areas of Yorkshire.[85] The *Victoria County History* mentions Baptists and Quakers in Durham during the 1650s, and cautiously notes 'in the religious confusion of the period, other sectaries may well have maintained themselves'.[86] It is only surprising, perhaps, that the Sabbatarian movement which came most clearly into the

[82] Tillam, *The Temple of Lively Stones*, 2–4.
[83] DDR, Visitation Records, *passim.*
[84] Barbour, *The Quakers in Puritan England*, 41.
[85] Ibid., fig. 2, facing p. 43.   [86] *VCH* Durham, ii. 54–5.

light in this region in the late 1660s appears to have been centred around Raby Castle, former home of Sir Henry Vane the younger, a 'religious enthusiast', whose tolerance of a wide spectrum of views was probably one reason for both his influence and his eventual downfall.[87] In 1662, shortly after Vane's execution, the bishop of Durham was reported to have been apprehensive of activities at Raby, since it was rumoured that sectaries in the area were 'loyal to the late Sir Henry Vane'.[88] Indeed, the meetings which were held there throughout the 1660s consisted variously of Quakers, or Quakers and Baptists, or of both Quakers and Baptists with Sabbatarians. The Durham and Northumberland Sabbatarians, usually only vaguely discernible through the shadows, are most likely to have emerged from the Baptist tradition. No Quaker Sabbatarians are known anywhere in the country, and it is highly unlikely that there were any.

Thomas Tillam had founded the Baptist church at Hexham in 1652, and remained there as its leader until 1655.[89] Contrary to earlier opinion, there is no trace whatsoever of Sabbatarianism at Hexham during Tillam's ministry, or thereafter.[90] In 1653, a group of Hexham

[87] e.g. PRO, SP 29/263/54:I, SP 29/232/10. Henry Vane has more recently been described as 'an ardent millenarian' who believed that his age 'stood on the brink of the Age of the Spirit, when through a glorious outpouring of the Holy Ghost, the church and indeed all creation, would be "restored to its primitive purity" and Christ would rule with his saints for a thousand years'; *BDBR* iii. 263. Vane's eschatology, and its implications, are set out in *The Retired Mans Meditations, or the Mysterie and Power of Godliness* (1655), *An Epistle General, to the Mystical Body of Christ on Earth, the Church Universal in Babylon* (1662), and *The Face of the Times* (1662). Vane's concern for 'the scattered seed and sheep of Christ, the true Israel by faith', and his desire to 'awaken up the present generation of God's people . . . to a more diligent and curious observation of the present signs of the new approaching day of the Lord, that they may be more carefully minding and doing what most concerns them by way of preparation', undoubtedly contributed to his toleration of radical views, and to the hopes placed in him by those who shared such views, and, after his death, in Raby Castle.

[88] Greaves, *Deliver us from Evil*, 106.

[89] Hexham church book, AL, MS 2/2/9, fo. 1; David Douglas, *History of the Baptist Churches in the North of England from the Year 1648 to 1845* (1846), 11. Tillam arrived in Hexham to begin his ministry on 27 Dec. 1651. On early Baptist history in the north-east, see also S.L. Copson, *Association Life of the Particular Baptists of Northern England, 1699–1732* (1991), who says that Tillam left Hexham for Colchester by May 1655: p. 14.

[90] *SO* 1/12 (1907), 93 lists a Sabbatarian church at Hexham *c.*1653. *SDBEA* 1: 49 claims that a Seventh-day Baptist church 'certainly' existed at Hexham *c.*1652, becoming extinct by 1715. For the reasons contrary, see Appendix II. Tillam wrote to the church at Hexham in 1654 of his fellowship with Peter Chamberlen, 'in whose sweet society I enjoyed ye blessing of my God by ye laying on of hands', AL, MS

Baptists, led by Tillam, were involved in a public disputation over baptism at Muggleswick, which resulted in the baptism of six persons. Subsequently, in 1656, as the result of an amicable secession from Hexham, a Baptist congregation was established at Muggleswick, which soon became one of the most important centres of Baptist activity in the region.[91] By 1665, Henry Blackett of Witton-le-Wear, 'a great Anabaptist', and soon to be associated with Foxey and Pooley at Raby Castle and its vicinity, had become co-pastor at Muggleswick, and the mainstay of the church at Hexham.[92] The Baptist cause had also been planted in the north-east of the county, in the South Shields–Sunderland–Washington area. In its early years, at least, Baptist work here was probably linked with the endeavours of Paul Hobson and Thomas Gower at Newcastle.[93] The diocesan records for these and other areas in Durham and for neighbouring parts of Northumberland throughout the 1660s provide evidence of the diffusion of Baptist principles and of the evolution of thought taking place in the minds of some Baptists and other radicals in the area.

Thus, at Durham in 1662, a man and his wife were presented for working on the Lord's day and for commanding their servants to do the same.[94] At Washington, in 1665, Henry Hallyday was reported for not bringing a child for baptism, and for calling young people together to dance on the Lord's day.[95] At Muggleswick in the same year, and at Ovingham, Slayley, and Shotley in Northumberland, there were several presentations of Anabaptists,[96] and in Newcastle, George and John Ellison were presented for winnowing corn on Sunday and for maintaining that they might as well plough on that day as on any other.[97] In 1669 it was reported from Witton-le-Wear to the Bishop of Durham that Henry Blackett 'hath entertained diverse and several times at his own house at private conventicles', and between 1665 and 1669 several individuals from parishes in the vicinity of Witton-le-Wear were presented as Anabaptists.[98] In

---

2/2/9. This probably explains the 'fourth principle' adopted by Tillam during his Hexham years. It was, in any case, prior to his acceptance of the Seventh-day Sabbath.

[91] Douglas, *History*, 32; DRO, B/Ham/1; AL, MS 2/2/9; Child, 'Prelude to Revolution', 294.

[92] PRO, SP 29/232/10; INB, *TBHS*, 7: 188. The Northern Baptist Association was founded in Blackett's house in 1699.   [93] Douglas, *History*, 6–7.

[94] DWL, GLT MS 89/12.   [95] Ibid.   [96] Ibid.

[97] DDR, II/3, fo. 1ʳ.   [98] DDR, Loose Papers 29; II/3, fos. 19ʳ, 20ʳ.

1669 it was reported from Stanhope that numerous conventicles had been held throughout the forest of Weardale over the preceding two or three years, attended by many persons from Cumberland and Northumberland.[99] A nineteenth-century historian maintained that during the 1660s conventicles in the house of John Ward at Muggleswick had attracted people from as far away as South Shields, and Sunderland, and from Eddesbridge, Crankley, Birchenfields, Edmondbyers, and Birchenhaugh.[100] In the episcopal returns for 1669, fifty-two Anabaptists and 'Freewillers' were reported at South Shields.[101] From the evidence provided in earlier chapters for the development of Sabbatarianism at other locations in the country similarities can be seen between many of these presentments and those in connection with which a Sabbatarian presence is explicitly mentioned. It would seem perfectly clear that 'the many . . . out of Northumberland', and from Muggleswick and Cleadon 'and other neighbouring parts', who met at Henry Blackett's house in company with Foxey and Pooley in 1667[102] were following a well-established pattern.

There are two documents in particular which elucidate the nature and extent of Northumberland–Durham Sabbatarianism. The first is a letter written in December 1666 from Egglestone, on the Durham–Yorkshire border, by Christopher Sanderson to Joseph Williamson, purporting to convey news 'from among Anabaptists and Fifth Monarchy Men', but which in fact was more a report on the activities of Foxey and Pooley.[103] The authorities at the time were still wary of any clandestine activity in the north which reasonably, or even unreasonably, could be construed as tending to unrest or rebellion. Discontent at the failure of the government to provide greater freedom in matters of religion was still strong in the north, as were reminders of the Farnley Wood plot of 1663 and other stirrings,[104] and although it is extremely doubtful that

---

[99] Ibid.

[100] William Fordyce, *The History and Antiquities of the County Palatine of Durham*, ii (Newcastle, 1857), 206–8, citing a deposition by John Ellerington of Blanchland.   [101] Cited in Child, 'Prelude to Revolution', 287.

[102] PRO, SP 29/232/10.   [103] Ibid.

[104] G.F. Nuttall suggests that the Farnley Wood plot, known also as the Yorkshire plot, was prompted by the desire 'to gain the liberty to tender consciences promised by Charles II in the Declaration of Breda,' 'English Dissenters in the Netherlands, 1640–1689', *Nederlands Archief voor Kerkgeschiedenis*, 59/1 (1979), 46. See also Greaves, *Deliver us from Evil*, Ch. 6: 'From Derwentdale to Kaber Rigg: Risings in the North', *passim*, esp. 173–85, for the plot's Fifth Monarchist overtones.

Foxey, or Pooley, or Tillam were intent on anything but a pacifist Sabbatarian settlement in the Palatinate, they could nevertheless not avoid suspicion. Sanderson's letter confirms such fears, as it also provides valuable information regarding the Northumberland–Durham Sabbatarian movement as a whole. Of Foxey and Pooley, Sanderson wrote:

They are reported as saying that they came out of Bohemia, and were sent by their Judge or leader, one Tillam, which I believe you have heard of, into England to acquaint all of their judgement, what great favours they receive from the Palsgrave there, and what a pleasant part of the country he hath assigned them to live in, and they doubt not but in a short time (as they do report) but that they will gain him to their opinion. Ever since June last they have been ranging in several counties amongst their brethren, endeavouring by all the arguments they can use to persuade them to repair into those parts out of this kingdom, telling them that they must separate because the sins of this kingdom are so great, that our Lord will destroy it; that they hope they must be the prophets that must restore and set up the kingdom of Christ here, but that whilst they are thus dispersed abroad, as they are, they can never do anything. I send you here enclosed their covenant, which they are very timorous to give a copy but to such as subscribe it. Yet by persuasion and riding a week with them in this county he got it; they are now in Northumberland, and intend to be in this county next week at a place where several of them are to give their resolution whether they will go into the Palatinate or not. He tells me that they do assure him that these people are upon no other designs in England, this being the way they intend to go at present. These two men intend within these fourteen days to be gone out of this county into the East Riding of Yorkshire, where they have not been as yet. I desire you immediately upon receipt hereof to let me have your answer, whether or not I should . . . cause them to be apprehended.[105]

The fact that Foxey and Pooley had been visiting 'brethren' in 'several counties' for some months in an attempt to recruit Sabbath-keepers for the Palatinate settlement is the most decisive single piece of evidence indicative of widespread Sabbatarianism in the north. The extent of their travels in Durham and Northumberland points to a diffuse movement, rather than one concentrated at a few specific points. Lack of further evidence precludes extended discussion, but it may be observed that the failure of the Llanwenarth record of 1690 to include any reference to surviving Sabbatarian churches north of Nottingham and Boston,[106] may indicate that

---

[105] PRO SP 29/181/116.   [106] *BQ* 14: 165.

Sabbatarians in Northumberland and Durham, and perhaps in Yorkshire as well, practised their religion as participants in mixed-communion churches, or in isolation, rather than in congregational community. It may also indicate, of course, that northern Sabbatarians were rather more careful to keep concealed the identity of any congregations which may have formed in these difficult years. The lack of precision in distinguishing between Anabaptists, Sabbatarians, Fifth Monarchy Men, and other 'sectaries', which appears to have been particularly marked in the north, may have made such concealment a practical necessity.[107]

The second document, originating probably no later than 1665,[108] is the covenant referred to by Sanderson, a copy of which he had managed to obtain for Williamson's information. It is an interesting and rare document, although probably of greater value in throwing light on the more extreme Pooley–Tillam Sabbatarians than it is in assessing the broader Sabbatarian movement elsewhere in England and Wales. The 'Solemne Covenant' apparently required the subscription of those willing to cast in their lot with the Tillam Sabbatarians. It is reproduced here in full, together with the caveats and clarifications added by the covenanting Sabbatarians after the document had been in use for some months:

In ye spirit & power of Christ our king we do utterly renounce all powers and rulers who are contrary to his Goverment with all their laws Courts & Customs in Church & state detesting all oathes of obedience to them or to bear arms or offices for them & do resolve in ye strength of God to cast off their Coin with all possible speed & wholly to separate from all relations who shall continue linked to AntiChristian Religion.

We do solemnly swear to ye Lord, our only Judge Lawgiver and king whom we choose for our God with our whole hearts in whose ways through grace we will walk and religiously obey all his laws, statutes, and Judgements which he hath commanded for all Israel, & particularly those first foundation truths, ye seventh day sabbath and marriage, and never give our daughters to ye sons of strangers, nor take their daughters for our wives.

We do freely & entirely devote our selves to ye Lord our God and with hands lifted up do vow to be his people, and to take hold of all opportunities

---

[107] Thus Henry Blackett was presented as an Independent in 1665, DDR, II/3, fo. 19ʳ.

[108] The covenant had been 'renewed' on the 14th of the 'first month'. The copy transcribed below is marked 'end 1666 Dec 14'.

we can to find out a place for ye Lord an habitation for ye mighty God of Jacob, where we may advance his holy throne & righteous sceptre, as a distinct people dwelling alone & not being reckoned among ye nations, but improve all our interest & abilities for conversion of ye Ancients and this Covenant we subscribe our hands to ye Lord surnameing ourselves by ye name of Israel.

We ye hand-maids and servants	We ye Ministers of our God do hereby bind ourselves to
of our Lord & king having solemnly separated from all polluted persons & things, to follow ye Lamb fully, shall faithfully endeavour to redeem others also from ye earth and from among men, witness our hands.	our soveraign lord in this Covenant breaking day to improve our uttermost power for ye destruction of Babilon by separating from yt mountain of confusion all ye precious Children of God which we testify by our hands and seals.

Upon ye renewing of this Covenant on ye 14th day of ye first month when we set ourselves consciensciously to inquire into ye scope thereof more fully than ever before & that by examining each sentence and expression that might admit seemingly of our debate, these following Conclusions were drawn up as our joint understanding concerning such causes therein and assented unto by all before their renewing hereof.

As to ye utter renouncing of all powers and rulers contrary to Christs government with their laws and customs that it is concluded:

> Utterly to renounce all powers that ever were, are, or shall be, opposers and persecutors of ye subjects of Christs kingdom.

> We do not utterly renounce such powers as are only different from Christs Government though we cannot subject to them or own communion with them.

By their Laws Courts & Customs

> We do not renounce any of Gods laws practiced by them but only those their own invention contrary to ye laws of God.

From these words The Lord our only Judge Lawgiver & King

> We conclude not to admit of any to be a Judge or ruler over us but such as are in communion with us.

By strangers in Marriage

> We understand all both natural Israelites and others that are not in ye faith of Christ Jesus.

As concerning Casting away of Coin

> We understand all such coin as hath Images & superscriptions contrary to ye word of God.

By freely and entirely devoting ourselves to ye Lord our God

> We do understand athrough [*sic*] Conformity to all that God requireth of us.

By seeking out a place an habitation for ye mighty God of Jacob

> We conclude that not withstanding we have a place found out for ye fulfilling of prophecy where his throne and sceptre is advanced yet it is our duty to be pressing forwards to that place of promise in ye holy land.

By a distinct people dwelling alone & not reckoned among ye nations

> We understand that every person is bound to keep close to all that keep this Covenant, and that is either in Community or propriety as providence shall order it according to persons freeness [*sic*].[109]

While this covenant in some respects resembled other church covenants of the time, it was sufficiently radical in tone to warrant the most thoughtful deliberation. Not every Sabbatarian would have found its claims to his liking. Sanderson's letter suggested that many of the local Sabbatarians had asked for time to consider its requirements, and the wider implications of emigration. There were, no doubt, honest Sabbath-keepers in Northumberland and Durham who did not feel able to subscribe.

Foxey and Pooley proceeded from Durham, via Yorkshire, to Nottinghamshire, where they were reported to be by February 1667.[110] By June of that year, Pooley, 'a person of dangerous principles', was in prison at Ipswich for refusing to take the oath of obedience or to acknowledge himself subject to the king.[111] It was a stance in harmony with the terms of the covenant, for presumably Charles II could have been regarded as an 'opposer' and 'persecutor' of loyal 'subjects of Christ's kingdom'. A warrant was issued for Pooley to be brought before Lord Arlington, Secretary of State, but he must have escaped or been released, for by the end of the year he was back in Durham, in company with John Foxey.[112] A letter from William Haggett to Sir Philip Musgrave, governor of Carlisle,

---

[109] PRO, SP 29/181/116. Two copies of the Solemne Covenant have survived. Both are included in the State Papers, one bearing the names of Pooley and Foxey.
[110] PRO, SP 29/190/104. [111] PRO, SP 19/207/1.
[112] *CSPD* 1667–8, 154.

2 June 1668, indicated that the writer had been with Henry Blackett and John Cocks at Raby Castle, and that Foxey and Pooley had been entertained there and at Blackett's house, and that 'many upon their view out of Northumberland' had been in attendance at these meetings.[113] Cocks and Blackett were evidently the local leaders of those attending the gatherings in Raby Castle and at Blackett's home in the latter part of 1667. Pooley and Foxey were there 'out of Germany . . . from Tillam', and Cocks was reported to be 'much against the ministry . . . making them no better than Roman Catholics, teaching for doctrine the traditions of men'.[114] Neither Cocks nor Blackett are known as Sabbatarians, but these were surely the sentiments that initially had made Puritans out of Anglicans, Baptists out of Puritans, and ultimately Sabbatarians out of Baptists. Tillam had said that the change of the Sabbath from Saturday to Sunday was the 'masterpiece of the man of sin', and that true Sabbath-keepers, 'by their entire separation, are become victors over the Beast, his image, his mark, and the number of his name'.[115] Pooley and Foxey would not have travelled so widely in Durham and Northumberland during 1667 and 1668 among 'their brethren', or have spent so much time in the Raby district amongst those of 'their view' merely to demonstrate sympathy for fellow Baptists, or Fifth Monarchists, who by then were a spent force in any case. Such language, if it means anything, indicates a brotherhood bound together by ties peculiar to a specific cause. It would be churlish to conclude that anything but the Sabbatarian interest is intended here.

What happened thereafter to Pooley and Foxey, or to the Sabbatarians of Northumberland and Durham, are largely matters for conjecture. Foxey disappears, and Pooley is not heard of again in the north. Tillam and Pooley are believed to have devoted their energies over the next six or seven years to consolidating the settlement on the Continent.[116] On account of the excesses widely reported to have developed in connection with that venture, they

---

[113] PRO, SP 29/232/10.   [114] Ibid.

[115] Tillam, *The Temple of Lively Stones*, 2, 203. This was standard doctrine amongst all Sabbatarians throughout the seventeenth and eighteenth centuries. Brabourne maintained that 'the Romish church' had 'blotted out the fourth Commandment, as they had done the second', *Discourse*, 114. Thomas Bampfield explained that 'the law to alter the seventh day to the first . . . was by the Bishops of Rome', *An Enquiry*, 135.

[116] Edward Stennett noted that those who followed Tillam were only 'a small number of those that keep the Sabbath', *The Insnared Taken*, sig. A2ᵛ.

were shortly thereafter described by a Sabbatarian contemporary as 'men of bad practices' and Tillam and, by implication, Pooley, as 'a very great blemish to the truth'.[117] Tillam is said to have died on the Continent, perhaps early in 1674,[118] and Pooley to have returned to England 'and professed repentance'.[119] It would be at least of passing interest to know whether that repentance included regret for his misguided involvement with Tillam and the havoc caused to so many churches and families in the north and east. No doubt there were many Sabbatarians in the northern counties in later years who, in retrospect, were profoundly glad to have decided against the Palatinate scheme, and who believed with even greater conviction that they were as able to 'keep the commandments of God, and the testimony of Jesus'[120] equally as well in England as on the Continent.

[117] Letter from Bell Lane to Newport, Rhode Island, 17 Sept. 1674, in SDBHS, MS 194x.6, 73, and letter of Joseph Davis to Newport, 5 Aug. 1674, ibid. 76. Developments in the Palatinate community by 1668 seem to have exceeded the bounds of the Solemn Covenant of 1666.

[118] Capp gives c.1676 as the date for Tillam's death: *FMM* 266. Joseph Davis, however, informed Sabbatarians in New England that Tillam was already dead by August of 1674: SDBHS, MS 194x.6, 76.

[119] Stennett, *The Insnared Taken*, 7.

[120] Rev. 12: 17; cf. Edward Stennett to the Sabbatarian church in Newport, SDBHS, MS 194x.6, 56.

Conclusion

I N the preceding chapters we have encountered a movement diffused widely across the country, and manifesting itself in congregational life and individual observance in many places hitherto unrecorded. It was vigorous enough to produce a literature that engaged some of the keenest minds of the time,[1] and resilient enough to survive by a century or more the rigours of an extended period of repression and harassment. Some of its more eminent ministers were in their own day and later regarded as being among the most able of Nonconformists.[2] Many of its prominent members were respected men of influence.[3] Its apologists produced persuasive and erudite works that measured favourably with those of the more recognized biblical and theological writers of the time.[4] Among its ranks were other authors whose works on wider topics contributed to the life and learning of their age.[5] Judged by some, in its early years at least, to be peripheral and transitory, it ultimately outlived most other contemporary sects and religious impulses, surviving long enough to see its most distinctive tenet firmly rooted

---

[1] Francis White, Bishop of Ely, responded to Brabourne's *Discourse* (1628) and *Defence* (1632) with *A Treatise of the Sabbath-Day; containing a Defence of the Orthodoxall Doctrine of the Church of England, against Sabbatarian Novelty* (1635). John Owen, *Exercitations* . . . (1671), Richard Baxter, *The Divine Appointment of the Lord's Day Proved* (1671), and John Wallis, *A Defence of the Christian Sabbath in answer to a Treatise of Mr Tho. Bampfield* (pt. 1, 1692, pt. 2, 1694), were all part of a considerable literature provoked by the publications of the Seventh-day Men, for which see Appendix IV, 'A Chronological Bibliography of Seventh-day Literature to 1750'.

[2] e.g. Joseph Stennett I, Joseph Stennett II, Samuel Stennett, Daniel Noble, Philip Jones. Micklewright noted that some Sabbatarian ministers 'were far more learned than were the majority of Baptist Puritan preachers', *Notes and Queries*, 191: 96.

[3] e.g. Peter Chamberlen, Mordecai Abbott, Sir William Tempest, Arthur Squibb, Thomas Bampfield.   [4] See Appendix IV.

[5] e.g. Jehudah Stennett, *A Comprehensive Grammar . . . for the Reading and Attaining the Hebrew Tongue* (1685); Peter Chamberlen, *A Voice in Rhama* (1647), which advocated state regulation of midwives; Nathaniel Bailey, *English and Latin Exercises for School Boys* (1706), which reached eighteen editions by 1798, and *An Universal Etymological English Dictionary* (1721), which reached thirty editions by 1802.

in the North American continent. From there it would be transplanted again in Europe and in many other countries around the world, eventually winning the minds of more adherents than its original protagonists could possibly have envisaged.[6] And yet by 1800, or shortly thereafter, only a remnant, a handful of small and ever-diminishing Sabbatarian congregations remained.

That the designation of Saturday as the weekly day of rest and worship was contrary to religious custom and established social practice is patently clear. It has been thus, whenever the Saturday Sabbath has been advocated, for most of the Christian era. Persistent divergence from prevailing norms has not of itself, however, been sufficient to eliminate Seventh-day observance at any period of its manifestation. Even the conclusion that Saturday Sabbatarianism in England failed 'through the inconvenience of Saturday worship when accompanied by a rigid Sabbatarian practice' is qualified by a recognition that the combination of dissonance and rigidity in practice was only partially responsible for its perceived failure.[7] Several other possible causes for the demise of the seventh day in the eighteenth century can be detected in the original sources, in the observations of contemporaries of seventeenth- and eighteenth-century Sabbatarians, and in the comments of later critics.

Such reasons may have contributed to the disappearance of a specific congregation, or collectively they may have accelerated the more gradual decline of the movement as a whole. They are perhaps no more than indications of trends and circumstances which arose as the Sabbatarian movement became more established and which tended to congregational stagnation and denominational decay. They are surveyed briefly here as factors which ultimately may have led to the virtual disappearance of a distinctive doctrine which in its heyday drew men and women from a wide cross-section of the social spectrum.

Issues which may have precipitated decline within the Sabbatarian community itself, must be seen in the context of the age as a whole. Profound changes in the way men thought about God and the

---

[6] In Dec. 1992, Seventh-day Adventists totalled approximately 7.5 million members in 187 countries. The latest estimate for Seventh Day Baptist world membership, 1991, is approximately 55,000. Both communions trace their Sabbatarian convictions back through English and European Reformation and post-Reformation Sabbatarianism to the early Church.

[7] Micklewright, *Notes and Queries*, 191: 96.

Bible had taken place between the middle of the seventeenth century when the Sabbatarian movement first began openly to flower and the middle of the eighteenth century when it began finally to wither. The effects of rationalism, deism, empiricism, and the Enlightenment were keenly felt in the Church from the later decades of the seventeenth century on. Certainly by the 1750s, if not by the end of the 1600s,[8] it was much less fashionable to believe in revelation as traditionally understood. To be sure, Nonconformity as a whole formally stood for the old truths, but even in Nonconformist circles the ripples of rationalistic thought were evident. By the end of the eighteenth century Enlightenment thinking had all but triumphed and belief in the Bible as the inspired and authoritative word of God, fundamental to Sabbatarian doctrine and practice, no longer held sway in the churches as it had 150 years earlier. When Sabbatarians spoke of the authority of Scripture and of the binding obligations of the Moral Law and the Ten Commandments, they addressed an increasingly smaller audience and with decreasing relevance. Long before 1800 Saturday Sabbatarianism had become more of an eccentricity than it had been in 1650. One observer speaks of the Sabbatarian movement possessing all 'the narrow scripturalism of seventeenth-century Puritanism', and being thereby 'unable to survive the changing intellectual climate'[9] of succeeding generations. More than they themselves may have realized the times had an adverse impact on the fortunes of the Seventh-day Men.

Of course, it is quite possible to overemphasize the effects of rationalism and the Enlightenment, profound and pervasive though they were. The decline of the Seventh-day Baptist cause, for that is essentially what the Sabbatarian movement in England and Wales had become by 1750, has to be seen in the context of a general decline in Nonconformity and Dissent during the eighteenth century, a trend recognized and lamented in most contemporary records. A twentieth-century Baptist historian designates rationalism as one of two forces which threatened the Baptist Church during the eighteenth century, 'more perilous than Roman Catholicism'.[10] However, the Baptist Church survived this difficult period, and the Methodist Church arose from it, as did the Evangelical Revival, both reactions

---

[8] John Locke, *The Reasonableness of Christianity as Delivered in the Scriptures* (1695), and John Toland, *Christianity not Mysterious* (1696), were important to the propagation of deist and rationalist views.

[9] Micklewright, *Notes and Queries* 191: 96.   [10] Brown, *English Baptists*, 5.

to the perceived formalism and lethargy of the Anglican Church as affected by Enlightenment thought. These and similar movements ensured that acceptance of the Bible as inspired revelation and sole authority in matters of faith and doctrine were to continue right down to the present time. So it is rather too facile to argue that rationalism and a new attitude to the Bible were solely, even largely, responsible for the disappearance of the Seventh-day Men. There were other factors, of varying significance, which together were probably of greater import. They may be categorized in general as pertaining to the structure of the movement, or lack of it, and to its ethos. Perhaps in the end they precipitated the disappearance of English Sabbatarianism as an identifiable movement even more than any prevailing spirit of the age, however rampant and pervasive that spirit may have been.

With structure, we come first to ministry. It has frequently been observed that the health of a congregation is related directly to the degree of edification and pastoral care it receives. This would have been thought particularly apt by Dissenting and Nonconformist congregations after the heady and tumultuous years of the Commonwealth and Restoration. Speaking specifically of Baptist congregations in Devon during the late seventeenth century, Allan Brockett remarks, 'The fortunes of the Baptists varied . . . according to the abilities and enthusiasm of their pastors.'[11] Following the Great Ejection of 1662 in the diocese of Oxford, it has been noted that Nonconformist conventicles with the largest congregations were those ministered to by eminent ejected ministers.[12] Similarly, in the same diocese shortly thereafter, lack of adequate pastoral ministry in the established Church was felt to encourage the growth of Dissent. Robert Atkyns wrote to Bishop Fell in 1683 complaining about 'hasty prayers' and short homilies 'read to us in the afternoon', which were leading to a drift of communicants to the Quakers and Anabaptists.[13]

What was true of Nonconformists in Oxfordshire and of Baptists in south Devon was equally true of Seventh-day Baptists throughout the country. Their fortunes flourished where they sat under able preachers and received the care of their souls from godly and concerned pastors. And therein lies one of the keys to the rise and

---

[11] Brockett, *Nonconformity in Exeter*, 109.
[12] Clapinson (ed.), *Bishop Fell*, p. xv.
[13] Bodl., MS Rawl. D. 399, fo. 279, cited in Clapinson (ed.), *Bishop Fell*, p. xxix.

fall of Sabbatarian congregations. Relatively few of them enjoyed such a ministry. The greater proportion of congregations identified in this study are not recorded as having an able, adequately trained pastor in charge. With a few notable exceptions, most Sabbatarian congregations were led by dedicated and zealous members of the flock who perhaps demonstrated a natural ability to lead but who lacked any formal training. It was precisely this situation which prompted Francis Bampfield to suggest that Sabbatarians show greater interest in the training of young men for ministry, and which led him to bequeath his own personal library for that purpose. Bampfield's hopes in this respect came to nothing when, after his death, representatives of the three London Sabbatarian churches declined to take the matter further.[14] If a congregation did at one time or another have such a leader, and he died or left, the chances were high that he would not be replaced. In either case the flock would eventually suffer from lack of a shepherd. Edward Stennett's Sabbatarian congregation at Wallingford is a case in point. After Stennett's death the congregation, which had flourished under his care, was ministered to by a local Presbyterian, since no Sabbatarian could be found to succeed him. Ivimey comments, 'At his death it is probable the Sabbatarian Baptist Church became extinct.'[15] In fact, it did, very soon afterwards.

The three Sabbatarian churches which survived the longest, Mill Yard, Pinners' Hall, and Natton were all served by able, dedicated, and educated men for the greater part of their existence. Ingham, Salisbury, Woodbridge, and Colchester likewise benefited from a settled ministry for many years and similarly persisted well into the eighteenth century. Under Joseph Stennett, Pinners' Hall flourished as few other Sabbatarian churches before or after. Stennett is still remembered for his learning, fluency, diligence, and moderation. When Robert Cornthwaite accepted the call to Mill Yard in 1720, the congregation, after a period of stagnation and decline, began to prosper once more. Cornthwaite, a man of great mental vigour and tenacity of argument and purpose, was correspondingly 'faithful and assiduous in the discharge of his ministerial duties'.[16] The effect was evident at Mill Yard. But the Cornthwaites and the Stennetts were exceptions rather than the rule. As the years passed, pastors

---

[14] 'Bampfield's Plan for an Educated Ministry', *TBHS*. 3.
[15] Ivimey, *History*, ii. 74.   [16] *PDM* 6: 2.

of any kind became fewer, and Sabbatarian congregations, General and Particular alike, dwindled accordingly. The thesis that an able and spiritual ministry is indispensable to the well-being of the church seems adequately demonstrated in Sabbatarian history.

The lack of such ministry was paralleled in many Sabbatarian congregations by lack of church buildings in which to meet and worship. There were even fewer churches which owned a permanent congregational home than there were those with a settled and continuous ministry. The story of Sabbatarian witness and worship is often a story of meetings held in cottages and barns, hired halls and private homes, frequently in a side street or alley or tucked away in some corner of an isolated hamlet or village. One of the last comments on the Natton church is very much to the point, 'The tiny congregation—the only meeting of the kind out of London—is one of the oddest things in the ecclesiastical world . . . the place of assemblage is a remote corner—in a farmyard.' And the question follows, 'How could there be anything but decline under the circumstances?'[17]

Mill Yard owned a place of worship from 1691 until 1885 when it was requisitioned to make way for the London, Tilbury, and Southend Railway. Natton members worshipped in their own chapel from 1746, albeit in part of a reconstructed barn in a remote hamlet, and Salisbury shared the Brown Street church with First-day Baptists for much of the eighteenth century and the early years of the nineteenth century. It may be coincidental, but Mill Yard, Natton, and Salisbury were three of the four most long-lived English Sabbatarian congregations. Ingham also built a meeting-house, but not until 1745 by which time the Sabbatarian cause in that community was in decline. The new building probably helped Ingham survive as a congregation until the present time, even though it lost its Sabbatarian identity in the process. Perhaps it was true of many Sabbatarian congregations as it was said of Pinners' Hall, 'It never plucked up heart to own a building, and flickered out.'[18] While buildings were not crucial to the success of New Testament Christianity, it seems to have been true in succeeding ages, perhaps especially among Nonconformists, that a vibrant witness has frequently emanated from a church or chapel dedicated to the glory

[17] *Birmingham Weekly Post*, 13 Apr. 1901; *SDBEA* 1: 49.
[18] *TBHS* 5: 78.

of God and known in the community as the focus of a living, dynamic congregation.

Most religious bodies that have survived for any appreciable period seem to have felt the need at some point for some kind of inter-congregational structure. The form and degree of such organiza-tion have usually been dictated by theological and ecclesiological convictions, but congregational independence to the point of iso-lation has been the exception rather than the rule. Baptists recog-nized the value of intercongregational relationships at an early date, and already by the 1640s the first steps to the eventual Associations of Baptist churches were being taken. Dr B.R. White notes 'the active concern' of Particular Baptists regarding 'unity of doctrine, polity and action among their churches, and their recognition that the tool for building that unity was "the counsel and help one of another" '.[19] The formation of the Abingdon Association in 1652 seems to have been the signal for other Baptist churches to follow suit, and within a few years similar Associations of Particular Baptists had been established around the country. The early Baptist move-ment derived much strength and mutual edification from these Associations, specifically by seeking solutions to problems which individual churches found difficult to resolve alone, financial assist-ance to needy congregations, and planning for the advancement of the work of the gospel in general.[20] The function of such Associa-tions was understood and appreciated amongst the churches and their members, and it is hard to visualize the development of the Baptist church and its expansion during the seventeenth century without them. A century later Associations were still making a sig-nificant contribution to the life and witness of Baptist churches throughout the country. Of General Baptist Associations at the time, Dr Raymond Brown remarks that they 'were not simply occasional gatherings of like-minded church representatives; they were an essential corporate expression of General Baptist inter-dependency'.[21]

The role of Associations amongst both General and Particular Baptists was known and understood by the Sabbatarian churches and their teachers well before the end of the seventeenth century. Indeed, in the early days, congregations which included Sabbat-arians or which had Sabbatarian neighbours had been present at

[19] White, *English Baptists*, 65.   [20] Ibid. 69.
[21] Brown, *English Baptists*, 60.

Association meetings in some areas.[22] Yet one of the unexplained questions relative to congregational life within the Sabbatarian movement and one of its inherent weaknesses, was its failure to associate as other Baptists had done. Francis Bampfield's unsuccessful call for an Association of all Sabbatarian churches in 1679 has already been discussed.[23] It is hard to see why this progressive suggestion from a leader of some influence in the Sabbatarian community fell on deaf ears, since it had the support of Edward Stennett, and since the arguments in favour of such a move had been convincingly set forth. Did the suggestion that churches in Holland and Rhode Island be included make the idea seem impracticable? Was the time inappropriate? Were the objectives outlined in the proposal too ambitious? Were the theological differences between General and Particular Seventh-day Baptists a stumbling block? Was the eschatological rationale for the proposed association too much emphasized? Was Bampfield's initiative, as a relative newcomer to the London Sabbatarian cause, resented? Did Bampfield's eccentricities generate caution?[24] While, with hindsight, some of these issues might have presented some difficulties, none of them seem in themselves sufficient cause to turn away from a proposition that offered so much potential for consolidation and growth. Yet the fact remains that the Sabbatarian congregations were not sufficiently motivated to associate, and what appears to have been an auspicious opportunity passed without action. The strength of a centralized organization, however loose, was never brought to the Sabbatarian movement.

Whitley believed that Calvinistic Seventh-day churches were considering an Association in 1689, and for that reason did not send representatives to the Assembly of Particular Baptist churches held in London that year.[25] Their absence might have been on other grounds, however. Whitley also noted that the Assembly addressed a number of issues, 'the most lengthy being a reasoned upholding of the Lord's Day as against the Seventh Day'.[26] Dr Raymond Brown believes that the 'deliberate rejection' of the Seventh-day churches

---

[22] White, *Association Records*, iii. 158, 191, 195.

[23] Bampfield, *A Name*, 24–5; see above, Ch. 4.

[24] His proposal, addressed to 'All the Churches of Seventh-day-Sabbath-Observers', was signed 'Shem Acher', the pseudonym he adopted after passing into 'the state of grace': ibid. 1, 25.   [25] Whitley, *British Baptists*, 176.

[26] Ibid.

from the Assembly was on account of their Sabbatarian principles.[27] If it had been known in advance that the Sabbath question was to be raised for discussion, that would have been reason enough to exclude Sabbatarians who might have wanted more than a fair hearing on the subject. It has also been suggested that the Sabbatarian churches were excluded from the Assembly by a desire to avoid radicalism—the inherent danger of Judaizing associated with Seventh-day worship, and the movement's past associations with millennialism—and on account of resistance from country churches.[28] Whatever the reality, Sabbatarians were neither represented at the 1689 Assembly nor formed an Association of their own, and as far as is known never returned to the idea again.[29] It must be concluded that they were poorer and weaker without the support and counsel, the resolution of mutual problems, the training of suitable young men for ministry, possible financial assistance, and the other benefits which association would undoubtedly have brought.

In addition to structural and organizational deficiencies, there were within the Sabbatarian movement problems of a more fundamental nature relating to its inner life, which in the end may have contributed more to its decline than matters of form, or a lack of facilities. From the standpoint of influence within a community, and thereby stability and growth, the ethos of a congregation may be thought of not only as that which it is, but also as that which it is perceived to be. Sometimes the real character of a congregation or a movement is incorrectly conveyed by the attitudes and actions of a few unrepresentative individuals. The image thus projected from time to time by over-enthusiastic or misguided zealots did little to enhance the credibility of the Sabbatarian cause at several periods in its history. Fanaticism has always been one of the hazards of any religious movement, and the Seventh-day Men did not lack for extremists. In fact, it is probable that the movement never wholly emerged from the shadow cast over it in the early years by John Traske and his followers. Traske, 'an unworthy person, and a Jew', was described by another contemporary as 'mutable and unconstant

---

[27] Brown, *English Baptists*, 34.

[28] Murdine McDonald, 'London Calvinistic Baptists, 1689–1727: Tensions within a Dissenting Community under Toleration' (D.Phil. thesis, Oxford University, 1982), 34–5.

[29] Joseph Stennett appeared at later Assemblies, and served as moderator in 1706: ibid. 139, 149.

... in his doings all his life long'.[30] Even allowing for some bias here, it was mud thrown and some of it stuck. For a long time, in some circles, Sabbatarians were collectively known as Traskites. The picture was not a good one.

Even if Sabbatarianism did overcome the Traskite image, it suffered further calumny from the aberrations of Thomas Tillam and his associates in the 1660s and 1670s. Reference has been made earlier to the damage caused by the Tillam faction, countered to some extent, but not completely, by the 1667 *Faithful Testimony Against the Teachers of Circumcision and The Legal Ceremonies.* John Cowell, as we have observed, eventually withdrew from the Sabbatarian community on account of Tillam's excesses, and the extremism of other Sabbatarians he had personally encountered.[31] There were probably others like him. The Sabbatarian who tore the New Testament from her Bible, vowing she needed only the Old Testament for her salvation, would have raised more than a few eyebrows.[32] Even the illustrious Peter Chamberlen cannot be entirely exonerated from any taint of suspicion which may have hung over the Sabbatarians of his time. Despite his undoubted accomplishments in medicine and his standing in the community as physician-in-ordinary to successive royal households, he was argumentative, overbearing, and possessed of a keen sense of his own importance. Bibliographies of the time reveal his penchant for publicity and debates on controversial issues.[33] His less celebrated enterprises include schemes to invent horseless coaches and carts, and to revise the English alphabet. There can be little doubt that he liked the limelight and generally knew how to look after himself. Despite his undoubted energy and talent, he did comparatively little to build up the Sabbatarian cause, preferring it seems to invest both in other directions.[34] In retrospect one wonders whether he was always an

---

[30] *CSPD* 1627–8, 281; Norice, *New Gospel,* 6.
[31] Cowell, *The Snare Broken,* 2–6. [32] Ibid. 12.
[33] e.g. *BB* i, s.v. Peter Chamberlain, 213.
[34] Late in life he did make a concerted effort to bring the Sabbath issue to the attention of the nation. In May and June of 1682 he wrote separately to the archbishops and bishops of the realm, to the judiciary, and to the universities of Oxford and Cambridge, urging them to give attention to the prophecies of Daniel, and to restore the times and laws which had been changed by the Little Horn. The latter was responsible for the confusion over the Sabbath, 'giving the lie to the Seventh day, and [saying] (in plain terms) that the First day is the Sabbath of the Lord'. The letters were published under the title *Englands Choice,* which was a choice between truth and falsehood; Peter Chamberlen, *Englands Choice* (1682), *passim.*

asset to his church. In the eighteenth century, Edward Elwall's Unitarian views and eccentric manner of dress did little to enhance the image of the Sabbatarian fraternity in Wolverhampton or London. John Ridley, the last pastor of Woodbridge, was known locally as 'Jew Ridley' on account of his appearance and eccentricities. The title of an eighteenth-century manuscript in the Bodleian Library may reflect a continuing degree of legalism amongst some Sabbatarians, 'The Seventh Day Man, or Restless Christian, in the Vanity of his Jewish Sabbath, and presumptuous contempt of Gospel-Rest . . .'.[35] While, again, too much should not be made of a relatively few instances of extremism in doctrine and dress, there is sufficient evidence of a fringe element in the Sabbatarian movement which inevitably coloured the perceptions of those who looked on. To many, such an image would have suggested caution.

It was fear of fanaticism and extremism, fear of appearing too isolated from the rest of the body of Christ, which perhaps pushed some Sabbatarians in the opposite direction. Compromise is an unpleasant word, but it seems to have been the case that a spirit somewhat akin to that entered Sabbatarian ranks around the turn of the century, to the detriment of many Seventh-day churches and the movement as a whole. Joseph Stennett I saw nothing wrong in preaching regularly to First-day congregations which did not share his own Sabbatarian convictions, and even in accepting the pastorate of one of them while he continued to serve the Pinners' Hall Sabbatarians. Attention has already been drawn to the effects of Stennett's divided ministry on the Pinners' Hall church. His example was followed by his son and grandson, Joseph II and Samuel. Joseph Stennett II, whose wife was the daughter of a Sabbatarian, ministered for most of his life to First-day churches,[36] while Sabbatarian congregations languished for want of pastoral care. Samuel Stennett, who succeeded his father at Little Wild Street,[37] preached regularly at Pinners' Hall and administered the Lord's Supper there, but declined a formal call to the pastorate. It would be easy enough to say that the appeal of Little Wild Street was too strong. Samuel Stennett was recognized as one of the most prominent Baptists of his age. Those who attended Little Wild Street during Stennett's ministry and who were influenced by his preaching, included Caleb

---

[35] Bodl. MS Rawl. D. 1350.
[36] At Exeter, 1721–37, and Little Wild Street, London, 1737–58.
[37] 1758–95.

Evans, later Principal of Bristol College, Joseph Hughes, secretary of the British and Foreign Bible Society, and John Howard, the noted philanthropist.[38] Stennett was even personally known to George III, who, it is said, held him in high esteem. A sympathetic comment on the Stennett family would be that they consistently felt that a wider ministry would enhance the standing of the Sabbatarians in the Baptist community. In fairness, it should also be said that the relatively small Sabbatarian congregations were probably unable to maintain a full-time minister and his family. A harsher critic, how-ever, might be excused for concluding that the later Stennetts' personal Sabbatarian convictions did little to advance the wider Sabbatarian cause.

Something of a similar nature took place at Mill Yard. Daniel Noble, who had succeeded Robert Cornthwaite as minister at the height of Mill Yard's prosperity, shortly thereafter also accepted the pastorate of the Barbican/Glasshouse Street Baptist church.[39] Noble was one of the few Sabbatarian ministers to hold the DD degree, and was obviously attractive to a number of congregations. He continued in that dual capacity until his death in 1783, or for seventeen years of his time as the Mill Yard minister. Noble also taught in a boys' school at Peckham during the week. It is hardly surprising, as noted earlier, that Mill Yard's decline began within a few years of his appointment.

An even more patent instance of compromise is provided by the case of Thomas Whitewood, who, in 1749, accepted a call from the Salisbury Sabbatarians to the First-day Baptist church in Reading. The record of negotiations between him and the church which preceded the formal call is revealing. The church appointed three representatives to meet with Whitewood 'to inform him with our circumstances . . . and he being a Sabbatarian to know how he should choose to act towards us on that point, being a First-day people'.[40] Whitewood understood the situation well and gave an undertaking 'not to give the people any uneasiness on that subject, and always observe whenever he was treating of the moral law, to recommend it in general'.[41] The terms were satisfactory to the church and Whitewood was duly installed, being ordained on 10 Decem-ber, Joseph Stennett II participating. The church at Reading knew

[38] *SR* 65/8: 237.   [39] *BQ* 1: 136–7.
[40] Davis, *History of the Baptist Church . . . Reading*, 30.   [41] Ibid.

that Whitewood was a Sabbatarian, but never knew why, and probably concluded it was not a matter of any significance. To a later generation, it is a classic example of compromise.

Interestingly enough, sixteen years later, Whitewood was asked by the church to vacate the pastoral office due to a 'visible decrease' in the congregation, and their desire to appoint a minister more able 'to call sinners to embrace the gospel of a crucified Jesus'.[42] Whether this reflected the influence of the Evangelical Revival then sweeping England, or a degree of Sabbatarian legalism which may have marked Whitewood's ministry, or both, or merely the fact that he was not a very popular or successful minister in any case, it is difficult to judge. He had previously left Salisbury depleted and unable to maintain a minister. He now left Reading as requested and went to Curriers' Hall to rejoin a Sabbatarian congregation, which from the point of view of principle, might have been a better move in the first place.

The later years at Natton are also relevant. From 1770, when Thomas Hiller succeeded Philip Jones at Natton and added the Seventh-day congregation there to his First-day responsibilities at Tewkesbury, Natton never again benefited from the undivided attention of a pastor wholly committed to the Sabbatarian cause. The fact that the cause at Natton continued for a further 130 years is more a testimony to the faithfulness of its members and the deep roots which Sabbatarian doctrine had put down in that part of Gloucestershire than to effective ministry. In any case, the records show that the Natton membership had noticeably declined during Hiller's tenure.[43] A later Sabbatarian believed it was not possible for a minister 'who is at the same time pastor of one church worshipping on the seventh day . . . and another church worshipping on the first day' to be faithful to both.[44] A similar view prevailed at Natton itself. In 1902, shortly before Natton's long history finally came to an end, deacon John Purser, last descendant of the original Purser family, commented, 'My opinion is that Natton will not go well until there is a true Sabbatarian pastor there.'[45] In fact Purser had never experienced that kind of minister, and it was never again to be. There can be few more obvious examples of men attempting to serve two masters, with the predictable results, than the Stennetts, Thomas Whitewood, Daniel Noble, and Thomas Hiller.

---

[42] Ibid. 34.   [43] DWL, Wilson MS 63, I, 5, fo. 8; *BAR* i 6.
[44] *SR* 2/1: 1.   [45] *SDBEA* 1: 47.

In this context, a word concerning mixed-communion churches is appropriate. Those who have followed carefully the development of Sabbatarian convictions in various parts of the country, will have noted occasional references to churches which accepted both First-day and Seventh-day members. There are hints that this was the case in a number of instances. Certainly in Gloucestershire and at Colchester during the eighteenth century it was acceptable for Sabbatarians to belong to Sunday-keeping congregations. Ingham became a mixed-communion church before capitulating completely to First-day worship, and may have been mixed-communion from the beginning. The Llangwm–Llantrissant church in Monmouthshire was mixed-communion with reference to both Baptist and Sabbatarian views. Tewkesbury was probably mixed-communion before Sabbatarians there established their own congregation in the Ashchurch–Natton district. Sabbatarians in the north-east may have worshipped in mixed-communion congregations, at least for a time. But the practice seldom, if ever, favoured the Sabbatarian cause, and was usually a concession to a Sabbatarian minority. There is not one known instance of a mixed-communion church ever having become Seventh-day, or having worshipped on the seventh day. The trend was always in the opposite direction. Thomas Rees makes an apt comment on the 'ruinous effect of mixed communion' in principle. With particular reference to the joint fellowship of paedobaptists and antipaedobaptists in Llangwm–Llantrissant, Rees observes:

No sight could be more agreeable to a Christian's feelings, than to see multitudes of Christ's followers, of evangelical denominations, uniting occasionally to commemorate their Lord's death; but the history of Nonconformity in Wales proves to a demonstration that nothing has proved a greater hindrance to the progress of religion than the attempt, though well meant, to unite permanently in church fellowship parties of different religious views, especially on the subject of baptism. History testifies that unmixed churches of both persuasions have been the most prosperous from age to age, while the mixed ones continued in the most declined state, until one party had so preponderated as to make the other's influence too weak to be felt.[46]

There were many Sabbatarians around the country who would have concurred with such sentiments. In particular, what was true of paedobaptists and antipaedobaptists at Llangwm–Llantrissant was

---

[46] Rees, *Nonconformity in Wales*, 190–1.

equally true of Sunday-keepers and Sabbatarians there. The Sabbatarian William Milman in consenting to assist Thomas Quarrel, thereby testified, if only unintentionally, that the Sabbath was a matter that might be compromised. Or so it may have appeared to some. What other circumstances contributed to this particular situation may never be known. What is beyond doubt is that Sabbatarianism in the Usk–Monmouthshire region petered out early in the eighteenth century. The witness of Sabbatarian history is that mixed-communion churches never eventuated to the lasting benefit of Sabbatarians.

Henri Misson had observed that already by the end of the seventeenth century, Sabbatarians made 'but little noise'. While this quiescence may signify one consequence of having recently emerged from a lengthy period of intermittent persecution, it may also denote something more fundamental. By the eighteenth century most Sabbatarians were Particular Baptists, espousing a Calvinistic theology. Mill Yard was by then the only known remaining General Seventh-day Baptist church. Sabbatarians may have been a quiet people because to all appearances they did not feel it necessary to press their views on others. Their congregational life centred more on the Word and worship than on witness. A theology undergirded by Calvinistic determinism does not in general see an urgent need to share the faith and invite unbelievers to accept the promises and obligations of the gospel. Brown speaks of a 'pre-occupation with election' in wider Baptist circles which led Particular Baptists in the eighteenth century 'to minimize the church's evangelistic imperative'.[47] While there is no reason to suppose that Sabbatarian Baptists were high Calvinists, the majority did share an underlying theology which made active promulgation of their faith a matter of little urgency. All the works written in England during the eighteenth century to advance the cause of the seventh day issued from Mill Yard.[48] It was said of Natton in its later years that there was 'little attempt to propagate the faith' and hence the number of adherents was 'not likely to increase'. For some years little or nothing had been said to advance 'the peculiar views whose prevalence founded the sect'.[49] Natton expired shortly afterwards.

Another instance is that of Watlington. By 1738, the Sabbatarian

[47] Brown, *English Baptists*, 5.   [48] See Appendix IV.
[49] *Birmingham Weekly Post*, 13 Apr. 1901.

interest here had subsided to a monthly meeting held in the home of its leader, Nathaniel Nash, said to be 'very wary', and inclined 'but little to promote their interest'.[50] Twenty years later the Sabbatarian cause at Watlington still remained within the Nash family, who continued to 'keep themselves much to themselves', and who did not 'endeavour to draw others over to their persuasion'.[51] It is not surprising that the local Anglican incumbent reported to the Bishop of Oxford that the Sabbatarians 'are decreased' and their numbers 'dwindle by disregard'.[52] While the Watlington Sabbatarians did not disappear finally until 1808, they had been little more than a curiosity in the community for the previous half-century or more. Whether the cause of such passivity was Calvinism or merely spiritual lethargy, the failure of later Sabbatarians to communicate their beliefs as their predecessors in the seventeenth century had done must be regarded as a principal reason for their decline.

Closely akin to this quiet reticence to become involved in persuading others of their views, there can be detected in the Sabbatarian movement an even more insidious cause of decay. There is a noticeable lack of reference to children and young people in the contemporary records of Sabbatarian history. One of the few exceptions is Francis Bampfield's plea for Sabbatarians to take a greater interest in the religious education of their children 'in Families, and in Schools', advanced in 1679 as one of the benefits to be derived from association.[53] It was presumably argued on the basis of a need perceived within the Sabbatarian community at the time. In 1682, John Bushell, vicar of Lewknor, reported to Bishop Fell of Oxford that all the 'sectaries', including Sabbatarians, had recently lost ground in his parish. One of the reasons singled out by Bushell for their decline was the failure of Dissenting congregations to hold their young people, 'None of them, in all the time I have been here, which is fifteen years, having proselytized any one of their children to their own persuasion.'[54] If true, it was a sad reflection on the Dissenting interest in Lewknor.

A similar situation pertained in Peter Chamberlen's large family. It is recorded that eighteen children, forty-five grandchildren, and eight great-grandchildren were born during Chamberlen's lifetime, but that not one of them appears to have been sufficiently persuaded

[50] *VCH* Oxon., viii. 246.   [51] Ibid.
[52] ORO, MS Oxf. Dioc. d. 554, fo. 1604ᵛ.   [53] Bampfield, *A Name*, 25.
[54] ORO, MS Oxf. Dioc. c.430, fo. 27.

of any form of the Christian faith to become a member of a church, 'Baptist, Seventh Day, or any other'.[55] Given the norms of Nonconformist family life and pretensions to household religious instruction then current, it seems almost beyond belief that a man so singularly successful in the world and prominent in the Church, should be so singularly unsuccessful in communicating the essentials of his faith within the confines of his own family. Even if Peter Chamberlen and the Lewknor Sabbatarians were exceptions, there are strong hints here of a failure to make the religious observation of the Sabbath, and perhaps even other aspects of Christian faith, attractive to younger generations. Francis Bampfield's concerns were evidently not without foundation.

We have been reflecting in the last few paragraphs on an ethos within the Sabbatarian movement and around it, which, particularly as the eighteenth century progressed, propelled it more towards decline than towards growth. A combination of differing factors, undoubtedly some stronger in certain circumstances than others, united to make the Sabbatarian cause increasingly unattractive, insignificant, and anachronistic. There is one more, perhaps in the end more directly pertaining to ethos than any other issue which may have influenced perceptions of Sabbatarians and Sabbatarianism in the popular mind. At the risk of appearing to conclude on a negative note, reference must be made to a contentious spirit which manifested itself from time to time within Sabbatarian congregations and between Sabbatarian believers. To admit that this spirit was present in other communions,[56] is not to lessen its effect on the Sabbatarian community.

It is most clearly demonstrated in the records of the More–Chamberlen church of the early 1650s. This detailed account of congregational life over an eleven-month period is largely given to the particulars of various disputes within the church and between its members. It presents a sad story to eyes looking in at a distance of three and a half centuries. In 1654 Elizabeth More wrote to the church justifying her absence from meetings and expressing regret at the 'malicious spirit' she found in the congregation. 'The first reason of my absence,' she explained, 'is because when I met with

---

[55] Whitley, 'Men of the Seventh Day', 5/8.

[56] e.g. of the Congregational church at Woodbridge, 'Tis reported that a rigid, censorious spirit that prevailed . . . stinted its growth and brought it into a dwindling state', DWL, Harmer MS 76, 5, p. 6.

you time after time with an intention to seek God, there I found confusion, falling out, and railing amongst you.'[57] Arise Evans had recently terminated his association with the congregation, 'being weary to see their corruption, division, malice, and enmity toward one another'.[58] How much of the wrangling resulted from Chamberlen's own disputatious nature, and how much from similar attitudes in other members is a matter for conjecture. The records contain a letter from Chamberlen to Dr Theodore Naudin in which Chamberlen refers pointedly to the latter's 'Pride, contention, and stubborn-ness of spirit', his 'anger and petulancy . . . false aspersions and high accusations'.[59] Even allowing for the bias of involved parties, it is clear that this particular congregation was in a sorry condition. That it was even considered necessary to record the details of congregational disputes in such minute fashion might be judged evidence of a morbidity quite out of harmony with the true spirit of love, forgiveness, and acceptance normally associated with Christ's gospel. Certainly it did little to make the More–Chamberlen church an attractive fellowship, and Elizabeth More and Arise Evans may have been illustrative of others who eventually found the situation intolerable.[60]

This was all in the early days of the Sabbatarian movement. Towards its end a somewhat similar attitude appears to have surfaced once more. The *Evesham Journal and Four Shires Advertiser* of 11 July 1903, purported to cite a manuscript which commented on the state of the two Sabbatarian churches then extant in England—Mill Yard and Natton. The report noted the 'lack of harmony amongst members' and 'differences . . . of such a nature' that no successful future could be envisaged.[61] The writer observed, 'Such extracts throw a very lurid light on the reasons for the sect's failure to permanently establish itself in England.' Whether or not the consequences were quite as far-reaching as that, is debatable, for strictly speaking this comment should be limited to the congregations in

[57] Bodl., MS Rawl. D.828, fo. 121.

[58] Arise Evans, *An Eccho to the Voice from Heaven* (1652), 92.

[59] Bodl. MS Rawl. D.828, fos. 95–111. Apparently the letter was 'not sent'.

[60] John Cowell complained of an antagonistic spirit manifested towards him in letters from Sabbatarians reacting to his break with the movement in 1674. Richard Parnham accused him of 'going to perdition', and a Mr Lawrence described his attack on the Sabbatarian doctrine 'a groundless, damnable fancy'; Cowell, *The Snare Broken*, 69.

[61] *Evesham Journal and Four Shires Advertiser*, 11 July 1903, 7.

question. Certainly Mill Yard's later years were fraught with trouble. However, there had been many Sabbatarian churches in the preceding years which had enjoyed harmonious fellowship amongst themselves, between each other, and with non-Sabbatarian congregations. Their decline was due to other causes. Yet Christ's own words would stand as a measure of all who claimed to be His disciples, Sabbatarians included, 'Ye shall know them by their fruits'. Discord, division, disharmony, and a contentious spirit would always be seen as fruits of another tree, and would always tend in another direction. At no time could such attitudes have enhanced the Sabbatarian churches or their prospects.

Beyond all this, of course, lay the indisputable consequences of civil and ecclesiastical opposition, and persecution. With smaller numbers overall, and generally smaller congregations, Sabbatarians would have been able to withstand the application of hostile legislation much less than Nonconformists of larger denominations. Dorothy Traske and Francis Bampfield ended their days in prison, and John James died on the scaffold. Robert Shalder died soon after a period of imprisonment, and his body was said to have been exhumed and left at his gate as a warning to others who might have been like-minded. The repressive measures against Nonconformists in the diocese of Salisbury under Bishop Seth Ward and in the West Country under the notorious Judge Jeffreys, where Sabbatarians were relatively strong, were as severe as anywhere in the country. In Gloucestershire, John Purser was disinherited on account of his Seventh-day convictions, and in Oxfordshire a Sabbatarian couple boarded up their house and left in order to avoid the attention of the authorities. John Rhys Howell, Stephen Mumford, and William Gibson emigrated to escape the possibility of similar harassment. Howell eventually returned, but Mumford and Gibson did not. Without doubt there were others like them who preferred the promised freedom of the Continent or the New World to the certain oppression of post-Restoration England. The total number of Sabbatarians who willingly followed Thomas Tillam to the Palatinate in order to avoid the penal code of the 1660s is unknown, but it was not inconsiderable.

In 1668 Edward Stennett had written to fellow believers in Rhode Island of the nine or ten Sabbatarian congregations and 'many scattered disciples' still in existence in England, noting that 'many once

eminent churches' had been 'shattered in pieces'.[62] Two years later,
Joseph Davis had similarly written to Rhode Island concerning the
Sabbatarian cause in England, observing that 'many shining lights'
had 'decayed . . . and lost their splendour'.[63] They were difficult years
for Sabbatarians, as they were for other Nonconformists. It appeared
to those caught up in those tumultuous times that the end of an era
had arrived. The future looked bleak indeed, and eschatological
hope seemed the only antidote for Stennett's 'thick clouds of
darkness' in 1671.[64] Stennett and Davis, then, and many others of
their persuasion, would have been much fortified could they have
known that the cause they cherished was to survive the clouds and
darkness of those troubled times. They would have rejoiced in the
knowledge that after the times of persecution, shattered congregations would regroup and that others previously unknown would
appear. They would have been greatly encouraged to learn that
many of the movement's most illustrious lights were yet to shine,
that some of its best literature was yet to be published, and that its
most distinctive doctrine would ultimately flourish in parts of the
world yet undiscovered. Perhaps most of all they would have been
gratified by the judgements of later generations. A nineteenth-century observer noted that their Sabbath doctrine was 'perfectly logical', and in terms of biblical interpretation 'impregnable'.[65] John Evans
wrote in 1795 in his survey of Christian denominations that
'Sabbatarians hold in common with other Christians the distinguishing doctrines of Christianity and, though much reduced in numbers,
deserve a distinct mention . . . on account of their integrity and
respectability.'[66] Despite the flaws and failures, the lost opportunities, and the times of hardship which may have contributed to the
disappearance of most of the Seventh-day Men by 1800, they would
surely have been pleased to know that posterity was to hold them
in such esteem.

[62] *SDBM* 1/1: 27.   [63] *SDBM* 1/2: 75.
[64] SDBHS, MS 194x.6, 67.   [65] Mellone, *JQR* 10: 407.
[66] John Evans, *A Sketch of the Several Denominations into which the Christian
World is Divided* (1795), 100.

APPENDIX I

Ireland

A SEVENTEENTH-CENTURY manuscript in Trinity College Library, Dublin, points to an interest in the Saturday Sabbath in Ireland which may, in its early years, have had links with the English Traskites.[1] The undated and untitled manuscript begins with the assertion, 'We are now to keep our Sabbath and rest upon Saturday the seventh and last day of the week from the beginning of creation, and not upon the first day.'[2] The manuscript discusses the reasons for Seventh-day observance, including its foundation in the Decalogue, the binding obligations of the moral law, and the formalization of Sunday observance in the fourth-century legislation of Constantine.[3] It is possible that another anonymous Dublin manuscript written in 1618 *contra* Traske, 'The Sabbath not to be kept on Saturday',[4] was a reply to the Trinity College work which had advocated Saturday observance. John Falconer's *A Briefe Refutation of John Traskes Judaical and Novel Fancyes*, published at St Omer in 1618, confirms that Traske's brand of Saturday Sabbatarianism was known in Ireland within a year or two of its appearance in London.

Christopher Sands (or Sandes, or Sandys), who had been known in London as one of Traske's chief aides during the formative years of the Traskite movement, appeared in Ulster during the 1630s as 'of Lysen, Co. Tyrone'.[5] Other reports indicated that Sands, in company with Hamlet Jackson, another prominent Traskite, had, in the interim, made contact with the Jewish community in Amsterdam, with a view to becoming an outright proselyte to the Jewish faith.[6] On learning that such a step required circumcision, Sands is reported to have declined admission to the Jewish faith, even though he continued to be suspected of maintaining antichristian doctrine.[7] Sands's reputation as a Traskite, and perhaps a genuine conviction about the significance of the Seventh-day Sabbath, if not other Old Testament practices, appear to have followed him for the rest of his known life. In 1633, Archbishop Laud wrote to the Lord Deputy

---

[1] TCD, MS 233, fos. 53–60.   [2] Ibid., fo. 53.   [3] Ibid., fos. 54–6.

[4] Noted by Whitley, commenting on a transcription of Bodl. MS Add. C.303, fos. 38–45, 'Trask in the Star-Chamber, 1619', *TBHS* 5: 12 (see Introd. n. 11, for comment on the date given in this title).   [5] *CSPD* 1635–6, 86.

[6] Katz, *Philo-Semitism*, 28.

[7] *TJHSE* 15: 70. Cf. *King-Killers*, 41, where it was also reported that Mary Chester, a convert of Sands, was 'as absolute against Christ, as Sands himself'.

of Ireland regarding ecclesiastical matters, noting that Christopher Sands, then a teacher at Londonderry, was 'a Jew and a dangerous person to teach the Youth'.[8] Laud directed that Sands should be seized and sent to England for interrogation. He subsequently appeared before the Court of High Commission in 1635, when it was stated that he had 'disclaimed all judaical or heretical opinions'.[9] This confession, if true, was nevertheless ambiguous, and not surprisingly the authorities in London seem not to have been convinced. Sands's case was referred to Francis White and Thomas Eden, Bishop and Chancellor of Ely, respectively, for further consideration.[10] Bishop White at the time was also dealing with Theophilus Brabourne, which probably helps to account for the fact that in the eyes of the establishment there was little difference between Brabourne's brand of Sabbatarianism, and that of Traske, Sands, and their followers. The proceedings against Sands in the Court of High Commission dragged on until 1636, when it seems that he eventually made a statement satisfactory to the court.[11] Sands is not heard of thereafter, either in London or in Ireland.

Sands's case was in some respects similar to that of James Whitehall, a decade or more earlier. Whitehall had been imprisoned in England for preaching 'Judaisme' and 'many things tending' thereto at Oxford, but had escaped to Ireland in 1624.[12] Katz believes that Whitehall's activities may have tended to Saturday Sabbatarianism, although definite evidence is lacking.[13] Whitehall had already been reported as the incumbent at Fearness (Ferns) in Co. Wexford in 1623, 'infected with Jewish opinions',[14] and on his return to Ireland in 1624 continued to preach 'Judaism' as he had recently done at Oxford. He was soon apprehended again, questioned by the Archbishop of Armagh, found to be 'obdurate' in his opinions, and committed to prison once more 'to prevent him from infecting others'.[15] Later that year he was sent back to England for further questioning by order of the Council for Ireland and at the personal request of the Archbishop of Canterbury.[16] The records make no mention of Seventh-day observance as such, but Whitehall's case included a defence of the continuing validity of the 'Law of Moses'. Ussher described Whitehall to James I as a 'true Israelite',[17] which could be interpreted to indicate an overt Sabbatarianism. The cases of Whitehall and Sands, if nothing more, show

[8] *CSPI* 1633–47, 21.   [9] *CSPD* 1635–6, 88.   [10] Ibid.

[11] Ibid. 469, 488, 497.   [12] *CSPD* 1623–5, 435.

[13] Katz, *Sabbath and Sectarianism*, 15.

[14] *CSPI* 1615–25, 435. A letter from the Bishop of Meath to James Ussher, Archbishop of Armagh, in 1621 noted that Whitehall believed in the restoration of the Jews, and that although 'Mosaical rites [were] not to be practised until the general calling of the Jews', his opinions had 'of old been condemned for heretical in the Nazarites'; James Ussher, *The Whole Works of the Most Rev. James Ussher, D.D.*, ed. C.R. Elrington, xv (Dublin, 1864), 161–2.

[15] *CSPI* 1615–25, 469.   [16] *CSPD* 1623–5, 435.

[17] PRO, SP Ireland, 238/1/26A, fos. 26–7.

that there were those in Ireland in the 1620s and 1630s who were willing to entertain the exposition of 'Jewish opinions'. Whitehall may have preached a kind of Sabbatarianism, Jewish or Christian. There can be no such ambiguity regarding Sands.

By 1653 at least ten Baptist churches had been established in Ireland, largely due to the influence of Cromwell's New Model Army.[18] There is no evidence of a specific Sabbatarian congregation and the precise nature of any Irish Sabbatarianism is difficult to determine. If, as has been suggested elsewhere,[19] the More–Chamberlen church which met at Lothbury Square in London at this time was Seventh-day, it could help to explain why seven members from Ireland were listed as transient members at Lothbury Square in 1653/4.[20] Philip Tandy, the York Sabbatarian, appears first as a school-teacher at Lisnagarvey (Lisburn), Co. Antrim, in 1635,[21] and again in 1658 as the Presbyterian incumbent there in succession to Henry Wyke, when he is described as a 'rare preacher', much liked in the parish, and as having 'first been an Episcopalian, then a Seventh-Day Baptist'.[22] He was also recorded in that same year as a Baptist minister in Lisburn. Tandy, 'of Westminster', is first noted in Ireland during Commonwealth times in 1654 as a landowner in Co. Meath.[23] Mordecai Abbott, later to be Receiver General of Customs in London, and a member of Pinners' Hall under Joseph Stennett, was known as a Baptist leader in Dublin *c.*1657.[24] While the evidence is often tentative and at times confusing, it points at least to an openness to Sabbatarian doctrine throughout Ireland for much of the first half of the seventeenth century. It may also help to account for a reported visit to Ireland by Thomas Tillam in 1666.[25]

The few recorded references to Seventh-day Sabbatarianism in Ireland during the 1700s are thus better viewed as traces of a seventeenth-century phenomenon, rather than as isolated occurrences of an eighteenth-century movement without previous ancestry. Minutes in the Mill Yard records in 1718 state that the church had ordered that answers to letters from Natton, New England, 'and to the letter from Ireland' be sent as soon as convenient.[26] There are hints here of an Irish Sabbatarianism with General Baptist sympathies. In 1732 the same records note that a letter had been received by the Mill Yard church from a Mr MacCollah from Connor.[27] Further

---

[18] *An Account of the Baptist Churches in Ireland* (1653) 13, 14. Cf. White, *English Baptists*, 66, 79. The significance of the Fifth Monarchy influence in the Baptist churches in Ireland at this period should not be overlooked as a trend parallel to the development of Sabbatarian views.　　　　　　[19] See Appendix III.

[20] Bodl. MS Rawl. D.828, fo. 17.　　[21] *CSPI* 1633–47, 118.

[22] *CSPI* 1647–60, 673; Seymour, *The Puritans in Ireland, 1647–1661,* 171–2, who records that Tandy was viewed by some locally as 'a Presbyterian and a madman'.

[23] *CSPI*, Adventurers for Land, 1642–59, 9, 95.

[24] *BB* i. 66, 210; INB, *TBHS* 7: 182.　　[25] *BQ* 17: 66.

[26] MYM 228.　　[27] Ibid. 265.

correspondence from Sabbatarians in Ireland is noted in the minutes of 1733.[28] Sabbatarian congregations are said to have existed at Londonderry, Banagher, Belfast, and in Tyrone during the nineteenth century,[29] but the sources are not reliable and further investigation lies beyond the scope of this study. Even if such groups did exist, there is no available evidence that would link them to a seventeenth-century origin. It may be worth noting in this respect that only in a few instances did seventeenth-century Sabbatarianism in England and Wales persist beyond 1800.

[28] Ibid. 267.   [29] *SDBEA* 1: 59–61.

APPENDIX II

Notes on Supposed Sabbatarian Congregations, 1650–1750

EARLIER this century three Seventh Day Baptist publications[1] maintained that a further five Sabbatarian congregations had existed during the seventeenth and early eighteenth centuries, for which no contemporary evidence is currently known. An uncritical acceptance of these assertions probably accounts for continued support in more recent literature for the existence of at least some of these congregations.[2] The information presently available suggests that few, if any, of these churches actually existed, and that assumption, misinterpreted data, and/or unfamiliarity with English topography were in most instances responsible for supposing the existence of these ghost congregations.

Hexham (Northumberland)

A Sabbatarian congregation is said to have been formed at Hexham in 1652 or 1653, and to have become extinct by 1715.[3] Thomas Tillam founded a Baptist church at Hexham early in 1652, and it appears that the association with Tillam is the main reason for attributing Seventh-day beliefs to this congregation. It should be noted, however, that Tillam left Hexham in 1655 and that there is no evidence that he publicly advocated Sabbath-day observance prior to his arrival in Colchester later that year.[4] The Hexham church book, still extant, whose early records are written in Tillam's own hand, lacks any reference to Sabbatarianism during the years of Tillam's ministry.

It is true that the church book contains a letter to the congregation from Tillam from London in 1654 when he was in contact with Peter Chamberlen,

---

[1] *SO* 1/11 (July–Sept. 1907) and 12 (Oct.–Dec. 1907) give two somewhat differing lists of Sabbatarian churches in or before 1706. The other sources are *SDBEA* 1: 39–56, and *SR* 83/16 (15 Oct. 1917), 497–9. In most instances *SDBEA* and *SR* appear to have followed *SO*. A further eleven Seventh Day Baptist congregations are said to have existed at various locations in England, Scotland, Ireland, and Wales during the nineteenth century, of which Westmancote in Worcestershire may have had seventeenth-century antecedents.

[2] Katz lists Burton-on-Trent and Hexham as 'Sabbath-keeping churches of the Interregnum', *Philo-Semitism*, 41. Katz also incorrectly designates Mill Yard as 'later, Bell Lane'.   [3] *SO* 1/12: 93; *SDBEA* 1: 49.

[4] See above, 269.

who by then was himself a practising Sabbatarian.[5] Tillam writes: 'I was by a blessed hand guided to my most heavenly brother, Doctor Chamberlen one of ye most humble mortified souls (for a man of parts) that ever yet I met with, in whose sweet society I enjoyed ye blessing of my God by ye laying on of their hands'.[6] Although again there is no reference to the Sabbath issue, it is possible that Tillam's attention had been drawn to the seventh day as well as to the necessity of laying on of hands through his association with Chamberlen at this time. It might also be argued, however, that had the Sabbath question been of such significance to Tillam at this point as was the imposition of hands, he would have at least mentioned it in his pastoral letter.

The Hexham church book also contains a letter from the Baptist church in Swan Alley, London, in 1653, one of the signatories to which was Henry Jessey,[7] who was also a convinced Sabbatarian by this date. Once again, there is no mention of the Saturday Sabbath. Jessey's congregation in Swan Alley was unquestionably a Sunday-keeping church, and correspondence between Baptist congregations at this period certainly cannot be taken to indicate doctrinal convergence in all points.

The lack of any reference to Seventh-day observance in the church book, the absence of any external evidence, and Tillam's own later conversion to the seventh day, together point to the conclusion that Hexham, certainly in its formative years, did not subscribe to Sabbatarian doctrine. It is not clear whether individual members at Hexham adopted Seventh-day views later when Sabbatarianism became more widespread in Durham and Northumberland. A book list in the Hexham church book includes a copy of Benjamin Keach's *The Jewish Sabbath Abrogated* (1700).[8]

It may also be noted that there is no indication of Seventh-day doctrine in the charges laid against Tillam and his ministry at Hexham by the New-castle Baptists over the case of Joseph ben Israel, the false Jew whom Tillam baptized in 1653.[9] Given the nature of the case and the degree of animosity it aroused between the Newcastle and Hexham churches, it may safely be assumed that, had Tillam's doctrine been tinged with Sabba-tarianism, his antagonists at Newcastle would have been quick to allude to it.

---

[5] See above, 81.

[6] The Hexham church book, AL, MS 2/2/9; cf. Underhill (ed.), *Records*, 323. A controversy over laying on of hands troubled the More–Chamberlen church itself at this period, Bodl. MS Rawl. D. 828, fos. 20–2; *TBHS* 3: 178.

[7] AL, MS 2/2/9, fo. 26^v, dated '2d of 8t month', 1653; cf. Underhill, *Records*, 346–8.   [8] AL, MS 2/2/9, fo. 39^r.

[9] A full account of this episode is given by Katz, *Sabbath and Sectarianism*, 21–34.

Burton-on-Trent (Staffordshire)[10]

Research in the Staffordshire and Derbyshire archives has failed to locate any evidence in support of the assertion that a Sabbatarian congregation existed at Burton-on-Trent from c.1650 and that a later derivative of this group was known at nearby Repton in Derbyshire during the nineteenth century. The principal evidence for these claims is an article in The *Birmingham Weekly Post* of 13 April 1901, which has been incorrectly interpreted to refer to 'a Sabbatarian church at Burton'.[11]

On examination, however, this reference proves to be a misreading of Burton[-on-Trent] for Bourton[on-the-Water]. The article concentrates on Sabbatarianism in the Ashchurch–Tewkesbury district of Gloucestershire during the seventeenth and eighteenth centuries, and refers to an eighteenth-century manuscript (now lost) which gave details of Seventhday Baptist congregations in the area from 1650 onwards. The manuscript is quoted as saying, 'There were in the last century a small society who kept the seventh day according to the ancient Scripture way, and there were some about Bourton in this last century.'[12]

It was in the Bourton-on-the-Water area and not at Burton-on-Trent that a Sabbatarian congregation was known 'in a flourishing condition in the middle of the seventeenth century'.

Norweston (Oxfordshire)

The attribution of a Seventh-day congregation in the tiny hamlet of Norweston c.1706 is similarly due to a misunderstanding of English placenames and their contracted forms. The evidence for a strong Sabbatarian presence in parts of Oxfordshire and Buckinghamshire adjacent to Norweston has been detailed elsewhere.[13] It is understandable that without further information this vigorous movement could be thought to have extended to Norweston from Bledlow or Watlington.

In 1706 Joseph Davis, sen., of Mill Yard, made provision in his will for an annuity of £5 to be paid to the ministers of nine Sabbatarian churches, including the church at North Walsham, Norfolk.[14] Later documents relating to the Joseph Davis Charity specified eight congregations, referring to North Walsham by its colloquially contracted form 'Norwalson',[15] or to 'Norweston'.[16] The editors of *SDBEA* presumably followed this latter source,

---

[10] *SDBEA* 1: 49 and *SR* 83/16: 497 give Burton-on-Trent in 'Derbyshire'.

[11] 'A Sabbatarian church at Burton, mentioned in the *Birmingham Weekly Post*', *SDBEA* 1: 49.   [12] *Birmingham Weekly Post*, 13 Apr. 1901.

[13] Above, Ch. 6.   [14] Black (ed.), *Last Legacy*, p. xii.

[15] *Case Submitted to the General Body of Protestant Dissenting Ministers of the Three Denominations*, 9.

[16] *Reports from the Commissioners for Charities*, xix, pt. I, 871. This source lists one of the congregations as at 'Sherbourn, in Buckinghamshire', instead of listing Sherborne in Dorset, *and* a congregation in Buckinghamshire, an error perpetuated

or the *Sabbath Recorder* of 1847, which also referred to Norweston. The allusion to 'Norwatson' as being identified in the Mill Yard minutes of 1719 is again a misrepresentation of 'North Walsom'.[17]

Manchester (Lancashire)[18]

A Sabbatarian group may have existed at Manchester during the eighteenth century (and earlier?), although extensive research in the relevant archival collections in Manchester has failed to reveal any substantiating evidence. Parker notes the wider Sabbatarian movement in Manchester, a 'protestant stronghold', and at other locations in the Chester diocese during the sixteenth and seventeenth centuries,[19] and suggests that John Traske 'may have influenced some in that diocese'.[20] The evidence for both conclusions is, at best, extremely tenuous. Manchester, like Hexham, Burton-on-Trent, and Norweston, is not mentioned by Joseph Davis.

Swansea (Glamorgan)

SDBEA cites a letter from Thomas Hollis to 'Elder Wheaton' of 'Swanzey' (*sic*), Wales, *c.*1730, recorded in the *Baptist Cyclopedia*: 'God, that hath shined into our hearts by his gospel, can lead you sleeping Sabbatarians from the Sinai covenant and the law of ceremonies into the light of the new covenant and the grace thereof.'[21] Theology apart, it appears that this is a simple, if substantial, geographical error. The existence of a Seventh-day church in Swanzey, New England, is clear from Samuel Hubbard's Journal.[22] Evidence for Sabbatarianism in Swansea, Glamorgan, during the seventeenth or eighteenth centuries is lacking.

by some later Seventh Day Baptist authors, cf. *SDBEA* 1: 55. Cox, also following the Charities Commissioners' *Reports*, incorrectly lists both Norweston and 'Sherburn in Buckinghamshire' as two of the original congregations, *Literature of the Sabbath Question*, ii. 81. This confusion has resulted in the assertion that there were only eight congregations originally endowed by Davis, when in fact there were nine.

[17] *SDBEA* 1: 56; MYM 231.
[18] *SDBEA* 1: 56, gives 'Manchester, Lancastershire, 1730'.
[19] Parker, *The English Sabbath*, 140–9, 69.   [20] Ibid. 162.
[21] *SDBEA* 1: 56, 111.   [22] e.g. SDBHS, MS 194x.6, 79, 132, 139.

APPENDIX III

The More–Chamberlen Church Reconsidered

THE question of whether the John More–Peter Chamberlen church which met in Lothbury Square *c*.1653–4 observed Saturday or Sunday was discussed in early issues of *TBHS*.[1]

On the basis of Chamberlen's own writings[2] and the inscription on his tombstone at Woodham Mortimer, Essex,[3] J.W. Thirtle maintained that Chamberlen began to observe the seventh day in 1651, and that by 1654 a church which was then led by Chamberlen also observed the Saturday Sabbath.[4] It has been assumed, probably correctly, that this congregation was a continuation of the More–Chamberlen Lothbury Square church, whose existence is authenticated by the survival of its original church book, now in the Bodleian Library.[5] The greater part of this valuable document is written in Chamberlen's own hand. From a study of these and other records Champlin Burrage concluded that the More–Chamberlen church 'was not a Seventh-Day Anabaptist congregation, as has hitherto been supposed', and that Chamberlen himself did not begin to observe the Saturday Sabbath until *c*.1656.[6]

The case presented by Burrage, after W.T. Whitley,[7] that the More–Chamberlen church was not Sabbatarian at the time the records were

---

[1] See Thirtle, *TBHS* 2: 9–30, 110–17; Champlin Burrage, 'A True and Short Declaration, both of the Gathering and Joining Together of Certain Persons [with John More, Dr Theodore Naudin, and Dr Peter Chamberlen]: and also of the lamentable breach and division which fell amongst them', *TBHS* 2: 129–60; Whitley, *TBHS* 2: 190–2; Thirtle, *TBHS* 3: 176–89.

[2] e.g. Chamberlen, *The Sons of the East*, bds. Chamberlen was one of many Sabbatarians and others who demonstrated a keen interest in the conversion of the Jews. In 1680 Chamberlen complained to the Archbishop of Canterbury that he had recently been misrepresented as a Jew: Bodl. MS Tanner 160, fo. 71.

[3] The inscription records that Chamberlen was born 8 May 1601 and died 22 Dec. 1683 'being 82 years, 7 months, and 14 days . . . having travelled most parts of Europe, and speaking most of the languages. As for his religion, was a Christian keeping the commandments of God and faith of Jesus, being baptised about the year 1648, and keeping the 7th day for the Sabbath above 32 years.' John Belcher was a witness to Chamberlen's will: *TBHS* 3: 188.

[4] *TBHS* 2: 22–3. Thirtle subsequently changed his opinion following the publication of Burrage's annotated transcription of the More–Chamberlen church records: ibid. 3; 176.

[5] Bodl. MS Rawl. D. 828. Burrage's transcription can be found in *TBHS* 2: 132–60.

[6] *TBHS* 2: 131.   [7] Ibid. 131 n. 9.

written, is not entirely convincing. The argument is based on the fact that these original records do not show any Saturday meetings in the five-month period between 25 December 1653 and 23 May 1654, when the records are at their fullest and all meetings of the congregation appear to have been recorded. Of twenty-three meetings recorded in total, fourteen were held on Sundays, and nine on other days of the week. There are a further nine Sundays on which no meeting is recorded. Although there is some evidence that preaching or exhortation occurred on some of these occasions, all meetings recorded seem principally to have been concerned with order and discipline, rather than for worship or edification.[8] This accords better with Chamberlen's heading for the record, 'Acts of the Church. Delivery to Satan'. A thoroughly Sabbatarian congregation might be expected to have dealt with its problems at times other than on the Sabbath. At a later date, the Mill Yard records note that a church meeting was scheduled for 'the next first day'.[9]

While there are references to the 'Lord's day' in the records, they do not appear to suggest meetings for worship.[10] The only clear indication of a Sunday meeting for religious purposes occurs near the beginning of the record, with reference to Sunday, 25 December 1653. On that occasion the church apparently met for 'breaking of bread' and prayer.[11] There is no suggestion that this was a regular feature of congregational life at Lothbury Square, and indeed mention of it at all in the records may indicate that it was rather an unusual occurrence. This particular meeting may well have been called in anticipation of the events of the following day, when Peter Chamberlen was arrested and detained in custody on a charge of threatening Cromwell's life.[12] It should also be remembered that the Pinners' Hall church, under Edward Stennett, celebrated the Lord's Supper on the first day.[13]

It is furthermore a questionable methodology to reject the accuracy of the inscription on Chamberlen's tombstone, which is the primary evidence for his 1651 acceptance of the seventh day, in order to conclude that he was not Sabbatarian by the time he assumed leadership at Lothbury Square. Even if an error had crept into the reckoning that Chamberlen had observed the seventh day for more than thirty-two years prior to his death in 1683, it would hardly have been of the magnitude of the six or seven years required by Whitley and Burrage to put the beginnings of his Sabbatarianism *c*.1656–7.[14] An early date for his acceptance and observation of the Saturday Sabbath also accords well with Chamberlen's own testimony.[15]

It has been further suggested that the absence of any substantial reference

---

[8] Bodl. MS Rawl. D.828, *passim.*   [9] MYM 212.
[10] *TBHS* 2: 155.   [11] Ibid. 136.   [12] Ibid.
[13] PHCB 10.   [14] Whitley, 'Men of the Seventh Day', 6/6; cf. *TBHS* 2: 131.
[15] *Sons of the East*, bds. Chamberlen would not have been able to claim that he was the first to have advocated observance of the seventh day, even if that claim was dubious, if he had only adopted the practice *c*.1656.

to the Seventh-day Sabbath in these original records indicates that the church was not Sabbatarian. However, there is a similar lack of reference to Fifth Monarchy views, which in the light of other evidence certainly could not be taken to mean that the church was not Fifth Monarchist. Sabbatarian churches did not always emphasize their Sabbath doctrine. The covenant between the founding members of Francis Bampfield's Seventh-day church made no reference at all to the Saturday Sabbath.[16] Correspondence between Peter Chamberlen and Theodore Naudin,[17] which is included in the Lothbury Square records, does refer at one point to certain articles 'agreed upon by the church, the 31 of the month, Shabat last'.[18] 'The merits or demerits of these arguments must be evaluated in light of the fact that the entire document concentrates on the life of the congregation rather than on its doctrinal stance or its worship practices.

The balance is perhaps finally tipped in favour of the earlier Sabbatarian tradition for the Lothbury Square church from an exchange between Chamberlen and John Graunt in June–July 1652.[19] Chamberlen had defended his congregation against a charge of being a false church, 'That whereby we aver our selves to be the true church of Christ, is by keeping the pure ordinances of Christ, according to his Word.'[20] Although there is no specific mention of Sabbatarianism here, Graunt's reply indicates that he was aware of practices within Chamberlen's congregation. 'Your lascivious washing your damsels' feet, and legs also' and 'keeping the Commandments of God', were the issues that Graunt specifically raised.[21] It is known from other sources that the More–Chamberlen church practised footwashing,[22] and the inscription on Chamberlen's tomb recorded that he was a 'Christian keeping the Commandments of God and faith of Jesus'. In 1652 John More also wrote that a true disciple would follow Christ not in 'one, or two, or three, or four particulars, but in the observing of all the Commandments, [and] a resolution to follow all and every particular thereof'.[23]

In Graunt's view, the Chamberlen church in 1652 was 'drawn out from others into separated congregations, according to the traditions of men's

---

[16] 'We own the LORD Jesus Christ to be the One & Only LORD & Lawgiver to our Souls & Consciences. And we own the Holy Scriptures of Truth as ye One & only Rule of Faith Worship & Life, According to which we are to Judge of all our Cases.'

[17] References to the radical activities of the French physician, Theodore Naudin, c.1654, can be found in Whitley, *BB* i. 39–654 and 47–654, and *FMM* 106, 256. Naudin was a member of the More–Chamberlen church.

[18] Bodl. MS Rawl. D. 828, fo. 93.

[19] John Graunt, *The Shipwrack of all False Churches: and the Immutable Safety and Stability of the True Church of Christ* . . . (1652), 'occasioned by Doctor Chamberlen, his mistake of her, and of the Holy Scriptures', title-page.

[20] Ibid. 4. The argument between Chamberlen and Graunt revolved around baptism and the Lord's Supper.   [21] Ibid.

[22] *TBHS* 2: 130.   [23] More, *Generall Exhortation*, 6–7.

devices, filling themselves with the old wine of Pharisaical righteousness'.[24] Graunt's comments reflect the practices of the Chamberlen church from at least the summer of 1652, and probably earlier. If, as seems likely, the Chamberlen congregation of 1652 was in fact the same as the More–Chamberlen church of 1653–4 and was Seventh-day by the time its records began in the latter part of 1652, it could help to explain two further features of this congregation: the hitherto unexplained existence of the 'separated assembly' referred to in the records, the members of which are listed without reason for their separation,[25] and the inclusion in the Lothbury Square roll of members from Ireland, Yorkshire, Devon, and Lincoln.[26]

In view of all the available evidence it seems preferable to retain the traditional view that the More–Chamberlen church at Lothbury Square, and the congregations identified only with Chamberlen which preceded and followed it, were Seventh-day from at least June 1652. Certainly, as has been indicated elsewhere, observance of the Saturday Sabbath had been advocated and practised in London from at least the early 1640s.[27]

---

[24] Graunt, *False Churches*, 6.   [25] Bodl. MS Rawl. D. 828, fo. 18.
[26] Ibid., fo. 17.   [27] See above Ch. 3.

An Annotated Chronological Bibliography of Seventh-day Literature to 1750

WORKS with substantial or significant contributions to the Seventh-day position are included, as well as works wholly on the topic. Abbreviated titles are normally given. Full titles or longer extracts are cited when they illuminate the Sabbatarian debate. References are to Wing, *Short-title Catalogue . . . 1641–1700*, 1st edition, and Whitley, *A Baptist Bibliography*, i. An asterisk indicates works of which no extant copy is known.

1628   Brabourne, Theophilus: *A Discourse upon the Sabbath Day: wherein are handled these particulars ensuing:—1. That the Lord's Day is not Sabbath Day by Divine institution. 2. An exposition of the iiii Commandment . . . 3. That the Seventh-day Sabbath is not abolished. 4. That the Seventh-day Sabbath is now still in force. 5. The author's Exhortation and reasons, that nevertheless there be no Rent from our Church as touching practice.*

(Not, as Whitley indicates, *BB* i. 2–628, the 1st edition of the 1632 *Defence.*)

1632   Brabourne, Theophilus: *A Defence of that most Ancient, and Sacred ordinance of* GODS, *the Sabbath Day . . . A Defence of the iiijth Commandement . . . of the integrity and perfection of the Decalogue. . . . A Discovery of the Superstition, impurity and corruption of Gods worship . . . committed by multitudes, in sanctifying the Lords Day for a Sabbath Day. . . . Undertaken against all Anti-Sabbatharians, both of Protestants, Papists, Antinomians, and Anabaptists; and by name and especially against these X Ministers, M. Greenwood, M. Hutchinson, M. Furnace, M. Benton, M. Gallard, M. Yates, M. Chappel, M. Stinnet, M. Johnson, and M. Warde.*

(But not, as Brabourne himself indicates, an amended 2nd edition of the 1628 *Discourse*. The *Defence* is essentially a new work.)

1647   J(essey), H(enry): *A Scripture Almanack, or, A Calculation for the year 1647.*

(From 1645 Jessey's *Almanack* was published annually for several years. Other editions also contained allusions to the Sabbath.)

1650   Ockford [or Oakford], James: *The Doctrine of the Fourth Commandement, Deformed by Popery; Reformed and Restored to its Primitive purity.*

(Cox, *Literature of the Sabbath Question*, i. 226, no. 111, incorrectly gives 1642 as the date of publication. Whitley, *BB* i. 93–649, gives 1649.)

1652   *The Moralitie of the Fourth Commandement.*

[*c.*1653]   Salter (Saller), William: *Sundry Queries Tendred to . . . Ministers of Jesus Christ, for clearing the Doctrine of the Fourth Commandement, And the Lords Sabbath Day.*
   (In the 2nd edition, *c.*1660, the date for this 1st edition is given as 'about the year 1653'.)
   Wing: S 400aA.

1653   Brabourne, Theophilus: *Of the changing of Church-Discipline.*

1654   Brabourne, Theophilus: *A Reply to the Indoctus Doctor Edoctus.*

1654   Brabourne, Theophilus: *The Second Part of the Change of Church Discipline.*
   (*Ad cal.* with the previous work. This, and others in similar vein, are part of Brabourne's controversy with John Collings.)
   Wing: B 4096.

1654   Brabourne, Theophilus: *A Reply to Mr Collings Provocator Provocatus.*
   Wing: B 4095.

1654   Brabourne, Theophilus: *An Answer to M. Cawdry's two Books of the Sabbath.*
   Wing: B 4088.

1654   Brabourne, Theophilus: *The Second Vindication of my first Book of the Change of Discipline.*

1656   Oockford (Ockford), James: *The Tryal of the Truth; or, rather the Law is the Truth.*
   BB i. 65–656.

1657(?)   S(pittlehouse), J(ohn): *The Unchangeable Morality of the Seventh-day Sabbath.* *
   (May have been published in 1656.)
   BB i. 23–657.

[1657]   Spittlehouse, John: *A Manifestation of sundry gross absurdities . . . in reference to the abrogating of the seventh-day-Sabbath, as commanded in the fourth Precept of the Royal Law of Jehovah.*
   Wing: S 5010 (gives 1656); *BB* i. 38–657.

[1657]   Spittlehouse, John: *A Return to some Expressions published in a Sermon preached by Mr John Simpson . . . Whereby He indeavored to prove that the seventh day Sabbath . . . is abolished by Christ, He being that Rest which Believers enter into by Faith.*
   Wing: S 5011 (gives 1656); *BB* i. 39–657.

1657   Saller, William and Spittlehouse, John: *An Appeal To the Consciences of the chief Magistrates of this Commonwealth, touching the Sabbath-day . . .*

   Wing: S 397; *BB* i. 4–657.

   (Reprinted 1679, with some further material; Wing: S 398.)

1657   Tillam, Thomas: *The Seventh-Day Sabbath Sought out and celebrated, or, the Saints last Design upon the Man of sin . . . being a clear discovery of that black character in the head of the little Horn, Dan. 7. 25. The Change of Times & Laws. With the Christians glorious Conquest over that mark of the Beast, and recovery of the long-slighted seventh day, to its antient glory.*

   Wing: T 1166; *BB* i. 40–657.

   (Whitley says this work was reprinted in 1683, but no extant copy is known.)

1658   Stennett, Edward: *The Royal Law Contended for, or, Some Brief Grounds serving to prove that the Ten Commandments are yet in full force, and shall so remain till Heaven and Earth pass away; also, The Seventh Day Sabbath proved from the Beginning, from the Law, from the Prophets, from Christ and his Apostles, to be a Duty yet incumbent upon Saints and Sinners.*

   BB i. 57–658.

   (Reprinted 1667, with a modified title: Wing: S 5403. The name Stennett is spelt here and throughout as above, following the *DNB*, in preference to other forms, some of which appear on some title-pages.)

[1658] Tillam, Thomas: *The Lasher Proved Lyer.*

   Wing: T 1165A.

   (A reply to W. Jennison, *A Lash for a Lyar.*)

1659   Brabourne, Theophilus: *An Answer to Two Books on the Sabbath. 1. To Mr Ives of London, his Book Intituled Saturday no Sabbath Day. 2. To Mr Warren of Colchester, his book intituled, The Jews Sabbath Antiquated, and the Lords day Instituted by Divine Providence.*

   BB i. 88–659.

1660   Brabourne, Theophilus: *Of the Sabbath Day, which is now, the Highest Controversie in the Church of England. For on this Controversie, Dependeth the Gaining or loosing one of Gods Ten Commandments, by name, the 4th Command, for the Sabbath day.*

   BB i. 91–660.

   (Only known copy missing from Dr Williams's Library.)

1660   J(essey) H(enry): *The Scripture Kalendar.*

   Wing: A 1841.

[1660] Saller, William: *An Appendix to a late* BOOK INTITULED *The Unchangeable Morality of the Seventh-day-Sabbath, OR, A letter written to some Friends, for the further satisfaction in that point.*

1660   Pooley, Christopher: *Unwarranted Principles.*
Wing: P 2859A.

[1660]   Salter (Saller), William: *Sundry Queries formerly tendred to the Ministers of London, for clearing the Doctrine of the fourth Commandment, and the Lord's SABBATH-DAY, but now tendred to the Consideration of all Men.*
Wing: S 400.

[1660]   Tillam, Thomas: *Sat. Vas. Subd.**
(Referred to by Cowell, *Divine Oracles.*)

1660   Tillam, Thomas: *The Temple of Lively Stones. Or the Promised glory of the last days.*
Wing: T 1167; *BB* i. 115–660.

1664   Cowell, John: *A Beame of Sabbath Light Breaking forth through a Cloud of Witnesses. Or, The Holy, Just, Good, Spiritual Law of God confirmed (and as included therein the seventh-dayes Sabbath to be observed) as a Rule of Life to Believers in Christ.*
Wing: C 6639.
(Later retracted in *The Snare Broken.*)

1664   Pooley, Christopher, and Skipp, Edward: *Propositions and Queries.**
(Referred to by Cowell, *The Snare Broken.*)

1664   Cowell, John: *Divine Oracles: or, A Testimony to Established Truths in a Declining Day.*
Wing: C 6640; *BB* i. 16–664.
(Later retracted in *The Snare Broken.*)

1664   Saller, William: *A Preservative against Atheism and Error, Wherein some fundamental points in religion . . . Are by way of question and answer, handled, and with much brevity and clearness proved. . . . To which is added, A brief answer to William Russell in a book of his, also entituled, No Seventh-day-Sabbath in Christs New Testament.*
Wing: S 399.

1664   Stennett, Edward: *The Seventh Day is the Sabbath of the Lord. Or An Answer to M William Russel his book, Entituled, No Seventh Day Sabbath Comanded* [sic] *by Jesus Christ in the New Testament .*
Wing: S 5404; *BB* i. 23–664.

[1667]   Eve, George; Squibb, Arthur; Belcher, John; Stennett, Edward; Gardner, John; Parnham, Richard; Woods, Robert, *A Faithful Testimony Against The Teachers of Circumcision and the Legal Ceremonies; who are lately gone into Germany .*
(Although this tract refers to the Sabbath, it is mainly directed against the excesses of the Tillam/Pooley group. It is included here on account of its significance in the development of the Sabbatarian movement.)
Wing: F 290A, where the date is incorrectly given as 1662; *BB* i. 14–667.

1667   Saller, William: *The Seventh-day Sabbath no Ceremony.**
(Referred to by Cowell, *The Snare Broken.*)

1671   Saller, William: *An Examination of a late Book published by Dr Owen, Concerning a Sacred Day of Rest. Many Truths therein as to the Morality of a Christian Sabbath assented to. With a Brief Inquiry into his Reasons for the change of it from the seventh day to the first, by way of denial.*
Wing: S 398D; *BB* i. 7–671.

1672   Benn, William: *The Judgment of Mr Francis Bampfield . . . for the Observation of the Jewish or Seventh Day Sabboth . . . and a vindication of the Christian Sabboth against the Jewish.*
Wing: B 624; *BB* i. 2–672.

1676   W.J., *Selah . . . Or, an appeal to the Scriptures . . . Whether the Seventh, or last day of the week . . . is a weekly Sabbath-day . . .*
Wing: W 44.

1677   Bampfield, Francis: *All in One. All Useful Sciences and Profitable Arts in one Book of Jehovah Aelohim . . . Comprehended and discovered in the Fulness and Perfection of Scripture-Knowledges.*
Wing: B 619; *BB* i. 8–677.

1677   Bampfield, Francis: *. . . Septima dies, Dies Desiderabilis, Sabbatum Jehovae. The Seventh-Day-Sabbath the Desirable Day . . .*
Wing: B 628; *BB* i. 9–677.

1677   Stennett, Edward: *The Insnared Taken in the Work of his Hands, or an Answer to Mr John Cowell . . .*
(BL copy has a second title-page, dated 1679.)
Wing: S 5402; *BB* i. 14–677.

1681   Bampfield, Francis: *A Name, an After One, or, A Name, A New One . . . or An Historical Declaration of the Life of Shem Acher.*
Wing: B 627; *BB* i. 22–681.

1682   Chamberlen, Peter: *The Sons of the East.*
Wing: C 1905; *BB* i. 17–682.

1683   Soursby, Henry, and Smith, Mehetabel: *A Discourse of the Sabbath, or The Controversies about the Sabbath Stated and Examined, with reference unto the Law of Nature, the Law of Moses, and the Law of Christ.*
Wing: S4722A; *BB* i. 24–683.

1692   Bampfield, Thomas: *An Enquiry Whether the Lord Jesus Christ made the World, and be Jehovah, and gave the Moral Law? And Whether the Fourth Command be Repealed or Altered?*
Wing: B 629; *BB* i. 8–692.

1693   Bampfield, Thomas: *A Reply to Doctor Wallis, his Discourse Concerning the Christian Sabbath.*
Wing: B 630; *BB* i. 9–693.

*c.*1693–5   Redford, Elizabeth: *The Widow's Mite, Shewing why the seventh day is to be kept in Christ.**
   (Incorrectly dated at 1716 by Whitley, *BB* i. 1–716, and in *SDBEA* 2: 1353. Both these sources also give the author as 'Bedford'.)
   Wing: R 662.

1696   [Soursby, Henry]: *The New Testament Sabbath.*
   (Attributed to Soursby by Benjamin Keach in *The Jewish Sabbath Abrogated* (1700).)
   Wing: N 784.

1707   [Davis, Joseph]: *The Last Legacy of Mr Joseph Davis, Senr.*
   BB i. 6–707.
   (Reprinted 1720 and 1869.)

1708   Philotheos [Maulden, John]: *A Threefold Dialogue, Concerning the Three Chief Points in Controversy amongst Protestants in our Days. viz. I. Whether the Holy Scriptures do prove the doctrine of Free Grace, or Free Will? II. Whether believers, or Infants-baptism, be the Ordinance of Christ? III. Whether the Seventh, or First Day of the Week, be the Sabbath of the Lord?*
   BB i. 11–708.
   (Whitley lists a 1728 edition, *BB* i. 7–728.)

1708   [Maulden, John]: *The pious Young Man's Guide, Or a Compendious and Useful Catechism.*
   BB i. 10–708.

1724   Maulden, John: *The Ancient and Honourable Way and Truth of God's Sacred Rest of the Seventh-Day Sabbath. Plainly discovered, to be the One and only Weekly-Day, by Divine Appointment, for the worship of God; binding all Men, in all Ages, from the Beginning to the End of Time, to its strict and intire Observation.*
   BB i. 7–724.

1724   Carlow, George: *Truth Defended; or, Observations on Mr Ward's Expositary Discourses, from the 8th, 9th, 10th, and 11th verses of the 20th chapter of Exodus, concerning the Sabbath.*
   BB i. 5–724.
   (Reprinted 1802 and 1847.)

[1725]   Elwall, Edward: *Dagon Fallen before the Ark of God. Or: the Inventions of Men not able to stand against the Ten Commandments of God.*
   BB i. 5–725.

1726   Elwall, Edward: *Dagon fallen upon his stumps, or the Inventions of Men not able to stand before the First Commandment of God.*
   BB i. 9–726.

1727   Elwall, Edward: *True Testimony for God, and for His Sacred Law;*
Being a Plain and Honest Defence of the Fourth Commandment of God:...
(Published as 'The Third Edition', probably after Elwall's *A True Testi-*
mony for God . . . against All the Trinitarians under Heaven (1724).)

1729   C(arlow), G(eorge): *The Excellency and Equity of God's Law* . . .
(This, and Carlow's *Dialogue* [1733], are attributed to him by W.H. Black
in *Catalogue of valuable manuscripts & printed books forming the . . . li-*
brary of . . . William Henry Black [1873].)

[1731]   Cornthwaite, Robert: *Reflections on Dr Wright's Treatise on the*
Religious Observation of the Lord's Day, According to the express Words
of the Fourth Commandment. Shewing the Inconclusiveness of the Doctor's
Reasoning on that Subject, and the Impossibility of grounding the First-
Day Sabbath on the Fourth Commandment, or any other Text of Scripture,
produced by him for that Purpose.
  BB i. 4–730.

1731   W(incop), N(icholas): *Remarks on Dr. Wright's Treatise . . . The In-*
violable Obligations Remaining on the Christian Church to the Religious
Observance of the Seventh Day.
  BB i. 14–731.

[1733]   C(arlow), G(eorge): *A Dialogue between a Sabbath Keeper and an*
Antinomian.

1734   Elwall, Edward: *A Declaration Against all the Kings and Temporal*
Powers under Heaven. Shewing that they have no authority over their
subjects in spiritual things. . . . With the Case of the Seventh Day Sabbath-
Keepers considered . . . that all such may have the Liberty to work Six Days
at their honest Vocations, and rest the Seventh Day, according to the
Commandment of God.
  BB i. 6–734.
  (3rd edition. Some earlier editions lack the section on Sabbath-keepers.
Reprinted 1741.)

1735   [Cornthwaite, Robert]: *The Seventh Day of the Week, the Christian*
Sabbath.
  BB i. 8–735.

1736   Cornthwaite, Robert: *The Seventh-Day Sabbath Farther Vindicated,*
or, a Defence of some Reflexions on Dr Wright's Treatise on the religious
observation of the Lord's Day, according to the express words of the fourth
commandment.
  BB i. 6–736.

1736   Cornthwaite, Robert: *A Second Defence of some Reflections on Dr*
Wright's Treatise on the Religious Observation of the Lord's-day . . . and

the Seventh-Day-Sabbath is prov'd to oblige all Christians, on Protestant Principles.

BB i. 8–736.

[1736] Elwall, Edward: *The Grand Question in Religion Consider'd, Whether we shall obey God or Man; Christ, or the Pope; the Prophets and Apostles, or Prelates and Priests.*

BB i. 10–736.

1738 Elwall, Edward: *The True and Sure Way to Remove Hirelings out of the Church . . . with an Answer to . . . Chubb's Dissertation Concerning the . . . Sabbath.*

BB i. 6–738.

1740 Cornthwaite, Robert: *An Essay on the Sabbath; or, a Modest Attempt towards a plain, scriptural Resolution of the following Questions:—I. Whether the Seventh Day Sabbath was given to Adam in Paradise? II. Whether the same now obliges Christians?*

BB i. 6–740.

1745 Cornthwaite, Robert: *Mr Foster's Sermon, of the Sabbath, and the Moral Ground of Public Worship . . . examined with candour.*

BB i. 1–745.

Note 1. The following 'Advertisement' at the end of Edward Stennett's rare *The Insnared Taken in the Work of his Hands* (1677) suggests that other seventeenth-century publications in favour of the seventh day have not survived:

Books promoting the seventh-day sabbath, but much out of print are Brabourne's *Answer to ten Ministers*, printed 1628 and reprinted 1632.[1] Two or three small treatises in answer to Mr Warren, Mr Ives, etc., by the same author. Mr Ockford, Mr Spittlehouse,[2] and Mr Cowe[3] on the same subject. Those things more easily gotten are, Mr Stennett's *Royal Law Contended For.* Also his *Answer to Mr Russell,*[4] A thin Folio by Mr Bampfield,[5] *An Answer* to Dr Owen's *Exercitations* by Mr Salter,[6] his *Answer* to Mr Grantham.[7] Likewise his sheet of *Queries* presented to the London Ministers, for their approbation or confutation.[8] A single sheet partly collected from Dr Heylin, called, *A Ram's Horn Sounding.*[9]

[1] *A Defence of . . . the Sabbath Day* (1632). On the relationship of this work to his earlier *Discourse Upon the Sabbath* (1628), see above, 342.

[2] Above for Brabourne's other works, and those by Ockford and Spittlehouse.

[3] Presumably John Cowell.

[4] *The Seventh Day is the Sabbath of the Lord* (1664).

[5] *All in One,* and *Septima dies* (1677).

[6] Saller, *An Examination of a late Book published by Dr Owen* (1671).

[7] *The Seventh-day Sabbath no Ceremony* (1667).

[8] *Sundry Queries* (1653 and 1660).

[9] Not otherwise known. No copy extant.

Another sheet entitled, *Scripture Light the Surest Light*, by W.G.[10] Also a useful tract, not exceeding two sheets, entitled, *The Churches Friend, fit to be considered by all Church Members.*[11]

Note 2. John Spittlehouse is said to have written another book in favour of the seventh day, entitled *Error Blasted.** See Jeremiah Ives, *Saturday No Sabbath* (1659), Ep. Ded., sig. A4ʳ.

Note 3. A further work by Thomas Tillam, *A Present From Prison,** is referred to by Cowell in *Divine Oracles*, without date.

Note 4. Whitley, *BB* i. 9–708, lists: B. C., *The Picture of a First-rate Jack.**

[10] Not otherwise known. No copy extant.
[11] Not otherwise known. No copy extant.

APPENDIX V

Distribution of the Sabbatarian Movement to 1800 by Counties

BASED on evidence available to date. It is possible, in some instances probable, that a Sabbatarian presence and/or congregation existed for which no evidence has survived or come to light. 'Congregation' refers to a group which met for worship and is not necessarily synonymous with 'church', which after seventeenth-century Nonconformist practice often consisted of more than one congregation. 'Mixed-communion' refers to First-day and Seventh-day believers.

Key:

*	Confirmed Sabbatarian congregation.
+	Probable Sabbatarian congregation, unconfirmed due to lack of definitive evidence.
●	Mixed-communion congregation.
o	Possible mixed-communion congregation.
×	Sabbatarian presence not identified with a congregation. In some instances, may also indicate an unconfirmed congregation.
∧	Possible Sabbatarian interest.

Double designations shewn thus, e.g. ×/o, indicate alternative possibilities, based on available evidence. Double designations shewn thus, e.g. ●–*, indicate a known progression.

Berkshire

+/o	Abingdon (now in Oxon.)
*	Wallingford (now in Oxon.)
×/o	Wantage

Breconshire (Brecknockshire) (now Powys)

∧	Olchon
∧	Probably in connection with Hay-on-Wye

Buckinghamshire

*	Amersham
●–*	Bledlow
*	Chalfont St Giles
∧	Chesham

*   Chorley Wood (now in Herts.)
×   Ibstone

Cambridgeshire

×   Burwell
●–+   Downham
∧   Eltisley
∧   Littleport

Devon

*   Exeter
×/o   Plymouth
∧   Prescott
×   Tiverton

Dorset

*   Beaminster
×   Castleton
*   Dorchester
*   Dorchester gaol
×   Holnest
*   Sherborne
*   Sturminster Newton

Durham

●   Raby Castle
∧   Witton-le-Wear
×/o/+   Other unspecified locations

Essex

*   Braintree
*   Colchester (Congregations of General and Particular Seventh-day Baptists)
∧   Langham
*   Harwich
+   Mersea

Gloucestershire

×/+   Badgeworth
*   Bibury
×   Bishop's Cleeve
×/+   Bourton-on-the-Water
*   Cheltenham
∧   Chipping Sodbury

∧   Fairford
×   Haresfield
●   Hillesley
∧   Horsley
*/o King's Stanley
×   Mickleton
*   Natton (Ashchurch, Aston-upon-Carrant)
*   Naunton
*   Notgrove
*   Oddington
*   Oxenton
+   Paxford
*   Stapleton (now in Avon)
×   Stow-on-the-Wold
●   Tewkesbury
×   Wheatenhurst (Whitminster)

Hampshire

∧   Cowes (Isle of Wight)
×   Gosport
*   Southampton/Portsmouth

Herefordshire (now Hereford and Worcester)

×   Broadmeadow
×   Clifford
*   Hay-on-Wye
*   Leominster

Hertfordshire

∧   Bishop's Stortford
∧   Brent Pelham
∧   Rickmansworth
*   Watford

Huntingdonshire (now Cambs.)

×   Holywell

Kent

×   Cranbrook

Lincolnshire

*   Boston
×   Croft
∧   Lincoln

London/Middlesex

* * Bell Lane
* * Mill Yard
* * Mill Yard, Huguenot
* * Pinners' Hall/Curriers' Hall
* * The Henry Jessey Congregation

Monmouthshire (now Gwent)

* ● Abergavenny (Llanwenarth)
* ●/o Llandegveth
* ●/o Llangibby
* ● Llangwm
* ● Llantrissant
* ∧ Magor
* ● Usk

Norfolk

* * East Ruston
* * Gt. Yarmouth
* ●–*–● Ingham (Stalham)
* + Lessingham
* * North Walsham
* * Norwich
* ∧ Pulham Margaret (Pulham Market)
* * Walcott
* ● Worstead
* ∧ Wymondham

Northamptonshire

* × Northampton
* ∧ At other unspecified locations

Northumberland

* ×/o At unspecified locations

Nottinghamshire

* * Nottingham
* × Ratcliffe (or Radcliffe)

Oxfordshire

* * Berrick Salome
* × Chipping Norton
* × Duxford

●/*	Kingston Blount
×	Lewknor
●	Oxford
*	Warborough
*	Watlington

Radnorshire (now Powys)

∧	Probably in connection with Hay-on-Wye

Somerset

×/+	Dunkerton (now in Avon)
×	Taunton

Staffordshire

×	Dudley (now in West Midlands)
∧	Wolverhampton

Suffolk

×	Beccles
*	Hasketon
×	Ipswich
×	Melton (with Woodbridge)
*	Woodbridge

Surrey

*	Chertsey

Warwickshire

×	Warwick

Wiltshire

*	Salisbury

Worcestershire (now Hereford and Worcester)

*	Alderminster (now in War.: known also as Aldermaston)
*	Ashton-under-Hill
×	Birlingham
×	Bredon
∧	Bredon's Norton
×	Kemerton
×	Overbury
*	Upton-on-Severn
×/o	Westmancote

Yorkshire

✕	Kingston upon Hull
✕/+	York
✕	Other unspecified locations

BIBLIOGRAPHY

MANUSCRIPT SOURCES

Visitation and conventicle returns, presentments, depositions, and consistory court records are not included.

The Angus Library, Regent's Park College, Oxford

F.P.C.F1b: Bourton-on-the-Water church book, 1719–1802.

F.P.C.F1c: Bourton-on-the-Water church book; pastoral diary, 1745–73.

F.P.C.c8: Benjamin Stinton, 'A Repository of Divers Historical Matters relating to the English Antipedobaptists', 1712.

2/2/9: 'Records and Letters Relative to the Baptist Church at Hexham, October, 1651–July 1680'.

30.a.8: 'An Outline of the History of the Baptist Church at Ingham, Norfolk'.

36 G.A.e.10: Benjamin Stinton, 'An Account of Some of the Most Eminent and leading Men among the English Antipaedobaptists'.

41.e.1: W.T. Whitley, 'Men of the Seventh Day'.

Bodleian Library

Rawl. D.399: Robert Atkyns to John Fell, 26 Aug. 1683.

Rawl. D.828: Register of the acts of an Anabaptist congregation in London, 22 Aug. 1652–23 May 1654 (records of the More–Chamberlen, Lothbury Square, church).

Rawl. D.846: 'Of the Sabbatarian Controversy'.

Rawl. D.1350: 'The seventh day man, or restless Christian, in the vanity of his jewish Sabbath and presumptuous contempt of Gospel-rest . . . and the Lord's Day justified, as the true Christian Sabbath'.

Tanner 35: Peter Chamberlen to William Sancroft, Apr. 1682.

Tanner 56: Francis Dove, Mayor of Salisbury, to the Speaker of the House of Commons, Feb. 1649/50.

Tanner 160: Peter Chamberlen to William Sancroft, July 1680.

Tanner 311: Statement of John Hobart to Roger Mingay, mayor of Norwich, Aug. 1658.

Tanner 378: Theophilus Brabourne, 'A Discourse upon the Sabbath Daye'.

Bodley 538: Theophilus Brabourne, 'An answer to Mr. Burton on the Lords Day Sabbath'; Thomas Broad, 'Two Treatises: The one Concerninge the Sabboath or seventh day. The other Concerninge the Lords day or first of the week', [1632]; Thomas Broad, 'A Confutation of Mr. Brabournes

Sabbath-doctrine, which is, that we Christians ought to keep holy the Jewes Sabbath, or Saterday'.

Add. C.303: 'The Sentence in the Starr-Chamber against Jo. Traske', 16 June, Anno Jacobi, 16.

Bristol Baptist College Library

G 98a(1): Joshua Thomas, 'The History of the Baptist Churches in Wales'.

G 98a(5): Joshua Thomas, 'Queries and Answers'.

The British Library

Harl. 2339: 'A litil tretys agens ye opynyon of sum men yt seyn yat no man hath powr for to chaunge ye Saboth fro ye Satirday to ye Sonday. And here is pleynly proved ye contrarie, bi Holi Writt, and Doctouris sentence, accordinge herewit'.

Sloane 63: James Toppe, 'Christs Monarchicall and personall Reigne upon Earth over all the Kingdoms of this world'.

Dr Williams's Library

38.4: John Evans, 'Dissenting Congregations and Ministers in England and Wales, 1715–29'.

38.5: Josiah Thompson, 'The State of the Dissenting Interest in England and Wales, 1772–3'.

38.6: Josiah Thompson, 'The Dissenting Interest in England and Wales, 1772–3'.

38.10: Josiah Thompson, 'History of Protestant Dissenting Congregations', 1772.

59.6: Richard Baxter to Thomas Bampfield, 16 Jan. 1671.

63.I, 1–5: Walter Wilson, 'An Account of Various Congregations in England, among the Presbyterians, Independents, and Baptists'.

76.5: Joseph Davey, 'Copy of the records of the Congregational Church worshipping at the Quay meeting, Woodbridge, 1651 to 1851'.

76.13: Joseph Davey, 'Copy of The Church Book of the United churches of Tunstead, Bradfield, and North Walsham'.

533.B.1: The Mill Yard Minutes: the Church book of the Seventh Day General Baptist Congregation meeting at Mill Yard, Goodman's Fields, 1673–1840 (MYM, Xerox copy).

533.B.2: Francis Bampfield Seventh Day Baptist Congregation (Curriers' Hall, and elsewhere). Records of the congregation, 1686–1843 (the Pinners' Hall/Curriers' Hall church book; PHCB, Xerox copy).

New College, L6/15: Joseph Meen, 'Collections Biographical, Historical and Miscellaneous Relating to the History of Dissenting Churches'.

Essex Record Office (Colchester)

Quarter Sessions Roll, Epiphany 1705/6: Registration of Meeting House.

Friends House Library

Vol. v, 178/1: J.J. Green, 'A Biographical Account of Samuel Cater, of Littleport in the Isle of Ely, Baptist Elder and Quaker Preacher, 1627–1711'.

Gloucestershire Record Office

D 2889, 2/1: Hillesley church book.
D 4944, 2/1: Tewkesbury Baptist church book.
D 4944, 10/1/4: Kinsham church book.
PA 178/3: K. Chappell, 'Hillesley Baptist Church, 1730–1980'.

Guildhall Library

9579: Certificates for Dissenters' Meeting Houses in the Diocese of London.

Lambeth Palace Library

Tenison MS 639.
MS 951/1.

Lincolnshire Archives Office

2, Brace 4: W. Elliott, 'Notes on the Baptists', in *Local Historian*, 34, 35.

National Library of Wales

409 B: Llanwenarth church book.
10620 E: Joshua Thomas, 'History of Welsh Baptists'.
11095 E: Exeter Baptist church to Leominster Baptist church, 7 Mar. 1721.
Minor Deposit 614 A: Joshua Thomas, 'History of Leominster Baptist Church'.

Norfolk Record Office

FC42/1: Worstead church book.
4260–1: M.F. Hewett, 'Historical Record of the Baptists of Norfolk and their Churches'.
NCC Wills 1662, OW80: Will of Theophilus Brabourne.

Oxfordshire Record Office

W.J. Oldfield (ed.), 'Oxfordshire Quarter Sessions Rolls', viii.

Public Record Office

SP 16/72/45: 'A true report of Mr. Traske, his proceedings'.
SP 16/73/64: Examination of John Traske, 9 Aug. 1627.
SP 16/261/55, 6: Deposition *contra* Sir Richard Stroud of Cattistock, Dorset, June 1634.
SP 29/4/18: James Hickes to Sir Edward Nicholas, 13 June 1660.
SP 29/41/1: Sir William Killigrew, report on Tillam and Pooley, 1 Sept. 1661.
SP 29/106/11: W.B. to Henry Muddiman, 5 Dec. 1664.

SP 29/181/116: Christopher Sanderson to Joseph Williamson, 14 Oct. 1666, including 'The Solemne Covenant'.

SP 29/190/104: Christopher Sanderson to Joseph Williamson, 5 Feb. 1667(8).

SP 29/207/1: Luke James, Miles Wallis, and John Sicklemore to the Duke of Albermarle, 25 June 1667.

SP 29/232/10: William Haggett to Sir Philip Musgrave, 2 Jan. 1667(8).

SP 29/233/207: Sir John Robinson to Joseph Williamson, 18 July 1671.

SP 29/236/14: Silas Taylor to Joseph Williamson, 5 Mar. 1667(8).

SP 263/54/1: William Haggett to Sir Philip Musgrave, July 1669.

SP, Ireland, 238/1/26A: James Ussher to James I, Mar. 1624.

Seventh Day Baptist Historical Society

194x.6: 'Samuel Hubbard's Journal, c.1633–1686'.

C.H. Green, Notebook 10: A transcript of W.T. Whitley, 'A Century of Sabbath Doctrine, 1595–1695'.

Trinity College Library, Dublin

TCD 233.53–60: Anonymous and untitled manuscript, 'We are now to keep our Sabbath and rest upon Saturday . . .'.

Church Books (held by respective churches and not listed above)

Brown Street, Salisbury, church book, 1766–82.

Eld Lane, Colchester, church book.

Leominster Baptist church book.

Naunton Baptist church book, 1849–65.

Upton-on-Severn Baptist church book.

Theses

CHILD, MARGARET, 'Prelude to Revolution: The Structure of Politics in County Durham, 1678–88' (Ph.D. thesis, University of Maryland, 1972).

McDONALD, MURDINE, 'London Calvinistic Baptists, 1689–1727: Tensions within a Dissenting Community under Toleration' (D.Phil. thesis, Oxford University, 1982).

Other Manuscripts

Baptist Church House: Deeds relating to the Brown Street Baptist church, Salisbury.

BURDICK, OSCAR, 'Seventh Day Baptist Origins in England, 1650–1683: A Bibliography', 1984.

CARTER, N., 'Wiltshire Nonconformity', Brown Street, Salisbury, church records, J.5.

Commissioners for Charities MSS 210274/A/1, 3, 7: Notes relating to the Joseph Davis Charity.

William Salt Library, Stafford: MS 33.

PRINTED SOURCES

Place of publication, unless otherwise indicated, is London.

1. *Primary works*

An Account of the Baptist Churches in Ireland (1653).

ALSOP, ANN, *Remarks on the Rev. T. Edmond's pamphlet . . . and an attempt to vindicate their conduct who observe the Seventh-day Sabbath . . .* (1801).

ANDREWES, LANCELOT, *A Patterne of Catechisticall Doctrine* (1630).

Articles to be Enquired of by the Churchwardens and Swornmen within the Archdeaconry of Middlesex (1582).

ASPINWALL, WILLIAM, *The Abrogation of the Jewish Sabbath* (1657).

The Authority and Sanctification of the Lord's Day Explained and Enforced (1786).

BACKUS, ISAAC, *A Church History of New-England . . . With, A Particular History of the Baptist Churches* (3 vols., Boston, Mass., 1777–96).

BAILEY, NATHANIEL, *English and Latin Exercises for School Boys* (1706).

—— *An Universal Etymological English Dictionary* (1721).

BALL, JOHN, *A Treatise of Faith, divided into two Parts. The First shewing the Nature, the Second, the Life of Faith* (1632).

BALL, JOHN, *The Anabaptist Teachers no Ministers of Christ, proved in a letter to Mr Charsley, an Anabaptist Teacher at Agmondesham* (1708).

BAMPFIELD, FRANCIS, *All in One. All Useful Sciences and Profitable Arts in one Book of Jehovah Aelohim . . . Comprehended and discovered in the Fulness and Perfection of Scripture-Knowledges* (1677).

—— *The House of Wisdom* (1681).

—— *A Name, an After One, or, A Name, a New One . . . or An Historical Declaration of the Life of Shem Acher* (1681).

—— *The Lords Free Prisoner* (1683).

—— *Septima dies, Dies Desiderabilis, Sabbatum Jehovae. The Seventh-Day-Sabbath the Desirable Day . . .* (1677).

BAMPFIELD, THOMAS, *An Enquiry Whether the Lord Jesus Christ made the World, and be Jehovah, and gave the Moral Law? And Whether the Fourth Command be Repealed or Altered?* (1692).

—— *A Reply to Doctor Wallis, his Discourse Concerning the Christian Sabbath* (1693).

BARATTI, GIACOMO, *The Late Travels of S. Giacomo Baratti, an Italian Gentleman, into the Remote Countries of the Abissins, or of Ethiopia, Interior,* tr. G.D. (1670).

BAXTER, RICHARD, *Aphorismes of Justification, with their Explication Annexed* (1649).

—— *The Divine Appointment of the Lords Day Proved . . . And consequently the Cessation of the Seventh day Sabbath* (1671).

BAXTER, RICHARD, *The Saints Everlasting Rest* (10th edn. 1669).

BECON, THOMAS, *The Early Works of Thomas Becon*, ed. J. Ayre (Cambridge, 1843).

BEEVAN, JOHN, *A Loving Salutation To all People who have any desire after the Living God; But especially to the Free-Will-Anabaptists* (1660).

BENN, WILLIAM, *The Judgment of Mr. Francis Bampfield . . . for the Observation of the Jewish or Seventh Day Sabboth . . . and a vindication of the Christian Sabboth against the Jewish* (1672).

BERNARD, NICHOLAS, *The Judgement Of the Late Archbishop of Armagh, and Primate of Ireland . . . Of the Sabbath, and observation of the Lords Day . . .* (1657).

BERNARD, RICHARD, *A Threefold Treatise of the Sabbath: distinctly divided into the Patriarchall, Mosaicall, and Christian Sabbath . . .* (1641).

BIRCHLEY, WILLIAM, *The Christian Moderator* (1652).

BOLTON, SAMUEL, *The True Bounds of Christian Freedom* (1656).

BOWNDE, NICHOLAS, *The Doctrine of the Sabbath* (1595).

—— *Sabbatum Veteris et Novi Testamenti: or, The True Doctrine of the Sabbath, held and practised by the Church of God, both before and under the Law, and in the time of the Gospel . . .* (1606).

BRABOURNE, THEOPHILUS, *A Defence of that most Ancient, and Sacred ordinance of GODS, the Sabbath Day. Consequently, and together with it, 2. A Defence of the iiijth Commandement: 3. A Defence of the integrity and perfection of the Decalogue, Morall Law, or X Commandements. 4. A Defence also, of the whole and intire worship of God, in all the partes thereof, as it is prescribed, in the first Table of the Decalogue. 5. A Discovery of the Superstition, impurity and corruption of Gods worship; yea, and Idolatry, committed by multitudes, in sanctifying the Lords Day for a Sabbath Day, by the iiijth Commandement. Undertaken against all Anti-Sabbatharians, both of Protestants, Papists, Antinomians, and Anabaptists:;and by name and especially against these X Ministers, M. Greenwood, M. Hutchinson, M. Furnace, M. Benton, M. Gallard, M. Yates, M. Chappel, M. Stinnet, M. Johnson, and M. Warde* ([Amsterdam], 1632).

—— *A Discourse upon the Sabbath Day; wherein are handled these particulars ensuing.—1. That the Lord's Day is not Sabbath Day by Divine institution. 2. An exposition of the iiii Commandment . . . and particularly here it is shown at what time the Sabbath day should begin and end . . . 3. That the Seventh-day Sabbath is not abolished. 4. That the Seventh-day Sabbath is now still in force. 5. The author's Exhortation and reasons, that nevertheless there be no Rent from our Church as touching practice* (1628).

—— *Of the changing of Church-Discipline* (1653).

—— *The Second Part of the Change of Church Discipline* (1654).

BRABOURNE, *The Second Vindication of my first Book of the Change of Discipline* (1654).

—— *An Answer to M. Cawdry's two Books of the Sabbath* (Norwich, 1654).

—— *An Answer to Two Books on the Sabbath. 1. To Mr. Ives of London, his Book Intituled Saturday no Sabbath Day. 2. To Mr. Warren of Colchester, his book intituled, the Jews Sabbath Antiquated, and the Lords day Instituted by Divine Providence* (1659).

—— *Of the Sabbath Day, which is now, the Highest Controversie in the Church of England. For on this Controversie, Dependeth the Gaining or loosing one of Gods Ten Commandments, by name, the 4th Command, for the Sabbath day* (1660).

—— *A Reply to Mr. Collings Provocator Provocatus* (1654).

—— *A Reply to the Indoctus Doctor Edoctus* (1654).

BRERERWOOD, EDWARD, *A Learned Treatise of the Sabaoth* (Oxford, 1630).

BROAD, THOMAS, *Three Questions Answered* (Oxford, 1621).

The Brownists Conventicle (1641).

BURNET, WILLIAM, *The Capital Principles of the People called Quakers Discovered and Stated out of their own Writings* (1668).

CALAMY, EDMUND, *A Continuation of the Account of the Ministers . . . Ejected and Silenced . . . by or before the Act for Uniformity* (2 vols., 1727).

CARLOW, GEORGE, *Truth Defended; or, Observations on Mr Ward's Expositary Discourses from the 8th, 9th, 10th, and 11th verses of the 20th chapter of Exodus, concerning the Sabbath* (1724).

CAVE, WILLIAM, *Primitive Christianity: or the Religion of the Ancient Christians in the first Ages of the Gospel* (1673).

CAWDREY, DANIEL, and PALMER, HERBERT, *Sabbatum Redivivum, or the Christian Sabbath Vindicated: in a full Discourse concerning the Sabbath and the Lord's Day*, part I (1645); parts II, III, IV (1652).

Certaine Sermons appoynted . . . to be declared and read . . . for the better understanding of the simple people (1563).

CHAMBERLAYNE, EDWARD, *Angliae Notitia* (20th edn., 1702).

CHAMBERLEN, PETER, *Englands Choice* (1682).

—— *The Sons of the East* (1682).

—— *A Voice in Rhama* (1647).

CHUBB, THOMAS, *Dissertation concerning the Time for Keeping a Sabbath* (1737).

CLARK, ROBERT, *The Lying-Wonders* (1660).

COLLIER, THOMAS, *The Seventh Day Sabbath Opened and Discovered* (1658).

COLLINGS, JOHN, *A New Lesson for the Indoctus Doctor* (1654).

A Comprehensive Account of the General Baptists with respect to Principle and Practice (Coventry, 1795).

CORNTHWAITE, ROBERT, *An Essay on the Sabbath; or, a Modest Attempt towards a plain, scriptural Resolution of the following Questions:—I.*

Whether the Seventh Day Sabbath was given to Adam in Paradise? II. Whether the same now obliges Christians? (1740).

CORNTHWAITE, ROBERT, *Reflections on Dr. Wright's Treatise on the Religious Observation of the Lord's Day, According to the express Words of the Fourth Commandment. Shewing the Inconclusiveness of the Doctor's Reasoning on that Subject, and the Impossibility of grounding the First-Day Sabbath on the Fourth Commandment, or any other Text of Scripture, produced by him for that Purpose* ([1731]).

—— *The Seventh-Day Sabbath Farther Vindicated, or, a Defence of some Reflexions on Dr Wright's Treatise on the religious observation of the Lord's Day, according to the express words of the fourth commandment* (1736).

COVEN, STEPHEN, *The Militant Christian* (1668).

COWELL, JOHN, *A Beame of Sabbath Light Breaking forth through a Cloud of Witnesses. Or, The Holy, Just, Good, Spiritual Law of God confirmed (and as included therein the seventh-dayes Sabbath to be observed) as a Rule of Life to Believers in Christ* (1664).

—— *The Snare Broken: Being a true and faithful account of the Authors Grounds for his leaving off the observation of the Sabbath of the First or Old Covenant: Wherein his Beam of Legal-Covenant-Light is darkned by the more clear shineing forth of Gospel Light and Truth* (1677).

COX, JOHN, *Articles of Christian Faith Believed and Written by me, John Cox, of York* (1689).

—— *An Epistle to all the Lord's People* ([1685]).

—— *A General Epistle to the Christian Churches* (1683).

—— *To All that Believe in God* ([1687]).

COXE, WILLIAM, *An Historical Tour in Monmouthshire* (1801).

CROSBY, THOMAS, *The History of the English Baptists* (4 vols., 1738–40).

[DAVIS, JOSEPH], *The Last Legacy of Mr. Joseph Davis, Senr.* (1707, 1720)

A Declaration of several of the Churches of Christ . . . Concerning the Kingly Interest of Christ, and The present Suffrings of His Cause and Saints in England (1654).

DENNE, HENRY, *Antichrist Unmasked in two Treatises . . . The second, The man of Sinne discovered in Doctrine; the root and foundation of Antichrist laid open* (1645).

Dissenters and Schismaticks Expos'd (1715).

DOBEL, DANIEL, *The Seventh-Day Sabbath not obligatory on Christians* (Canterbury, 1739).

DOD, JOHN, and CLEAVER, ROBERT, *A Plaine and Familiar Exposition of the Ten Commandments* (1615).

EDWARDS, THOMAS, *Gangraena: or A Catalogue and Discovery of many of the Errours, Heresies, Blasphemies and pernicious Practices of the Sectaries of this time . . .* (2nd edn. 1646).

—— *The third Part of Gangraena, or, A new and higher Discovery of the*

Errors, Heresies, Blasphemies and insolent Proceedings of the Sectaries of these times (1646).

ELLIOTT, EDWARD, *Plain Scripture-Proof that the Christian Church is under no obligation to keep any of the Jewish Sabbaths* (1708).

ELWALL, EDWARD, *A Declaration Against all the Kings and Temporal Powers under Heaven. Shewing that they have no authority over their subjects in spiritual things. . . . With the Case of the Seventh Day Sabbath-Keepers considered . . . that all such may have the Liberty to work Six Days at their honest Vocations, and rest the Seventh Day, according to the Commandment of God* (4th edn. 1741).

—— *The Supernatural Incarnation of Jesus Christ proved to be false . . .* (1743).

—— *True Testimony for God, and for His Sacred Law; Being a Plain and Honest Defence of the Fourth Commandment of God . . .* (3rd edn., 1727).

ERASMUS, D., *De amabili Ecclesiae concordia* (Antwerp, 1533).

EVANS, ARISE, *An Eccho to the Voice from Heaven* (1652).

EVANS, JOHN, *A Sketch of the Several Denominations into which the Christian World is Divided* (2nd edn. 1795).

EVE, GEORGE; SQUIBB, ARTHUR; BELCHER, JOHN; STENNETT, EDWARD; GARDNER, JOHN; PARNHAM, RICHARD; and WOODS, ROBERT, *A Faithful Testimony Against The Teachers of Circumcision and the Legal Ceremonies; who are lately gone into Germany* (1667).

The Faith and Practice of Thirty Congregations Gathered according to the Primitive Pattern (1651).

[FALCONER, JOHN] B.D., *A Briefe Refutation of John Traskes Judaical and Novel Fancyes* (St Omer, 1618).

FIELD, JOHN, *A godly exhortation, by occasion of the late judgement of God . . . concerning the keeping of the Sabboth day* (1583).

FLAVEL, JOHN, *The Whole Workes of the Reverend Mr. John Flavel* (2nd edn. 1716).

FLEMING, CALEB, *The Fourth Commandment Abrogated by the Gospel: Or, the Fourth Commandment's enjoining the Observance of the Seventh Day of the Week as a Religious Rest, was only obligatory and binding within the Jewish State. But the Law of the Sabbath being destroy'd, the Christian Institution authoriseth the Christian's Observance of the First Day of the Week, as an Holy Festival* (1736).

—— *A Plain and Rational Account of the Law of the Sabbath; Being a Defence of a late Pamphlet, intitled, 'The Fourth Commandment abrogated by the Gospel'; or An Answer to Mr. Robert Cornthwaite's farther Defence of the Seventh-Day Sabbath; in which Gen. ii, 2, 3 (called by him the Original Institution) is more particularly considered, and his most material Objections and Criticisms refuted* (1736).

FOXE, JOHN, *The Actes and Monuments of John Foxe*, ed. G. Townsend (8 vols., New York, 1965; facsimile of 1843–9 edn.).

FRANCIS, BENJAMIN, *An Elegy on the Death of the Reverend Mr. Philip Jones, late Minister of the Gospel at Upton-on-Severn* (1771).

FULLER, THOMAS, *The Church-History of Britain, from the Birth of Jesus Christ until the year 1648* (1655).

GRANTHAM, THOMAS, *Christianismus Primitivus: or, the Ancient Christian Religion . . . vindicated . . .* (1678).

—— *The Seventh-Day Sabbath Ceased as Ceremonial, and yet the Morality of the Fourth Command remaineth* (1667).

GRAUNT, JOHN, *The Shipwrack of all False Churches: and the Immutable Safety and Stability of the True Church of Christ . . .* (1652).

GREENHAM, RICHARD, *The Workes of . . . Richard Greenham* (3rd edn. 1601).

HALLETT, JOSEPH, *A Free and Impartial Study of the Holy Scriptures recommended* (1729).

—— *A Third Volume of Notes on Several Texts of Scripture* (1736).

HANSON, JOHN, *A short Treatise shewing the Sabbatharians confuted by the new Covenant* (1658).

HEBDON, RETURNE, *A Guide to the Godly* (1648).

HEYLYN, PETER, *Cosmography* (5th edn. 1674).

—— *The History of the Sabbath* (2nd. edn. 1636).

—— *Respondet Petrus: or the Answer of Peter Heylyn, D.D., to so much of Dr. Bernard's book, entituled 'The Judgement of the late Primate of Ireland', etc., as he is made a party to by the said Lord Primate in the point of the Sabbath* (1658).

HILL, ROBERT, *A Discourse upon the Fourth Commandment* (1728).

HILLER, THOMAS, *The Doctrine of Grace* (1740).

The History of King-Killers (1719).

HOOKER, RICHARD, *The Lawes of Ecclesiasticall Politie* (Oxford, 1622).

HOOPER, JOHN, *A Declaration of the Ten Holy Commaundements of almyghty God* (1548).

HORNIUS, GEORGIUS, *De statu Ecclesiae Britannicae hodierno* (Danzig, 1647).

HOSPINIAN, RUDOLPH, *De Origine, Progressu, Ceremoniis, et Ritibus Festorum Dierum Iudaeorum, Graecorum, Romanorum, et Turcarum* (Zurich, 1592).

IRONSIDE, GILBERT, *Seven Questions of the Sabbath briefly disputed, after the Manner of the Schools* (Oxford, 1637).

IVES, JEREMIAH, *Saturday No Sabbath: Or, the Seventh-Day Sabbath Proved To be of no force to the Beleeving Gentiles in the times of the Gospel* (1659).

IVIMEY, JOSEPH, *History of the English Baptists* (4 vols., 1811–30).

JEPHSON, ALEXANDER, *A Discourse Concerning the Religious Observation of the Lord's Day* (1737).

J[ESSEY] H[ENRY], *A Calculation for this present year, 1645* ([1645]).

—— *Miscellanea Sacra, or Diverse Necessary Truths* (1665).

—— *A Scripture Almanack, or, A Calculation for the year 1647* ([1647]).

JOSSELIN, RALPH, *The Diary of Ralph Josselin 1616–1683*, ed. A. MacFarlane (1976).

Journals of the House of Commons, vi (2 Sept. 1648–14 Aug. 1651).

KEACH, BENJAMIN, *The Jewish Sabbath Abrogated, or The Saturday Sabbatarians Confuted* (1700).

KILLINGWORTH, GRANTHAM, *A Supplement to the Sermons . . . at Salters-Hall against Popery . . . with the Appendix: concerning the First Day of the Week* (1738).

KNEWSTUB, JOHN, *Lectures . . . upon the twentieth Chapter of Exodus* (1577).

LATIMER, HUGH, *The Works of Hugh Latimer*, ed. G.E. Corrie (2 vols., Cambridge, 1844–5).

LEY, JOHN, *Sunday a Sabbath: or, a Preparative Discourse for Discussion of Sabbatory Doubts* (1641).

LLOYD, DAVID, *Memoires of the Lives, Actions, Sufferings & Deaths of those . . . Excellent Personages that Suffered . . . for the Protestant Religion* (1668).

LOCKE, JOHN, *The Reasonableness of Christianity as Delivered in the Scriptures* (1695).

LUTHER, MARTIN, *Werke*, xlii (Weimar, 1911).

MARLOW, ISAAC, *A Tract on the Sabbath Day. Wherein the keeping of the First Day of the Week a Sabbath is justified by a Divine Command and a Double Example contained in the Old and New Testament. With Answers to the chiefest Objections made by the Jewish Seventh-day Sabbatharians and others* (1694).

MAULDEN, JOHN, *The Ancient and Honourable Way and Truth of God's Sacred Rest of the Seventh-Day Sabbath. Plainly discovered, to be the One and only Weekly-Day, by Divine Appointment, for the worship of God; binding all Men, in all Ages, from the Beginning to the End of Time, to its strict and intire Observation* (1724).

—— [Philotheos], *A Threefold Dialogue, Concerning the Three Chief Points in Controversy amongst Protestants in our Days, viz. I. Whether the Holy Scriptures do prove the doctrine of Free Grace, or Free Will? II. Whether believers, or Infants-baptism, be the Ordinance of Christ? III. Whether the Seventh, or First Day of the Week, be the Sabbath of the Lord* (1708).

MILTON, JOHN, *A Treatise of Christian Doctrine*, trans. C.R. Sumner (Cambridge, 1825).

The Moralitie of the Fourth Commandement (1652).

MORE, JOHN, *A Generall Exhortation to the World* (1652).

—— *Moses Revived; or a Vindication of an ancient Law of God. . . . wherein the Unlawfulness of eating blood is clearly proved by the Word of God* (1670).

—— *A Trumpet Sounded: or The Great Mystery of the two Little Horns Unfolded* (1654).

MYERS, GEORGE, *A Serious Examination of a Pretended Answer to a Paper of Judgement past at Yorke, with a Reply thereto* (1686).

A Narrative of the Apprehending, Committment, Arraignment, Condemnation, and Execution of John James (1662).

NORICE, EDWARD, *The New Gospel not the True Gospel, or, A Discovery of the Life and Death, Doctrin and Doings of Mr John Traske, and the effects of all, in his Followers* (1638).

OCKFORD, JAMES, *The Doctrine of the Fourth Commandement, Deformed by Popery; Reformed and Restored to its Primitive purity* (1650).

—— *The Tryal of the Truth; or, rather the Law is the Truth* (Amsterdam, 1656).

OWEN, JOHN, *Exercitations Concerning the Name, Original, Nature, Use, and Continuance of a Day of Sacred Rest. Wherein the Original of the Sabbath from the Foundation of the World, The Morality of the Fourth Commandment, with the Change of the Seventh Day are inquired into. Together with an Assertion of the Divine Institution of the Lord's Day, and Practical Directions for its due Observation* (1671).

—— *The Nature, Power, Deceit, and Prevalency of the Remainders of Indwelling Sin in Believers* (1668).

OZELL, JOHN (tr.), *M. Misson's Memoirs and Observations in his Travels over England* (1719).

PAGITT, EPHRAIM, *Heresiography, or a Description of the Heretics and Sectaries of these Latter Times* (6th edn. 1661).

PALMER, S. (ed.), *The Nonconformist's Memorial* (3rd edn., 3 vols., 1802–3).

PARDOE, WILLIAM, *Antient Christianity Revived; Being a Description of the Doctrine, Discipline, and Practice of the Little City of Bethania . . .* (1688).

PARRY, HENRY (trs.), *The Summe of Christian Religion* (1595).

PENINGTON, ISAAC, *An Epistle to all such as observe the Seventh-day of the Week for a Sabbath to the Lord* (1660).

—— *The New-Covenant of the Gospel Distinguished from the Old Covenant of the Law, and the Rest or Sabbath of Believers, from the Rest or Sabbath of the Jews* (1660).

—— *To the Jews Natural and to the Jews Spiritual* (1677).

PLOT, ROBERT, *The Natural History of Oxfordshire* (Oxford, 1677).

POCKLINGTON, JOHN, *Sunday No Sabbath* (1636).

PORTER, EDMUND, *Sabbatum: The Mystery of the Sabbath Discovered* (1658).

PRIDEAUX, JOHN, *The Doctrine of the Sabbath, Delivered in the Act at Oxon, anno 1622* (1634).

PRIESTLEY, JOSEPH, *An Appeal to the Serious and Candid Professors of Christianity* (1791).

PURCHAS, SAMUEL, *Hakluytas Posthumus, or Purchas his Pilgrims* (1625).

REDFORD, ELIZABETH, *The Widow's Mite. Shewing why the seventh day is to be kept in Christ* ([1693–5]).

RIPPON, JOHN, *The Baptist Annual Register* (4 vols., 1790–1809).

Ross, Alexander, Πανσεβεια: or, A View of all Religions in the World (6th edn. 1683).

Russell, William, No Seventh-Day-Sabbath Commanded by Jesus Christ in the New-Testament (1663).

Russen, David, Fundamentals without Foundation, or, a True Picture of the Anabaptists in their Rise, Progress and Practice. Written for the use of such as take 'em for saints, when they are not so much as Christians (1703).

Rutland, John, A Vindication of the Divine Decrees of Election and Reprobation (1720).

Ryland, John, The Presence of Christ the Source of Eternal Bliss (n.d.).

Saller [Sellars], William, An Examination of a late Book published by Dr. Owen, Concerning a Sacred Day of Rest. Many Truths therein as to the Morality of a Christian Sabbath assented to. With a Brief Inquiry into his Reasons for the change of it from the seventh day to the first, by way of denial (1671).

—— A Preservative against Atheism and Error, Wherein some fundamental points in religion . . . Are by way of question and answer, handled . . . To which is added, A brief answer to William Russell in a book of his, also entituled, No Seventh-day-Sabbath in Christs New Testament (1664).

—— [Salter], Sundry Queries Tendred to . . . Ministers of Jesus Christ, for clearing the Doctrine of the Fourth Commandement, And the Lords Sabbath Day ([1653]).

—— [W.S.], Sundry Queries formerly tendred to the Ministers of London, for clearing the Doctrine of the fourth Commandment, and the Lord's SABBATH-DAY, but now tendred to the Consideration of all Men ([1660]).

—— and Spittlehouse, John, An Appeal To the Consciences of the chief Magistrates of this Commonwealth, touching the Sabbath-day . . . (1657).

Seagar, John, A Discoverie of the World to Come According to the Scriptures (1650).

Sibbes, Richard, Christs Exaltation Purchast by Humiliation (1639).

Soursby, Henry, and Smith, Mehetabel, A Discourse of the Sabbath, or The Controversies about the Sabbath Stated and Examined, with reference unto the Law of Nature, the Law of Moses, and the Law of Christ (1683).

Spittlehouse, John, A Manifestation of sundry gross absurdities . . . in reference to the abrogating of the seventh-day-Sabbath, as commanded in the fourth Precept of the Royal Law of Jehovah (1657).

Sprint, John, Propositions Tending to Prove the Necessary Use of the Christian Sabbath, or Lord's Day (1607).

Stennett, Edward, The Royal Law Contended for, or, Some Brief Grounds serving to prove that the Ten Commandments are yet in full force, and shall so remain till Heaven and Earth pass away; also, The Seventh Day Sabbath proved from the Beginning, from the Law, from the Prophets, *from Christ and his Apostles, to be a Duty yet incumbent upon Saints and Sinners* (1658).

—— *The Seventh Day is the Sabbath of the Lord. Or An Answer to M William Russel his book, Entituled, No Seventh Day Comanded by Jesus Christ in the New Testament* (1664).

—— *The Insnared Taken in the Work of his Hands, or an Answer to Mr John Cowell . . .* (1677).

STENNETT, JEHUDAH, *A Comprehensive Grammar . . . for the Reading and Attaining the Hebrew Tongue* (1685).

STENNETT, JOSEPH, *An Answer to Mr David Russen's Book Entituled, Fundamentals Without a Foundation, or a True Picture of the Anabaptists* (1704).

—— *The Groans of a Saint under the Burden of a Mortal Body* (1695).

—— *The Works of the late Reverend and Learned Mr Joseph Stennett* (4 vols., 1732).

STOCKWOOD, JOHN (tr.), *A Verie Profitable and Necessarie Discourse Concerning the observation and keeping of the Sabboth Day* (1584).

Strange and True Newes from Glocester (1660).

STRYPE, J., *Historical Memorials, Ecclesiastical and Civil*, iii (1721).

SYMONS, HENRY, *The Lord Jesus His Commission* (1657).

TANDY, PHILIP, *Christ Knocking at the Door* (1655).

TAYLOR, JOHN, *A Swarme of Sectaries and Schismatiques* (1641).

THOMAS, JOSHUA, *Hanes y Bedyddwyr, Ymblith Y Cymry* (Caerfyrddin, 1778).

—— *The History of Antipaedobaptists in Wales* (1778).

—— *A History of the Baptist Association in Wales, 1650–1790* ([1795]).

TILLAM, THOMAS, *The Lasher Proved Lyer* ([1658]).

—— *The Seventh-Day Sabbath Sought out and celebrated, or, the Saints last Design upon the Man of sin . . . being a clear discovery of that black character in the head of the little Horn, Dan. 7. 25. The Change of Times & Laws. With the Christians glorious Conquest over that mark of the Beast, and recovery of the long-slighted seventh day, to its antient glory* (1657).

—— *The Temple of Lively Stones. Or the Promised glory of the last days* (1660).

TOLAND, JOHN, *Christianity not Mysterious* (1696).

TOMBES, JOHN, *Anti-Paedobaptism, or the Third Part, Being a full review of the dispute concerning infant Baptism* (1657).

—— *Saints no Smiters: or Smiting Civil Powers not the Work of Saints. Being a Treatise Shewing the Doctrine and Attempts of Quinto-Monarchians, or Fifth-Monarchy-Men, about Smiting Powers, to be damnable and Antichristian* (1664).

—— *Two Treatises . . . concerning Infant Baptism* (1645).

TRASKE, JOHN, *The Power of Preaching* (1623).

—— *A Treatise of Libertie from Judaisme . . .* (1620).

Truth Exalted and the Peaceable Fellowship and Exercise thereof Vindicated Against the Abusive Clamours of a Dividing False Spirit (1685).

TYNDALE, WILLIAM, *An Answer to Sir Thomas More's Dialogue*, ed. H. Walter (Cambridge, 1850).

URSINUS, ZACHARIAS, *The Summe of Christian Religion*, trans. H. Parry (Oxford, 1595).

USSHER, JAMES, *The Whole Works of the Most Rev. James Ussher, D.D.*, ed. C.R. Elrington (17 vols., Dublin, 1847–64).

VANE, HENRY (the Younger), *An Epistle General, to the Mystical Body of Christ on Earth, the Church Universal in Babylon* (1662).

—— *The Face of the Times* (1662).

—— *The Retired Mans Meditations, or the Mysterie and Power of Godliness* (1655).

WALLIS, JOHN, *A Defence of the Christian Sabbath in answer to a Treatise of Mr. Tho. Bampfield*, 2 parts (Oxford, 1692, 1694).

WARREN, EDMUND, *The Jews Sabbath Antiquated* (1659).

WATTS, ISAAC, *The Holiness of Times, Places, and People under the Jewish and Christian Dispensations Considered and Compared, in several Discourses, viz.: 1. On the Perpetuity of a Sabbath, and the Observation of the Lord's-Day . . .* (1738).

[WHISTON, EDWARD], *The Life and Death of Mr. Henry Jessey* (1671).

WHITE, FRANCIS, *A Treatise of the Sabbath-Day; containing a Defence of the Orthodoxall Doctrine of the Church of England, against Sabbatarian Novelty* (1635).

—— *An Examination and Confutation of a Lawlesse Pamphlet, Intituled, A Briefe Answer to a late Treatise of the Sabbath Day* (1637).

WHITE, JOHN, *A Way to the Tree of Life* (1647).

WHITEHEAD, GEORGE, *The Christian Quaker and his Divine Testimony Vindicated* (part II) (1673).

—— *The Light and Life of Christ within* (1668).

WILKINS, DAVID, *Concilia Magnae Britanniae et Hiberniae ab Anno MCCCL ad Annum MDXLV* (4 vols., 1737).

WILLETT, JOSEPH, *Some Observations on a Pretended Dialogue Between a Baptist and a Quaker* (1720).

[WRIGHT, SAMUEL], *A Treatise on the Religious Observation of the Lord's Day, according to the express Words of the Fourth Commandment* (1724).

WYCLIF, JOHN, *Select English Works of John Wyclif*, ed. T. Arnold (3 vols., Oxford, 1869–71).

2. Secondary works

ANDERSON, A.O. and M.O. (eds), *Adomnan's Life of Columba* (1961).

ARNOLD, T. (ed.), *Select English Works of John Wyclif* (3 vols., Oxford, 1869–71).

AVELING, J.H., *The Chamberlens and the Midwifery Forceps* (1882).

AYRE, J. (ed.), *The Early Works of Thomas Becon* (Cambridge, 1843).

BALL, B.W., *A Great Expectation: Eschatological Thought in English Protestantism to 1660* (Leiden, 1975).

BALLEINE, G.R., *A History of the Evangelical Party in The Church of England* (1933).

BANNISTER, A.T. (ed.), *The Register of John Stanbury, Bishop of Hereford 1453–1474* (1918).

The Baptist Union Directory (1985–6).

BARBOUR, H., *The Quakers in Puritan England* (1964).

—— and ROBERTS, A. (eds.), *Early Quaker Writings 1650–1700* (1973).

BARNETT, T.R., *Margaret of Scotland: Queen and Saint* (Edinburgh, 1926).

BASSETT, T.M., *Bedyddwyr Cymru* (Llandysul, 1977).

—— *The Welsh Baptists* (Swansea, 1977).

BEARD, J.R., *Unitarianism Exhibited in its Actual Condition* (1846).

BENEDICT, D., *A General History of the Baptist Denomination* (Boston, Mass., 1813).

BEUZART, P., *Les Hérésies pendant le Moyen Âge et la Réforme dans la région de Douai, d'Arras et au pays de l'Alleu* (Le Puy, 1912).

BLACK, W.H. (ed.), *The Last Legacy of Joseph Davis, Snr.* (1869).

BLACKER, B.H. (ed.), *Gloucestershire Notes and Queries*, ii (1884).

BLOMEFIELD, F., *An Essay towards a Topographical History of the County of Norfolk . . .* (5 vols., 1805–10).

BLUNT, J.H., *Dictionary of Sects, Heresies, Ecclesiastical Parties, and Schools of Religious Thought* (1886).

BRAITHWAITE, W.C., *The Second Period of Quakerism* (1919).

BROCKETT, A., *Nonconformity in Exeter, 1650–1875* (Manchester, 1962).

BROOK, B., *The Lives of the Puritans* (3 vols., 1813).

BROWN, R., *The English Baptists of the Eighteenth Century* (1986).

BROWNE, J., *History of Congregationalism, and Memorials of the Churches in Norfolk and Suffolk* (1877).

BUDGE, E.A.W., *By Nile and Tigris* (2 vols., 1920).

BUICK-KNOX, R. (ed.), *Reformation, Conformity and Dissent* (1977).

BURNSIDE, R., *Remarks on the Different Sentiments Entertained in Christendom Relative to the Weekly Sabbath* (1825).

CAPP, B. S., *The Fifth Monarchy Men* (1972).

The Case Submitted to the General Body of Protestant Dissenting Ministers of the Three Denominations (n.d.).

CLAPINSON, M. (ed.), *Bishop Fell and Nonconformity* (Oxford, 1980).

CLIFFORD, H., *History of Bourton-on-the-Water, Gloucestershire* (Stow-on-the-Wold, 1916).

COLLINSON, P., *The Elizabethan Puritan Movement* (1967).

—— *Godly People: Essays on English Protestantism and Puritanism* (1983).

COOMER, D., *English Dissent under the Early Hanoverians* (1946).

COPSON, S.L., *Association Life of the Particular Baptists of Northern Eng-land, 1699–1732* (1991).

CORRIE, G.E. (ed.), *The Works of Hugh Latimer* (2 vols., Cambridge, 1844–5).

COX, H.W., *A Short History of the Upton Baptist Church: Its Origin, Growth, and Progress 1653–1953* (n.p., 1953).

COX, R., *The Literature of the Sabbath Question* (2 vols., Edinburgh, 1865).

CROSS, C., *Church and People, 1450–1660* (1976).

DASENT, J.R. (ed.), *Acts of the Privy Council of England*, iii (1891).

DAVIDS, T.W., *Annals of Evangelical Nonconformity in the County of Essex from the time of Wycliffe to the Restoration* (1863).

DAVIS, C.A., *History of the Baptist Church, Kings Road, Reading* (Reading, 1891).

DENNISON, J.T., Jr., *The Market Day of the Soul: The Puritan Doctrine of the Sabbath in England, 1532–1700* (1983).

DENSHAM, W., and OGLE, J., *The Story of the Congregational Churches of Dorset* (Bournemouth, 1899).

DICKENS, A.G., *The English Reformation* (1964).

DOUGLAS, D., *History of the Baptist Churches in the North of England from the Year 1648 to 1845* (1846).

DUGMORE, C.W., and DUGGAN, C. (eds.), *Studies in Church History*, i (1964).

EEDLE, M., *A History of Beaminster* (1984).

ELWELL, C.J.L., *The Iron Elwells* (Ilfracombe, 1964).

FLICK, A.C., *The Rise of the Mediaeval Church* (1909).

FORBES-LEITH, W. (ed.), *The Life of St. Margaret, Queen of Scotland* (Edinburgh, 1896).

FORDYCE, W., *The History and Antiquities of the County Palatine of Durham* (2 vols., Newcastle, 1855–7).

FROOM, L.E., *The Prophetic Faith of our Fathers* (4 vols., Washington, DC, 1946–64).

GABB, A., *A History of Baptist Beginnings, with an Account of the Rise of the Baptist Witness in Exeter and the Founding of the South Street Church* (Exeter, 1954).

GAIRDNER, J., and SPEDDING, J., *Studies in English History* (Edinburgh, 1881).

GEORGE, C.H. and K., *The Protestant Mind of the English Reformation 1570–1640* (Princeton, NJ, 1961).

GILFILLAN, J., *The Sabbath Viewed in the Light of Reason, Revelation, and History . . .* (Edinburgh, 1861).

GREAVES, R.L. (ed.), *A Biographical Dictionary of British Radicals in the Seventeenth Century* (3 vols., 1982–4).

—— *Deliver us from Evil: The Radical Underground in Britain, 1660–1663* (New York, 1986).

GREEN, V.H.H., *Bishop Reginald Pecock* (Cambridge, 1945).

HARDINGE, L., *The Celtic Church in Britain* (1972).

HART, W.H., *Index expurgatorius Anglicanus* (5 vols., 1872–8).

HEARNSHAW, F.J.C., *The Life of Sir Henry Vane the Younger, Puritan Idealist* ([1910]).

HILL, C., *Society and Puritanism in Pre-Revolutionary England* (1969).

HINE, R., *The History of Beaminster* (Taunton, 1914).

HINTON, J.H., *A Biographical Portraiture of the Late Rev. James Hinton, M.A.* (1824).

Historical Manuscripts Commission, *Calendar of the Manuscripts of the . . . Marquis of Salisbury*, x (1904).

—— *Report on the Records of the City of Exeter* (1916).

A History of the English Church . . . 1640–1660, ii (1900).

HITCHCOCK, E.V. (ed.), *R. Pecock: The Donet* (1921).

HOLMES, C., *Seventeenth-Century Lincolnshire* (Lincoln, 1980).

HOSKEN, T.J., *History of Congregationalism and Memorials of the Churches . . . in Suffolk* (Ipswich, 1920).

HOWELL, T.B. (ed.), *Cobbett's Complete Collection of State Trials*, vi (1810).

JACKMAN, D., *300 Years of Baptist Witness in Dorchester, 1645–1945* (Dorchester, 1945).

JEAFFRESON, J.C. (ed.), *Middlesex County Records*, iv (1892).

JEWSON, C.B., *Stalham Baptist Church, 1653–1953* (n.d.).

—— *The Baptists in Norfolk* (1957).

KATZ, D.S., *Philo-Semitism and the Readmission of the Jews to England, 1603–1655* (Oxford, 1982).

—— *Sabbath and Sectarianism in Seventeenth-Century England* (Leiden, 1988).

KENNEY, J.F., *The Sources for the Early History of Ireland* (2 vols., New York, 1929).

KEVAN, E.F., *The Grace of Law* (1964).

KING, H.P.F. (ed.), *Fasti Ecclesiae Anglicanae 1300–1541, i: Lincoln Diocese* (1962).

King's Stanley Baptist Church: 330th Anniversary (1970).

KIRBY, I.M. (ed.), *Diocese of Gloucester: A Catalogue of the Records of the Bishop and Archdeacons* (Gloucester, 1968).

KLAIBER, A.J., *The Story of the Suffolk Baptists* (1931).

LAISTNER, M.L.W., *Thought and Letters in Western Europe, A.D. 500 to 900* (1957).

LANG, A., *A History of Scotland from the Roman Occupation* (4 vols., Edinburgh, 1900–7).

LE HARDY, W. (ed.), *Calendar to the Sessions Records (Buckinghamshire), i: 1678–1694*; Aylesbury, 1933; ii (Aylesbury, 1939).

—— *Calendar to the Sessions Records (Middlesex)*, NS iii: *1615–1616* (1937).

LLOYD JUKES, H.A. (ed.), *Articles of Enquiry Addressed to the Clergy of the*

Diocese of Oxford at the Primary Visitation of Dr. Thomas Secker, 1738 (Oxford, 1957).

MACFARLANE, A. (ed.), *The Diary of Ralph Josselin 1616–1683* (1976).

MAGALOTTI, L., *The Travels of Cosmo the Third, Grand Duke of Tuscany, through England . . . in 1669* (1821).

MATTHEWS, A.G., *Calamy Revised* (Oxford, 1934).

MILTON, J., *A Treatise of Christian Doctrine*, tr. C.R. Sumner (Cambridge, 1825).

MOFFAT, J.C., *The Church in Scotland* (Philadelphia, 1882).

MOORE, G.A., *The Story of Brown St. Baptist Church, Salisbury* (n.d.).

MOSHEIM, J.L. VON, *Institutes of Ecclesiastical History*, ed. H. Soames (4 vols., 1841).

NEAL, D., *The History of the Puritans* (5 vols., 1822).

NOTESTEIN, W., RELF, F.H., and SIMPSON, H. (eds.), *Commons Debates, 1621* (7 vols., New Haven, Conn., 1935).

NUTTALL, G.F., *The General Body of the Three Denominations: A Historical Sketch* (1955).

—— (ed.), *Letters of John Pinney 1679–1699* (Oxford, 1939).

—— *Visible Saints: The Congregational Way 1640–1660* (Oxford, 1957).

OLSEN, V.N., *John Foxe and the Elizabethan Church* (1973).

OWEN, D.M., *Church and Society in Medieval Lincolnshire* (Lincoln, 1971).

PARKER, K.L., *The English Sabbath: A Study of Doctrine and Discipline from the Reformation to the Civil War* (Cambridge, 1988).

PARKER, T.M., *The English Reformation to 1558* (1950).

PATTENDEN, C., *Tiverton Baptist Church* (n.p., n.d.).

PAYNE, E.A., *The Baptists of Berkshire through Three Centuries* (1951).

PENNEY, N. (ed.), *The First Publishers of Truth* (1907).

—— (ed.), *Extracts from State Papers Relating to Friends, 1654–1672* (1913).

PIKE, G.H., *Ancient Meeting Houses* (1870).

QUIN, W.F., *A History of Braintree and Bocking* (Lavenham, 1981).

REDSTONE, V.B., *Bygone Woodbridge* (Woodbridge, 1893).

REES, T., *History of Protestant Nonconformity in Wales* (2nd edn. 1883).

Reports and Transactions of the Devonshire Association (1935).

Reports from the Commissioners for Charities, xix (1840).

RICHARDS, T., *A History of the Puritan Movement in Wales . . . 1639–1653* (1920).

—— *The Religious Census of 1676* (1927).

—— *Religious Developments in Wales, 1654–1662* (1923).

—— *Wales under the Indulgence 1672–1675* (1928).

—— *Wales under the Penal Code, 1662–1687* (1925).

RIPPON, J., *The Baptist Annual Register* (4 vols., 1793–1802).

ROOTS, I., *The Great Rebellion 1642–1660* (1966).

Rowe, V.A., *Sir Henry Vane the Younger* (1970).

Sanford, D.A., *A Choosing People: The History of Seventh Day Baptists* (Nashville, 1992).

Seventh Day Baptists in Europe and America, i and ii (1910); iii (1972).

70th Annual Report of the Seventh Day Baptist Historical Society, document E (1986).

Seymour, St J.D., *The Puritans in Ireland, 1647–1661* (Oxford, 1921).

Shipley, C.E. (ed.), *The Baptists of Yorkshire* (1912).

Skene, W.F., *Celtic Scotland: A History of Ancient Alban* (3 vols., Edinburgh, 1876–80).

Smith, W., and Wace, H., *A Dictionary of Christian Biography* (4 vols., 1877–87).

[Spurrier, E.], *Memorials of the Baptist Church Worshipping in Eld Lane Chapel, Colchester* (Colchester, 1889).

Stokes, Whitley, *The Tripartite Life of Patrick* (1887).

—— and Strachan, J., *Thesaurus Palaeohibernicus: A Collection of Old Irish Glosses* (3 vols., Cambridge, 1901–10).

Stokes, William, *The History of the Midland Association of Baptist Churches 1655 to 1855* (1855).

Stuart, J., *Beechen Grove Baptist Church, Watford* (1907).

Summers, W.H., *History of the Congregational Churches in the Berkshire, South Oxon, and South Bucks Association* (Newbury, 1905).

Swinburn, L.M. (ed.), *The Lanterne of Light* (1917).

Taylor, A., *The History of the English General Baptists* (2 vols., 1818).

Thompson, J.A.F., *The Later Lollards 1414–1520* (Oxford, 1965).

Townsend, G.F., *The Town and Borough of Leominster* (Leominster, 1863).

Townsend, W.J., Workman, H.B., and Eayrs, George, *A New History of Methodism* (1919).

Trask, W.B., *The Traske Family in England* (Boston, Mass., 1900).

Turner, G.L., *Original Records of Early Nonconformity under Persecution and Indulgence* (3 vols., 1911–14).

Tyerman, L., *The Oxford Methodists* (1873).

Tyndale, W., *An Answer to Sir Thomas More's Dialogue* (1850).

Underhill, E.B. (ed.), *Records of the Churches of Christ, Gathered at Fenstanton, Warboys, and Hexham 1644–1720* (1854).

—— *Records of a Church of Christ, Meeting in Broadmead, Bristol* (1847).

Urwick, W., *Nonconformity in Herts* (1884).

Wallen, W., *The History and Antiquities of the Round Church at Little Maplestead, Essex* (1836).

White, B.R. (ed.), *Association Records of the Particular Baptists of England, Wales and Ireland to 1660* (3 parts, 1971–4).

—— *The English Baptists of the Seventeenth Century* (1983).

Whiting, C.E., *Studies in English Puritanism from the Restoration to the Revolution 1660–1688* (1931).

WHITLEY, W.T., *A Baptist Bibliography* (2 vols., 1916, 1922).

—— *The Baptists of London* ([1928]).

—— (ed.), *The Church Books of Ford or Cuddington and Amersham* (1912).

—— *A History of British Baptists* (1923).

—— (ed.), *Minutes of the General Assembly of the General Baptist Churches in England* (2 vols., 1909, 1910).

WILBUR, E.M., *Our Unitarian Heritage* (Boston, Mass., 1926).

—— *A History of Unitarianism: In Transylvania, England, and America* (Cambridge, Mass., 1952).

WILKINSON, T., *Sketch of the History of the Baptist Church, Tewkesbury* (n.d.).

WILLCOCK, J., *The Life of Sir Henry Vane the Younger* (1913).

WILLCOX, W.B., *Gloucestershire: A Study in Local Government 1590–1640* (New Haven, Conn., 1940).

WILLIAMS, G.H., *The Radical Reformation* (1962).

WILSON, W., *The History and Antiquities of Dissenting Churches and Meeting Houses in London, Westminster and Southwark* (4 vols., 1808–14).

WITARD, G.D., *The History of Braintree Baptist Church, Essex* (1955).

—— *Bibles in Barrels: A History of Essex Baptists* (1962).

3. Journals and articles

BEEMAN, G., 'Notes on the Sites and History of the French Churches in London', *Proceedings of the Huguenot Society of London*, 8 (1909).

BLACK, W.H., 'The Mill Yard Seventh-day Baptist Church', *SR* 14/32 (14 Jan. 1858).

BROCKETT, A.A., 'The Presbyterian Committee of Thirteen in Exeter', *TUHS* 11 (1958).

BURGESS, W.H., 'James Toppe and the Tiverton Anabaptists', *TBHS* 3 (1912–13).

BURRAGE, C., 'A True and Short Declaration, both of the Gathering and Joining Together of Certain Persons [with John More, Dr. Theodore Naudin, and Dr. Peter Chamberlen]: and also of the lamentable breach and division which fell amongst them', *TBHS* 2 (1910–11).

COLLINSON, P., 'The Beginnings of English Sabbatarianism', *Studies in Church History*, 1 (1964).

DALAND, W.C., 'Letter from London', *SR* 51/25 (20 June 1895).

DE WIND, H.A., 'A Sixteenth Century Description of Religious Sects in Austerlitz, Moravia', *Mennonite Quarterly Review*, 29 (1955).

DOYLE, A.I., 'A Treatise of the Three Estates', *Dominican Studies*, 3/4 (1950).

EVANS, J., 'The Baptist Interest under George I', *TBHS* 2 (1910–11).

GORDON, A., 'Theophilus Brabourne, M.A.' *SM* 49–50 (1887).

GREAVES, R.L., 'Francis Bampfield (1615–1684): Eccentric Hebraist and Humanitarian', *Bulletin of the Institute of Historical Research*, 44 (1971).

GREENE, C.H., 'History of Seventh Day Baptists', *SO* 1/4–28 (1905–11); 2/1–28 (1912–18); 3/1–8 (1919–20).

HASEL, G.F., 'Sabbatarian Anabaptists of the Sixteenth Century', *AUSS* 5/2 (1967), and 6/1 (1968).

HAYDEN, R., 'The Particular Baptist Confession 1689 and Baptists Today', *BQ* 32 (1987–8).

JEWSON, C.B., 'St. Mary's, Norwich', *BQ* 10 (1940–1).

JONES, W.M. (ed.), *The Sabbath Memorial: A Journal of Sabbath Literature, Biblical Archaeology, and Christian Life* (Jan. 1875–Dec. 1889).

KENYON, I.F., 'English Sabbath-Keepers in the Seventeenth Century', *SR* 32/17 (11 May 1876).

'A List of Seventh Day Baptist Churches in the British Isles, 1617–1917, with their Earliest Known Dates', *SR* 83/16 (15 Oct. 1917).

MELLONE, W.E., 'Seventh-Day Christians', *JQR* 10 (1898).

MICKLEWRIGHT, F.H.A., 'A Congregation of Sabbatarian and Unitarian Baptists', *Notes and Queries*, 191/5 (7 Sept. 1946).

—— 'Some Further Notes on Mill Yard Meeting House', *Notes and Queries*, 191/7 (5 Oct.); 8 (19 Oct.); 9 (2 Nov. 1946).

—— 'A Mill Yard Layman', *Notes and Queries*, 192 (1947).

NUTTALL, G.F., 'Association Records of the Particular Baptists' (review), *BQ* 26 (1975–6).

—— 'English Dissenters in the Netherlands, 1640–1689', *Nederlands archief voor kerkgeschiedenis*, 59 (1979).

—— 'George Whitefield's "Curate": Gloucestershire Dissent and the Revival', *JEH* 27 (1976).

—— 'The Lollard Movement after 1384: its Characteristics and Continuity', *TCHS* 12 (1935).

—— 'Questions and Answers: an Eighteenth-Century Correspondence: Joshua Thomas and Benjamin Francis', *BQ* 27 (1977–8).

—— 'The Fifth Monarchy Men: a Study in Seventeenth-Century Millenarianism' (review), *JTS* 24 (1973).

PAYNE, E.A., 'More about the Sabbatarian Baptists', *BQ* 14 (1951–2).

—— 'Thomas Tillam', *BQ* 17 (1957–8).

PHILLIPS, H.E., 'An Early Stuart Judaising Sect', *TJHSE* 15 (1946).

Protestant Dissenters' Magazine (6 vols., 1794–9).

RANDOLPH, C.F., 'The Sabbath and Seventh Day Baptists', *SR* 65/8 (24 Aug. 1908).

'The Seventh Day Baptist Church in Newport, R.I.', *SDBM* 1/1 (Jan. 1852); 1/2 (Apr. 1852).

THIRTLE, J.W., 'Dr. Peter Chamberlen: Pastor, Propagandist, and Patentee', *TBHS* 3 (1912–13).

—— 'A Sabbatarian Pioneer—Dr. Peter Chamberlen', *TBHS* 2 (1910–11).

THURSTON, H., 'The Mediaeval Sunday', *Nineteenth Century*, 46 (July 1899).

[UTTER, G.B.], 'Daniel Noble', *SR* 3/2 (2 July 1846).

—— 'The Sabbath-Keeping Church at Natton', *SR* 2/1 (26 June 1845).

WHITE, B.R., 'Henry Jessey: A Pastor in Politics', *BQ* 25 (1973–4).

—— 'John Traske (1585–1636) and London Puritanism', *TCHS* 20 (1968).

[WHITLEY, W.T.], 'Bampfield's Plan for an Educated Ministry', *TBHS* 3 (1912–13).

—— 'An Index to Notable Baptists', *TBHS* 7 (1920–1).

—— 'Chamberlen's First-Day Church', *TBHS* 2 (1910–11).

—— 'Daniel Noble', *BQ* 1 (1922–3).

—— (ed.), 'Salisbury and Tiverton about 1630', *TBHS* 3 (1912–13).

—— 'Seventh Day Baptists in England', *BQ* 12 (1946–8).

—— 'Some Norwich Notes', *BQ* 10 (1940–1).

—— 'South Wales till 1753', *TBHS* 6 (1918–19).

—— (ed.), 'Trask in the Star-Chamber, 1619', *TBHS* 5 (1916–17).

'Wiggenton's Visitation', *TCHS* 3 (1907).

4. General reference works

Alumni Cantabrigienses (4 vols., 1922–7).

Alumni Oxonienses, Early Series (4 vols., Oxford, 1891–2).

Athenae Oxonienses (2 vols., 1691–2).

Calendar of State Papers, Domestic.

Calendar of State Papers, Ireland.

Chambers's Encyclopaedia (1874).

The Concise Dictionary of National Biography, i, to 1900.

The Dictionary of National Biography.

The Dictionary of Welsh Biography.

The New International Dictionary of the Christian Church (1974).

The Oxford Dictionary of the Christian Church (2nd edn., revised, 1983).

A Select Library of Nicene and Post-Nicene Fathers of the Christian Church, NS (Oxford, 1890–1900).

Short-Title Catalogue . . . 1641–1700 (3 vols., New York, 1972).

The Victoria History of the Counties of England.

5. Newspapers

Birmingham Weekly Post (13 Apr. 1901).

Diary (3 Oct. 1651).

Evesham Journal and Four Shires Advertiser (11 July 1903).

Publick Intelligencer (21–8 Feb 1650).

INDEX OF PLACES

Bold numbers denote references to illustrations

INDEX OF PERSONS

Bold numbers denote references to illustrations

GENERAL INDEX